Young People and the Labour Market

T0295866

Young people are a vulnerable category of workers, finding themselves in a delicate phase of their working life: their first entry into the labour market. In many European countries, youngsters are unemployed or have difficulty finding and obtaining jobs. This situation has deteriorated particularly after the crises, recessions and stagnation that have impacted European economies in recent years. In addition to the cyclical or crisis impact, structural factors are also very important. Additionally, prolonged crises, as in some Eurozone countries, have transformed a significant part of cyclical unemployment in structural (long term) unemployment.

Young People and the Labour Market: A Comparative Perspective explores the condition of young people in the labour market. The authors present new evidence from several countries, with a special focus on Europe, and offer a comparative perspective. They investigate questions such as which structural conditions and labour market institutions guarantee better youth performance, which education systems and school-to-work processes are more effective and in which countries is gender differentiation less of an issue. All of the aforementioned, as well as many other comparisons which the authors make, are significant in helping to facilitate the successful design of labour and education policies.

As the first investigation by economists to explore the complexity of this topic, this book will be useful to both economists and sociologists who are interested in the role of young people in the labour market, and the problem of youth unemployment.

Floro Ernesto Caroleo is Full Professor of Labour Economics at the Parthenope University of Naples and Director of the Research Centre on Development Economics and Institutions (CRISEI). His research interests are in the field of labour market policies. He has been the president of the Italian Association of Labour Economics.

Olga Demidova is Associate Professor at the Department of Applied Economics and Academic Director of the Doctoral School of Economics in the National Research University Higher School of Economics, Moscow. She carried out postgraduate studies at Lomonosov Moscow State University. Her main research interests are in applied micro-econometrics and comparative economic studies.

Enrico Marelli is Full Professor of Economic Policy at the University of Brescia, Italy. He studied, taught and carried out research at Bocconi University, Italy, London School of Economics and the University of Pennsylvania. His current research activity is primarily in labour economics, economic policy and European integration.

Marcello Signorelli is Associate Professor of Economic Policy at the Department of Economics, University of Perugia, Italy. He carried out postgraduate studies and research at the University of Siena (PhD), Italy, Columbia University, USA and the University of Warwick, UK. He has been the president of the European Association for Comparative Economic Studies.

Routledge Studies in Labour Economics

Young People and the Labour Market

A Comparative Perspective

Edited by
Floro Ernesto Caroleo,
Olga Demidova,
Enrico Marelli and
Marcello Signorelli

Routledge
Taylor & Francis Group

LONDON AND NEW YORK

First published 2018 by Routledge

2 Park Square, Milton Park, Abingdon, Oxfordshire OX14 4RN
52 Vanderbilt Avenue, New York, NY 10017

Routledge is an imprint of the Taylor & Francis Group, an informa business

First issued in paperback 2019

British Library Cataloguing in Publication Data
A catalogue record for this book is available from the British Library

Library of Congress Cataloging in Publication Data
Names: Caroleo, F. E. (Floro Ernesto), editor.
Title: Young people and the labour market : a comparative perspective / edited by Floro Ernesto Caroleo [and three others].
Description: Abingdon, Oxon ; New York, NY : Routledge, 2018. | Series: Routledge studies in labour economics | Includes bibliographical references and index.
Identifiers: LCCN 2017032293| ISBN 9781138036680 (hardback) | ISBN 9781315178424 (ebook)
Subjects: LCSH: Youth–Employment–Europe. | Unemployed youth–Europe. | Labor market–Europe.
Classification: LCC HD6276.E852 Y6795 2018 | DDC 331.3/4094–dc23
LC record available at https://lccn.loc.gov/2017032293

ISBN: 978-1-138-03668-0 (hbk)
ISBN: 978-0-367-88863-3 (pbk)

Typeset in Times New Roman
by Wearset Ltd, Boldon, Tyne and Wear

Contents

Contributors

Tindara Addabbo (PhD European University Institute, MSc London School of Economics, national scientific qualification as Full Professor in economic policy) is currently Associate Professor at the University of Modena, Italy and Reggio Emilia, Department of Economics Marco Biagi. He is also a member of the Centre for Analysis of Public Policies and Interuniversities Research Centre Ezio Tarantelli (CIRET).

Vasilis Angelis, PhD, is Professor Emeritus of quantitative methods at the University of the Aegean, Greece; his main fields of research are business and regional economics.

Francesco Bartolucci is Full Professor of Statistics at the Department of Economics, University of Perugia, Italy. His research interests are focused on the analysis of complex data structures, in particular longitudinal and multilevel data, through latent variable models.

Aleksandra Bashina is a Lecturer at the Department of Applied Economics, National Research University Higher School of Economics, Moscow. She has an MSc in Economics. Her main research interests are in human capital, education and public procurements.

Giovanni S. F. Bruno (PhD, University of Southampton, UK) is a Researcher at Bocconi University, Milan. His research interests lie in the field of applied econometrics. He has published several articles in scholarly journals.

Floro Ernesto Caroleo is Full Professor of Labour Economics at the Parthenope University of Naples and Director of the Research Centre on Development Economics and Institutions (CRISEI). His research interests are in the field of labour market policies. He has been the president of the Italian Association of Labour Economics.

Elvira Ciociano used to work in a bank as an HR specialist. She has a PhD (labour economics – youth unemployment and VET systems) from the Parthenope University of Naples. Currently she is studying labour and tax law for the examination of employment consultant (professional association in Italy).

Olga Demidova is Associate Professor at the Department of Applied Economics and Academic Director of the Doctoral School of Economics in the National Research University Higher School of Economics, Moscow. She carried out postgraduate studies at Lomonosov Moscow State University. Her main research interests are in applied microeconometrics and comparative economic studies.

Sergio Destefanis is Professor of Economics at the University of Salerno, Italy. He took his PhD at Cambridge, UK, and was awarded the Tarantelli and Banco di Napoli prizes. He was president of the Italian Association of Labour Economics from 2010 to 2013.

Hans Dietrich is Senior Researcher at the Institute for Employment Research (IAB), Nürnberg, Germany; his main fields of research are the education and labour market of young people.

Katerina Dimaki, PhD, is Associate Professor at the University of Economics and Business, Athens, Greece; her main research fields are statistics and regional economics.

Lina Gálvez-Muñoz (PhD European University Institute) is Economic History Professor and Director of the Master programme on Gender and Equality at the Pablo Olavide University, Spain, where she was Vice-Rector of graduate studies from 2007 to 2012. She leads the Gender, Economy, Politics and Development Observatory (GEP&DO).

Anette Haas is Senior Researcher at the Institute for Employment Research (IAB), Nürnberg, Germany. Her main fields of research are regional economics and migration.

Elish Kelly is Senior Research Officer in the Economic Analysis Division at the Economic and Social Research Institute (ESRI) and Adjunct Assistant Professor at Trinity College Dublin. Her postgraduate studies and research were conducted at Trinity College Dublin (PhD).

Randi Kjeldstad (MSc in Sociology, Oslo University) is a sociologist and former senior researcher and head of research (retired since 2015) at the Research Department, Statistics Norway. She was a member of the Nordic network on part-time research, financed by the Swedish Research Council.

Enrico Marelli is Full Professor of Economic Policy at the University of Brescia, Italy. He studied, taught and carried out research at Bocconi University, Italy, London School of Economics and the University of Pennsylvania. His current research activity is primarily in labour economics, economic policy and European integration.

Paula Rodríguez-Modroño (PhD in Economics, University of Seville and MPhil in Development, University of Cambridge) is a Lecturer in the Department of Economics, University Pablo de Olavide, Spain. She is a member of the UN Women Roster on Macroeconomic Policy and the UNDP Group of Experts in Unpaid Work, Economic Development and Human Wellbeing.

Seamus McGuinness is Research Professor and Research Area Co-ordinator for labour market research at the Economic and Social Research Institute (ESRI), a research fellow in the Institute of Labour Studies (IZA) at the University of Bonn and Adjunct Professor at Trinity College Dublin. He obtained his PhD from Queens University Belfast.

Maria Laura Parisi is Associate Professor of Economics at the University of Brescia, Italy. She gained her PhD in Economics at Boston College, USA. Her research interests include productivity, innovation, R&D, economic growth and inequality. She is currently Associate Editor of the Economics Book Program at DeGruyterOpen.com.

Francesco Pastore is Associate Professor of Economics (with habilitation as Full Professor of Economic Policy) at University of Campania Luigi Vanvitelli, Italy. He is an IZA research fellow, the country lead for Italy of the Global Labor Organization (GLO) and Associate Editor of the *Journal of Population Economics*.

Cristiano Perugini is Associate Professor of Political Economy and Jean Monnet Professor of European Integration Studies at the University of Perugia, Italy. He is a research associate at FREN (Foundation for the Advancement of Economics) in Belgrade. His research interests include income and wage inequality.

Fabrizio Pompei is Associate Professor of Applied Economics at the University of Perugia, Italy. His main research interests are focused on relationships among labour, productivity and innovation, and their effects on wage inequalities in a comparative perspective.

Brigitte Schels is Senior Researcher at the Institute for Employment Research and Junior Professor at the Friedrich-Alexander University Erlangen-Nürnberg (FAU), Germany; her main fields of research are benefit recipience and labour market integration of young people.

Ekaterina Selezneva is a researcher at the Institute for East and Southeast European Studies in Regensburg, Germany. Her research interests include subjective well-being, poverty, inequality and gender studies, especially in the context of post-socialist economies.

Marcello Signorelli is Associate Professor of Economic Policy at the Department of Economics, University of Perugia, Italy. He carried out postgraduate studies and research at the University of Siena, Italy (PhD), Columbia University, USA and the University of Warwick, UK. He has been president of the European Association for Comparative Economic Studies.

Ioanna Tsoka is a Lecturer at the University of the Aegean, Greece; her main field of research is business economics.

Annie Tubadji is a Lecturer at the University of Bologna, Italy; her main fields of research are cultural and regional economics.

Adele Whelan is Research Officer in the Economic Analysis Division at the Economic and Social Research Institute (ESRI) and Adjunct Assistant Professor at Trinity College Dublin. Her postgraduate studies and research were conducted at Maynooth University, Ireland (PhD).

Young people and the labour market

A review

Floro Ernesto Caroleo, Olga Demidova,
Enrico Marelli and Marcello Signorelli

Only since the beginning of the new millennium has the political, economic and social importance of guaranteeing decent and productive employment for youth in developing and developed countries finally been recognized as a priority challenge requiring decisive policy responses. Although an urgent concern at the global level, youth employment is not only an issue for developing countries: in recent decades, both developed countries and countries in transition have also seen their labour markets incapable of integrating newcomers. Youth unemployment is at present a crucial issue on the EU policy agenda. The EU Youth Strategy recognizes the importance of increasing participation in the labour market to mitigate the effects of social exclusion amongst young people; to limit, as much as possible, the effects of an ageing population; and to overcome the negative economic consequences of a declining European labour force from 2010 onwards. Several policy instruments have been designed to improve the labour-market integration of young people; nonetheless, to date the situation of youth in employment has not been substantially improved.

Youth unemployment and underemployment is one of the most arduous questions for politics and economics, given that young people are considered a vulnerable category of workers since they are in a delicate phase of their working lives – first entry into the labour force; that is to say, they are involved in the school-to-work transition. Therefore, when analysing youth unemployment, several factors should be considered: the institutions governing the school-to-work transition (including the quality of the education system and the integration between school and work-based training), labour-market regulation (hiring and firing rules, safety nets and industrial relations systems), but also demographic and cyclical patterns.

Moreover, the economic crisis which began in most European countries in 2008 has had severe effects on EU and Eastern Europe labour markets. Although no country has been able to escape the crisis, the extent of output loss and the number of jobs lost, as well as the resulting rise in unemployment, vary considerably among countries and regions. Overall, the recession has not affected all workers in the same way: low-educated young people and women have proved to be the groups most vulnerable to the crisis. Several explanations have been advanced to justify this evidence and, without claiming to be complete, we may mention the following: the role of structural change and the spatially asymmetric impact on local labour markets; the size and the speed of the labour market's response to output shocks in different EU countries due to a different composition of labour-market institutions and of labour-market policies; the impact of labour-market institutions, and in particular those governing the school-to-work transitions, on youth labour-market performance; the structural factors determining the gender disparities in the labour market.

This book is the outcome of the EU IRSES project[1] *The Political Economy of Youth Unemployment.* The project has been an opportunity to set up a network of scholars (mainly from Italian and Russian universities) dealing with youth labour market and policies, viewed in a perspective of comparison among countries. There has been a good exchange of opinions and knowledge among the researchers involved that has led to fruitful teamwork, creating a long-lasting relationship among the participating institutions. This cooperation has in turn resulted in joint papers and joint research initiatives through continuous interchange and dissemination of the research results, and the participation in several international meetings and workshops. This has also made it possible to produce a rich body of ideas relevant for scholars and policy makers.

More specifically, comparing West-East European countries, the general aim has been to provide a comprehensive understanding of the causes of a very high unemployment rate among young people, in a period of deep recession and financial crisis, and to assess the effectiveness of labour-market policies designed to mitigate this phenomenon. The scholars involved in this joint exchange programme have attempted to answer these questions with an in-depth and systematic investigation in several directions.

Four broad themes have been examined:

1   The analysis of certain key issues determining the disadvantage of young people in the labour market, such as the role played by individual and family characteristics, wage discrimination across age cohorts, genders and sectors, the different sensitivity of young workers to economic fluctuations.
2   The impact of the financial crises and of the productivity slowdown on young workers. An important question explored has been the extent to which the increase in youth unemployment in many European countries has been caused by the Great Recession and how much it has been due to structural factors. Another issue addressed has been whether financial crises have something special, in the sense that they have effects on unemployment additional to the direct impact caused by the recession.
3   The third theme investigated has been a review of alternative youth labour-market policies and the evaluation of youth unemployment programmes. Analysed in particular have been the role of temporary contracts, and, in general, labour-market flexibility on youth unemployment; the role of education and training institutions in enhancing school-to-work transitions; the effects of active labour-market policies and in general of labour-market institutions on youth unemployment.

4   Finally, all these features have been analysed from the point of view of comparison among countries and regions. Techniques of spatial analysis have been implemented to verify if the Eastern regions of new member states have responded to the crisis in a different way compared to the Western regions and to identify different determinants of youth unemployment in Eastern and Western regions of Russia, between the regions of Italy and Russia, and between EU-28 countries as well.

The socio-economic impact of the project is self-evident. Indeed, the rich body of deliverables produced by the researchers has made it possible to learn more about the problems that youth face in their approach to the labour market. Scholars may find suggestions concerning the empirical approach and econometric methodologies applied in the analysis of youth labour markets. On the other hand, policy makers can benefit and draw assessments from the analyses of the micro and macro policies adopted to address youth unemployment and to mitigate the effect of financial crises. In this Introduction, we first briefly summarize the most relevant articles already published by the authors involved in the EU project and then present the studies included in the ten chapters of this book.

During the preparation of the European project, some preliminary studies were carried out. In particular, it was necessary to conduct an initial comparison of the international evidence on youth unemployment (YU).[2] Marelli and Signorelli (2011)[3] presented and discussed, in a first study, some empirical evidence on YU, before and during the global financial crisis and the Great Recession. The paper focused on EU countries, but it comprised some comparative data regarding many world regions. It also included a preliminary review of the existing literature on the determinants of YU.

After the start of the European project, already in the first year some interesting empirical investigations were carried out by our research group. A first investigation focused on the impact of financial crises on YU: see Choudhry Tanveer *et al.* (2012). It used fixed effects panel estimations on a large panel of countries (about 70) around the world for the period 1980–2005; an Arellano–Bond dynamic panel was also employed. The two key results were: (i) financial crises have a large impact on YU (beyond the impact resulting from GDP changes); (ii) the effect on YU is greater than the effect on overall unemployment. These results remained significant also on including many control variables. In particular, financial crises affect YU for five years after the onset of the crises, but the most adverse effects are found in the second and third year.

A similar strand of investigation focused on the impact of the crises on female work. Signorelli *et al.* (2012) studied the impact of financial crises, in the period 1980–2005, on female labour force participation and female unemployment. A random effects panel estimation method was applied; also in this case, many control variables were considered. One feature of this paper is that the crises impact was investigated separately for economies at different levels of development; furthermore, the persistence of the impact on female unemployment was also evaluated. The key finding was that both female participation rates and female unemployment rates have been deeply affected by financial crises; moreover, the impact for women has been greater than in the general case. Finally, it has been found that the impact has been greater (and the results more robust) in the case of high-income countries.

A different research question was raised in a third line of inquiry, which focused on the regional differentiation of the impact of the crisis. Marelli *et al.* (2012a), by considering the EU states, were not only able to include an analysis of unemployment at the regional level, but also to use fresh data for the 2007–2010 period (i.e. including the "Great Recession"), that is, compared to the previous trends for the 2004–2007 period. From a methodological viewpoint, a spatial filtering technique was applied to the regional data. The specific research questions referred not only to a possible reversal in employment and unemployment dynamics (from the first to the second sub-period previously mentioned), but also to whether the Eastern regions of new member states have responded to the crisis in a different way compared to the Western regions. The different responses thus established were then related to the characteristics of the regions, both structural (sector specialization) and institutional (share of temporary workers and long-term unemployment). Although not explicitly considering YU (because of a lack of such data at the regional level), the latter results are particularly relevant to young people.

A final line of inquiry, commenced in the first year of the project, again concerned the European countries, but focused on the links between employment and productivity. Marelli *et al.* (2012b) analysed the short-term joint dynamics of productivity and employment; they considered the economic down cycles over a period of 20 years, on the basis of quarterly data, and focused on the peculiarities of the latest recession. In order to identify the peaks, the Hodrick and Prescott filter was applied. The authors were thus able to distinguish four major types of adjustments caused by the fall in output.

In the second year of the project, a more comprehensive investigation of the impact of policies and institutions on the YU was conducted. Marelli *et al.* (2013), after a review of the relevant literature, used a fixed effect panel analysis – on a large set of developed countries during the last three decades – to single out the key determinants of YU. In addition to economic growth, four specific factors – economic freedom, labour-market reforms, share of part-time employment and active labour-market policies – proved to play a greater role in reducing unemployment.

By contrast, Marelli and Signorelli (2013) revisited the basic factors by analysing the links among changes in YU, the business cycle and big economic shocks, e.g. those caused by the financial crises. Starting from Okun's law, they proposed a model able to detect the additional impact determined by financial crises, compared to that operating through GDP changes alone. In fact, financial crises cause larger effects, compared to normal recessions, because the falls in production are accompanied by an increase in "systemic" uncertainty. The model was applied to data concerning a large panel of countries, for the period

1980–2005, and was able to distinguish the specific impact of particular types of financial crises (e.g. systemic and non-systemic bank crises). The empirical results are also presented considering different scenarios of GDP change.

Demidova *et al.* (2013) opted to resume the regional dimension by considering 75 Russian regions over the 2000–2010 period. They tried to identify the common and different determinants of YU in Eastern and Western regions of Russia. The econometric estimation applied the Arellano–Bond methodology, but also searched for the existence of boundary and distance spatial effects. Four types of explanatory variables were considered: demographic variables, variables on migration processes, variables characterizing the economy and structure of regions, and variables on regional trade. Besides the significant role played by some of these variables, the general outcome was that, also in Russia, there is a more serious situation for YU compared to general unemployment; furthermore, the impact of the 2008–2009 crisis has been significant. As for the policy implications, since several variables seem to affect YU levels and dynamics, there is no single policy intervention suitable for all regions.

Altavilla and Caroleo (2013) analysed the different regional effects on employment of the Active Labour Market Policies (ALMPs) in Italy. Their broad conclusion was that a strategy of policy established at the national level may not take sufficient account of region-specific economic structures, especially in the presence of significant differences among regional economies. Indeed, the results suggest that the timing and magnitude of the reaction of the employment rate to ALMP shocks in two different areas of Italy (Northern regions and Southern regions) are substantially different. For example, in the South, employment is mainly driven by its own shocks and by social and economic context variables. By contrast, in the Northern regions, the employment dynamics are significantly explained by the dynamics of nominal and policy variables such as remunerations and ALMPs.

The papers by Bruno *et al.* (2013, 2014a) studied the temporary contract, one of the key reforms aimed at flexibilizing and liberalizing the labour market, implemented mainly in the Mediterranean countries. In particular, Bruno *et al.* (2013) focused on labour-market transitions out of temporary jobs among young people in Italy. By means of a discrete-time duration analysis and estimating a competing-risk model, the authors assessed the extent to which, and for whom, starting a temporary job after 2004 resulted (within a three-year span) in a stepping stone to permanent employment rather than a dead end outside the labour market or in a precarious job. They found that temporary contracts have a positive impact on men's transitions to permanent employment only. School leavers, workers in the South, as well as women, are instead rather penalized after a temporary job. They have a higher probability than men of remaining trapped in temporary contracts and a higher probability of exiting the labour market. In particular, school leavers entering the labour market with a temporary contract experience relatively high exit-rates to non-employment just after the first year of the contract.

Bruno *et al.* (2014a) tried to shed light on the quality of these temporary jobs, which are particularly diverse among young workers. They estimated a regression model of perceived overall job satisfaction of young workers, controlling for the various types of temporary contracts (temporary workers and autonomous collaborators) and for perceived satisfaction with nine aspects of the job. They found that lack of job stability is the most serious cause of lower satisfaction for both temporary employees and autonomous collaborators. However, while temporary employees compensate concerns of job stability with other job aspects, attaining satisfaction levels comparable to those of permanent employees, autonomous collaborators do not, and are thus significantly the least satisfied.

The third year of the European project involved systematization of the previous surveys of the literature on the determinants of YU, and updating the empirical evidence to include pre- and post-crisis periods (2007 and 2013). Brada *et al.* (2014) thus presented a special Symposium on labour markets (published in *Comparative Economic Studies*). The empirical evidence collected in the paper referred not only to YU, compared to total unemployment, but also to the NEET indicator.

In the same Symposium, Bruno *et al.* (2014c) reconsidered the regional differentiation of YU. This paper evaluated the impact of the recent crisis not only on YU rates (compared with total unemployment rates) but also on the NEET indicator. The key control variable was regional GDP growth. The estimation applied GMM and bias-corrected LSDV dynamic panel data estimators; moreover, all models incorporated dynamic feedbacks to identify the degree of persistence; and spatial interactions were also considered. The paper focused on changes, in both indices, from 2000–2008 to 2009–2010 and considered the EU regions classified into five groups (Continental, Northern or Scandinavian, Anglo-Saxon, Southern, and regions in new EU member states). The key finding was that NEET rates were persistent, and persistence increased over the crisis period, although this result varied according to which of the five regional groups was considered.

A more general model of the determinants of YU was proposed by Bruno *et al.* (2014b). It not only considered the impact of GDP growth and financial crises, but also estimated the role played by more general macroeconomic and structural conditions (inflation, real interest rate, demographic variables, education, etc.) as well as institutions and policies (e.g. labour-market reforms, ALMPs, overall economic freedom). The econometric analysis was based on a panel of OECD countries for the period 1981–2009 and used different fixed effect panel models. The greater impact – of both GDP growth and financial crises – on YU, compared to total unemployment, was confirmed by this study. Among the control variables, the labour-market reforms index proved to have a (statistically significant and robust) impact on YU; active labour-market policies and unemployment benefits were also generally significant.

In the fourth year of the project, 2015, on the one hand some comparisons between the labour-market situation of the two countries directly involved in the project – Italy and Russia – were completed; on the other hand, a final systematization of the different determinants of YU was accomplished. The corresponding papers have been published either in the cited year or in the subsequent one.

Demidova *et al.* (2015) compared YU in the Russian and Italian regions. In both countries, YU rates were found to be higher than adult (or total) ones, but in the presence – in both cases – of a huge regional differentiation. Above-average YU regions tend to cluster close to each other, and a distinction between "North" and "South" regions resulted appropriate for both countries. Key determinants of YU were identified, for both groups of regions and for the period 2000–2009, by applying a modified Arellano–Bond model including some explanatory and control variables; the existence of distance spatial effects was detected through the use of distance matrixes. Also the negative impact of the 2008–2009 crisis was statistically confirmed. The main policy implication concerned the need to adopt appropriate labour policies, but taking into account that ALMPs, although differentiated across regions, may produce significant spillover effects on nearby regions.

A comparison between YU in Italy and Russia was also made by Marelli and Vakulenko (2016), but it focused on the relationship between individual and family characteristics and the risk of unemployment. After overviewing aggregate youth unemployment trends in several European countries, besides Italy and Russia, a Heckman probit model was used to estimate the unemployment risk of young people, compared to adults, during the period 2004–2011. Despite many differences between the two countries, most of the explanatory variables acted in a similar way in each country (for example gender and education). The strongest marginal effect on the probability of being unemployed, for both countries, was exerted by socio-economic status and, once again, by the regional unemployment situation.

The regional dimension also characterized the investigation by Bruno *et al.* (2016b). They compared the responsiveness of male and female YU and NEET rates, as well as aggregate unemployment rates, to GDP in the European regions. The main focus was on the changes that occurred during the crisis (2009–2011) with respect to the previous period. The method of investigation consisted in a sophisticated dynamic generalized method of moments. On considering different groups of regions, the best performance was recorded in Continental and Northern regions, while the worst ones were found in the Southern regions and among new member states. A significant conclusion, also because of its policy implications, referred to the high persistence of NEET and YU rates, together with their low responsiveness to GDP: thus, even when the economy does recover, many years will elapse before the situation of young people may improve, unless policy makers rapidly adopt effective structural policies.

Marelli and Signorelli (2016) analysed and discussed the key disadvantages of young people in the labour market by considering the evolution of different youth labour-market performance indicators in the EU-28 countries: not only the YU rates, but also youth to total unemployment ratios, long-term unemployment rates, employment rates, NEET rates, part-time and temporary employment, hourly earnings. The disadvantage of young people emerged as a persistent phenomenon, and the impact of the recent crises has been particularly damaging. The worsening of the relative position of young people in the labour market, in terms of quantity and quality of job opportunities, thus requires careful consideration at the policy level.

Bruno *et al.* (2016a) reassessed the impact of financial crises on the YU rate, compared to the total unemployment rate (UR), in a model that also included the unemployment impact of GDP growth (lagged one year) and some institutional variables. The focus of the paper, however, was on the distinction between short- and long-run coefficients, estimated using bias-corrected dynamic panel data estimators. The observations concerned a panel of OECD countries over the period 1981–2009. Both short- and long-run effects of financial crises proved to be significantly greater on YU rates compared to total unemployment rates (some 1.9 and 1.5–1.7 times higher for the short- and long-run effects respectively). Similar results were obtained for the unemployment impacts of lagged GDP, and they appeared to be robust to various dynamic specifications. Although both YU rates and total rates were found to be significantly persistent, the short-run impact of a crisis appears to be so much higher for YU that it eventually triggers also a higher long-run impact, highlighting the need for specific labour policies.

The paper by Caroleo and Pastore (2016) surveyed the theoretical and empirical literature on cross-country differences in overeducation, which is the mismatch between the educational level of workers and that required by the jobs available in the labour market. In general, overeducation penalizes individuals in terms of earnings and employment opportunities and causes wasted resources of society at large in terms of state investments in education that do not yield sufficient benefits. The authors point out that both penalties are higher not only where the demand for skills is lower, but also where school-to-work transition systems fail effectively to address the aim of generating competences rather than only education for their graduates. As known, the recent literature tends to interpret the phenomenon in terms of human capital theory, whereas the disorganization of the educational system, and its degree of integration with the labour market, may play an important role in helping young graduates to develop the work experience and the skills necessary to prevent them from experiencing overeducation.

Caroleo *et al.* (2017) explored the impact of labour- market and educational institutions on youth labour-market performance across OECD countries for the 1985–2012 period. They found that the tax wedge, changes in union density, the minimum wage, educational attainment and the level of economic activity stand out as the key determinants of youth employability. Moreover, participation in VET (vocational education and training) programmes also matters, although only in the short run. There are also some interesting differences across age and gender groups. In particular, labour-market institutions seem to have a stronger impact for women.

Some of the topics regarding young people and the labour market reviewed thus far can also be found in the contributions selected for this book, where nonetheless new and original material is assembled. Short summaries of the content of each chapter are now presented.

In Chapter 1, Caroleo, Ciociano and Destefanis explore the impact of labour-market and educational institutions on youth labour-market performance across OECD countries for the 1985–2013 period. They draw on various sources to build a data set including series about labour-market institutions, youth population, schooling, and VET participation rates. They estimate a dynamic panel model, building upon Bassanini and Duval (2006a), and articulating the analysis among various age groups (15–24, 20–24). Union density, the minimum wage and the level of economic activity stand out as important determinants of youth employability; educational attainment and expenditure on public education matter to a lesser extent. VET participation also matters, although only in countries where the dual apprenticeship system is important.

Pompei and Selezneva analyse in Chapter 2 the influence of country-level education mismatch and individual-level educational attainment on the probability of being unemployed or remaining in alternative labour force statuses for young people aged 15–34 and living in 21 EU countries (years 2006, 2008 and 2010). The authors perform a multinomial logit model taking into account both the multilevel structure of data (country- and individual-level variables) and the endogeneity between education and labour force status. The aggregated measure of mismatch enables them to study its overall impact not only on employability but also on other possible individual labour statuses in which young people may be, especially unemployment and inactivity. The results show that more years of education are important to reduce the probability of being unemployed, and they slightly raise the probability of being self-employed with respect to the probability of being an employee. An extra year of education seems particularly effective (considering interaction terms) in reducing the probability of being unemployed in countries that experienced a higher mismatch after 2008. Therefore, improving access to university degrees remains the main means to tackle youth unemployment caused by education mismatch, even after the outbreak of the current economic crisis.

In the third chapter, Parisi, Marelli and Demidova describe the evolution of four macroeconomic phenomena and their wide heterogeneity across European and Anglo-Saxon countries: labour productivity, youth unemployment rate, strictness of employment protection legislation, the share of youngsters with a temporary job. They begin by observing the well-known productivity slowdown in Southern Europe, starting in 1995, and the dramatic increase in youth unemployment, especially after the onset of the financial and economic crisis in 2007; in this regard, they also document countries' differences and policy choices to combat unemployment. The authors show whether the data support different hypotheses about labour-market reforms and firms' productivity dynamics. One hypothesis is that temporary work reduces the capital-labour ratio and, being cheap work, mostly substitutes riskier (ICT-enabled) innovations, thus reducing productivity. The second one is the "matching hypothesis" which affirms that short-term contracts allow the better matching of workers to jobs or projects, thus increasing productivity. The third hypothesis regards weak firms' incentives to employ, invest in and train temporary labour: such weak incentives decrease productivity. A glance at the data shows that the matching hypothesis is most plausible for Anglo-Saxon (after 2005) and Southern European countries, in the 1992–2012 period. The other two hypotheses may be plausible – at least for specific periods – for Continental, Scandinavian countries and new EU countries. Until the crisis years, countries with a medium level of labour protection were also those with the highest level of youth unemployment, but the trend was decreasing. After 2007, all groups on average showed an upward swing of youth unemployment. Finally, the greater use of temporary work for youngsters does not seem to be associated with either higher or lower unemployment.

In Chapter 4, Perugini and Pompei investigate the temporary/permanent contracts' wage gap for young and older workers in EU-28 countries by employing EU-SILC microdata for the period 2010–2013. The analysis is carried out by focusing on the wage levels of temporary workers (compared to permanent ones), distinguished by broad age classes (16–39 and 40–64 years old) and level of education attained (primary, secondary and tertiary). The results reveal a remarkable cross-country variability in the incidence of fixed-term contracts and in the temporary/permanent wage disparity. However, albeit with significant exceptions and heterogeneity, the share of temporary contracts is normally higher for young workers; moreover, older workers tend to suffer a significantly deeper wage penalty when they are fixed-term employees. This result suggests that a large share of those temporary workers who are not able to attain a permanent job when they grow older may be caught in a trap of repeated temporary positions/low pay. The analysis of the personal characteristics associated with fixed-term positions for the pool of older workers reveals that higher levels of education undoubtedly reduce the probability of temporary, and therefore low-wage, employment.

In Chapter 5, Addabbo and Kjeldstad analyse living arrangements among young Italian and Norwegian adults by gender. The starting point is the wide difference between the two countries as regards the propensity of young adults to remain in their parents' home after compulsory schooling. A general consideration is that young Europeans leave their parents' home at different ages: Southern Europeans leave at the highest ages and, in Italy, postponement of leaving the parental home is widespread and increasing, even compared to other Mediterranean countries. Conversely, young Nordic adults, including Norwegians, are the youngest leavers; they establish independent households at much younger ages, either on their own or in cohabitation with a partner or friends. The study tries to answer various research questions: (i) the reasons for the different behaviours of young Italians and Norwegians; (ii) the characteristics of young adults who stay with their childhood family long into adulthood and of those who form independent households, either with or without a partner; (iii) what are the propensities in the two countries to stay with parents compared to living alone or with a partner, and what conditions and what characteristics are associated with the various propensities; (iv) the existence of gender differences, because in both countries adult men stay longer in their parents' homes than adult women do. Regarding the last point, the authors investigate whether there are reasons to believe that leaving the parents' home is related to dissimilarities in events and characteristics between women and men, between the two countries, and possibly even between Italian and Norwegian women and men. They examine these questions by means of a comparative data set (EU-SILC) containing demographic and standard-of-living information for both individuals and households in Italy and Norway. The year of the analysis is 2007, a time when the economic prospects and the labour markets were relatively stable in both countries.

In Chapter 6, Dietrich *et al.* explore the risk of being unemployed during the Great Recession, from a school-to-work transition perspective, in two quite different countries: Germany and Greece. In contrast to the commonly used definition of young people based on age cohorts, Dietrich *et al.* introduce a framework where the unemployment risk of school graduates is analysed within the first five years after entry into the labour market. Besides individual characteristics, the study includes institutional characteristics and macro level information varying over time and country. Logit models are employed for estimations. The results confirm not only clear differences in the situation of the two countries but also some similarities: for example, the protective function of education for the unemployment risk. Country-specific effects are considered to analyse individual characteristics regarding, for instance, gender and migration background.

Addabbo, Rodríguez-Modroño and Gálvez-Muñoz analyse in Chapter 7 the factors that increase the risk of being NEET in Spain and Italy. The authors also investigate its costs in terms of life satisfaction, meaning of life and financial satisfaction, distinguishing by gender. They use a multivariate analysis based on EU-SILC 2013 data for youths aged 15–34. The results reveal that being NEET in Italy and Spain is more likely for older individuals, while a higher educational level protects against the risk of being NEET. This risk depends not only on gender but also on differences regarding living arrangements, since women are more likely to be NEET and live as a couple, whereas men are more likely to be NEET while living with their parents, living alone or in other living arrangements. The analysis also shows the high cost of the effect of the NEET status on subjective measures of well-being, in terms of reduced life satisfaction, lower satisfaction with the financial situation, and negative impact on the overall meaning of life.

In Chapter 8, Bartolucci *et al.* analyse job satisfaction among young Russian workers. The corresponding response variables are divided into five ordered categories, from "completely unsatisfied" to "completely satisfied". Ordered logit models of job satisfaction have been estimated with individual fixed effects for a panel data analysis of young male and female Russian workers. The wage plays a prominent role as an explanatory variable in the model specifications; indeed, for all but one sample considered, there is at least one job satisfaction variable with a significantly positive wage effect. This result can be interpreted as a failure of the theory of compensating wage differentials in the Russian youth labour market. Interestingly, compensating wage differentials only appear to be at work among the older subjects. The estimates also show strong gender and location effects.

Pastore provides in Chapter 9 an interpretative framework to understand the reasons why school-to-work transition is so hard and long in Italy. The country is a typical example of the South European school-to-work transition regime, where the educational system is typically rigid and sequential, the labour market has been recently made more flexible through two-tier reforms, and the family has an important role in absorbing the cost of the passage to adulthood. The main thesis of this study is that the disorganization of the educational and training system, rather than the supposedly low degree of labour market flexibility, explains the high (youth) unemployment rate. Regarding the policy implications, the chapter concludes by assessing the potentialities and shortcomings of the European Youth Guarantee as a tool to fight youth unemployment in the country.

In Chapter 10, Kelly, McGuinness and Whelan examine whether young people qualifying from the educational system in Ireland have had a greater or lesser exposure to unstable employment following the Great Recession. In particular, the study examines the extent to which individuals qualifying at various education levels faced an increased likelihood of temporary employment between 2006 and 2012. The research initially examines the descriptive evidence on temporary versus permanent employment among newly qualified young people, before assessing the extent to which the marginal impact of various credentials on the likelihood of temporary compared to permanent employment changed over the time period considered. The sample (for the main part of the study) is restricted to individuals under the age of 26 who entered employment after obtaining a formal qualification in the previous 12 months. A significant finding is that student status and being employed in sectors such as Education and Industry substantially increase the probability of non-permanent employment (in both pre- and post-recession periods). Finally, a particularly worrying aspect of the analysis is that obtaining a third-level qualification does not provide a buffer against temporary employment for young people.

Notes

1 EU FP7 "The Political Economy of Youth Unemployment", Marie Curie Actions "People" – International Research Staff Exchange Scheme – Project IRSES GA-2010-269134.
2 For simplicity, we use YU also when the analysis specifically concerns youth unemployment rates (YUR).
3 All references are listed in the Bibliography at the end of the book.

1 Youth unemployment, labour-market institutions and education

A cross-country analysis

Floro Ernesto Caroleo, Elvira Ciociano and Sergio Destefanis

1 Introduction

The effects of youth unemployment can be particularly serious, because they occur at the beginning of the working life of a person and may have substantial scarring effects (O'Higgins, 2010; Manfredi *et al.*, 2010; Caporale and Gil-Alana, 2014). Moreover, youth unemployment has very detrimental effects on welfare and, in the longer term, on future employment prospects and earnings (Gregg and Tominey, 2005; Mroz and Savage, 2006), on human capital accumulation (Caroleo, 2012) and on fertility rates (Jimeno and Rodríguez-Palenzuela, 2002). Besides, the long-lasting global crisis begun in 2008 has disproportionately affected young people and exacerbated the weakness of their condition in the labour market.

Education and skills formation are generally related to the possibilities of a young worker of being employed: indeed, the observed differences in the severity of youth unemployment across countries can also depend on how the national school-to-work institutions are organised (Ryan, 2001). Young people with low levels of qualification facing higher risks of exclusion and lacking access to employment are a feature common to many economies. Unemployment rates of higher skilled people tend to be lower than those of low skilled and their average employment rates are higher (Zimmermann *et al.*, 2013). In developed countries (Quintini and Martin, 2014) the crisis has made harder the transition from school to work, especially for young people without an educational background matching the needs of the structural and technological change. Some countries have therefore created or reinforced institutions to support entry into the labour market. Yet, while the expansion of general education occurred in many countries in recent years has led to a substantial increase in overall levels of educational attainment, the quality of the education system and its linkage to the labour market have very often been questioned (Eichhorst *et al.*, 2015).[1]

This chapter focuses on the role of education systems and labour-market institutions in determining youth employment in a cross-country framework. We allow for various institutional and structural factors, building upon Bassanini and Duval (2006a), and extend the literature in considering with some detail participation rates to vocational programmes at the secondary level of education

(ISCED levels 2 and 3, according to the ISCED classification), and expenditures in education across OECD countries. Our analysis is articulated across two age groups (15–24, 20–24) and makes full allowance for the dynamic structure of the data.

The rest of the chapter has the following outline. In Section 2 we review the debate on youth labour-market performance and school-to-work transition. Section 3 presents the empirical framework and the main results. Some concluding remarks are provided in Section 4.

2 The youth labour market

2.1 Determinants of youth labour-market performance

When analysing youth labour-market performance, several factors should be considered: the institutions governing the school-to-work transition (including the quality of the education system and the integration between school and work-based training), labour-market regulation (hiring and firing rules, safety nets and industrial relations systems), as well as demographic and cyclical patterns (Zimmermann *et al.*, 2013).

Demographic structure affects young employability for two reasons: it influences the size of younger cohorts determining youth labour supply (Korenman and Neumark, 1997; Shimer, 2001); and it affects the social and cultural approach of a country towards young people. It is obvious that the more young people are in the labour market, the more jobs will be needed to accommodate them. This is the so called "cohort crowding hypothesis", according to which larger youth cohorts face reduced job opportunities in the presence of imperfect substitutability between workers of different ages and wage rigidities. When the entity of younger cohorts is very high, their entry into the labour force under bad economic conditions or sluggish demand can cause the origin of longer queues, since the labour market will absorb these young people slowly and/or insufficiently (Korenman and Neumark, 1997; Bassanini and Duval, 2006a; Zimmermann *et al.*, 2013). According to Jimeno and Rodríguez-Palenzuela (2002), demographic developments have a significant but limited impact on relative youth unemployment rates: youth workers mostly play a role of "buffer" to absorb macroeconomic shocks, through wider fluctuations in their unemployment rates: this is reflected in the very significant impact of cyclically related variables on the relative youth unemployment rates.

It has long been known that younger workers tend to be more severely affected by economic fluctuations (Clark and Summers, 1982; Manfredi *et al.*, 2010; Bell and Blanchflower, 2011; Verick, 2011; Bernal-Verdugo *et al.*, 2012; Choudhry Tanveer *et al.*, 2012; O'Higgins, 2012; Zimmermann *et al.*, 2013; Ghoshray *et al.*, 2016). This phenomenon has various reasons: a disproportionate presence of youth among temporary jobs, their high concentration in some cyclically sensitive industries, as for example construction (Manfredi *et al.*, 2010), and the so-called LIFO principle (last-in-first-out), applied by firms in times of crisis: they prefer to fire workers hired more recently, than the ones employed for a longer time. More recently hired people tend to be younger, with higher mobility and opportunities to find a job somewhere else (this is the inclination to job shopping highlighted in Caliendo *et al.*, 2011); moreover, they have less experience (Caroleo and Pastore, 2007). Bell and Blanchflower (2011) also find that the least educated young workers have been hit harder by the Great Recession.

Following the seminal papers of Nickell (1997) and Blanchard and Wolfers (2000) (see also Nickell *et al.*, 2005), a wide consensus has formed around the belief that the rigidity of labour-market institutions plays a major role in the determination of long-run labour-market performance. These institutions cover the unemployment benefits system, the extent of active labour-market policies, the wage determination system (union density, union coverage, degree of coordination, minimum wages), the tax wedge, the pervasiveness of employment protection legislation and the strictness of the legislation regarding the use of temporary contracts (OECD, 1994). In Jimeno and Rodríguez-Palenzuela (2002) two institutional features stand out as the most relevant for the study of youth unemployment rates: those that increase the overall cost of the standard labour contract, for instance employment protection, and those which do not make provision for some contractual flexibility for the specificities of young workers. The first ones could make younger workers less attractive than the prime age ones, because the average lower job experience tends to decrease their average productivity. The second characteristics leave youth in a relative disadvantage with respect prime age workers, if the general labour-market setting is predominantly rigid.

The literature has conflicting views on the impact of temporary employment on the school-to-work transition. This contract type may increase labour-market flexibility in those European countries with excessive employment protection regulation or that need to speed up the transition process towards a market economy. The widely debated issue is whether temporary jobs are actually a stepping-stone to permanent work, without causing a long-lasting wage penalty, or a dead end. Indeed, temporary work often becomes a low-pay trap as young people tend to accept low-pay jobs. Instead of accumulating work experience to find high pay-high quality jobs later, they remain trapped for many years or even for the rest of their lives (Bruno *et al.*, 2013).

In this chapter we lay stress on the institutions concerning schooling, training and school-to-work transition, which can also play a key role in determining the success of the younger workers, especially during the phase of the transition from school to work (O'Higgins, 2001; Choudhry Tanveer *et al.*, 2012; Cahuc *et al.*, 2013; Eichhorst *et al.*, 2013; Banerji *et al.*, 2015; Ghoshray *et al.*, 2016). The different institutional environment could explain cross-country and intertemporal variations of youth integration into employment, and institutions targeted at the activation, the employability, the skills and knowledge improvement of youth, can play a role in fighting youth unemployment, and different strategies could be implemented to contrast it (Eichhorst, 2016).

2.2 School-to-work transition

Youth are considered a vulnerable category of workers since they are in a delicate phase of their working life, the first entry into the labour force. They are involved in the school-to-work transition (Piopiunik and Ryan, 2012), typically defined as the period between the end of compulsory schooling and the attainment of full-time and/or stable employment.[2] Several reasons justify a particular vulnerability. Workers at the first experience do not have the same knowledge, skills, competences that can be learnt only at work. As a result, young workers often show high turnover rates (this is the *youth experience gap* highlighted in Caroleo and Pastore, 2007 and Pastore, 2011). Many young workers conciliate part-time jobs with study and/or the searching activities for work, frequently alternating periods in the work force with periods of inactivity, which gives rise to a not always smooth school-to-work transition that entails growing precariousness and less job satisfaction (Martin *et al.*, 2007). This situation can be worsened by other specific characteristics: gender, ethnicity, disability, regional disparity, the organisation of the family economy (Berloffa *et al.*, 2015), initial differences in skills and education, and rigidities on the side of institutions (school, university, training system, labour agencies as well as labour-market legislation; see on this Caroleo and Pastore, 2007, 2009).

Piopiunik and Ryan (2012) propose a useful classification of the policy interventions specific for the school-to-work transition into three groups: a) active labour-market programmes (ALMP) (see also Martin *et al.*, 2007; Caliendo *et al.*, 2011; Caliendo and Schmidl, 2016) based on short-run strategies aimed at improving labour-market efficiency, increasing the labour supply, integrating unemployed workers into the labour market (Escudero, 2015)[3]; b) vocational education and training (VET) systems aimed at equipping people with knowledge, know-how, skills and/or competences required in particular occupations or class of occupations or trades on the labour market (Cedefop, 2008); in this case effects are expected over a longer time spectrum; c) apprenticeship, that is a system of cooperation between firms and vocational schools in initial training (Ryan, 2001) allowing the acquisition of general and transferable skills during class-based VET, and combining structured learning on the job and actual work experience within a training company (Eichhorst *et al.*, 2015).

Generally ALMPs are characterised by a lack of integration with the educational system, whereas in VET systems the continuity with schooling is fundamental. Competences and qualifications acquired should be made comparable to those acquired in the academic tracks to promote possibilities of transfers between the two systems (Eichhorst *et al.*, 2015). On the other hand, the distinction between VET and apprenticeship can be ambiguous, as vocational education may have work-based components (e.g. apprenticeships, dual-system education programmes). Depending on how VET systems are organised and implemented in the institutional setting, are integrated into the formal educational path, on the place where it is carried out (at general schools, and/or at specific training centres or colleges), on the degree of specificity of the provided skills, Eichhorst *et al.* (2015) identify three types of VET systems: a) a school-based education system, b) a dual apprenticeship system in which school-based education is combined with firm-based training, c) informal training.

Our interest in VET systems finds, in particular, its motivation to the fact that, during the current recession, the best performances in terms of youth labour-market outcomes have been observed in the countries where a dual apprenticeship system is prevailing, that is Germany, Austria, Denmark. More generally, it could be asked which VET systems are more conducive in the long run to favourable youth labour-market outcomes (Ryan, 2007; Hanushek *et al.*, 2011; Zimmermann *et al.*, 2013; Rodríguez-Planas *et al.*, 2015; van Ours, 2015), and whether more VET increases youth employment. Evidence in this field is by no means as abundant as the findings related to cycle, demographics and (to a lesser extent) overall labour-market institutions. In the next section, we provide first some descriptive evidence about this issue, and then some econometric estimates considering VET participation alongside with other educational and institutional variables.

3 Youth employment, institutions and VET systems: some dynamic panel estimates

3.1 Analysing youth employment: the empirical issues

Analysing from an empirical standpoint the relationship between youth employment, labour-market institutions and VET systems is an undertaking potentially affected by various problems. One has to allow for various measures of performance, due to the multi-dimensionality of the problem under scrutiny. Furthermore, since schooling potentially interacts with other institutions, the issue must be analysed taking into account as wide a set of institutions as possible. The likely endogeneity of institutions is another source of problems for the analysis: reverse causality may run from labour-market changes to policy changes (Bassanini and Duval, 2006a). Moreover, there is not a uniform definition across countries of VET systems, nor are data complete or available, at least for quite long time series. The lack of data and precise definitions for VET programmes could make useless the implementation of usual estimation methods.

Finally, and perhaps foremost, differences in economic conditions, labour-market institutions, education and labour-market policies may result in systematic cross-country differences in the chances of youth to enter the labour market. This suggests that empirical analysis should make distinctions across countries according to their different institutional arrangements.

Cross-country classifications of institutional differences are based on theories, prevailing regimes and laws, organisational philosophies (see Wilkinson and Wood, 2012). Generally speaking, the most famous classification among countries based on institutional attributes is the Varieties of Capitalism approach, proposed by Hall and Soskice (2001) in which two types of market economy are defined: Liberal Market Economies and Coordinated Market Economies (LMEs and CMEs, respectively). Another classification, particularly helpful in order to distinguish countries on the basis of labour-market institutions, is proposed by Esping-Andersen (1990) and relates to the welfare state systems.

Recently, there has been an increasing interest in defining identification criteria based on the relationship between national institutional archetypes and educational and training systems, and in general school-to-work transition institutions (Caroleo and Pastore, 2007; Hanushek *et al.*, 2011; Goergen *et al.*, 2012; Piopiunik and Ryan, 2012; Zimmermann *et al.*, 2013; Dolado, 2015). As a broad rule they distinguish economies in which VET involves largely or entirely full-time schooling, and economies in which part-time schooling is combined with work-based learning as part of apprenticeship.

In this chapter we adopt two types of classification of the OECD countries under scrutiny. The first one builds upon Hall and Soskice, as well as Esping-Andersen, and is based on differences in the economic and institutional structures. The resulting groups are: "Central European" countries (dubbed as *Central*): Austria, Belgium, Germany, Netherlands, Switzerland; "Anglo-Saxon" countries (*Anglo*): Australia, Canada, Ireland, New Zealand, UK, USA; *Mediterranean* countries: France, Italy, Portugal, Spain; and *Nordic* countries: Finland, Norway, Sweden, Denmark.

The second criterion takes into account the distinction between countries on the basis of the different VET systems. Following Hanushek *et al.* (2011) we distinguish: "highly vocational" countries (dubbed as *hi-vet*), having a high share of participants to VET: Belgium, Finland, Norway, Sweden; "dual" vocational countries (dubbed as *dual*), having not only a high share of VET participation but also a high percentage of participants in combined school and work-based programmes: Austria, Denmark, Germany, Netherlands, Switzerland; "non-firm vocational" countries, having some school-based VET in a system geared toward general education and dubbed as *nofirm*: Australia, France, Italy, Portugal, Spain; "non-school vocational" countries (dubbed as *noschool*) having little or no VET but relying on in-firm apprenticeship: Canada, Ireland, New Zealand, UK, USA.[4]

Following our discussion at the end of the previous section, we now provide some descriptive evidence on youth employment across these country groups.

Table 1.1 Some descriptive evidence on youth employment by country groups

Economic-institutional classification	Employment rate, age 15–24 (mean and s.d.)	Employment rate, age 20–24 (mean and s.d.)	VET-based classification	Employment rate, age 15–24 (mean and s.d.)	Employment rate, age 20–24 (mean and s.d.)
Central	49.58, 13.22	65.44, 10.37	Dual	57.20, 7.89	70.59, 4.65
Anglo	55.07, 7.94	68.30, 4.92	Hi-vet	44.67, 11.70	60.79, 9.69
Mediterranean	33.64, 8.36	48.71, 8.40	Nofirm	53.83, 8.18	67.19, 4.69
Nordic	52.81, 9,64	66.02, 8.44	Noschool	39.18, 13.31	53.71, 12.47

This descriptive evidence shows that, by and large, dual apprenticeship countries do better than the other ones. However, it is not possible to deduce a simple relationship between youth employment and VET. European countries with a high share of VET participants fare almost as well as dual countries, but are outperformed by the "noschool" Anglo-Saxon countries.

3.2 The empirical set-up

We now try to shed some further light on these issues by providing some econometric evidence within a dynamic panel data model. We use the study on labour-market institutions done by Bassanini and Duval (2006a, 2006b) as starting point, since it explores the effect of the main labour-market institutions on different workers' groups. The following remarks are in order. First Bassanini and Duval only consider workers aged 20–24: we also consider the more traditional definition of young people aged 15–24. Second, additionally to labour-market institutions, they also consider some demographic and educational variables standing for VET and other educational features (relative youth cohort and education). We add to these the VET participation rates. Finally, Bassanini and Duval only provide static estimates (actually Jimeno and Rodríguez-Palenzuela, 2002, do the same). But lagged dependent variables could be very useful proxies both for the persistence associated with labour-market performances and the relationships between past performances and policy actions. Evidence evocative of both phenomena is found in Destefanis and Mastromatteo (2010, 2012). Furthermore Pena-Boquete (2016), when analysing the aggregate determination of female labour force participation, has recently found that static estimates may give rise to misleading inference. Hence we proceed to the estimation of full-fledged dynamic estimates, selecting our preferred specifications through a general-to-specific search maximising coefficient significance. The estimated equation is:

$$emp_{it} = \beta\, emp_{it-1} + \Sigma\, v_j X_{it-j} + \Sigma\, \chi_j Si_{t-j} + \Sigma\, \lambda_j Z_{it-j} + \alpha_i + \tau_i + \delta_t + \varepsilon_{it} \qquad (1.1)$$

where emp_{it} is the youth employment rate (in the country i and in the year t), and $j=0, 1$. X_{it} is a vector of variables representing specific policies and institutions: employment protection legislation, tax wedge, the percentage of active labour-market policies expenditures over GDP, minimum wages, unemployment benefits and union density. S_{it} is the vector of the education-related variables: VET participation, educational attainment, relative youth education and the percentage of expenditures in public education. Z_{it} is a vector of control variables: the relative cohort of youth population on total population, and the output gap. The equations include country fixed effects, α_i, country-idiosyncratic linear trends, τ_i, and time dummies, δ_t. Equation (1.1) follows a basically linear specification (Bassanini and Duval did the same). Only educational attainment is taken in natural logarithms. We have also attempted with full-fledged loglinear specifications, but they entailed a lower fit.

We have data for nineteen OECD countries: Australia, Austria, Belgium, Canada, Denmark, Finland, France, Germany, Ireland, Italy, Netherlands, Norway, New Zealand, Portugal, Spain, Sweden, Switzerland, United Kingdom, United States, for the 1985–2013 period. Our main source has been the OECD statistics portal. We have taken from it the employment rates, the indicator of employment protection legislation, the tax wedge measure, the percentage of active labour-market policies expenditures over GDP, the minimum to median wage indicator[5] and union density. The relative youth cohort, youth population over total working age population, the percentage of expenditure in public education[6] and the output gap, also come from the OECD statistics portal. On the other hand, in order to measure duration and replacement rate of the unemployment benefit system, we use the indicators of duration and generosity proposed by Scruggs *et al.* (2014). These data have been integrated with other (mainly education-related) variables. The VET participation, that is the ratio of technical/vocational (ISCED 2 and 3) over total secondary enrolment, comes from the UNESCO UIS statistics portal. Educational attainment and relative youth education, the difference between the number of education years of total population aged 15 and over and the number of education years of total population aged 25 and over come from the Barro-Lee website (these data are given only over five-year intervals, which meant that we had to interpolate them for the missing years; in this exercise we also used the 2015 predicted data). There are missing data for some countries and years, and hence we end up with an unbalanced panel data set. Further details about the data set are available upon request.

The choice of schooling variables is highly driven by the availability of the data. The VET participation has been chosen because it derives from one of the richest data archives about VET systems. The fact that the related data are collected on the basis of the ISCED classification, allows, at least partially, to overcome the lack of homogeneous juridical definitions for VET and apprenticeship across countries.

Our econometric approach is based upon the ARDL estimator proposed in Pesaran and Shin (1999). Provided the correct order is chosen for the ARDL model, this estimator provides consistent estimates of the short-run parameters and super-consistent estimates of the long-run coefficients. Some recent works (Destefanis and Mastromatteo, 2015; Pena-Boquete, 2016) find that regressor endogeneity is likely to be important in this ambit, strengthening the case for the adoption of estimation techniques dealing with this problem. In a dynamic panel framework, system GMM would appear as a natural choice, but in our case the number of countries is too small for appropriate application of this technique. On the other hand, when dealing with the estimation of the long-run coefficients, an appropriate choice of the orders of the ARDL model is sufficient to correct for the problem of endogenous regressors. This also means that, in commenting upon our results, we shall focus on the estimates for the long-run coefficients.

3.3 The main results

For every dependent variable (the time variations of emp and emp2024; see the Legend in the Appendix for the list of abbreviations we used), we estimated a different equation for each country group. We used the Akaike Information Criterion (AIC), and the Schwarz Criterion (SC) to select the orders of the ARDL model, obtaining in all cases the (1, 1) specification. The estimated equations are shown in Tables A1.1–A1.4 in the Appendix.

Generally speaking, our estimates indicate that dynamics is important and that both structural and educational variables and institutional variables are needed in order to make sense of the evolution of youth employment in the countries under scrutiny. The results for institutional variables mark some novelties vis-à-vis the literature on youth labour-market performance. Employment protection legislation is only significant, with a positive sign, for both *Anglo* samples. Unemployment benefit generosity is never significant.[7] Both results starkly differ with respect to those obtained in Bassanini and Duval (2006a), who obtain a strong negative impact on employment for both variables. Differences in the sample period and the robustness of the adopted indicators seem to matter more than those in the estimation method and in the dynamic specification (we estimated some static equations, but their results differ considerably from Bassanini and Duval's ones. Results are available upon request. A similar comment may apply to the tax wedge, which is only significant in the *Dual* and *Nofirm* samples (both for age 20–24) with a different sign.

Active labour-market policies are significant for both *Anglo* samples, and again for the *Dual* and *Noschool* samples (age 20–24), but the *negatively* affect employment. They only are significant with the expected positive sign for the *Hi-vet* sample (age 20–24). We note that this particular variable was never included in macroeconomic estimates (such as Bassanini and Duval's ones). On the other hand, Caliendo and Schmidl (2016), reporting results from the micro-econometric literature, write that

> The particularity of the youth labor market situation and the results from the meta-analyses suggest that assessments of the effectiveness of ALMP for adults are most likely not valid for youth. So far, no consensus exists on the effectiveness of the different ALMP programs for this age group. … Overall, the aggregate evidence of the effectiveness of ALMP is somewhat discouraging, suggesting that some – but not all – elements of ALMP programs can be a solution for the youth unemployment problem.
>
> (Caliendo and Schmidl, 2016, p. 3)
> (see also Escudero, 2015; Eichhorst, 2016)

We will pick up this point again in our concluding remarks.

The other institutional variables provide results that, although circumscribed to some country samples, are more in line with a priori expectations. The minimum wage reduces employment for the *Central* and *Anglo* samples (not so much for the age 20–24 subset in the latter case), and again in the *Noschool* (age 15–24) and *Hi-vet* (age 20–24) samples. Union density negatively affects employment for the *Anglo* samples, and approaches significance (always with a negative sign) for the *Noschool* and *Nofirm* samples (age 15–24).

By and large, the *Anglo* and the *Noschool* samples (which are closely related) are the ones most affected by institutional variables. The samples based on the VET classification, especially for the 20–24 age segment, are, on the other hand, the most impervious to institutional influences.

Regarding the education-related variables, VET participation is significant and positive in the *Central* and *Dual* samples. This is rather in line with a priori expectations. On the other hand it is significant and positive for the *Anglo* (age 20–24) sample and again approaches significance with a negative sign for the *Noschool* (age 20–24) sample. This suggests that the outcome of this variable is highly context-dependent and that policy advice about it should be carefully considered. The other educational variables are mostly significant for the *Mediterranean* and *Anglo* samples, and, to a lesser extent, for the similar *Nofirm* and *Noschool* samples. Relative youth education has the expected negative sign, while educational attainment increases employability. The percentage of expenditure in public education over final government consumption expenditure is only significant for the *Mediterranean* and *Nofirm* samples, where indeed it could be surmised that it should matter most.

Turning finally to the control variables, the relative youth cohort favours employment in the *Anglo* and *Noschool* samples, and rather less expectedly, in the *Nofirm* (age 20–24) sample. Only in the *Dual* (age 20–24) sample there is the a priori expected negative effect. The output gap is always significant with the expected positive sign, but never for the *Mediterranean* and *Nofirm* samples. In this case, the presumption of a strong cyclical sensitivity of the youth labour market is not borne out by our results.

4 Concluding remarks

In this chapter we study the effects of labour-market institutions and education-related variables on youth employment rates in a sample of nineteen OECD countries through the 1985–2013 period. We provide some panel estimates, paying attention to a proper dynamic specification of our equations, and splitting our countries in two different classifications (each composed of four country samples).

Looking at the labour-market institutions, minimum wage and union density seem the institutions that have more significant effects on youth employment. These results are in line with a priori expectations, but further research may be needed to make sense of the insignificant results we find for EPL, unemployment benefits and tax wedge. As far as the unexpected sign of active labour-market policies are concerned, it is worthwhile quoting again Caliendo and Schmidl (2016), who say that

> Overall, the findings with respect to employment outcomes are only partly promising. While job search assistance (with and without monitoring) results in overwhelmingly positive effects, we find more mixed effects for training and wage subsidies, whereas the effects for public work programs are clearly negative.
>
> (Caliendo and Schmidl, 2016, p. 1)

Hence in future research, we plan to experiment with disaggregated measures of active labour-market policies.

VET participation has positive effects on youth employment, but only in the country samples where it could be expected a priori to have such effects. Other educational variables have a (mostly positive) impact on youth employability in the samples where VET participation is supposed not to be very important. Finally, we find little support for the crowding-out effect of the relative youth cohort, and the a priori idea of a strong cyclical sensitivity of youth employment is not fully supported by our evidence.

In the future we want to pursue this research by analysing other types of country classification (eventually exploring data-based classifications). Another issue worth of future research relates to the type of employment contracts. The empirical framework used in this chapter can be easily extended to allow for this important feature of labour markets in advanced countries.

Appendix – The econometric estimates

Table A1.1 The employment rate, age 15–24, the economic-institutional classification

		Central	Anglo	Mediterranean	Nordic
emp	t–1	−0.40***	−0.39***	−0.31***	−0.33***
		(0.00)	(0.00)	(0.00)	(0.00)
epl	Δ	−1.81	1.92	−0.66	1.66
		(0.16)	(0.14)	(0.53)	(0.32)
	t–1	−0.47	2.42**	−0.36	−0.38
		(0.72)	(0.03)	(0.74)	(0.80)
taxWedge	Δ	−0.20	−0.02	0.23	−0.07
		(0.18)	(0.73)	(0.15)	(0.74)
	t–1	−0.55	−0.92	−1.81	1.92
		(0.29)	(0.20)	(0.20)	(0.28)
almpgdp	Δ	5.18*	−3.03*	2.11	−1.70
		(0.05)	(0.07)	(0.34)	(0.23)
	t–1	2.95	−3.16	−0.55	−0.93
		(0.21)	(0.06)	(0.75)	(0.62)

continued

Table A1.1 Continued

		Central	Anglo	Mediterranean	Nordic
minW_medW	Δ	0.25	−0.03**	−0.14	–
		(0.62)	(0.03)	(0.54)	–
	t−1	−1.04*	−0.05***	−0.28	–
		(0.05)	(0.00)	(0.15)	–
gener	Δ	−10.26	−4.90*	4.29	4.13
		(0.28)	(0.07)	(0.17)	(0.60)
	t−1	−11.33	4.46	4.96	−0.85
		(0.31)	(0.13)	(0.27)	(0.89)
ud	Δ	−0.26	−0.23**	−0.12	−0.15
		(0.41)	(0.01)	(0.59)	(0.59)
	t−1	−0.09	−0.20**	−0.05	−0.45
		(0.67)	(0.01)	(0.77)	(0.14)
vet	Δ	0.07	−0.08	0.11	−0.03
		(0.57)	(0.16)	(0.39)	(0.86)
	t−1	0.29**	−0.03	−0.07	−0.14
		(0.02)	(0.44)	(0.94)	(0.50)
EducExp	Δ	−0.01	−0.05	0.17**	0.07
		(0.73)	(0.32)	(0.02)	(0.68)
	t−1	0.02	−0.05	0.32***	0.11
		(0.71)	(0.19)	(0.00)	(0.56)
Educ		−7.73	19.30	40.72**	−26.24
		(0.33)	(0.14)	(0.03)	(0.45)
relEduc		−1.88	−3.99	−10.00*	−5.65
		(0.73)	(0.15)	(0.06)	(0.30)
relcoh	Δ	−2.01	1.62*	−1.87***	−0.35
		(0.14)	(0.06)	(0.00)	(0.67)
	t−1	−0.13	0.77**	−0.16	−0.44
		(0.80)	(0.02)	(0.66)	(0.20)
ygap	Δ	0.13	0.40***	0.27	0.87***
		(0.57)	(0.00)	(0.25)	(0.00)
	t−1	0.55*	0.44***	0.03	0.59***
		(0.09)	(0.00)	(0.92)	(0.00)
N		**124**	**157**	**107**	**111**
R2–adj		**0.50**	**0.75**	**0.71**	**0.70**
AR(1)		**0.17**	**0.11**	**0.28**	**0.36**

Note
Heteroskedasticity-robust significance; * means $p < 0.10$, ** $p < 0.05$, and *** $p < 0.01$.

Table A1.2 The employment rate, age 20–24, the economic-institutional classification

		Central	Anglo	Mediterranean	Nordic
emp2024	t–1	–0.51***	–0.45***	–0.43***	–0.35***
		(0.00)	(0.00)	(0.00)	(0.00)
epl	Δ	0.48	1.22	–0.76	0.80
		(0.76)	(0.41)	(0.56)	(0.61)
	t–1	0.09	1.88*	–0.52	–0.27
		(0.96)	(0.09)	(0.77)	(0.84)
taxWedge	Δ	–0.12	–0.04	0.15	–0.28
		(0.50)	(0.70)	(0.46)	(0.18)
	t–1	–0.05	–0.02	0.08	0.07
		(0.79)	(0.77)	(0.75)	(0.68)
almpgdp	Δ	1.27	–3.13*	0.68	–1.97
		(0.60)	(0.07)	(0.80)	(0.12)
	t–1	2.63	–3.23*	–1.75	0.23
		(0.31)	(0.08)	(0.42)	(0.87)
minW_medW	Δ	0.39	–0.02	–0.12	–
		(0.50)	(0.41)	(0.68)	–
	t–1	–1.19**	–0.03	–0.40	–
		(0.02)	(0.14)	(0.13)	–
gener	Δ	–3.16	–3.80	5.60	–0.92
		(0.75)	(0.33)	(0.21)	(0.88)
	t–1	–14.44	1.71	5.26	–4.36
		(0.25)	(0.62)	(0.39)	(0.48)
ud	Δ	0.17	–0.25**	0.07	0.03
		(0.61)	(0.01)	(0.80)	(0.89)
	t–1	0.22	–0.15**	–0.05	–0.30
		(0.43)	(0.02)	(0.84)	(0.22)
vet	Δ	0.06	–0.08	0.20	–0.08
		(0.69)	(0.26)	(0.29)	(0.55)
	t–1	0.19*	–0.12**	–0.02	–0.03
		(0.08)	(0.01)	(0.90)	(0.85)
EducExp	Δ	–0.01	–0.05	0.12	0.16
		(0.86)	(0.26)	(0.24)	(0.29)
	t–1	0.04	–0.07	0.27**	0.12
		(0.57)	(0.10)	(0.04)	(0.46)
Educ		–10.94	18.27	35.81	–6.17
		(0.23)	(0.13)	(0.10)	(0.84)
relEduc	–4.02	–8.14***	–11.09	–7.15	
		(0.47)	(0.00)	(0.11)	(0.11)
relcoh2024	Δ	–1.12	1.37*	–0.52***	0.56
		(0.14)	(0.06)	(0.00)	(0.67)
	t–1	–0.28	0.23**	0.53	–0.87
		(0.80)	(0.02)	(0.66)	(0.20)

continued

26   *F. E. Caroleo* et al.

Table A1.2 Continued

		Central	Anglo	Mediterranean	Nordic
ygap	Δ	0.05	0.38***	0.56**	0.89***
		(0.84)	(0.00)	(0.06)	(0.00)
	t–1	0.58*	0.45***	0.41	0.81***
		(0.09)	(0.00)	(0.24)	(0.00)
N		122	157	107	111
R2=adj		0.41	0.70	0.64	0.80
AR(1)		0.40	0.08	0.38	0.03

Note
Heteroskedasticity-robust significance; * means $p < 0.10$, ** $p < 0.05$, and *** $p < 0.01$.

Table A1.3 The employment rate, age15–24, the VET-based classification

		Dual	Noschool	Nofirm	Hi–vet
emp	t–1	−0.41***	−0.38***	−0.27***	−0.38***
		(0.00)	(0.00)	(0.00)	(0.00)
epl	Δ	0.27	2.91	−0.61	2.75
		(0.88)	(0.14)	(0.44)	(0.09)
	t–1	0.04	1.66	−0.22	3.29
		(0.98)	(0.31)	(0.84)	(0.17)
taxWedge	Δ	−0.41**	−0.02	0.16	0.15
		(0.04)	(0.82)	(0.17)	(0.41)
	t–1	−0.56**	−0.09	0.43**	0.35**
		(0.02)	(0.23)	(0.01)	(0.04)
almpgdp	Δ	−1.68	−4.29	3.05	−0.94
		(0.52)	(0.13)	(0.10)	(0.55)
	t–1	−4.45**	−5.28*	1.18	1.41
		(0.03)	(0.05)	(0.45)	(0.34)
minW_medW	Δ	1.16	−0.03*	−0.26	0.87
		(0.21)	(0.07)	(0.10)	(0.15)
	t–1	0.11	−0.06**	−0.09	−0.60
		(0.84)	(0.01)	(0.52)	(0.26)
gener	Δ	4.15	−4.71	4.04	4.49
		(0.63)	(0.18)	(0.11)	(0.58)
	t–1	8.88	4.84	3.12	−5.81
		(0.38)	(0.16)	(0.42)	(0.38)
ud	Δ	−0.24	−0.19	−0.42**	−0.09
		(0.52)	(0.10)	(0.01)	(0.70)
	t–1	−0.07	−0.15	−0.23	−0.32
		(0.84)	(0.14)	(0.12)	(0.20)
vet	Δ	0.07	−0.17*	0.08	0.01
		(0.94)	(0.08)	(0.39)	(0.99)
	t–1	0.25*	−0.05	0.03	−0.05
		(0.09)	(0.53)	(0.57)	(0.79)

		Dual	Noschool	Nofirm	Hi–vet
EducExp	Δ	0.01	0.01	0.14*	0.01
		(0.85)	(0.98)	(0.06)	(0.64)
	t–1	–0.09	–0.05	0.24***	0.03
		(0.44)	(0.91)	(0.00)	(0.96)
Educ		–6.93	24.00	17.29	–7.69
		(0.41)	(0.12)	(0.20)	(0.80)
relEduc		1.15	–2.12	–8.05*	–8.82
		(1.02)	(1.43)	(–1.66)	(–0.88)
relcoh	Δ	1.02	1.43	–1.66***	–0.88
		(0.28)	(0.14)	(0.00)	(0.23)
	t–1	–0.20	1.14***	0.42	–0.59
		(0.57)	(0.00)	(0.19)	(0.12)
ygap	Δ	0.17	0.42***	0.39**	0.77***
		(0.52)	(0.00)	(0.01)	(0.00)
	t–1	0.32	0.42**	0.06	0.85***
		(0.31)	(0.01)	(0.73)	(0.00)
N		123	129	135	112
R2–adj	0.52	0.74	0.66	0.73	
AR(1)		0.19	0.34	0.01	0.78

Note
Heteroskedasticity-robust significance; * means $p<0.10$, ** $p<0.05$, and *** $p<0.01$.

Table A1.4 The employment rate, age 20–24, the VET-based classification

		Dual	Noschool	Nofirm	Hi-vet
emp2024	t–1	–0.41 ***	–0.47 ***	–0.34 ***	–0.52 ***
		(0.00)	(0.00)	(0.00)	(0.00)
epl	Δ	0.24	3.18	–0.79	3.07 *
		(0.90)	(0.23)	(0.47)	(0.06)
	t–1	–0.02	2.68	–0.12	3.04
		(0.99)	(0.14)	(0.94)	(0.24)
taxWedge	Δ	–0.29	–0.05	0.12	0.12
		(0.23)	(0.73)	(0.43)	(0.52)
	t–1	–0.31	–0.02	0.19	0.27
		(0.17)	(0.76)	(0.35)	(0.12)
almpgdp	Δ	–3.28	–3.11	1.89	–0.28
		(0.20)	(0.24)	(0.34)	(0.85)
	t–1	–1.50	–2.58	0.78	2.84 *
		(0.32)	(0.39)	(0.68)	(0.06)

continued

Table A1.4 Continued

		Dual	Noschool	Nofirm	Hi-vet
minW_medW	Δ	0.36	−0.08	−0.31	0.94
		(0.74)	(0.72)	(0.11)	(0.14)
	t−1	0.37	−0.03	−0.22	−0.93
		(0.44)	(0.29)	(0.23)	(0.11)
gener	Δ	−3.26	−4.79	7.40 **	3.69
		(0.69)	(0.29)	(0.03)	(0.58)
	t−1	0.09	1.90	6.93	−6.13
		(0.39)	(0.61)	(0.16)	(0.30)
ud	Δ	0.35	−0.21	−0.32	−0.26
		(0.25)	(0.10)	(0.12)	(0.31)
	t−1	−0.07	−0.11	−0.19	−0.46 **
		(0.77)	(0.30)	(0.26)	(0.03)
vet	Δ	−0.15	−0.14	0.22	0.02
		(0.33)	(0.26)	(0.11)	(0.88)
	t−1	0.34 *	−0.14	0.17	−0.23
		(0.07)	(0.11)	(0.19)	(0.99)
EducExp	Δ	−0.00	−0.02	0.06	−0.00
		(0.99)	(0.72)	(0.49)	(0.99)
	t−1	−0.97	0.78	1.56	−0.82
		(0.16)	(0.35)	(0.18)	(0.88)
Educ		−7.57	22.74	22.63	−16.85
		(0.45)	(0.13)	(0.14)	(0.60)
relEduc		1.25	−7.15 **	−12.44 **	−13.48 *
		(0.86)	(0.01)	(0.02)	(0.06)
relcoh	Δ	0.42	1.05	0.19	0.54
		(0.65)	(0.36)	(0.88)	(0.69)
	t−1	−0.20 *	1.14	0.42	−0.59
		(0.05)	(0.15)	(0.10)	(0.14)
ygap	Δ	0.31	0.38 **	0.53 ***	0.67 ***
		(0.14)	(0.01)	(0.00)	(0.00)
	t−1	0.60 **	0.48 **	0.22	1.06 ***
		(0.03)	(0.02)	(0.27)	(0.00)
N		121	129	135	112
R2–adj		0.50	0.68	0.63	0.78
AR(1)		0.51	0.19	0.01	0.13

Note
Heteroskedasticity-robust significance; * means $p < 0.10$, ** $p < 0.05$, and *** $p < 0.01$.

Legend – definitions and sources of the variables

emp	Employment-to-population ratio, age 15–24 (OECD).
emp2024	Employment-to-population ratio, age 20–24 (OECD).
epl	Employment Protection Legislation Indicator (OECD).
taxWedge	Measure of the difference between labour costs to the employer and the corresponding net take-home pay of the employee for a single-earner couple with two children (OECD).
almpgdp	Expenditure on Active Labour Market Policies as a percentage of GDP (OECD).
minW_medW	Minimum wage to median wage indicator (OECD).
gener	Unemployment benefit generosity (Scruggs *et al.*, 2014).
ud	Trade union density: union membership/employment (OECD).
vet	Technical/vocational (ISCED 2 and 3) over total secondary enrolment (UNESCO UIS).
EducExp	Percentage of expenditure in public education over final government consumption expenditure (OECD).
Educ	Average years of schooling (logarithm; Barro-Lee website, data downloaded in 2016; missing annual data have been interpolated; predicted data have been used for 2015).
relEduc	Difference between the number of education years of total population aged 15 and over and the number of education years of total population aged 25 and over (Barro-Lee website, data downloaded in 2016; missing annual data have been interpolated; predicted data have been used for 2015).
relcoh	Youth population (age 15–24) to the total working age population (OECD).
relcoh2024	Youth population (age 20–24) to the total working age population (OECD).
ygap	Output gap: deviation of actual GDP from potential GDP as % of potential GDP (OECD).

Each column refers to the country sample indicated in the table header and specified in the text. In all models we have included yearly dummies and country-idiosyncratic linear trends, not shown in the interest of parsimony. Δ is the difference operator, and t-1 refers to a one-period lagged variable. Coefficient significance levels are provided in italics. N is the number of observations. The *R2–adj.* is the coefficient of determination adjusted for degrees of freedom. Diagnostics are presented for the Arellano–Bond test for first order serial correlation (*AR(1)*, distributed as a normal). We provide p-values for all these tests.

Notes

1 Another important phenomenon affecting young workers is the growing mismatch between their educational or skill level and the level required by jobs available in the labour market. The quality and orientation (general versus vocational) of the educational programme (Leuven and Oosterbeek, 2011; Caroleo and Pastore, 2016) are found among the major factors explaining the cross-country variation in overeducation and its persistence.
2 This definition can vary according to the statistical uses and to the interpretations (Raffe, 2008; Elder, 2009; Manfredi and Quintini, 2009; Elder and Matsumoto, 2010).
3 The most recent European ALMP programme is the "Youth Guarantee" or "job guarantee". It is a system through which a government or local authorities and the public employment services commit to offering a young person a job, training or re-training within a certain period of being made unemployed or leaving formal education (Pastore, 2015b).
4 Neither classification can account for a country traditionally included in cross-country exercises for OECD countries, namely Japan. Subsequently, Japan is not included in our estimates.
5 Following the literature, we use this indicator for assessing the impact of minimum wages.
6 We have experimented with both the percentage of expenditure in public education over GDP, and the percentage of expenditure in public education over final government consumption expenditure. The latter gave slightly better results, which is comforting, because it is in principle a better measure of the focus of a given government on education.
7 The unemployment benefit duration indicator from Scruggs *et al.* (2014), or various indicators for the unemployment benefit system for the OECD, were equally not significant.

2 Education mismatch and youth labour force status in Europe

Fabrizio Pompei and Ekaterina Selezneva

1 Introduction

From a macroeconomic perspective, presence of the skills and education mismatches in labour markets got recently recognized as a possible explanation of the severe youth unemployment which is plaguing Europe (European Central Bank (ECB), 2012; European Commission, 2013; International Labour Office (ILO), 2013; OECD, 2014b). Indeed, the dramatic structural changes caused by the Great Recession have contributed to the appearance of the multiple forms of skill mismatch in the European labour markets. The process of labour reallocation from declining to emerging sectors is not free from frictions and may be a cause of long-lasting unemployment, especially among the youth. In any case, it is not clear yet whether this aggregate mismatch negatively affects all young people in the same way or, instead, heterogeneous and counter-balancing effects emerge as a result of the different education profiles of individuals. There is, in fact, theoretical and empirical evidence reporting a positive effect of human capital accumulation (i.e. increasing years of education) in reducing unemployment or inactivity risk (Spence, 1973; Mincer, 1991; Trostel and Walker, 2006). Consequently, the higher is the aggregate skill mismatch, namely lack of higher educated young people at the supply side of the labour market, the more favoured the scanty better educated youngsters should be. On the other hand, theories of job polarization question a positive monotonic relationship between formal education and the probability of being employed (Acemoglu and Autor, 2012). Intermediate and higher levels of education (compared with lower educational attainments) do not guarantee higher chances of finding a job, especially when they mainly involve the routinary tasks. Therefore, the effect of the aggregate education mismatch on the relationship between human capital accumulation and youth labour status remains a testable empirical question.

Starting from the considerations above, this chapter aims to bridge the gap between the macro- and micro-level literature on education mismatch. First, we investigate whether formal education helps the youth to avoid situations of unemployment and inactivity in favour of other labour force statuses, across EU countries over the period 2006–2010. Second, we analyse if the relationship between education and labour status is affected by different intensity of the country-level education mismatch and moreover, whether there is direct or indirect impact of the the current crisis on the strength of this relationship.

Following the ECB (2012), European Commission (2013) and ILO (2013), we use the country-level education mismatch index in form of a dissimilarity index which compares the shares of individuals with primary, secondary and tertiary education (three education groups) in employment (that is a proxy of labour demand) and shares of the same education groups either in the unemployment pool or in the total labour force (the latter two serve as proxies of labour supply). As we will explain in detail below, the higher the dissimilarity in terms of educational composition between labour demand and labour supply, the higher the country-level mismatch.

As regards the econometric method, we take into account the multilevel character of the data and the possible cross-level effects (interactions at the country-individual level). In order to do so, we implement the methodology described by Bryan and Jenkins (2013). We also deal with endogeneity between education and labour statuses by applying the two-stage residual inclusion approach (2SRI), suggested by Bollen *et al.* (1995) and Terza *et al.* (2010). The question of whether the crisis changed or not the urgency of improving access to tertiary education in order to reduce structural unemployment, investigated in this study, is highly topical from the political point of view. The chapter is structured as follows. In the next section, a thorough discussion of theoretical and empirical background supporting the hypotheses that drive the empirical analysis is reported. Section 3 presents the econometric strategy, whereas Section 4 shows data sources and variables that we use in the estimations. After a brief summary of statistics (Section 5), a detailed discussion of the econometric results is given in Section 6. The last section is dedicated to the final remarks.

2 Background and hypotheses

An abundant literature addresses the beneficial impact of human capital, and in particular of education, on labour market outcomes, as well as the variety of problems caused by a mismatch between (individually) acquired and (market or job) demanded skills at micro and macro-levels.[1]

First of all, a clear beneficial role of education in reducing the unemployment risk is identified (Spence, 1973; Nickell, 1979; Mincer, 1991; Blöndal *et al.*, 2002). Highly educated job seekers signalize to employers, through the education level achieved, their potentially greater productivity, which leads to the higher chances of being hired (Spence, 1973). When hired, college graduates demonstrate better ability to acquire firm-specific knowledge during the on-the-job training, than less educated workers; for this reason, college graduates experience lower job turnover and unemployment (Mincer, 1991).

Trostel and Walker (2006) focus on a set of both developed and emerging countries and highlight that individual decision to invest in human capital improves both intensive and extensive margins of employment in the first part of the life cycle, that is, it increases the hours worked and reduces the probability of being unemployed, respectively. In particular, the study clearly shows the endo-geneity of the choice to invest in human capital to the labour market status (employee, unemployed, etc.) and demonstrates that the beneficial impact of education on inactivity is significant. Trostel and Walker's article also fits the strand of literature on chances of the youth being in unemployment or other labour market statuses. According to this research line, a beneficial impact of secondary and tertiary educational attainment is established also for a broader set of labour market statuses including self-employment (Millàn *et al.*, 2012) and continuation of studies/education (Styczynska, 2013). Alongside individual education, some characteristics of household structure (marital status, presence of children), civic engagement and social activities (association memberships, meeting friends) help to reduce the unemployment and inactivity risk (Pfeiffer and Seiberlich, 2009; Dietrich, 2012; Millàn *et al.*, 2012).

From the evidence above one cannot automatically deduce the existence of a simple monotonic relationship between education and employability, namely that a linear increase in years of education is lowering the risk of being unem-ployed. Indeed, a discussion on job polarization is gaining momentum. Concen-tration of employees in either high-paying cognitive occupations or in low-paying manual-service jobs has been observed in both US and EU countries (Autor *et al.*, 2003; Goos and Manning, 2007; Dustmann *et al.*, 2009; Acemoglu and Autor, 2012). In addition, unlike in 1995–2008, the latest crises have caused extensive changes in the European job structure (Eurofound, 2013b). An acceler-ated task-biased technological change together with a profound institutional transformation of the labour markets have led to contraction of the mid-paying routine job segment both in manufacturing and in service sectors.

Above-mentioned discussion supports the formulation of our first hypothesis on the relationship between educational attainment and the probability of being in different labour status for people aged 15–34 across EU countries over 2006–2010.

H1: *the higher the length of individual education, the lower the risk of being unemployed or inactive and the higher the probability of being an employee or self-employed.*

This hypothesis stems directly from predominant evidence on a positive effect of education on employment chances, even though the job polarization theories are currently challenging this view. We to test this relationship for EU countries in the years around the crisis.

Recent studies also take into account macro-determinants of the individual labour status, namely the labour market institutions, unemployment rate and international trade (see Scherer, 2004; De Lange *et al.*, 2014). For example, higher expected lifetime earnings and higher unemployment rate at regional level support the decision to continue to study and to co-reside with parents over the alternative to work and live alone after having completed high school among Italians aged 18–32 (Giannelli and Monfardini, 2003a). In Poland, higher educational attainment reduces the unemployment risk, even though in a different way than in Italy; higher regional unemployment rates do not stimulate the further education decision (Pastore, 2012).

To the best of our knowledge there is no evidence on the effects of an aggregated measure of country-level mismatch on the relationship between education and labour status at individual level.

At the micro-level, the majority of studies combine the analysis of mismatch-caused problems with that of private returns to schooling and challenge the human capital theory of Becker (1964) and Mincer (1974). Other articles concentrate on the relationship between over-education and permanent jobs, where human capital might be traded off for job security (Ortiz, 2010). Relatively few studies have investigated the impact of mismatch on the unemployment and inactivity incidence in the working age population at individual level.[2]

However, from a macro-perspective matching problems in the labour markets remain one of the reasons for structural unemployment since the recent crisis outbreak, in both the European Union and the United States (Pissarides, 2000, 2013; ECB, 2012; European Commission, 2013; ILO, 2013; OECD, 2014b). Indeed, the crisis has aggravated the education mismatch between labour demand and supply, especially in the EU countries. These imbalances in the educational composition of the labour supply and demand, actuate frictions in the process of labour reallocation across sectors. Currently, the labour supply side is still characterized by an excess of low-educated people in opposition to a shortage of individuals with higher educational attainments (European Commission, 2013). One may deduce that at the micro-level, people with higher educational attainment should be favoured by this vertical and aggregated education mismatch. Marsden *et al.* (2002) provided indirect evidence on this point by showing that an increase in the share of individuals with higher education, remarkably reduces the aggregated education mismatch. It means that a higher education mismatch relates to a higher labour demand for educated workers.

The second and third working hypotheses of the study rely on these speculations and try to connect the macro- and micro-dimension by studying the effect of the country-level mismatch on the probability of the young being employees compared to the probability of being in alternative individual labour statuses, in particular, unemployment and inactivity.

H2: *the higher the country-level education mismatch, the stronger the positive effect of the number of years of education on reducing unemployment and inactivity risk, at the individual level.*

As discussed above, the overall effects of education mismatch on unemployment could be different from the specific effects calculated along individuals with different education profiles. For example, in situation of high education mismatch and hence a lack of highly educated young people on the supply side, the few individuals with these characteristics that enter the labour force should be in an advantageous position in terms of job finding rate.

In this way, the crisis through increased education mismatch, should have favoured higher educated youngsters in the labour market; different results could emerge for the different number of years of education accumulated. Therefore:

H3: *the higher the country-level education mismatch at the moment of the crisis, the stronger the positive effect of education in reducing unemployment risk or inactivity choice at the individual level.*

3 Method

Based on the conceptual framework discussed above, we assume that young people (15–34) may fall in five mutually exclusive unordered labour market statuses: 1) Employee; 2) Self-employed; 3) Unemployed; 4) In education; 5) Inactive. According to Luce (1959) and Cameron and Trivedi (2005, 2010), the multinomial logit model (MNL) is the econometric specification that best fits in studying determinants of multiple categorical outcomes:

$$\Pr(Y = m \mid X) = \frac{X\beta_{(m|b)}}{\sum_{j=1}^{J} [Exp(X\beta]_{(j|b)})}$$

where $J=1 \ldots, 5$, b is the base category (1 Employee), m and j are respectively the specific outcome (labour status) to be examined and the generic outcome, X is the matrix of regressors.

A restriction is needed to ensure the model identification, namely the sum of probabilities of alternatives has to equal 1. For the MNL the comparison is to a base category which is the alternative normalized to have coefficients equal to zero, $\beta_{b|b}=0$. In our case, this leads to estimation of four binary logit models for choice between a labour market status m and the base status (1 Employee).

$$\frac{\Pr(Y = m \mid X)}{\Pr(Y = b \mid X)} = \frac{\Pr(Y = m \mid X)}{\Pr(Y = 1)} = Exp(X\beta_{(m|b)}) \tag{1}$$

A positive value of the estimated parameter $\beta_{m|b}$, means that the higher the value of the regressor, the higher the likelihood of being in an alternative labour status m with respect to the probability of being employed. Therefore, the coefficient indicates a change in the relative probability for an outcome and not for the outcome itself.

In order to ensure that the relative probabilities of the alternatives are not correlated among themselves (for example, for statuses Inactivity and Unemployed), we test the validity of the irrelevant alternatives assumption (IIA). This is done with the help of the Small-Hsiao test, which does not reject the hypothesis for any set of outcomes (see Table A2.1 in the Appendix). This means that the alternative-specific errors are uncorrelated and that the odds-ratios for pairs of alternatives are invariant with respect to the expansion (and contraction) of the alternatives set.

Our baseline specification aims to test the validity of hypothesis 1 (H1). Therefore, by taking the log odds version of equation (1), we estimate the following equation (2) on a pooled sample of data taking into account country-level fixed effects and time dummies:

$$\ln \Omega_{(m|b)} = \alpha_{(m|b)} + EduYrs\beta_{(1,m|b)} + P\beta_{(2,m|b)} + F\beta_{(3,m|b)} +$$
$$S\beta_{(4,m|b)} + \delta_{(t.m|b)} + \eta_{(c,m|b)} \quad (2)$$

where m are the four outcomes alternative to the base category b (Employee).[3] *EduYrs* is the main variable of interest at the individual level (years of education); P, F and S are matrices including other personal, family and socio-political characteristics of young people,[4] $\delta_{t,m|b}$ are time dummies ($t=2006, 2008, 2010$), $\eta_{c,m|b}$ are country fixed effects and $c=1\dots,21$.

Afterwards, we augment equation (2) with the interaction term of the aggregated country-level education mismatch (EMI) and years of education completed by individuals in order to test the second hypothesis, i.e. the impact of the EMI on the relationship between the individual-level education and relative probabilities of choice of the outcomes:

$$\ln \Omega_{(m|b)} = \alpha_{(m|b)} + (EMI * EduYrs)\beta_{(1,m|b)} + EduYrs\beta_{(2,m|b)} + P\beta_{(3,m|b)} +$$
$$F\beta_{(4,m|b)} + S\beta_{5.m|b)} + \delta_{(t,m|b)} + \eta_{(c,m|b)} \quad (3)$$

We include EMI in the interaction term only, by omitting EMI as a main effect. In our specification, country dummies are intended to capture all other possible country-specific variables, such as business cycle and institutions.[5] However, as we will see below, the main effect of EMI will be thoroughly studied and it will play a central role in the econometric strategy.

Eventually, as explained in the previous section, we also pay attention to the impact of crisis on the picture described above, by adding the following interactions:

$$\ln \Omega_{(m|b)} = \alpha_{(m|b)} + (EMI * EduYrs * 2010)\beta_{(1.m|b)} +$$
$$([EduYrs * 2010)\beta]_{(2,m|b)} + (EMI * EduYrs)\beta_{(3.m|b)} + \quad (4)$$
$$X\beta_{(4.m|b)} + \delta_{(t.m|b)} + \eta_{(c.m|b)}$$

where now X is a matrix including all personal, family and socio-political characteristics reported in the previous terms P, F and S.

Two main problems undermine these specifications, the endogeneity of education with respect to labour status (Trostel and Walker, 2006; Riddell and Song, 2011) and the multilevel nature of the data that we use for the econometric analysis (Bryan and Jenkins, 2013).

As regards endogeneity, we follow several authors (Bollen *et al.*, 1995; Terza *et al.*, 2010; Wooldridge, 2010; Ivlevs and King, 2012) and prefer a two-stage residual inclusion regression (2RSI) in place of the conventional two-stage predictor substitution approach, given that all simulation studies conducted by the authors above confirm the superiority of 2RSI in the non-linear models. The 2RSI method consists in setting up an OLS regression in the first stage in which, similarly to the conventional two-stage predictor substitution approach, we regress our continuous endogenous variable *years of education* on instrumental variables.

$$EduYrs = \alpha + IV\beta_1 + P\beta_2 + F\beta_3 + S\beta_4 + \delta_t + \eta_c \tag{5}$$

where IV is a matrix containing a set of excluded instruments that we thoroughly discuss in the next section, P, F and S are the same matrices of equation (2), containing all the individual level control variables (included instruments), δ_t and η_c are time and country dummies respectively.

In the second-stage regression, however, the endogenous variables are not replaced. Instead, the first-stage residuals are included as additional regressors in second-stage estimation, besides the actual value of *EduYrs* (Terza *et al.*, 2010).

$$\begin{aligned} \ln \Omega_{(m|b)} = {}& \alpha_{(m|b)} + EduYrs\beta_{1,m|b} + 1\text{stage Resid}\beta_{(2,m|b)} + \\ & P\beta_{(3,m|b)} + F\beta_{(4,m|b)} + S\beta_{(5,m|b)} + \delta_{(t,m|b)} + \eta_{(c,m|b)} \end{aligned} \tag{6}$$

where **1stage Resid** are the included residuals stemming from the first stage.

According to Bollen *et al.* (1995) and Ivlevs and King (2012), we test the relevance of instruments in the first stage by means of an F test, discuss the endogeneity/exogeneity of *EduYrs* by simply reporting the Wald test for the coefficients of **1stage Resid** and take into account the exclusion restrictions by comparing the log-likelihood between the reduced form and the structural equation in the second-stage MNL model. As regards the exclusion restrictions, in the reduced form we replace *EduYrs* with the set of instruments IV, whereas in the structural equation we only include the predicted value for *EduYrs* and omit instruments. If the instruments only indirectly influence the labour status, through their effects on *EduYrs*, the log-likelihood of the reduced and structural equations should be similar (Bollen *et al.*, 1995). Therefore, we conduct this test on the identifying assumptions to prove the exogeneity of instruments. Moreover, we find *EduYrs* as being endogenous; consequently we include the residuals in specifications (2), (3) and (4).

Bryan and Jenkins (2013) highlighted problems arising with multi-country data sets in which there are observations at the individual level nested within a higher level (countries). On the one hand, this multilevel structure provides useful information about *country effects* as well as *individual effects*, and also about interactions between them (*cross-level effects*); on the other hand, the drawback due to the small number of groups (countries) is not alleviated by the large size of the sample at the individual level (thousands of observations). This means that the desirable properties of parameters estimated for individual-country-level interactions, such as consistency and efficiency, are questionable when the number of countries is below 30. For this reason, we follow Bryan and Jenkins (2013) in performing a two-step approach that is useful to disclose the statistical significance of the variable of interest at country-level. In other terms, we consider the baseline specification in our analysis with correction for endo-geneity (equation (6)) as the first step. The only difference is that we estimate separately three regressions of equation (6) for each year (2006, 2008, 2010). Afterwards, we take the country intercepts from these three regressions and express them as a linear function of EMI at country level. In the second step estimation, we therefore regress coefficients of country intercepts on the country-level variable EMI, using OLS. We repeat this regression for each outcome *m* (Unemployed, Self-employed, Education, Inactive) stemming from the first step.

$$\hat{\eta}_{c,t} = \alpha + EMI_{c,t}\beta_1 + LabMarkLiberal_{c,t}\beta_2 + GDP_{Shock_{c,t}}\beta_3 + \delta_t + \varepsilon_{c,t} \qquad (7)$$

where $c = 1, \ldots 21$ countries and $t = 2006, 2008, 2010$ years[6]; $\hat{\eta}_{c,t}$ are the estimated parameters for the country intercept c and year t, describing the relative prob-ability to be in labour status *m*; EMI is the same proxy for the education mis-match used in equations 4 and 5; *Lab.MarketLiberal*$_{c,t}$ and *GDP_Shock*$_{c,t}$ are two country-level control variables that take into account labour market institutions and business cycles, respectively.

This supplementary approach offers two advantages to our econometric analysis: 1) we have a preliminary assessment concerning the reliability of EMI as country-level effect, namely a significant coefficient for EMI means that its main effect on the average relative probability of being in a labour status is binding; 2) it provides useful information on the sign (direction) of the main effect of EMI in order to clarify the interpretation of cross-level effects (inter-action terms) in the main specifications (equations 4 and 5). Concerning this last point, independently from the statistical significance of the EMI coefficients that we obtain in regressions (7), we again follow a Bryan and Jenkin's suggestion and perform a graphical analysis by plotting $\hat{\eta}_{c,t}$ on EMI for each labour status.

4 Data sources and variables discussion

We collected all the individual-level variables from the European Social Survey (ESS).[7] The cumulative data files integrate cross-section information collected in 2006, 2008 and 2010, respectively. Unfortunately, the first edition of the sixth round (2012) excludes a large number of countries we wanted to take into account in this study, so we limited our investigation to the period 2006–2010. In any case, also for this period there are data missing for some countries, thus we considered only 21 European Union members and excluded Italy, Austria, Malta, Luxembourg, Latvia, Lithuania, Romania.

The key variable of interest represents a self-reported labour status at the moment of the interview for young individuals aged 15–34. More precisely, the status of *Employee* is our base outcome and includes all young employees (contract with limited and unlimited duration). *Self-employment* is the second status and includes self-employed and persons working for their own family business. Unemployed actively looking for a job is the third status (*Unemployed*), whereas youngsters still in education is the fourth one (*Education*). Eventually, *Inactive* is a residual category that includes unemployed young people who are not actively looking for a job and are not in education, and young people who are inactive for different reasons (permanently sick or disabled, community or military service, housework, looking after children, other).

As regards the key explanatory variable at the individual level, we took the full-time completed *years of education* that includes compulsory schooling. In addition, according to the literature mentioned above, we considered as controls a set of variables describing personal characteristics (age and gender), family characteristics (number of family members, presence of children, labour/capital income as main source of the household income), political rights (citizenship), social relationships (frequency of meetings with friends or colleagues, taking part of events with other people, membership in trade unions).

Additionally, we also drew four binary variables from ESS to instrument the *years of education* at the first stage of the 2SRI approach. These variables are the *father's tertiary education level* and three proxy variables for *altruism*, *equalitarianism* and *environmentalism* from the section of ESS database dedicated to the human scale values.[8] We assume that these four binary variables are correlated to the *years of education* while not having an impact on probability of being in any of the five labour statuses considered. The parents' educational attainment is largely used in literature as an instrument for education (Trostel *et al.*, 2002; Parker and Van Praag, 2006; Ivlevs and King, 2012) even though its exogeneity with respect to income or labour status has been questioned (Card, 1999). We only use the father's education due to the excessive number of missing data for the mother's education. As regards human scale values, there is a growing consensus in defining basic values as cognitive representations of desirable goals that serve as guiding principles in the life of a person. We defined as *altruism*, *equalitarianism* and *environmentalism* orientations that Piurko *et al.* (2011) grouped in the broader categories of *benevolence* and *universalism*, namely self-transcendence values located at the opposite of self-enhancement values (power, achievement) that instead encourage and legitimize the pursuit of self-interest. Therefore, it is plausible to guess that the presence/absence of these values could be correlated with increasing years of education to support mental openness and the desire to understand the world; instead, they should have nothing to do with the behaviour in pursuance of self-interest, that could be correlated with the probability of being employed, unemployed, inactive or self-employed.

As far as EMI is concerned, we followed the approaches of the ECB (2012), European Commission (2013) and ILO (2013), and constructed the country-level educational mismatch as a dissimilarity index. In particular, the index compares the differences in the educational attainment (coded as three levels of education completed) between two groups, of employed and unemployed (or labour force). Indeed, the index is estimated on two proxies of the labour supply, namely on the pools of unemployed (EMI_{un}) and of labour force (EMI_{lf}):

$$EMI_{un} = \frac{1}{2} \sum_{i=1}^{3} \left| \frac{E_i}{E} - \frac{U_i}{U} \right|$$

$$EMI_{lf} = \frac{LF_i}{LF} \sum_{i=1}^{3} \left| \frac{E_i}{E} - \frac{LF_i}{LF} \right|$$

where i is the level of education coherent with the International Classification of Education 2011(ISCED (2012))[9]; $\frac{E_i}{E}$ is the proportion of the employed with education level i; $\frac{U_i}{U}$ and $\frac{LF_i}{LF}$ the proportion of the unemployed and labour force respectively, with education level i.

According to the ILO (2013), if the unemployment rate in EMI_{un} is the same among the primary, secondary and tertiary education level graduates, the index equals zero; no dissimilarity between groups is observed. The index equals unity in the case of complete dissimilarity among groups; that is, for example, when all primary and tertiary education graduates are employed, while those with secondary education are unemployed. The index can also be interpreted as the percentage of unemployed individuals that should be reallocated across skill levels to balance labour supply and demand. EMI_{lf}, instead, does not range from zero to one, albeit also in this case the score of the indicator is low if the skill composition of the employed reflects the labour forces skill composition, while the value is high if the education groups that are highly represented in the labour force are not in terms of employment (European Commission, 2013). Our calculations, presented in the following section, show that the ranking of countries differs for these two definitions of EMI, therefore, both indices are used later in order to test the robustness of our results. Data on shares of employed, unemployed and labour force come from the Eurostat database (country-level labour force survey).[10]

Lastly, as regards the country-level variables that we inserted as control in equation 7, GDP–Shock was calculated from Eurostat data and it is the difference between the annual variation of GDP (e.g. 2005–2004 for the first year) and the five-year annual average of GDP (chain-linked volumes, reference year 2005);[11] the proxy for labour market liberalization is a composed indicator that comes from the Fraser Institute database and combines six different components of country-level labour market institutions: 1) hiring regulation and minimum wage; 2) hiring and firing regulations; 3) centralized collective bargaining; 4) hours regulation; 5) mandated cost of worker dismissal; 6) military conscription.

5 Descriptive statistics

Table 2.1 reports descriptive statistics for the whole sample that refers to the three rounds under scrutiny (2006, 2008 and 2010). The overall number of observations varies on average from about 9,000 in 2006 to more than 10,000 in 2008 and 2010.[12] The first five rows of Table 2.1 describe the five labour statuses of interest, whereas the remaining ones are the explanatory variables at the individual and country level. As expected, over the five years that include the outbreak of the recent crisis, the employment rate remarkably decreased from 48.6 to 43.53 per cent, whereas the percentage of unemployed on total population (15–34) increased from 5.27 to 7.64 per cent.[13] At the same time, the percentage of young people in education increased from 29.20 to 32.92 per cent and the share of inactivity slightly decreased from 12.08 to 11.42 per cent. Both average age and average years of education remained stable at around 24.7 years old and 13.30 years, respectively. According to ISCED (2012), the latter number corresponds approximately to the end of upper secondary education. Indeed, about half of all the young people in the sample have a secondary level of educational attainment, one-third shows only the primary education level, whereas the share of highly educated people varies between 16.26 and 18.20 per cent. Both the nature of household income and the number of family members are important determinants of inactivity and other labour statuses; Table 2.1 shows that the majority of youngsters in the sample live in households in which labour income is the main source of wealth and the average number of family members is slightly above three. However, the share of young people with children is not negligible, even though it decreased from 26.70 to 24.33 per cent.

Eventually, in line with the previous literature, we observe an overall increase in the two indices of the educational mismatch between 2006 and 2010, in both average and standard deviation. In particular, according to the ILO (2013) interpretation of the EMI_{un}, in 2010 about 20 per cent of youth unemployment needed to be reallocated according to the educational attainment composition of employment, to reduce the mismatch to zero. Figures 2.1 and 2.2 chart more detailed levels and variations of EMI_{un} and EMI_{lf} across countries. For the majority of them we observe a similar ranking between the two indexes (see the country localization in the quadrants). Sweden, Finland, France, Belgium and Estonia maintained a very high education mismatch, whereas for Greece, Portugal, Cyprus, Czech Republic, Slovenia and Denmark the two EMIs remained at the bottom of the ranking.[14] As regards the changes over time, the bulk of countries experienced an increase in EMI, especially Spain, Ireland, Portugal and Estonia. According to the theory discussed above, this fact adds to the output drop of the current crisis in explaining the rise in the ratio of unemployed to population for young people (see Figure A2.1 in the Appendix). However, both levels and variations of education mismatch could have had a different impact on individual labour statuses if youngsters decided to invest in education. Indeed, in all countries under scrutiny education mismatch means that besides an excess of low-educated people there is an important deficit of highly educated people on the

Table 2.1 Summary statistics for variables used in the econometric analysis

	2006			2008			2010		
	N	Mean	Std.Dev.	N	Mean	Std.Dev.	N	Mean	Std.Dev.
Employees	8,933	48.60	49.98	10,789	47.12	49.92	10,882	43.53	49.58
Self-employed	8,933	4.84	21.45	10,789	5.33	22.47	10,882	4.50	20.72
Unemployed	8,933	5.27	22.35	10,789	6.07	23.88	10,882	7.64	26.57
In Education	8,933	29.20	45.47	10,789	30.13	45.89	10,882	32.92	46.99
Inactive	8,933	12.08	32.60	10,789	11.35	31.72	10,882	11.42	31.80
Age	9,050	24.75	5.75	10,862	24.75	5.68	10,952	24.55	5.73
Gender (male=1)	9,041	49.70	50.00	10,858	48.77	49.99	10,944	48.44	49.98
Years of Education	8,949	13.30	3.37	10,794	13.32	3.29	10,836	13.39	3.31
Primary Ed.	5,731	30.91	46.22	7,294	31.02	46.26	10,899	33.52	47.21
Secondary Ed.	5,647	53.20	49.90	7,153	51.95	49.97	10,899	48.31	49.97
Tertiary Ed.	5,647	16.26	36.91	7,153	17.56	38.05	10,899	18.20	38.59
Citizenship	9,044	94.59	22.62	10,857	93.94	23.85	10,949	93.30	25.01
Disconnected	9,036	3.67	18.79	10,848	3.72	18.92	10,940	4.16	19.98
No Social Activ.	8,924	27.46	44.63	10,734	27.95	44.88	10,876	28.03	44.92
Children (yes=1)	9,002	26.70	44.24	10,826	24.36	42.93	10,946	24.33	42.91
H. Labour Income	8,730	88.26	32.19	10,625	88.74	31.62	10,594	86.98	33.65
H. Capit. Income	8,730	2.75	16.36	10,625	2.75	16.34	10,594	2.89	16.77
Trade Un. Member	8,994	13.26	33.91	10,815	11.99	32.49	10,906	11.71	32.16
Family Members	9,038	3.41	1.50	10,856	3.37	1.47	10,947	3.41	1.44
EMI_{un}	9,050	19.64	4.26	10,862	18.64	6.34	10,952	19.98	4.64
EMI_{lf}	9,050	1.10	0.38	10,862	0.94	0.31	10,952	1.22	0.52
GDP_shock (t-1)	9,050	42.60	50.50	10,862	29.73	92.07	10,952	-605.66	309.17
Lab.Market Liberal.	8,443	6.03	1.46	9,536	5.95	1.33	9,789	6.46	1.13

Notes

Weighted statistics according to the ESS sample weights. All variables are percentages, with the exception of Age, Family Members, Years of Education and Labour Market Liberal.

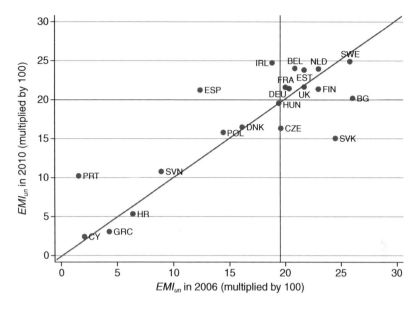

Figure 2.1 Education Mismatch Index (Employment vs Unemployment) between 2006 and 2010.

Notes
BG – Bulgaria, CY – Cyprus, CZE – Czech Republic, DEU – Germany, ESP – Spain, EST – Estonia, FIN – Finland, FRA – France, HR – Croatia, HUN – Hungary, GRC – Greece, NLD – The Netherlands, POL – Poland, PRT – Portugal, SVK – Slovak Republic, SVN – Slovenia, SWE – Sweden, UK – United Kingdom.

labour supply side, as the graphical representation of EMI_{un} and EMI_{lf} for 2010 clearly discloses (see Figures A2.2 and A2.3 in the Appendix). Therefore, the higher the education mismatch, the lower the risk of unemployment or inactivity should be for people with better education.

6 Estimation results

Table 2.2 shows the coefficients for the MNL model of the baseline specification (equation 2), estimated on the pooled sample with time and country dummies (27,887 observations). These results partially support the hypothesis 1, namely an extra year of education reduces the probability of being unemployed or inactive, compared to the probability of being employed. Apparently, the years of education have no effect on the relative probability of being self-employed, while they have a remarkable impact on the probability of staying in education. The latter is likely to signalize a persistence in the choice of education for the cohort aged 15–34. Almost all other control variable coefficients are significant with the expected sign, according to the literature on youth unemployment

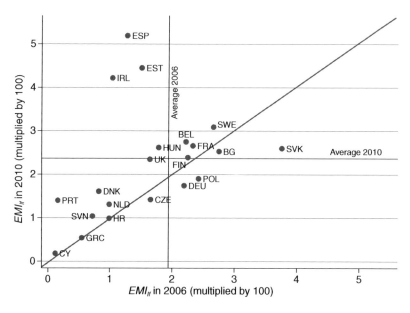

Figure 2.2 Education Mismatch Index (Employment vs Labour Force) between 2006 and 2010.

Notes
BG – Bulgaria, CY – Cyprus, CZE – Czech Republic, DEU – Germany, ESP – Spain, EST – Estonia, FIN – Finland, FRA – France, HR – Croatia, HUN – Hungary, GRC – Greece, NLD – The Netherlands, POL – Poland, PRT – Portugal, SVK – Slovak Republic, SVN – Slovenia, SWE – Sweden, UK – United Kingdom.

(Dietrich, 2012). In particular, until a certain threshold, an additional year of age reduces the relative likelihood of being unemployed, inactive or in education. The risk of being unemployed or inactive is lower for men compared to that of women. When capital income is the main source of the household's wealth, we observe higher relative probability of being self-employed, in education or inactive, whereas the opposite holds for cases where the labour income is the main source. Eventually, we also find that a relative probability of being unemployed or staying in education is remarkably higher for two years after the beginning of the crisis, in 2010. However, the coefficient of our main interest, related to the years of education, may be subject to a bias due to endogeneity (Trostel and Walker, 2006). As discussed in Section 3, we implemented the 2SRI method to tackle this problem and present the respective estimation results in Table 2.3.

First of all, the instruments (father's tertiary education, equalitarianism, altruism and environmentalism) are proved to be relevant and positively correlated to years of education, as the F-statistic value reported at the bottom of Table 2.3 suggests.[15] The test for validity of exclusion restrictions signals that the instruments are also exogenous with respect to the outcomes in the second stage.[16]

Table 2.2 Effects of education on labour status of young people aged 15–34. MLN model: baseline specification; raw coefficients (Base category: Employee)

	Self-employed	Unemployed	Education	Inactive
Years of Education	−0.002	−0.069***	0.202***	−0.052***
	(0.009)	(0.009)	(0.010)	(0.008)
Age	−0.469***	−0.264***	−1.658***	−0.814***
	(0.075)	(0.060)	(0.048)	(0.047)
Age2	0.009***	0.003***	0.025***	0.013***
	(0.001)	(0.001)	(0.001)	(0.001)
Gender (male=1)	0.676***	−0.153***	−0.544***	−1.136***
	(0.061)	(0.057)	(0.043)	(0.047)
Citizenship	0.396***	−0.059	0.010	0.002
	(0.137)	(0.108)	(0.109)	(0.092)
Disconnected	−0.234*	−0.304**	−0.702***	−0.060
	(0.138)	(0.127)	(0.141)	(0.089)
No Social Activities	−0.016	0.243***	−0.100**	0.339***
	(0.064)	(0.061)	(0.049)	(0.047)
Children	0.313***	−0.080	−0.647***	1.372***
	(0.076)	(0.077)	(0.078)	(0.059)
H. Labour Income	−0.272	−3.582***`	−2.789***	−3.066***
	(0.190)	(0.092)	(0.096)	(0.089)
H. Capital Income	1.228***	−0.384*	1.432***	0.409*
	(0.335)	(0.219)	(0.205)	(0.210)
Trade Un. Member	−0.952***	−0.374***	−0.684***	−0.657***
	(0.092)	(0.086)	(0.073)	(0.068)
Family Members	0.013	0.190***	0.153***	0.213***
	(0.025)	(0.021)	(0.017)	(0.017)
Year-2008	0.062	0.243***	0.025	0.022
	(0.073)	(0.078)	(0.054)	(0.055)
Year-2010	0.132*	0.659***	0.423***	0.060
	(0.074)	(0.075)	(0.053)	(0.057)
Country dummies	Yes	Yes	Yes	Yes
Obs.			27,887	
p-value-Overall Model			0.000	
Pseudo-R2			0.33	

Note
*** significant at 1% level; ** significant at 5% level; * significant at 10% level. Robust standard errors in parentheses.

In addition, the significant coefficients for *1-stage Residuals* indicate that the variable *years of education* is endogenous (Bollen *et al.*, 1995; Terza *et al.*, 2010). As we can see, controlling for endogeneity makes the impact of education in reducing the probability of unemployment stronger. Differently from results of Table 2.2, now a significant and positive effect of education on self-employment emerges and the impact of education on the relative probability of being inactive is slightly positive and significant. This last result apparently contradicts hypothesis 1 and needs some additional discussion. Indeed, by inserting the *1-stage Residuals* it is possible to take into account omitted variables such as innate ability, qualitative aspects of education and tasks, as job polarization

Table 2.3 Effects of education on labour status of young people aged 15–34. MNL model: endogeneity control with 2SRI method; raw coefficients (Base category: Employee)

	Self-employed	Unemployed	Education	Inactive
Years of Education	0.219***	−0.149***	0.573***	0.097**
	(0.049)	(0.056)	(0.035)	(0.041)
1-stage Resid.	−0.230***	0.083*	−0.389***	−0.155***
	(0.051)	(0.047)	(0.036)	(0.042)
Age	−0.784***	−0.141	−2.193***	−1.041***
	(0.108)	(0.105)	(0.072)	(0.079)
Age 2	0.014***	0.001	0.033***	0.017***
	(0.002)	(0.002)	(0.001)	(0.001)
Gender (male=1)	0.800***	−0.207***	−0.366***	−1.080***
	(0.065)	(0.065)	(0.047)	(0.053)
Citizenship	0.337**	−0.081	−0.315***	−0.089
	(0.149)	(0.117)	(0.115)	(0.102)
Disconnected	−0.055	−0.328**	−0.428***	0.086
	(0.146)	(0.138)	(0.150)	(0.096)
No Social Activities	0.047	0.220***	0.029	0.382***
	(0.067)	(0.065)	(0.052)	(0.050)
Children (yes=1)	0.653***	−0.196*	−0.135	1.635***
	(0.102)	(0.110)	(0.094)	(0.083)
H. Labour Income	−0.463**	−3.447***	−3.140***	−3.152***
	(0.201)	(0.108)	(0.105)	(0.100)
H. Capital Income	1.016***	−0.145	0.912***	0.288
	(0.348)	(0.242)	(0.221)	(0.227)
Trade Un. Member	−1.049***	−0.346***	−0.868***	−0.705***
	(0.096)	(0.092)	(0.078)	(0.072)
Family Members	0.030	0.189***	0.196***	0.224***
	(0.026)	(0.022)	(0.018)	(0.018)
Year-2008	0.018	0.253***	−0.044	−0.019
	(0.075)	(0.080)	(0.055)	(0.057)
Year-2010	0.068	0.652***	0.298***	−0.010
	(0.078)	(0.080)	(0.056)	(0.061)
Country dummies	Yes	Yes	Yes	Yes
Obs.		26,245		
p-value-Overall Model		0.000		
Pseudo-R2		0.33		

Notes

F test for the relevance of instruments in the first stage $F(4)=314.35$; p-value$=0.000$

Test for validity of exclusion restrictions

Log-Likelihood Reduced-Form Equation (a)$=-23,120.932$

Log-Likelihood Structural Equation (b)$=-23,127.321$

Ho: a=b; p-value$=0.385$

*** significant at 1% level; ** significant at 5% level; * significant at 10% level. Robust standard errors in parentheses. Significant t-test for the coefficients of 1-stage Resid. indicates that education is endogenous.

theories predict. These aspects might play a role in discouraging youngsters who made the wrong choice in the education field, from entering the labour market. Instead, if higher educated young people decide to seek a job, it may suggest a previous choice of a 'right education', hence the risk of being unemployed is inversely related to the years of education. The coefficients reported in Table 2.3 only tell us about relative probabilities, whereas they say nothing in terms of real magnitude and sign of the effects of years of education (Long and Freese, 2006; Cameron and Trivedi, 2010). For this reason, we calculated the marginal effects of the latter[17] and considered individuals in the sample at two different levels of cumulative years of education: 8 years of education, that approximately corresponds to the end of primary (lower secondary) education and the beginning of upper secondary education; 13 years of education, that is the end of upper secondary and the beginning of tertiary education (ISCED, 2012). As regards the other independent variables, we took age at 26 and the sample mean for all other regressors. At this stage of life, if we take into account *years of education*=8 we are studying the effect of an additional year of education for people aged 26 who completed at least primary education; whereas if we consider *years of education*=13 we are evaluating people aged 26 with more years of education than those with upper secondary educational attainment.

Marginal effects, depicted in Figure 2.3, suggest that an additional year of education for those with secondary education (*years of education*=8), reduces

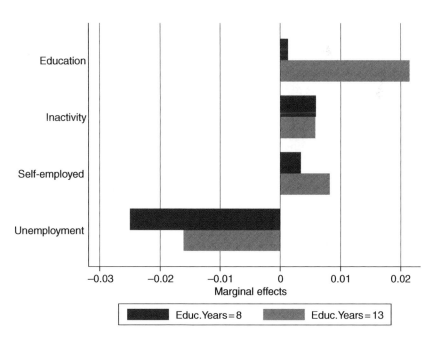

Figure 2.3 Marginal effects for years of education at age=26 and at the sample mean for other regressors.

the probability of being unemployed by –0.025 (2.5 per cent). This value largely offsets the positive effects on probabilities of being in alternative statuses and indicates that employment (the base category), as complement of unemployment, is the most probable outcome. In the case of *years of education* = *13*, an extra year of education reduces the probability of being unemployed by –0.016 and increases the probability of being in education by 0.021. However, the size of the effects on inactivity and self-employment is negligible and leads us to conjecture that human capital accumulation is especially important to reduce the risk of unemployment and to reinforce the choice to extend the period of education for higher educated people.

Now that we have established a beneficial impact of human capital in the form of formal education on youth employability, the question remains whether this strategy is successful for young people in countries heavily affected by educational mismatch (hypothesis 2). In addition, we want to investigate if the beginning of the current crisis introduced any changes in this relationship, given that in almost all countries there was a remarkable surge in the education mismatch (hypothesis 3). As Bryan and Jenkins (2013) suggest, we start with presenting the main effects of education mismatch at country level. Tables 2.4 and 2.5 report the results of OLS estimates in which we regressed the country intercepts of the MNL model in Table 2.3 on EMI_{un} and EMI_{lf}, respectively.[18] According to the macro-level theoretical and empirical evidence we mentioned in Section 2, EMIs positively and significantly affect the average probability of being unemployed at the country level. This holds especially for EMI_{un} (see Table 2.4), where a one-point increase in the mismatch index boosts the average relative probability of being unemployed by 0.015 both with and without macro-level control variables (*GDPshock* and *labour market institutions*). This result is less robust for EMI_{lf}, where the coefficient is not statistically different from zero if control variables are included (Table 2.5). As regards other labour statuses, education mismatch exerts a significant and positive impact only on the average relative probability of staying in education, whereas no significant influence has been found on self-employment and inactivity. Liu (2012) provides support for the positive relationship between country-level mismatch and probability of extending education by pointing out that very often people, experiencing job search difficulties due to education mismatch, decide to acquire new skills through vocational training or more formal education. A graphical analysis in the Appendix (see Figures A2.4 and A2.5) basically corroborates the evidence of OLS regressions.

Further in this section, we concentrate on the discussion of the combined effects of macro-and micro-level variables for which we obtained significant results. This means that we concentrate on the interpretation of the interactions with EMI_{un}, whereas the respective results for EMI_{lf} are presented in the Appendix.

Despite that both the country-level effects of education mismatch (Table 2.4) and the individual effects of years of education (Table 2.3) are significant, their cross-level effect, that Table 2.6 exhibits, is not. This holds for all alternative labour statuses. Especially for unemployment, the interaction term EMI_{un}* *Years of Education*, shows the right expected negative sign but it is not significantly

Table 2.4 Education mismatch effects at country level. EMI unemployment version (OLS regression)

	Unempl.	Self-empl.	Educ.	Inact.	Unempl.	Self-empl.	Educ.	Inact.
EMI_{un}	0.015**	−0.001	0.014	0.003	0.015***	0.008	0.021*	0.010
	(0.006)	(0.006)	(0.009)	(0.006)	(0.005)	(0.006)	(0.011)	(0.006)
Year-2008	0.813***	2.510***	−0.440**	3.178***	0.787***	2.454***	−0.437*	3.138***
	(0.104)	(0.086)	(0.205)	(0.114)	(0.107)	(0.089)	(0.225)	(0.115)
Year-2010	0.312***	1.547***	1.082***	2.272***	0.055	1.448***	0.742**	2.204***
	(0.110)	(0.093)	(0.183)	(0.113)	(0.173)	(0.162)	(0.337)	(0.176)
GDPshock					−0.037	−0.011	−0.054	−0.007
					(0.027)	(0.018)	(0.041)	(0.023)
Lab.Mark.Lib.					0.004	−0.054	−0.148*	0.027
					(0.035)	(0.041)	(0.079)	(0.049)
Constant	4.240***	4.527***	19.900***	8.199***	4.195***	4.718***	20.677***	7.882***
	(0.109)	(0.103)	(0.213)	(0.132)	(0.215)	(0.241)	(0.590)	(0.253)
Adj. R2	0.50	0.92	0.55	0.94	0.54	0.92	0.55	0.94
Obs.	60	60	60	60	52	52	52	52

Notes
*** significant at 1% level; ** significant at 5% level; * significant at 10% level. Robust standard errors in parentheses.

Table 2.5 Education mismatch effects at country level. EMI labour force version (OLS regression)

	Unempl.	Self-empl.	Educ.	Inact.	Unempl.	Self-empl.	Educ.	Inact.
SMI_{lf}	0.079*	-0.028	0.204***	0.015	0.047	-0.010	0.235***	0.042
	(0.040)	(0.037)	(0.050)	(0.039)	(0.041)	(0.045)	(0.062)	(0.036)
Year-2008	0.843***	2.505***	-0.393*	3.184***	0.816***	2.465***	-0.378*	3.157***
	(0.105)	(0.086)	(0.199)	(0.112)	(0.106)	(0.092)	(0.215)	(0.113)
Year-2010	0.268**	1.565***	0.958***	2.264***	0.051	1.452***	0.706**	2.199***
	(0.125)	(0.099)	(0.174)	(0.118)	(0.185)	(0.171)	(0.327)	(0.182)
GDPshock					-0.034	-0.012	-0.036	-0.005
					(0.029)	(0.020)	(0.044)	(0.025)
Lab.Mark.Lib.					0.031	-0.037	-0.124	0.043
					(0.033)	(0.041)	(0.078)	(0.045)
Constant	4.364***	4.556***	19.804***	8.228***	4.212***	4.765***	20.506***	7.879***
	(0.090)	(0.077)	(0.178)	(0.105)	(0.207)	(0.255)	(0.553)	(0.262)
Adj. R2	0.48	0.92	0.59	0.94	0.51	0.92	0.60	0.94
Obs.	60	60	60	60	52	52	52	52

Notes
*** significant at 1% level; ** significant at 5% level; * significant at 10% level. Robust standard errors in parentheses.

different from zero. It means that higher levels of individual human capital help to lower the risk of unemployment, regardless of the level of education mismatch in a country. Therefore hypothesis 2 is not confirmed after the empirical test.

Before considering hypothesis 3, we cannot neglect that the crisis, started in 2008, could have had an influence on the relationships between education and

Table 2.6 Combined effects of country-level EMI_{un} and individual education on labour status of young people aged 15–34. MNL model: endogeneity control with 2SRI method; raw coefficients (Base category: Employee)

	Self-employed	Unemployed	Education	Inactive
EMI_{un} *Education Years	−0.101	−0.037	−0.049	0.100
	(0.068)	(0.074)	(0.055)	(0.069)
Years of Education	0.237***	−0.143**	0.582***	0.077*
	(0.051)	(0.058)	(0.037)	(0.043)
1-stage Resid.	−0.231***	0.083*	−0.389***	−0.153***
	(0.051)	(0.047)	(0.036)	(0.042)
Age	−0.786***	−0.142	−2.194***	−1.036***
	(0.108)	(0.105)	(0.072)	(0.079)
Age2	0.015***	0.001	0.033***	0.017***
	(0.002)	(0.002)	(0.001)	(0.001)
Gender (male=1)	0.803***	−0.207***	−0.365***	−1.083***
	(0.065)	(0.065)	(0.047)	(0.053)
Citizenship	0.333**	−0.081	−0.315***	−0.086
	(0.149)	(0.117)	(0.116)	(0.102)
Disconnected	−0.052	−0.327**	−0.424***	0.081
	(0.146)	(0.138)	(0.150)	(0.096)
No Social Activities	0.046	0.219***	0.028	0.383***
	(0.067)	(0.065)	(0.052)	(0.050)
Children (yes=1)	0.654***	−0.196*	−0.134	1.631***
	(0.102)	(0.110)	(0.094)	(0.083)
H. Labour Income	−0.461**	−3.446***	−3.141***	−3.151***
	(0.201)	(0.108)	(0.106)	(0.100)
H. Capital Income	1.023***	−0.145	0.911***	0.289
	(0.348)	(0.242)	(0.222)	(0.227)
Trade Un. Member	−1.050***	−0.346***	−0.867***	−0.707***
	(0.096)	(0.092)	(0.078)	(0.072)
Family Members	0.031	0.189***	0.196***	0.223***
	(0.026)	(0.022)	(0.018)	(0.018)
Year-2008	0.031	0.255***	−0.037	−0.040
	(0.075)	(0.080)	(0.056)	(0.058)
Year-2010	0.081	0.660***	0.307***	−0.021
	(0.079)	(0.082)	(0.058)	(0.061)
Country dummies	Yes	Yes	Yes	Yes
Obs.		26,245		
p-value-Overall Model		0.000		
Pseudo-R2		0.33		

Notes
*** significant at 1% level; ** significant at 5% level; * significant at 10% level. Robust standard errors in parentheses. Significant t-test for the coefficients of the first-stage resid. indicates that education is endogenous.

alternative labour statuses (especially unemployment), independently of country-level education mismatch. The results for this test are reported in Table 2.7, where the coefficient of the variable capturing the point under scrutiny (i.e. the interaction term *Years of Education*Year-2010*) is not significant. This result is somehow coherent with recent empirical evidence (ILO, 2013; OECD, 2014b) in

Table 2.7 Effects of education in crisis time on labour status of young people aged 15–34. MNL model: endogeneity control with 2SRI method; raw coefficients; raw coefficients (Base category: Employee)

	Self-employed	*Unemployed*	*Education*	*Inactive*
Years of Education*Year-2010	0.015	−0.021	−0.015	−0.014
	(0.018)	(0.017)	(0.014)	(0.015)
Years of Education	0.214***	−0.141**	0.578***	0.101**
	(0.050)	(0.057)	(0.036)	(0.041)
1-stage Resid.	−0.230***	0.083*	−0.389***	−0.155***
	(0.051)	(0.047)	(0.036)	(0.042)
Age	−0.782***	−0.143	−2.195***	−1.042***
	(0.108)	(0.105)	(0.072)	(0.079)
Age2	0.014***	0.001	0.033***	0.017***
	(0.002)	(0.002)	(0.001)	(0.001)
Gender (male=1)	0.800***	−0.208***	−0.366***	−1.081***
	(0.065)	(0.065)	(0.047)	(0.053)
Citizenship	0.335**	−0.078	−0.314***	−0.087
	(0.148)	(0.117)	(0.115)	(0.102)
Disconnected	−0.055	−0.326**	−0.426***	0.088
	(0.146)	(0.138)	(0.151)	(0.096)
No Social Activities	0.047	0.219***	0.029	0.382***
	(0.067)	(0.065)	(0.052)	(0.050)
Children (yes=1)	0.652***	−0.196*	−0.137	1.635***
	(0.102)	(0.110)	(0.094)	(0.083)
H. Labour Income	−0.462**	−3.447***	−3.139***	−3.152***
	(0.201)	(0.108)	(0.105)	(0.100)
H. Capital Income	1.010***	−0.145	0.912***	0.289
	(0.348)	(0.242)	(0.221)	(0.227)
Trade Un. Member	−1.049***	−0.347***	−0.869***	−0.705***
	(0.096)	(0.092)	(0.078)	(0.072)
Family Members	0.030	0.189***	0.196***	0.224***
	(0.026)	(0.022)	(0.018)	(0.018)
Year-2008	0.018	0.251***	−0.044	−0.019
	(0.075)	(0.080)	(0.055)	(0.057)
Year-2010	−0.136	0.926***	0.500**	0.183
	(0.261)	(0.238)	(0.205)	(0.211)
Country dummies	Yes	Yes	Yes	Yes
Obs.		26,245		
p-value-Overall Model		0.000		
Pseudo-R2		0.33		

Notes
*** significant at 1% level; ** significant at 5% level; * significant at 10% level. Robust standard errors in parentheses. Significant t-test for the coefficients of the first-stage resid.indicates that education is endogenous.

which better-educated young people continue to be favoured with respect to their low-educated peers, regardless of the crisis.

Conversely, as stated in hypothesis 3, the crisis could have affected the relationships above through the education mismatch. Indeed, if we combine these three terms in the interaction $EMI_{un}*Years\ of\ Education*Year-2010$, significant coefficients emerge for unemployment, education and inactivity (see Table 2.8).[19] More precisely, an extra year of education in countries that experienced a remarkable increase in mismatch after the beginning of the crisis has an additional effect (-0.150) in reducing the relative probability of being unemployed. Therefore, as stated in hypothesis 3, it seems that the crisis, by aggravating education mismatch, is, on the one hand, worsening the position of low-educated youngsters and, on the other hand, favouring the employability of their better-educated peers. It is also worth noting that, in this case, an extra year of education, combined with mismatch and crisis, significantly decreases the relative probability of being in education (-0.209). This could be another sign for better employability of highly educated youth who, in these conditions, prefer to start seeking a job rather than extend their education period. Moreover, Table 2.8 shows a positive and significant sign of $EMI_{un}*Years\ of\ Education*Year-2010$ for inactivity. However, we should be very cautious in interpreting the result for inactivity status because of the lack of significance of the EMIs main effect at the country level on this outcome (see Tables 2.4 and 2.5).

The coefficients we present in Table 2.8 for $EMI_{un}*Years\ of\ Education*Year-2010$ only give us the information concerning relative probabilities, but tell us nothing about the real magnitude and sign of the effect of this combined variable on unemployment status.

Unfortunately, the computation of marginal effects for interaction terms in non-linear models is affected by many drawbacks that severely limit their interpretation (Ai and Norton, 2003; Greene, 2010). For this reason, we follow Greene (2010) and use a graphical representation of the sole marginal effects for *Years of Education* on unemployment, based on the model of Table 2.8 and conditional to EMI_{un} and *Year-2010*. Figure 2.4 depicts this interpretation by recovering the framework already used in Figure 2.3, where we take into account young people aged 26 with *years of education* = 8 and *years of education* = 13. In addition, these marginal effects are calculated at three different values of the distribution of EMI_{un}, the bottom decile (5.3), the median (16.3) and the top decile (21.4), in both the pre-crisis (*Year-2010* = 0) and post-crisis period (*Year-2010* = 1). As expected, in every category the marginal effects are negative, even though some differences are worth noting. Indeed, if we focus on the effect of an extra year of education for people aged 26 and provided with eight years of education, we can see that the negative impact decreases as the EMI_{un} increases. In 2010, the line connecting marginal effects for this cohort remarkably shifts upward. This indicates that for people who presumably have a secondary education, the guarantee to escape unemployment attenuates.

On the contrary, an extra year of education at the end of secondary education (*years of education* = 13), for people currently at the age of 26, makes the risk of being unemployed lower when the education mismatch is higher. Moreover, in

Table 2.8 Country-level EMI-un and individual education in crisis time, effects on labour
status of young people aged 15–34. MNL model: endogeneity control with
2SRI method; raw coefficients (Base category: Employee)

	Self-employed	Unemployed	Education	Inactive
EMI_{un} *Education	−0.071	−0.150**	−0.209***	0.115**
Years*Year-2010	(0.058)	(0.066)	(0.053)	(0.051)
EMI_{un} *Education Years	−0.077	0.013	−0.003	0.055
	(0.071)	(0.077)	(0.057)	(0.061)
Years of Education*Year-2010	0.029	0.009	0.029	−0.035*
	(0.022)	(0.022)	(0.018)	(0.019)
Years of Education	0.228***	−0.143**	0.580***	0.089**
	(0.051)	(0.058)	(0.037)	(0.043)
1-stage Resid.	−0.232***	0.082*	−0.391***	−0.152***
	(0.051)	(0.046)	(0.036)	(0.042)
Age	−0.785***	−0.144	−2.200***	−1.033***
	(0.108)	(0.105)	(0.072)	(0.079)
Age2	0.014***	0.001	0.034***	0.017***
	(0.002)	(0.002)	(0.001)	(0.001)
Gender (male=1)	0.804***	−0.207***	−0.365***	−1.085***
	(0.065)	(0.065)	(0.047)	(0.053)
Citizenship	0.328**	−0.081	−0.318***	−0.083
	(0.148)	(0.117)	(0.116)	(0.102)
Disconnected	−0.050	−0.323**	−0.416***	0.080
	(0.146)	(0.138)	(0.150)	(0.096)
No Social Activities	0.046	0.218***	0.028	0.382***
	(0.067)	(0.066)	(0.052)	(0.050)
Children (yes=1)	0.653***	−0.197*	−0.134	1.630***
	(0.102)	(0.110)	(0.094)	(0.083)
H. Labour Income	−0.462**	−3.448***	−3.145***	−3.153***
	(0.201)	(0.108)	(0.106)	(0.100)
H. Capital Income	1.014***	−0.154	0.889***	0.287
	(0.349)	(0.241)	(0.221)	(0.227)
Trade Un. Member	−1.050***	−0.345***	−0.864***	−0.708***
	(0.096)	(0.092)	(0.078)	(0.072)
Family Members	0.032	0.189***	0.197***	0.222***
	(0.026)	(0.022)	(0.018)	(0.018)
Year-2008	0.039	0.274***	−0.020	−0.050
	(0.075)	(0.081)	(0.056)	(0.059)
Year-2010	−0.155	0.900***	0.445**	0.180
	(0.268)	(0.240)	(0.206)	(0.211)
Obs.		26,245		
p-value-Overall Model		0.000		
Pseudo-R2		0.33		

Notes
*** significant at 1% level; ** significant at 5% level; * significant at 10% level. Robust standard
errors in parentheses. Significant t-test for the coefficients of 1-stage Resid. indicates that education
is endogenous.

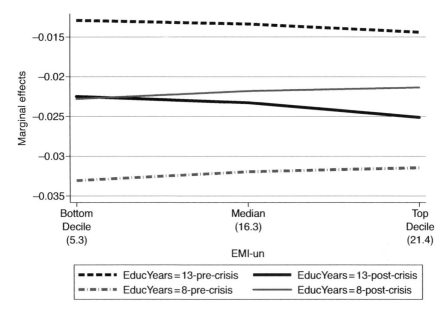

Figure 2.4 Marginal effects of years of education on unemployment according EMI-un and crisis effect (at age=26 and at the sample mean for other regressors).

this case the crisis shifts the line connecting marginal effects downward. The final result is that, in 2010, the risk of being unemployed for higher-educated people is lower than that of medium-educated people, as outlined by the two solid lines in the figure. This is an additional reinforcement for hypothesis 3 that is coherent with Figures A2.2 and A2.3. In other terms, if a high education mismatch means lack of young people with tertiary education on the labour supply side, by boosting mismatch the crisis aggravated the employment prospects for low- and medium-educated youngsters and favoured their highly educated peers.

7 Conclusions

This chapter analysed the effects of country-level education mismatch on the probability of being unemployed or staying in alternative labour statuses for young people living in 21 EU countries. Normally, education mismatch studies concentrate on structural unemployment at the aggregate level or focus on wages and productivity of mismatched workers at the individual level. Our contribution pointed out the effects of country-level education mismatch along individual profiles of young people that differ according the years of education they have accumulated. Unlike previous studies, we attempted to take into account how an aggregate phenomenon like education mismatch influences not only young employees or the unemployed, but also the conditions of all the population aged 15–34.

First of all, we provided new evidence that increasing years of education still matters to reduce the probability of being unemployed, it is important to lengthen the period of education, and slightly raises the probability of being self-employed with respect to the probability of being an employee. Therefore, our hypothesis 1, that we raised with the support of previous theoretical and empirical evidence upon the role of education, remains valid, especially for unemployment and self-employment. Second, we investigated whether education mismatch, measured at the country level, weakens or reinforces the results we found above. More precisely, we hypothesized that education mismatch should affect differently youngsters by only favouring better educated people (hypothesis 2). We did not find support for this evidence. This means that independently of the relevance of education mismatch, investing in education has the same effects we found for hypothesis 1 in all countries.

Finally, we considered the effect of the crisis on the relationships studied above. It is worth noting that the crisis per se did not significantly influence the impact of increasing years of education on labour status; in particular, it did not exert any additional effect on the probability of being unemployed. Instead, the crisis acted through education mismatch as we guessed in hypothesis 3. In other terms, an extra year of education is particularly effective in reducing the probability of being unemployed in countries that experienced a higher mismatch after 2008. This result particularly holds for young people who go beyond the secondary education level, whereas for those that do not, the guarantee of avoiding unemployment attenuates, especially after the beginning of the crisis.

Policy-relevant implications arise from these results and tell us that overall tertiary formal education still matters to avoid the negative effects of country-level education mismatch boosted by the recent crisis. This happens regardless of the specific field of study one makes. Thus, improving access to university degrees remains the main road to tackle unemployment caused by education mismatch. However, we need further research to prove that increasing education mismatch keeps qualitative changes in the labour demand for skilled workers out of sight. These changes, in turn, might affect the unemployment risk both for young people with intermediate education levels (aimed to routinary tasks) and for graduates who have acquired obsolete knowledge.

Appendix

Table A2.1 Small-Hsiao tests of IIA assumption

Omitted	lnL(full)	lnL(omit)	chi2	df	p-value	evidence
Self-employed	−9,593.874	−9,544.271	99.205	102	0.560	for Ho
Unemployed	−9,486.677	−9,440.177	93.000	102	0.727	for Ho
Education	−7,968.380	−7,916.704	103.352	102	0.444	for Ho
Inactive	−8,068.264	−8,020.706	95.116	102	0.672	for Ho

Notes
Ho: Odds (Outcome-J vs Outcome-K) are independent of other alternatives.

Table A2.2 2SRI-First stage estimation for results in Table 3: instrumentalization of years of education (OLS)

	Dependent Variable: Years of Education
Father's Tertiary Education	1.444***
	(0.042)
Equalitarianism	0.082*
	(0.048)
Environmentalism	0.291***
	(0.048)
Altruism	0.152***
	(0.058)
Age	1.502***
	(0.029)
Age^2	−0.025***
	(0.001)
Gender (male=1)	−0.462***
	(0.035)
Citizenship	0.775***
	(0.098)
Disconnected	−0.673***
	(0.093)
No Social Activities	−0.261***
	(0.039)
Children	−1.261***
	(0.053)
H. Labour Income	0.871***
	(0.064)
H. Capital Income	1.226***
	(0.116)
Trade Un. Member	0.396***
	(0.054)
Family Members	−0.087***
	(0.013)
Year-2008	0.182***
	(0.044)
Year-2010	0.331***
	(0.044)
Constant	−9.659***
	(0.388)
Country dummies	Yes
Adj. R^2	0.32
Obs.	26,410

Notes
Excluded instruments in bold. Robust standard errors in parentheses.
*** significant at 1% level; ** significant at 5% level; * significant at 10% level.

Table A2.3 Country-level education mismatch (labour force based) and individual education in crisis time, effects on labour status of young people aged 15–34. MNL
model: endogeneity control with 2SRI method; raw coefficients (Base
category: Employee)

	Self-employed	Unemployed	Education	Inactive
SMI_{lf}*Years of Education*Year-2010	0.105	−1.164**	−0.723*	1.393***
	(0.475)	(0.533)	(0.378)	(0.393)
SMI_{lf} *Years of Education	−0.198	1.717***	0.870**	−0.097
	(0.479)	(0.516)	(0.362)	(0.385)
Years of Education*Year-2010	0.014	−0.009	−0.006	−0.051***
	(0.021)	(0.021)	(0.016)	(0.017)
Years of Education	0.217***	−0.165***	0.567***	0.101**
	(0.050)	(0.057)	(0.036)	(0.042)
1-stage Resid.	−0.230***	0.081	−0.390***	−0.152***
	(0.051)	(0.057)	(0.036)	(0.042)
Age	−0.784***	−0.148	−2.199***	−1.038***
	(0.108)	(0.105)	(0.072)	(0.079)
Age2	0.014***	0.001	0.034***	0.017***
	(0.002)	(0.002)	(0.001)	(0.001)
Gender (male=1)	0.801***	−0.208***	−0.366***	−1.086***
	(0.065)	(0.065)	(0.047)	(0.053)
Citizenship	0.333**	−0.078	−0.316***	−0.091
	(0.148)	(0.117)	(0.115)	(0.102)
Disconnected	−0.054	−0.328**	−0.426***	0.074
	(0.146)	(0.138)	(0.151)	(0.097)
No Social Activities	0.047	0.225***	0.031	0.383***
	(0.067)	(0.065)	(0.052)	(0.050)
Children (yes=1)	0.652***	−0.191*	−0.133	1.631***
	(0.102)	(0.110)	(0.094)	(0.083)
H. Labour Income	−0.462**	−3.448***	−3.144***	−3.149***
	(0.201)	(0.108)	(0.106)	(0.100)
H. Capital Income	1.010***	−0.159	0.897***	0.295
	(0.349)	(0.241)	(0.221)	(0.227)
Trade Un. Member	−1.049***	−0.344***	−0.868***	−0.700***
	(0.096)	(0.092)	(0.078)	(0.072)
Family Members	0.030	0.188***	0.196***	0.223***
	(0.026)	(0.022)	(0.018)	(0.018)
Year-2008	0.011	0.302***	−0.018	−0.045
	(0.077)	(0.082)	(0.056)	(0.058)
Year-2010	0.000	−0.141	0.955***	0.531***
	(0.100)	(0.264)	(0.238)	(0.206)
Obs.		26,245		
p-value-Overall Model		0.000		
Pseudo-R2		0.33		

Notes
*** significant at 1% level; ** significant at 5% level; * significant at 10% level. Robust standard
errors in parentheses. Significant t-test for the coefficients of 1-stage Resid. indicates that education
is endogenous.

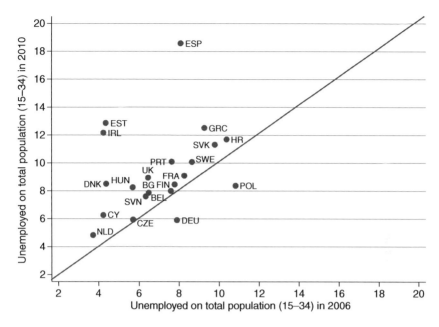

Figure A2.1 Unemployment on population ratio between 2006 and 2010.

Notes

BG – Bulgaria, CY – Cyprus, CZE – Czech Republic, DEU – Germany, ESP – Spain, EST – Estonia, FIN – Finland, FRA – France, HR – Croatia, HUN – Hungary, GRC – Greece, NLD – The Netherlands, POL – Poland, PRT – Portugal, SVK – Slovak Republic, SVN – Slovenia, SWE – Sweden, UK – United Kingdom.

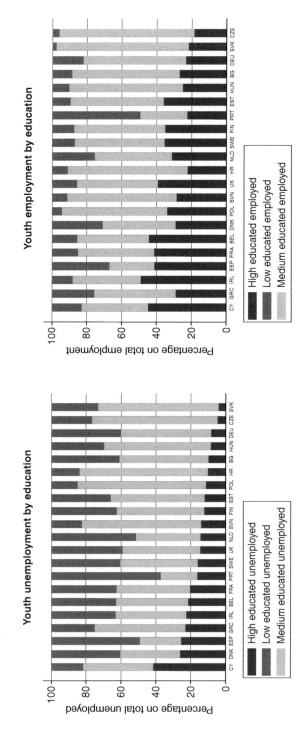

Figure A2.2 Education mismatch composition in 2010 (Employment vs Unemployment).

Notes

BG – Bulgaria, CY – Cyprus, CZE – Czech Republic, DEU – Germany, ESP – Spain, EST – Estonia, FIN – Finland, FRA – France, HR – Croatia, HUN – Hungary, GRC – Greece, NLD – The Netherlands, POL – Poland, PRT – Portugal, SVK – Slovak Republic, SVN – Slovenia, SWE – Sweden, UK – United Kingdom.

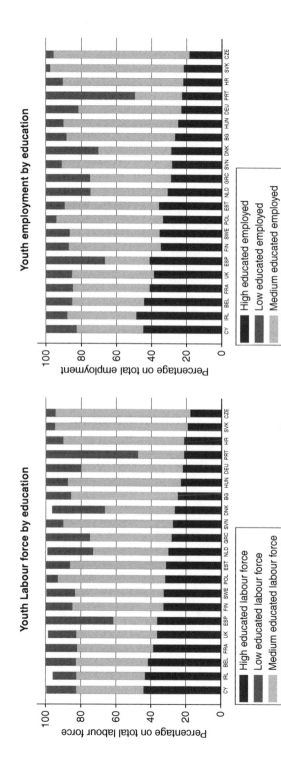

Figure A2.3 Education mismatch composition in 2010 (Employment *vs* Labour Force).

Notes

BG – Bulgaria, CY – Cyprus, CZE – Czech Republic, DEU – Germany, ESP – Spain, EST – Estonia, FIN – Finland, FRA – France, HR – Croatia, HUN – Hungary, GRC – Greece, NLD – The Netherlands, POL – Poland, PRT – Portugal, SVK – Slovak Republic, SVN – Slovenia, SWE – Sweden, UK – United Kingdom.

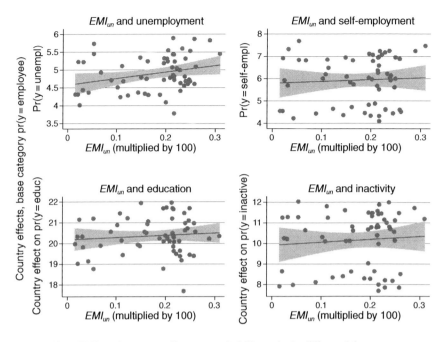

Figure A2.4 EMI$_{un}$ and country effects on probability to be in different labour status.

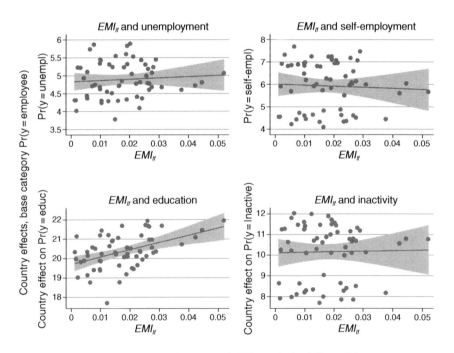

Figure A2.5 EMI$_{lf}$ and country effects on probability to be in different labour status.

Notes

1 Detailed reviews are in Mac Guinness, 2006; Desjardins and Rubenson, 2011; Leuven and Oosterbeek, 2011; Quintini, 2011; Acemoglu and Autor, 2012.
2 In this case, it is more difficult to analyse the effect of individual education mismatch on unemployment due to unavailability of data on vacancies by education composition. However, also studies concerning the simple effect of educational attainment on the probability of being unemployed are much less numerous than those addressing wages and productivity.
3 Hence our multinomial model includes four regressions to study the probability of being in labour market status 2; 3; 4; 5 (Self-employed, Unemployed, In education, Inactive) compared to the probability to be in 1 (Employee, the base category).
4 The components of these matrices are described in detail in Section 4.
5 Needless to say, that including EMI alone besides country dummies, would have caused multicollinearity problems.
6 This leads having approximately 60 observations or slightly under, due to missing data.
7 ESS is an academically driven multi-country survey aiming at developing a series of European socio-economic indicators.
8 These three proxy variables are coded as 1 when an individual responds *i) very much like me; ii) like me; iii) somewhat like me* to a relevant question, and zero in case of other answer. We deduced *altruism* from the question *important to help people and care for others' well-being*; *equalitarianism* from *important that people are treated equally and have equal opportunities*; and *environmentalism* from *important to care for nature and environment*.
9 1) Primary or less and lower secondary education (levels 1–2); 2) Upper secondary and post-secondary, non-tertiary education (levels 3 and 4); 3) from short-cycle tertiary education on, i.e. bachelor, master (levels 5–8).
10 It must be noticed that due to data availability, the cohort upon which these EMIs are built (persons 15–39 years old) is slightly different from the one we use at the micro-level (persons 15–34 years old). In addition, we suppose one year delay in the effect of aggregate mismatch on individual outcomes, therefore EMIs referring to 2006, 2008 and 2010 are actually calculated on 2005, 2007 and 2009 respectively.
11 We successfully confirmed the robustness of the estimation results with other several versions of this index, namely a three-year annual average and the annual change.
12 When interpreting the results, one should recall the (repeated) cross-section character of the data. Descriptive statistics in Table 2.1 are estimated on all the available observations for each variable; the number of observations vary due to presence of missing values for some variables. However, careful examination shows that the number of missing observations rarely exceeds 100 units out of 9–10 thousands of observations. The only exception is information on the ISCED levels of education. For Primary Ed., Secondary Ed. and Tertiary Ed. we have information for about 5–7 thousands out of 9–10 thousands of individuals. Further, we keep these dummy educational variables in Table 2.1 in order to give an idea of the approximate education composition in the sample we use. In the econometric estimations, the only variable describing education will be *Years of Education*, which has a negligible number of missing observations.
13 It is worth noting that this is not an unemployment rate, that normally corresponds to the ratio of unemployment to the labour force, but an unemployment to population ratio. However, the share of unemployment on population aged 15–34 that we show in Table 2.1 is not much different from that coming from Eurostat aggregate labour force survey data referring to the same countries: 7.74 per cent in 2006, 6.79 per cent in 2008 and 9.43 per cent in 2010.
14 The main differences between the two indexes concern the Netherlands, Germany and Poland. Especially the latter two countries show a slight increase in the mismatch

according to the unemployment based EMI_{un} (see also ILO, 2013, p. 93) and a reduction in the labour force version represented by EMI_{lf}. These differences support the choice to use both of them.

15 See also Table A2.2 in the Appendix. According to Bollen *et al.* (1995), excluded instruments are relevant when the adjusted R-squared in the first stage OLS regression is above 0.30.

16 The reduced and structural equations mentioned in Section 3 show a very similar Log-Likelihood and H0 cannot be rejected. It means that instruments influence the probability of being in an alternative labour status only through years of education and do not have any direct effect on these outcomes.

17 We used regression results from Table 2.3.

18 It must be remarked that we estimated three MNL models, one per year, similar to that of equation 2 and Table 2.3.

19 We also obtain very similar results with EMI_{lf}, see Table A2.3 in the appendix.

3 Youth unemployment, labour productivity and the evolution of the labour markets in Europe

Maria Laura Parisi, Enrico Marelli and Olga Demidova

1 Introduction

The latest crisis has exacerbated two negative macroeconomic phenomena, particularly in Southern Europe. First, the size and persistence of youth unemployment has become unacceptable after 2010. Second, stagnation in labour productivity goes back to the 1990s, but it has not improved since then and even worsened with the crisis. We document the evolution of these two macroeconomic phenomena and their wide heterogeneity across European and Anglo-Saxon countries. Moreover, we associate their trend with the evolution of the labour markets in the same period, starting from the mid-1990s.

Different labour market reforms at the end of the 1990s tried to solve the problem of "too high" unemployment. Many European governments for instance introduced a set of newly designed job-contracts that allowed the extensive use of temporary work. At the same time, Employment Protection Legislation schemes (measured by the OECD index EPLG) encompassed temporary workers too, allowing for special rules (EPLT).[1] In Section 4, we discuss the effects of EPLG on the flexibility of the labour market.

These rules might have affected both the youngsters' ability to find a job and the productivity of firms. The most common path today is that unemployed young people may re-enter the labour market almost exclusively through signing a temporary contract. At the end of the period, if not hired on a permanent position, they fall back into unemployment (see Di Giorgio and Giannini, 2012, or De Graaf-Zijl *et al.*, 2011).

The entry of temporary workers (who are relatively inexperienced if young) likely lowered the productivity of firms because it reduced their capital-labour ratio and, being cheap work, it mostly substituted riskier ICT-enabled innovations (see for example Gordon and Dew-Becker, 2008 or Daveri and Parisi, 2015).[2] Nonetheless, Cingano *et al.* (2010) observed that partial EPL reforms via the introduction of temporary contracts resulted in mixed impacts: temporary contracts used as screening devices may lead to better matches and higher productivity, but they may also lead to lower productivity if they provide weaker incentives for specific investments and less on-the-job learning.

We think that their conclusion is particularly serious for young people, who are more inexperienced and maybe have not accumulated enough skills and education yet.

We organized the chapter as follows. Section 2 discusses the path of youth unemployment in each observed country and its determinants. Section 3 describes the path of labour productivity in the selected countries. Section 4 discusses the policy rules adopted in each country in favour of labour market flexibility. Section 5 documents the cross-country time-varying heterogeneity in four dimensions: Labour Productivity, Youth Unemployment, Employment Protection and Temporary work. Section 6 concludes.

2 The pattern of youth unemployment and its determinants

By "youth unemployment", we mean the unemployment rate of the 15–24 year old population. Although in this age, typically, people attend school or university – in most countries education is mandatory up to 16 years old – those entering the labour force in the past 20 years contributed to swell the ranks of the unemployed. This characteristic is common to all advanced economies of the OECD, as Figure 3.1 shows. The figure represents the average youth unemployment rate, since 1990, for different groups of countries. These groups largely overlap with well-known classifications of European welfare systems proposed in the literature.[3]

The countries with the highest ever rate are in Southern Europe (France, Italy, Spain, Portugal and Greece), with the exception of the period 2000–2006, when youth unemployment was highest on average in the new EU member countries of Eastern Europe (Hungary, Czech Republic, Slovakia, Slovenia, Poland), for

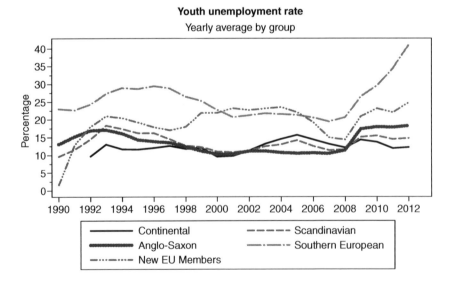

Figure 3.1 Trend of youth unemployment in the past 20 years by country groups.

which we have long enough observations. In 1990, Southern countries started already with a 23 per cent rate of youth unemployment, which reached more than 40 per cent on average in 2012 and beyond. New EU members had a very low rate of youth unemployment in 1990 (when they just started the transition to a market economy), less than 5 per cent, but over time, after 2000, it stepped above 20 per cent and stayed there. More stable, lower and converging was the youth unemployment rate of the three remaining groups until 2002: Continental (including Germany, Austria, Luxembourg, the Netherlands), Scandinavian (Finland, Norway, Sweden, Denmark) and Anglo-Saxon countries (including Ireland, Iceland and the UK in Europe, and New Zealand, Australia, Canada and the US outside Europe). In the year 2002, the average rate for all groups was slightly below 10 per cent. After the economic crisis, the average rate of these groups started diverging, with Anglo-Saxon increasing above 15 per cent, Continental decreasing below 10 per cent and Scandinavian in between.

However, heterogeneity is present within groups as well. Within the Continental group, for example, as in Figure 3.2, Germany's trend of youth unemployment started at a low 4 per cent in 1990, trending up to about 15 per cent in 2005, decreasing thereafter, even after the big world crisis. Austria, too, has a trend similar to Germany's, but constantly below by 4 percentage points until 2011. The Netherlands, which for some aspects regarding welfare and labour market policies can be assimilated to the Scandinavian countries, has a fluctuating unemployment rate converging to the average of the group after 2010.

Youth unemployment rates are heterogeneous in high unemployment countries too, including Southern Europe plus France and Belgium. Spain, Italy and Greece have the highest rates, even if, before the crisis, these countries were converging

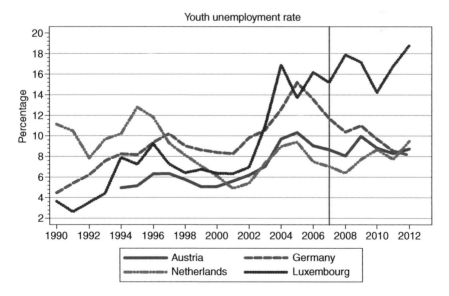

Figure 3.2 Fluctuating youth unemployment in Continental Europe.

towards the Portuguese rate, which was slightly above 15 per cent. After the crisis, with the exception of France and Belgium, the unemployment rates of young people in Southern Europe increased exponentially (see Figure 3.3).[4]

Although in a range between 5 and 15 per cent after 1995, Figure 3.4 shows that the Anglo-Saxon countries saw similar convergence in their youth unemployment rates, but right after the explosion of the crisis, the rates increased everywhere, especially in Ireland, with a rate above 30 per cent in 2012.[5] Nonetheless, these countries have never seen youth unemployment rates as high as in Italy or Spain.

Finally, the most heterogeneous countries in terms of youth unemployment dynamics are in the Scandinavian group. Figure 3.5 illustrates the trend of Sweden and Finland, the two countries with highest rates in the group. Finland halved its rate from a peak in 1994 to 15 per cent in 2007. Norway and Denmark saw a similar low and stable trend, very close to that of the Netherlands. Norway and the Netherlands seem to be the only two countries not suffering from the big crash in terms of unemployment.

In principle, there is no reason to think that the youth unemployment rate behaves differently from the general unemployment rate, in macroeconomics. A high GDP growth rate (above its "normal" rate or potential output) should reduce the unemployment rate, with much higher effect for those countries whose labour markets are more flexible (the so-called Okun's Law, as in Lee, 2000; Cazes *et al.*, 2012). Strong employment protection and labour hoarding explain why the impact of GDP growth in less flexible countries is weaker on reducing unemployment (IMF, 2010).

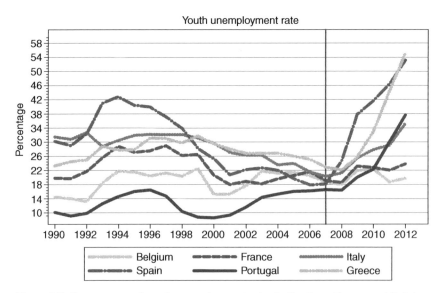

Figure 3.3 Convergence of youth unemployment rates in Southern Europe and Belgium until 2007.

Starting from the 1980s, many governments in Europe and elsewhere eliminated or relaxed the norms regulating hiring and firing, introduced new types of contracts, mainly atypical forms of temporary work, and competition increased in product markets. Therefore, we should observe the unemployment rate increasing drastically after an economic recession in the Anglo-Saxon countries,

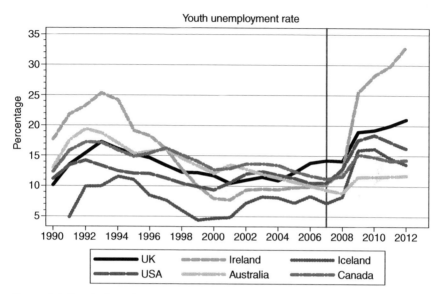

Figure 3.4 Trend of youth unemployment in Anglo-Saxon countries.

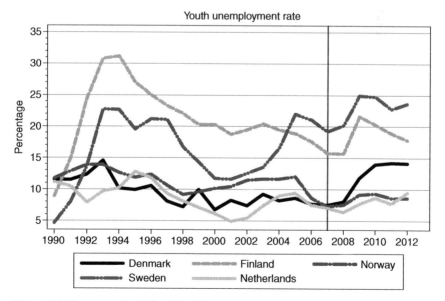

Figure 3.5 Heterogeneity in Scandinavian youth unemployment.

which typically have more flexibility (vice-versa after a boom). In general, Bar-tolucci *et al.* (2015) show that the impact on unemployment is amplified after a large financial shock, like that of 2007, due to a "systemic uncertainty" effect. Moreover, it seems that youth unemployment rate is more sensitive – compared to total unemployment rate – not only to GDP growth (with large effects both in the short and in the long run, i.e. a high degree of persistence) – but also to the occurrence of financial crises (Bruno *et al.*, 2016a).

What about youth unemployment trends? In 2001, the US entered a recession, but we observe a small increase in youth unemployment rate in 2002 and after-wards, both in the US and UK, the two countries with the most flexible labour markets. After 2007, however, the US youth unemployment rate almost doubled; in the UK, it started increasing in 2009 and peaking at above 20 per cent there-after. Indeed, this happened in all countries, with the exception of Germany, Austria, the Netherlands and Norway. Nonetheless, Italy and Spain suffered from the highest ever youth unemployment rates, although their employment protection legislation changed slowly (and lately).

Youth unemployment, therefore, must be affected by other (additional) factors, in particular institutional variables and labour policies.[6] To test whether labour market reforms in Southern European countries helped alleviate the problem of youth unemployment, Parisi (2016) estimates a model in which the unemployment rate of the youngsters is potentially affected by those reforms.[7] It turns out that, in the period ranging from 1998 to 2012, neither the share of young temporary workers, nor the share of adult workers had an effect on changing the youth unem-ployment rate. Some timid results indicate that after 2007, only increasing the share of adults on a temporary contract resulted in youth unemployment growing. Figure 3.12 in Section 5 of this chapter, indeed, shows that there is at least a non-linear (polynomial) relationship between temporary work shares (among the young) and youth unemployment in the South. On the other hand, the employment protec-tion legislation after the crisis helped restrain the growth of youth unemployment, given that some aspects of EPL were extended to temporary workers, too.

In a similar fashion, we can discuss the relationship between youth unem-ployment and inflation (Caporale and Gil-Alana, 2014). In a time in which central banks (including the "new" European Central Bank) had an inflation target, we should observe a stable unemployment rate, fluctuating very close to its natural rate. Indeed, as the figures above indicate, youth unemployment in the Eurozone countries was converging between 2000 and 2007, to a stable path, with the exception of Germany and Luxembourg. Parisi *et al.* (2014) estimate that inflation does not have any significant impact on youth unemployment, on average, in any group of countries.

3 The path of labour productivity: why is there such a decelerating growth in the South?

If we take a long look at labour productivity in the past 25 years, we observe that it has been growing on average in every country. Figure 3.6 reports the time

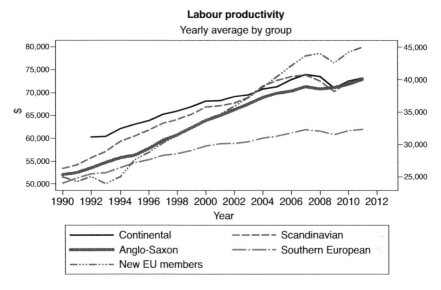

Figure 3.6 Productivity of labour in different groups of countries over time.

Note
New members' scale on the right axis.

series of labour productivity calculated as output per employee and as an annual average across countries for each group described in Section 2. Every group suffered from a large slowdown in 2009, during the economic crisis. However, Figure 3.6 shows that the Southern European countries level is much lower than other OECD economies (except for New EU) over the entire span, and labour productivity grew at lower rates too. While Continental, Scandinavian and Anglo-Saxon productivity converged in 2009, the New EU countries' productivity growth rate was the highest starting from 2004.

A bunch of empirical papers analysed the reasons why labour productivity in Southern Europe has slowed down in the 1990s and is still growing now at a slower pace than other advanced economies. At the micro level, Daveri and Parisi (2015) showed that Italian firms' productivity depends, among others, on the age and experience of the managers. Innovative firms are more productive than non-innovating firms, the latter adopting mostly a family-based management model, where education, abilities and young age is less important than other factors, like seniority, relationship and work experience. Moreover, the authors show that the share of temporary workers is associated with lower productivity, especially for innovative firms. Typically, after the mid-1990s, Italian firms – but also many firms in other countries of Southern Europe – started employing mostly workers under fixed-term contracts. Again, Bloom and Van Reenen (2010) showed how good management practices and product market competition are strongly related to productivity. They claim that France and the

UK's companies tend to use a family-based management model more than German and US firms do. Product market competition is another important factor, conducing to increase the market share of more efficient firms (moreover, improving managerial practices and effort) and to step inefficient firms out of the market. The OECD Regulatory Database (Woelfl *et al.*, 2009) provides a "product market reform" (PMR) index, revealing that Italy, France and Spain had the highest index in Europe in 1998, Germany, Belgium, Norway and the Netherlands an intermediate level, while the UK had the lowest PMR, setting the standard of the most competitive business environment. In ten years, however, Southern European countries adopted few liberalization policies under an EC/96 directive. Their PMR index indeed converged to the European average (yet their labour productivity has not grown, as a consequence).

Bassanini *et al.* (2009) studied the impact of regulations combination on the performance of industries in OECD countries in terms of Total Factor Productivity growth. Their main finding is that in countries with rigid dismissal regulations but lax legislation on the use of temporary contracts, firms can circumvent the constraints imposed by lay-off restrictions by opening fixed-term positions.

Another source of slow productivity may come from scarce investments in Research and Development and, in particular, the lagging adoption of Information and Communication Technology and the Internet. IT usage has been shown to increase labour productivity, especially when crucial sectors are considered (Daveri, 2004; Daveri and Mascotto, 2006). Differences between the US and Europe explain the gap in labour productivity (Van Ark, 2003).

4 Employment protection legislation and social spending: differences in rules and impacts on the labour market

The growing differences between unemployment dynamics in the US and Europe have been attributed to lack of labour market flexibility in the 1980s, giving rise to the first wave of employment protection legislation reforms, intended to liberalize the use of temporary fixed-term contracts in the 1990s (see e.g. Boeri and Garibaldi, 2007). The effect of such reforms resulted in a "two tier" labour market, which created high turnovers and flows in and out of unemployment for part of the labour force, while keeping intact the protection of permanent workers. The first unwanted effects of these asymmetric reforms were increasing employment at the "margin" and decreasing firms' productivity when they operate under decreasing returns to scale. Moreover, in times of downturns, inflows to unemployment, especially for youth and temporary workers, were larger. The countries experiencing the two tier reforms between the mid-1990s and the beginning of the 2000s were Italy, Portugal, Belgium, Germany, the Netherlands and Sweden. Spain is also considered as a country with a large two-tier labour market, even if it introduced such reforms back in the 1980s.

A second wave of reforms were introduced in most countries after the global crisis, in search of even greater labour market flexibility. Cazes *et al.* (2012) surveyed the existing literature on the impact of the reforms of employment protection legislation across countries, in particular after the global crisis. They document the number of countries reporting any reforms in legislation regarding permanent or temporary work and collective dismissals. Between 2008 and March 2012, about half of the advanced economies and Eastern European countries have altered their employment protection regulations for permanent employees, modifying in particular the regulation of severance payment and notice period. During the same period, about 60 per cent of these countries have relaxed their legislation on collective dismissals for economic reasons. Moreover, 66 per cent of these countries modified the regulation of temporary contracts, too, i.e. changing probationary periods and maximum length of fixed-term contracts, generally reducing their protection. For example, Greece in 2010 reduced the notice period for individual dismissal, reduced severance payment for white collars and allowed transforming fixed-term contracts into permanent after three years of work. Spain in 2010 and 2012 changed some rules of collective and individual dismissal, making them more flexible. The only exception (among those included in our focus) is Denmark, which increased protection after the crisis, by introducing severance payment in national agreements, and extending it also to hourly workers with a minimum work seniority. Austria in 2008 increased severance payments and improved the regulation against gender discrimination.

However, many studies found that the lack of employment protection might hamper employment and the labour market functioning, especially after recessions or negative shocks, requiring more "efficiency" in regulation design (among others, Bassanini and Duval, 2006a; Cazes and Tonin, 2010; Cazes *et al.*, 2012). The low variability of EPLG over time allows to group countries under three main categories: EPLG between 4 and 6 indicates a high level of protection. Since 1990, only Portugal has belonged to this category, but over time, it relaxed EPLG somehow (see Table 3.1). When EPLG takes the values 2 to 4, it indicates a medium level of labour protection. In this category, we find most Southern European, Continental, Scandinavian and New EU member countries. Notice that Germany and France increased protection until 2008. Spain reduced protection starting in 1994. Only Belgium and Denmark result to have an increasing index after 2008. When EPLG takes values below 2, then the level of protection is low or even zero, like in all Anglo-Saxon countries and Hungary. The US shows almost unprotected workers with an index close to zero. Estonia's EPLG index after 2010 reached this last group. Nonetheless, the UK, Australia and New Zealand increased labour protection already before the crisis.

Many countries adopt as well policies to protect those who are forced out of employment for different reasons, or those who belong to weak and disadvantaged social categories. Total social expenditure in a country includes spending for welfare, active and passive labour market policies, and other issues.[8] Table 3.2 summarizes the mean social expenditures of country groups as a percentage of GDP, in the period 1998–2014. Social expenditure is directed mainly towards welfare. Scandinavian countries reserve more than 1 per cent of GDP also to Active and Passive labour market policies, while Southern Europe devotes 1.2

Table 3.1 Level of EPLG and changes over time for observed countries

EPLG	1990–1994	1994–2002	2002–2008	2008–2013
0–2 Low	Aus, Can, Ice, Ire, Nzl, UK, US, Hun	Aus+ UK+	Ire– Nzl+	Aus–, Aus+ Est–
2–4 Medium	Aut, Bel, Ger, Nld, Esp, Fra, Gre, Ita, Dmk, Fin, Nor, Swe, Cze, Est, Pol, Svk	Dmk– Esp– Fin– Nld– Ger+ Swe–	Aut– Fin– Fra+ Ger+ Svk–	Bel+ Cze– Dmk+ Esp– Fra– Gre– Lux Svk– Svn
4–6 High	Por	Por–	Por–	Por-

Source: EPLG index from OECD and elaboration of the authors.

Note
Positive or negative changes of the EPLG index denoted by + or – indicate that the country has increased or reduced labour protection, respectively, in that time interval.

per cent of GDP on average to passive measures. The country ranking first in welfare expenditure is France (23.3 per cent), the country ranking last is Canada (11.6 per cent). The country ranking first in ALMP is Denmark (1.75 per cent), the country ranking last in ALMP is Iceland (0.075 per cent). Finally, the country ranking first in total social expenditures is again France (29.92 per cent) while the country ranking last is Estonia (15.06 per cent).

5 Heterogeneity in four dimensions

It is interesting to discuss the trend of youth unemployment and labour productivity conditional on the level of EPLG. It is evident from Figure 3.7 that, until the crisis years, countries with a medium level of labour protection were also those

Table 3.2 Social expenditures in the period 1998–2014 as a percentage of GDP

	Total	Welfare	ALMP	PLMP	Other
Continental	26.8	20.9	0.8	2.0	3.1
Scandinavian	25.3	18.3	1.2	1.6	4.2
Anglo-Saxons	17.9	13.1	0.4	0.7	3.7
Southern Europe	24.5	20.5	0.7	1.2	2.2
New EU members	19.1	15.8	0.3	0.5	2.5

Source: OECD.Stat data, elaborations of the authors.

Notes
ALMP=Active Labour Market Policy. PLMP=Passive Labour Market Policy.
Other=residual spending.

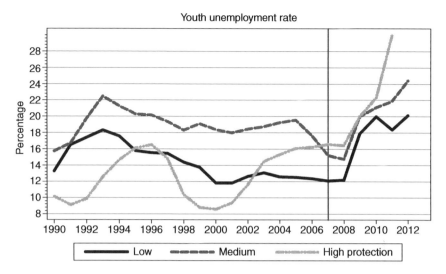

Figure 3.7 Average youth unemployment by level of EPLG.

with the highest level of youth unemployment, but the trend was decreasing (from 22 per cent in 1993 to about 15 per cent in 2008). Countries with medium and low protection had a decreasing trend in the 1990s, with the high-EPLG country having a largely fluctuating level of youth unemployment over the same time interval. From 2000 to 2008, the level of youth unemployment was stable at about 12 per cent in the low-EPL countries, and doubling in the high-EPL country. After 2007, all groups showed an upward swing of youth unemployment, no matter the level of EPLG, but in 2012 the low protection group stopped its youth unemployment rate at 20 per cent, the other groups going beyond 25 per cent.

On the other hand, Figure 3.8 indicates that labour productivity of low protection countries has been on average much higher than in the other countries. Until 2008, LP has increased constantly for all groups. The decrease after the burst of the crisis had different speeds: the high protection group saw its LP decreasing at a lower speed than the low protection group. The medium protection group saw an immediate decrease and an upward trend after 2009.

One important debate is whether strictness of employment protection caused the large recurrence of firms to temporary work. Indeed, Figure 3.9 shows that countries with medium or high level of employment protection have also experienced large and increasing shares of temporary (young) work. Only the medium-level countries experienced an average decrease of temporary work after 2007, which recovered from 2009. Countries with low level of EPL, nonetheless, recurred to more youth temporary work after 2005, peaking to 24 per cent share, on average, in 2011.

Countries have experienced different pattern of labour productivity and youth unemployment since 1990, as evident from Figure 3.10. During the 1990s, New

EU members, Anglo-Saxon and Scandinavian countries increased their labour productivity while reducing youth unemployment.

Southern Europe and Continental countries' growth of labour productivity, on the other hand, was accompanied by higher levels of youth unemployment. After the first wave of labour market reforms at the end of the 1990s, we still see an even more heterogeneous development across countries. New EU and Southern

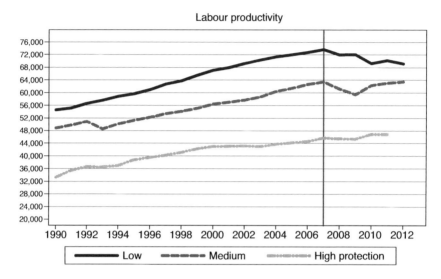

Figure 3.8 Labour productivity trend by level of EPLG.

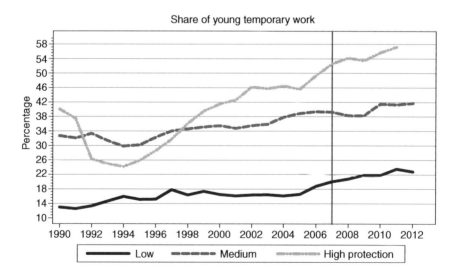

Figure 3.9 Share of young temporary workers by level of EPLG.

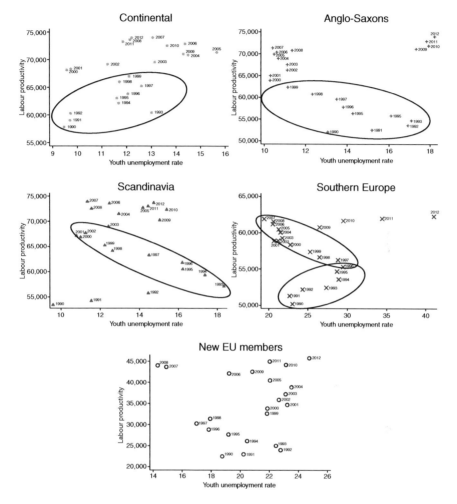

Figure 3.10 Labour productivity and youth unemployment rate.

countries managed to increase their labour productivity, while reducing youth unemployment, on average, until 2007. Both phenomena increased in Continental Europe, until 2007. Scandinavian and Anglo-Saxons did not see a clear path, their productivity increased but youth unemployment remained quite stable (and low in Anglo-Saxon countries). Finally, after 2007, only Continental and Scandinavian countries have not seen a significant increase in youth unemployment, while labour productivity continued to increase.

The regulation and extensive use of temporary work in Southern Europe and Continental countries accompanied labour productivity growth over time. Figure 3.11 shows that from 1991 to 2005 in Anglo-Saxon countries on average

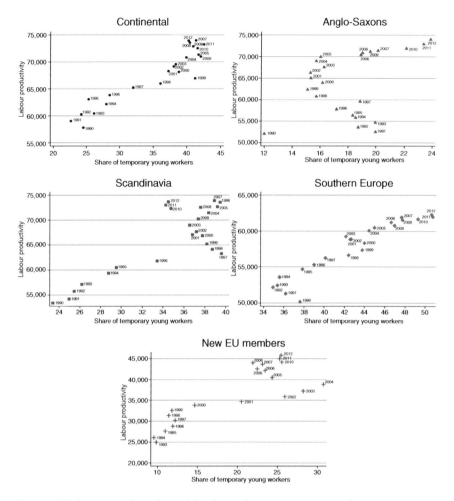

Figure 3.11 Labour productivity and the share of temporary young work.

there was a declining trend of the use of temporary young work, while productivity was increasing yet. After 2005, both labour productivity and temporary work increased. In Scandinavian countries, during the 1990s, labour productivity had been pushed by an increase in temporary work of the youngsters, but, after 1997, the reverse was true, while labour productivity was increasing, the share of young workers who had a fixed-term contract fell by four p.p. Finally, labour productivity was pushed by an increasing share of young temporary workers in New EU countries, until 2004, and Southern Europe, where the temporary share grew over 50 per cent of total employment. After that, the share of temporary work fell down by almost 10 percentage points in New EU, while their labour productivity was still increasing. This evidence gives support to Cingano *et al.*

(2010)'s matching hypothesis, but after the crisis, in Scandinavian and New EU countries, the hypotheses of weaker investment and on-the-job training (low) incentives for temporary workers appear to dominate. This evidence has important policy implications about the optimal way in which to organize labour market regulation (Lisi, 2013), that is different according to specific groups' characteristics.

In Figure 3.12, we learn that there is not a clear unique relationship between youth unemployment and the share of young temporary work across countries. While in Anglo-Saxons youth unemployment appears to decrease when the share of temporary work decreases as well, the opposite is true for Scandinavia and Southern Europe, until the beginning of the crisis. In the South, there is an "S" shape relationship: in the second half of the 1990s the increase in temporary

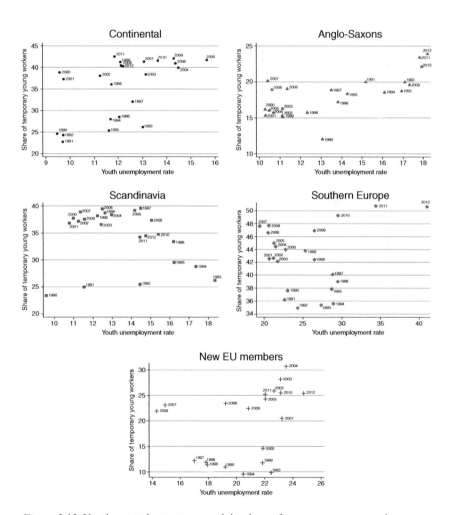

Figure 3.12 Youth unemployment rate and the share of temporary young work.

work helped at reducing youth unemployment, however, after 2007, the two phenomena grew together. In the New EU countries, even if the share of young temporary work increased significantly from 1999 to 2004, it did not help reduce the high rate of youth unemployment of that period.

6 Conclusions

We have described the evolution of four macroeconomic phenomena and their wide heterogeneity across European and Anglo-Saxon countries: labour productivity, youth unemployment rate, strictness of employment protection legislation, the share of youngsters with a temporary job. Moreover, we associated their trends with the evolution of the labour markets in the same period, starting from the mid-1990s.

We started from observing the well-known productivity slowdown in Southern Europe, starting in 1995, and the dramatic increase in youth unemployment, especially after the burst of the financial and economic crisis in 2007. We documented countries' differences and policy choices to contrasting unemployment. We showed whether the data support different hypotheses about labour market reforms and firms' productivity dynamics. One hypothesis is that temporary work reduced the capital-labour ratio and, being cheap work, mostly substituted riskier (ICT-enabled) innovations, thus reducing productivity. The second one is the "matching hypothesis" which affirms that short-term contracts allow a better matching of workers to jobs or projects, thus increasing productivity. The third hypothesis regards weak firms' incentives to employ, invest into and train temporary workforce: such weak incentives decrease productivity. A glance at the data shows that the matching hypothesis is most plausible for Anglo-Saxons (after 2005) and Southern European countries, in the 1992–2012 period (especially until the 2008 crisis in the Southern group). The other two hypotheses might be plausible for Continental, Scandinavian countries (after 1997) and New EU countries, after 2004.

Thus it seems, on the basis of our descriptive investigations (econometric analysis is due in future research), that the slow growth of Southern European labour productivity, cannot be attributed to the two waves of labour market reforms at the end of the 1990s and after 2007, when young workers entered the labour market under temporary fixed or short-term contracts. Indeed, the massive use of temporary fixed-term contracts for employing young workers helped – at least for a certain period – at sustaining labour productivity (not reducing it). On the other hand, it also seems that strict employment protection legislation makes the labour productivity level much lower than it would be with a lower level of employment protection. Moreover, the countries with low EPL managed to keep labour productivity growth at sustainable rates after the crisis. Nonetheless, Southern European countries have a medium level of EPLG, similar to that of Continental and Scandinavian countries (Belgium and Denmark even increased their EPLG after the crisis burst), yet their productivity growth has slowed down. For sure, other forces are at work in explaining cross-country differentiation in productivity trends.

Until the crisis years, countries with a medium level of labour protection were also those with the highest level of youth unemployment, but the trend was decreasing (from 22 per cent in 1993 to about 15 per cent in 2008). After 2007, all groups on average showed an upward swing of youth unemployment, no matter what level of EPLG was in place, but in 2012, the low protection index group stopped its youth unemployment rate at 20 per cent, the other groups going beyond 25 per cent.

Finally, a greater use of temporary work for the youngsters does not seem associated either to higher or to lower unemployment. Actually, in Continental countries there is no clear relationship. In Scandinavia, the increasing share of temporary work is associated with a decreasing rate of youth unemployment after 1993. In the South, however, the increasing share of temporary young work first decreased unemployment until 2007 the opposite happened thereafter. In the New EU countries, even if the share of young temporary work increased significantly from 1999 to 2004, it did not help reduce the high rate of youth unemployment of that period. Thus, appropriate policies are needed to reduce the youth unemployment rates, extremely high in many countries, and they are not incompatible with the support for creating "good" and more stable jobs.

Notes

1 EPLT extends EPLG including regulation of types of work allowed and duration of fixed-term contracts as well as rules governing the establishment and operations of temporary work agencies and agency workers' pay (OECD, 2013a).
2 Gordon and Dew-Becker (2008) made this point for Europe, showing that the labour market reforms that occurred in many European countries in the second half of the 1990s have been eventually detrimental to productivity growth.
3 See Esping-Andersen (1990). A similar classification can also be found in Vogel (2002), Caroleo and Pastore (2007b), and in our elaborations of OECD data on social expenditures.
4 We know that in these countries the youth unemployment rate continued to rise, e.g. it reached a 43.5 per cent peak in Italy in January 2014 – see Pica (2016) – slightly diminishing thereafter.
5 Then decreasing in the subsequent years.
6 Choudhry Tanveer *et al.* (2013) found that – in addition to economic growth and to a general index of "economic freedom" – labour market reforms, a high share of part-time employment and active labour market policies tend to reduce the unemployment rate.
7 At the end of the 1990s, many Southern European countries introduced the possibility to hire workers under temporary agreements. There were different kinds of contracts, ranging from fixed-term to collaborations or jobs finalized to the realization of a short-term project. Apprenticeship has been introduced, too. The aim of these reforms was to increase flexibility in the labour market.
8 OECD defines the different expenditures with the following taxonomy. Welfare expenditure: elderly pensions, survivors pensions, incapacity related spending, health expenditure. Active Labour Market Policy: programmes to improve Public Employment Service (PES) and administration, training, job rotation and job sharing, employment incentives, supported employment and rehabilitation, direct job creation, start-up incentives. Passive labour market policy: subsidies for unemployment. Other is residual spending.

4 Temporary-permanent contract wage gap for young and older workers in EU-28 countries

Cristiano Perugini and Fabrizio Pompei

1 Introduction

The relationship between flexible jobs and inequality in Europe has been largely analysed in the past two decades, both before and after the 2008–2009 crisis, with many contributions focusing on the impact of labour market reforms. Among them Jahn *et al.* (2012), despite a remarkable heterogeneity among EU-15 countries, also report some regularities from which we can deduce that the well-known trade-off between efficiency and inequality in implementing labour market reforms is still at work. By focusing on the 1985–2008 period these authors have found a positive correlation between liberalization of fixed-term contracts and employment (or productivity), but also a negative correlation between the same indicators for flexible labour (lower regulation for both regular and temporary workers) and the Gini Index.

In the years following the 2008–2009 crisis, a notable increase in the number of non-standard jobs for young people went hand in hand in Europe with persistent wage inequalities. According to Eurofound (2013b), between 2009 and 2012 the uncertainty about the economic prospects was dominant and forced employers to recruit large numbers of young people, for instance those needed to replace retiring workers, by means of fixed-term contracts. By focusing on young people, Eurofound (2013b) shows that about 57 per cent of the individuals who moved from education to employment in the EU between 2010 and 2011 were hired on a temporary basis. The same happened to those young workers who entered employment from the area of unemployment (61 per cent were hired with a fixed-term contract).

Several studies complement this evidence with information on the side of wage differences, showing in most cases non-negligible and pervasive negative wage gaps for temporary workers with respect to their permanent peers, not justified by education or other individual and job characteristics (Eurofound, 2015a). On the whole, the estimated temporary-permanent workers wage gap on cross-section data sets ranges from –13 per cent to –21 per cent, depending on the group of European countries considered (Stancanelli, 2002; Boeri, 2011; Comi and Grasseni, 2012; Kahn, 2012; Da Silva and Turrini, 2015; Perugini and Pompei, 2016, 2017). By adopting a dynamic framework, a recent OECD

Employment Outlook report (OECD, 2015b) has highlighted the notable role played by temporary jobs in worsening long-term earnings disparities in the majority of developed countries. What is also worth noting is that long-term wage inequality is mainly determined in the first ten years of workers' careers and inequality is normally exacerbated by age. Therefore, while for some workers a low quality job at the beginning of the working life represents a stepping-stone to better paid jobs, for others it is associated with a persistent impediment to career progression (a sort of scarring effect). The findings of the report confirm that a temporary job at the early stage of the worker's career is associated with a large persistent negative effect on the probability of having an open-ended contract in the future (OECD, 2015b).

Empirical evidence on wage inequality associated with temporary/permanent positions in the labour market leads to inconclusive results when the age profile is thoroughly taken into account along with other relevant individual characteristics. For example, by analysing thirteen EU countries in 1996 and 1998, Stancanelli (2002) finds that temporary workers are paid significantly less than permanent ones simply because they are less trained. Not only does this wage gap enlarge with age, but youngsters and individuals aged less than 35 are significantly more likely to make the transition to a stable job than older workers; the latter more often tend to fall into a trap of low-paid/low-productivity temporary jobs. In contrast, Kahn (2016), by focusing on the same thirteen countries between 1995 and 2001, observes that the gap for older temporary workers is smaller compared that for younger ones, because in some way also temporary workers benefit from experience and training, therefore being able to gain higher wages when age proceeds despite straying into the segment of temporary employment.

Other evidence upon the career effects of temporary employment seems to suggest that opposite results can emerge, depending on the countries under scrutiny (for a review see Gebel, 2013). In Germany and the UK, for example, temporary workers suffer from lower initial wages, but they later experience higher wage growth in comparison to permanent workers; this suggests that some sort of compensating effect is at work (Booth *et al.*, 2002; Mertens and McGinnity, 2004; Gebel, 2009). In particular Gebel (2009), finds that British and German young workers who start their working life in temporary jobs suffer from initial wage penalties and higher risks of temporary employment cycles. However, these differences, if compared to entrants with permanent contracts, diminish over time, especially in the UK. Although Barbieri and Scherer (2009) did not specifically focus on wages, they show that in Italy, entering the labour market via temporary jobs has strong and long-lasting negative career consequences in terms of lower employment chances and lower chances of ending up in permanent employment. According to Gebel (2013), an *integration versus entrapment* perspective of temporary jobs seems to follow a geographical/institutional pattern in which transitions from temporary to permanent positions are much less likely to occur in Continental, and particularly EU Southern welfare state regimes, and more likely in Anglo-Saxon and Nordic welfare state regimes.

In any case, the available evidence remains fragmented and no up-to-date and comparative perspective for all EU-28 countries exists. In addition, most of the studies discussed so far use an age profile in which young workers are those aged 16–24 years (older workers being the 25–64 year old ones). These age classes, despite having advantages, do not help analysing very crucial aspects; one of them is whether the fact that some older workers persist into temporary employment is due to entrapment or to the fact that they have just completed tertiary education (and are now in their late 20s or early 30s, thus classified as old) and did not have a reasonable time to complete their transition from education to work.

All these considerations led us to analyse the magnitude of the wage gap between temporary and permanent workers across all the EU-28 countries taking into account two age classes defined differently: from 16 to 39 years old (labelled as "young" workers) and from 40 to 64 ("old" workers). We use four waves of the EU-SILC cross-sectional database (with reference years from 2010 to 2013) to produce up-to-date evidence on the aspect we consider as crucial: the difference in temporary/permanent wage gap between the two groups of young and old workers. If the wage gap is more severe for young-sters, all other observable wage drivers being controlled for, this would suggest that employers apply a larger wage penalty/discount simply because these employees are less productive and need more training; once those temporary workers become more and more trained, experienced and productive, the gap with respect to the compensation of regular workers reduces (and the observed temp/perm wage gap for older workers narrows). In contrast, should the wage gap be larger for older workers, we might hypothesize that a sort of trap is at work. An important portion of the older temporary workers is not able to accumulate those skills that allow them to catch up with the pay of regular workers. Whatever would be the case, studying which factors favour staying in temporary employment or exiting from it when age proceeds seems a promising research perspective. The chapter is therefore organized as follows: in the next section we describe the data set used and provide some descriptive evidence on: (i) the share of temporary employment in the EU-28; (ii) its relative importance in age and education subgroups; (iii) the (hourly) wage levels and raw disparities across the EU-28 by job position (permanent or temporary), age (young and old workers, according to our definition) and education (primary, secondary or tertiary). In Section 3 we set up a micro-econometric model to study empirically the adjusted wage gap between temporary and permanent workers in the two age groups; once having ascertained that the gap is higher for older workers, we investigate the factors that can increase/decrease the probability of persisting into temporary employment (and the low-wage segment) also in later stages of the working life. Section 5 provides some concluding remarks.

2 Data, variables and preliminary descriptive evidence

2.1 Data and variables

Our empirical analysis covers the twenty-eight EU member countries in the years from 2010 to 2013. For the aggregate information used in the descriptive analysis on the share of temporary employment by age classes and education groups, we rely on Eurostat Labour Force Survey data (http://ec.europa.eu/eurostat/data/database). The individual data used for the analysis of wage disparities and in the micro-econometric models are instead drawn from the 2011–2014 cross-section releases of the European Union Statistics on Income and Living Conditions – EU-SILC. The number of individuals, aged between 16 and 65 years, included in the total sample is 1,015,487. Of them, 415,703 individuals are aged between 15 and 39 years (young workers, according to our definition) and 563,784 between 40 and 64 years (old workers). Similarly, 584,173 are employed as dependent workers and are the object of our empirical analysis on the temporary/permanent wage gap (see Tables 4.1 and 4.2 for the country/year details). The remaining 431,314 individuals (not in employment, in education, self-employed or retired) are used in the estimates to account and correct for sample selection bias. Due to the well-known challenges posed by self-employment in terms of income data availability and reliability, we decided not to include this segment of the labour market in our analysis. Within the sample of dependent workers, 216,577 individuals are aged between 15 and 39 years (young workers, according to our definition) and 367,596 between 40 and 64 years (old workers). The subsample of "old" workers (563,784 individuals, of which 367,596 are employees) is the object of the analysis of the factors affecting the probability of older workers to hold a temporary job. The subsample of "old" employees is composed of 341,646 permanent and 25,950 temporary workers, respectively.

Employees' income (variable PY010G) is defined as the gross total (yearly) remuneration, in cash or in kind, payable by an employer to an employee in return for the work done in the reference period. It includes wages and salaries paid in cash, holiday payments, thirteenth month and overtime payment, profit sharing, bonuses and productivity premia, allowances paid for transport or for working in remote locations, as well as the social contributions and income taxes payable by employees. The use of gross wages is common in the literature that considers within-countries wage and earnings inequality (Antonczyk *et al.*, 2010) and employs EU-SILC data (Brandolini *et al.*, 2010). In order to account for differences in hours worked, we computed all earning measures on hourly basis using the information on the number of hours usually worked per week in the main job and the number of months spent at work. Top and bottom 1 per cent of the hourly wage distributions in each country and year were trimmed in order to avoid distortions by outliers. All monetary values are expressed in 2015 Euro PPPs.

As explanatory variables of wages, besides the employment status (temporary or permanent), we use a large set of individual information which include:

gender of the worker, education (primary, secondary and tertiary, corresponding to the ISCED classification levels 0–2, 3–4 and 5–6, respectively), age (and its square), marital status, self-reported health status (on a 1 – very good to 5 – very bad scale), presence of a second job, control for part-time employment, type of occupation, sector and size of the firm in which the individual is employed.[1] In addition, we also considered geographical/institutional factors that influence the wage level, such as region (urban/non-urban) and, for the pooled estimations, the Central-Eastern vs Western countries divide. The latter, that is the dummy variable "East", is intended to capture all the structural differences underlying the rather systematic wage gap that the new EU members show when they are compared to the old EU members, Slovenia is the only exception[2] (see Table 4.1).

2.2 Temporary jobs, age and education in EU-28 countries

According to the aggregate data provided by the Eurostat Labour Force Survey, the proportion of temporary workers in the EU held quite steady between 2010 and 2013 (around 13.7 per cent). However, in line with evidence from previous studies (Jahn *et al.*, 2012) Figure 4.1 illustrates the huge heterogeneity of the share of temporary on dependent employment across the EU-28 countries.

It is worth noting that some Central and Eastern Europe Countries (CEECs) stand at both the top and the bottom of the ranking. In particular, after the 2008 crisis Poland leapfrogged Spain and Portugal and became the country with the highest share of temporary workers (26.8 per cent in 2013). According to Gora *et al.* (2016), the growth of temporary employment in Poland was partly due to the increase in civil-law contracts, which is a type of contract surveyed by LFS but not included in the Labour Code and not fully covered by social security, paid leave and minimum wage. This means that the surge in flexible work in

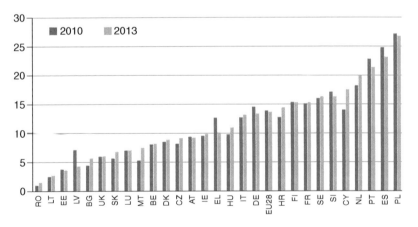

Figure 4.1 Temporary workers as a percentage of total employees (2010 and 2013).
Source: Eurostat online database.

Table 4.1 Mean hourly wages by education group and age (average 2010–2013; PPS)

Country	Obs	Pooled	Primary Ed.	Secondary Ed.	Tertiary Ed.	Young	Old
RO	18,209	3.845	2.759	3.460	5.363	3.736	3.910
BG	17,092	4.084	2.946	3.763	5.206	4.073	4.091
LV	17,492	6.100	4.386	5.056	8.374	6.269	6.015
LT	15,646	6.120	4.128	4.871	8.138	5.708	6.258
HU	31,900	6.173	4.241	5.461	8.864	5.979	6.301
SK	22,497	6.616	4.947	6.127	8.198	6.605	6.623
EE	18,280	7.365	6.285	6.583	8.974	7.675	7.197
HR	14,163	7.453	5.508	6.760	10.654	6.680	7.925
CZ	26,252	7.792	5.499	7.239	10.644	7.692	7.857
PL	37,173	8.057	5.491	6.926	11.157	7.524	8.472
PT	16,997	9.063	6.967	8.962	15.463	7.869	9.841
EL	10,226	10.763	8.344	9.326	13.088	8.763	12.105
SI	12,977	12.321	8.551	10.439	17.037	10.844	13.245
MT	10,584	13.286	10.887	13.016	17.881	12.454	14.130
ES	31,492	13.747	10.397	12.548	17.250	11.447	15.063
CY	16,041	14.101	9.960	12.110	18.119	11.245	16.212
IT	46,679	14.894	12.253	14.825	18.913	12.564	16.092
FR	35,158	15.120	12.840	13.589	17.934	13.527	16.131
UK	27,364	16.061	12.405	13.667	19.998	14.977	16.787
SE	11,720	17.013	14.638	16.078	18.662	14.291	18.600
DE	39,290	18.465	13.008	15.972	22.733	16.092	19.266
FI	14,207	19.125	15.463	15.743	22.590	16.849	20.192
IE	11,444	19.836	15.184	15.943	23.546	17.731	21.560
BE	17,508	19.987	16.262	17.568	23.091	17.573	21.694
AT	17,694	20.277	14.440	18.869	26.731	17.081	22.111
DK	9,658	21.972	18.223	20.263	24.641	20.076	22.599
LU	18,083	23.763	16.049	22.537	33.118	20.461	26.431
NL	18,347	24.882	18.765	21.815	29.915	21.696	26.341
EU-28 average	*584,173*	*12.929*	*10.658*	*10.857*	*17.306*	*11.372*	*13.847*

Source: Our elaborations on EU-SILC data.

Poland has been possible without remarkable liberalization on the side of employment protection legislation: in fact, the protection for temporary workers remained substantially high (OECD, 2013b; Arak *et al.*, 2014). In contrast, Romania and the Baltic countries are at the bottom of the distribution with percentages of temporary workers below 5 per cent. Eurofound (2013a), highlighted that these very low percentages could partly be explained by the presence of non-standard forms of temporary employment that are not fully captured by LFS or by flexible dependent employment disguised as bogus self-employment.

Western EU countries also appear to be dispersed around the EU-28 average, even to a greater extent compared to the Eastern counterparts. Many scholars agree on identifying labour market dualism and asymmetries in the protection levels of employment as the main reasons behind the high propensity to hire temporary workers (Boeri, 2011; Gora *et al.*, 2016). Besides the clear-cut example of Spain (23.2 per cent of temporary workers in 2013) that implemented two-tier reforms after 1984 (Bentolila and Dolado, 1994), the European Commission (2010) shows that this is also the case for Portugal, the Netherlands, Sweden, France, Finland, Germany and Italy. According to Figure 4.1, all these countries are above or slightly below (Germany, 13.4 per cent, and Italy, 13.2 per cent) the EU-28 average. However, differences in temporary worker shares of total employment among countries with similar labour market dualism remain important because different complementarities develop between the employment protection regimes and other institutions that influence the outside option of workers (see Bentolila *et al.*, 2012a for France and Spain; Berton and Garibaldi, 2012 and Cappellari *et al.*, 2012 for Italy).

In contrast, the UK shows the lowest share of temporary workers among Western countries (6 per cent in 2013). This evidence can be explained by the lowest levels of employment protection for both temporary and permanent employees; the low asymmetries resulting from these provisions would also explain the absence in this country of that hiring strategy aiming at replacing permanent with temporary workers (OECD, 2013a). For this reason, some authors considered the UK a sort of benchmark country in which the propensity to hire temporary workers only responds to technological and idiosyncratic features of industries and it is not affected by legislation (Bassanini *et al.*, 2009).

However, labour market institutions are not the only smoking guns; individual characteristics, such as education and age, are also thought to play a key role in complementing institutions and shaping different patterns of the temporary employment in the EU economies. First of all, even considering the aggregate of EU-28 countries (Figure 4.2), we observe that the incidence of temporary workers within the group of employees with primary education is almost double than the average (around 20.3 per cent versus 13.7 per cent). In contrast, the percentage of fixed-term employees for workers with secondary and tertiary education stands below the average (around 12.6 per cent and 11.5 per cent, respectively). The country-by-country profile of Figure A4.1 in the Appendix is coherent with the aggregated picture: in all twenty-eight EU economies the importance of temporary jobs swiftly falls when one turns from low to medium educated workers and then further declines from secondary to tertiary education. In any case, the diffusion of fixed-term contracts among low educated workers remarkably increased in those countries that were already at the top of the ranking in Figure 4.1 (47.9 per cent in Poland and 30.7 per cent in Cyprus in 2013). In addition, if we observe the distribution around the EU-28 average, some countries have a remarkably different position compared to the mean values charted in Figure 4.1. For example, the moderate use of temporary workers in Slovakia, Germany and Austria only holds for medium and highly educated workers, whereas it largely exceeds the EU-28 average within the group of the low educated employees (38 per cent in Slovakia, 31.7 per cent in Germany and 26.4 per cent in Austria, versus an average of 20.3 per cent). Italy is the only country that shows an opposite pattern: in this country the percentage of flexible and highly educated employment reached 13.9 per cent in 2013 (compared to an average of 11.4 per cent); this is a value very close to that for low educated temporary workers (14.2 per cent) and slightly larger than that for those with secondary education (12.2 per cent).

Age is another key dimension to discern the different patterns of temporary employment across EU countries. Figure 4.3 clearly shows that the incidence of flexible employment is for young workers nearly three times as large as for older

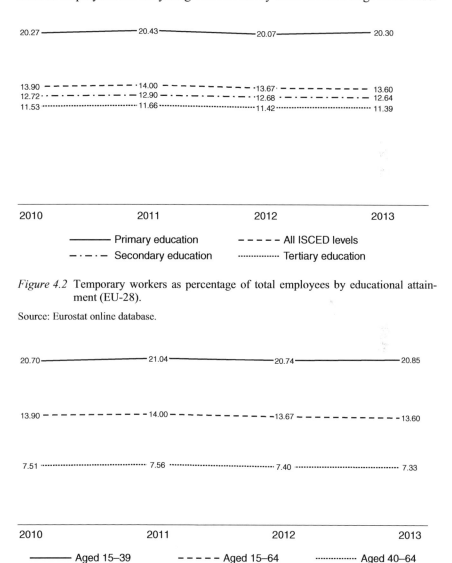

Figure 4.2 Temporary workers as percentage of total employees by educational attainment (EU-28).

Source: Eurostat online database.

Figure 4.3 Temporary workers as percentage of total employees by age (all ISCED levels and all 25 EU countries).

Source: Eurostat online database.

ones (20.8 per cent and 7.3 per cent, respectively). This evidence is consistent with most of the considerations that have been made regarding the large use of this type of contracts among younger workers (Eurofound, 2013b). Fixed-term contracts are screening devices that employers use to evaluate the newly hired personnel, especially those people in transition from education to employment and when uncertainty upon economic prospects is high, so that the need to increase numerical flexibility and reduce costs becomes dominant.

By combining age and education, we get more articulated country-by-country profiles (Figures A4.2, A4.3 and A4.4 in the Appendix), which better clarify the evidence presented earlier. As we discussed in Section 1, if temporary jobs in the age-class 40–64 partially reflects forms of *entrapment*, in which the transition from temporary to permanent job is not possible or very unlikely, Figure A4.2 reveals that low educated workers are those to be associated with the highest probability of staying in a temporary condition.

This is especially the case for Poland, Slovakia, Spain and Cyprus, positioned at the top of the ranking of flexible employment for both young and old workers (Figure A4.2). Spain and Cyprus, accompanied by Portugal, keep the same position also among workers with tertiary education (Figures A4.3 and A4.4). The possibility that some form of *entrapment* is at work within these countries seems to be confirmed by the high presence of involuntary temporary workers, highlighted by Eurofound (2013b). In contrast, the very high percentages of low educated flexible employment in Austria and Germany, already discussed, are confined to the younger workers (Figure A4.2) and could be explained by the specific vocational training and apprenticeship systems that in those countries are associated with temporary work (Eurofound, 2013b).

Being a temporary worker (before or after the age of 40) would not be a disadvantage if wage differentials were not important. Tables 4.1 and 4.2 compare levels and differentials of hourly wages in Purchasing Power Standards (2015 PPS) across EU countries.

According to our EU-SILC sample, during the period under scrutiny the hourly wage in the EU-28 amounted to about 13 euro (in 2015 PPS). The dispersion of countries around this mean value is consistent with evidence reported in other studies (Eurofound, 2015b; Perugini and Pompei, 2015) and mirrors the broad structural and historical differences shaping the EU national economies (Kornai, 2006). All central and Eastern EU members, accompanied by some southern EU countries (Croatia, Greece and Portugal) show wages below the EU-28 average (Table 4.1, column "Pooled"); however, if Romania and Bulgaria remain at the very bottom of the distribution (3.8 and 4 euro per hour, respectively), the Slovenian average hourly wage (12.3 euro) is very close to the EU-28 average. Large differences also exist across Western EU countries, with the Netherlands, Luxembourg and Denmark at the top of the ranking (24.9, 23.8 and almost 22 euro per hour, respectively) and Spain, Cyprus and Italy showing wages only slightly above the EU-28 average (13.7, 14.1 and 14.9 euro, respectively).

Education and age emerge as important drivers of within country wage differentials. It is worth noting that disparities associated with education, especially between workers with primary and tertiary education, play a more important role than those related to age. In the majority of countries, wages for highly educated workers are more than one and half times larger (often nearly double) than those earned by workers with primary education. Differences between old (40–64) and young (15–39) workers are, although remarkable, smaller.

As regards the unadjusted wage gap between temporary and permanent workers, Table 4.2 reveals that on average in the EU-28, aside from all workers' characteristics that we will consider in the econometric analysis, a temporary worker's wage is 71.8 per cent of the one earned by a permanent employee. Above average gaps emerge for those Western EU countries (or new EU members) that experienced a higher use of temporary jobs: Cyprus (51.4 per cent), Spain (67.5 per cent), but also Italy (67.7 per cent), Germany (68 per cent) and Sweden (70 per cent). Luxembourg is a particular case in the sense that, despite its very low percentage of fixed-term contracts (7 per cent in 2013), the temporary/permanent wage gap is

Table 4.2 Temporary/permanent mean hourly wage by education group and age

Country	Pooled	Primary Ed.	Secondary Ed.	Tertiary Ed.	Young	Old
CY	0.514	0.440	0.496	0.631	0.638	0.459
LU	0.657	0.717	0.632	0.687	0.750	0.614
ES	0.675	0.778	0.697	0.668	0.793	0.646
IT	0.677	0.748	0.657	0.671	0.753	0.678
DE	0.680	0.761	0.677	0.709	0.748	0.674
EL	0.696	0.827	0.759	0.679	0.825	0.651
SE	0.702	0.740	0.701	0.712	0.752	0.754
SI	0.703	0.839	0.775	0.649	0.761	0.706
LV	0.703	0.698	0.788	0.837	0.711	0.696
HU	0.709	0.815	0.796	0.801	0.730	0.696
PL	0.711	0.851	0.781	0.726	0.738	0.701
PT	0.752	0.821	0.624	0.663	0.871	0.701
FR	0.755	0.850	0.779	0.734	0.816	0.748
HR	0.771	0.889	0.814	0.708	0.830	0.772
BE	0.779	0.848	0.776	0.780	0.867	0.752
FI	0.785	0.853	0.814	0.766	0.851	0.784
BG	0.793	0.940	0.876	0.761	0.749	0.823
RO	0.797	0.844	0.876	0.750	0.819	0.784
NL	0.809	0.869	0.809	0.796	0.842	0.844
AT	0.824	0.827	0.772	0.841	0.926	0.807
CZ	0.824	0.939	0.821	0.828	0.824	0.827
SK	0.861	0.946	0.863	0.876	0.852	0.869
IE	0.862	0.910	0.932	0.834	0.942	0.817
MT	0.886	0.918	0.778	0.887	0.869	0.943
LT	0.918	0.955	1.008	1.035	0.881	0.948
DK	0.920	0.864	0.909	0.919	0.996	0.908
EE	0.935	1.022	0.917	0.988	0.832	1.021
UK	1.023	1.071	1.025	0.927	1.055	1.028
EU-28 average	*0.718*	*0.734*	*0.724*	*0.769*	*0.788*	*0.703*

Source: Our elaborations on EU-SILC data.

high (65.7 per cent.) However, the bulk of countries located at the bottom of Figure 4.1 (i.e. with the lowest use of temporary jobs), also show the lowest wage gap (Estonia, 93.5 per cent; Denmark, 92 per cent, Lithuania, 91.8 per cent; Malta, 88.6 per cent) or even no gap (the UK, 102 per cent).

It is worth noting that in twenty-three out of twenty-eight countries, the temporary/permanent gap is deeper in the group of workers with tertiary education compared to those with primary education. This is especially the case for Slovenia (65 per cent for highly educated workers versus 85 per cent for the low educated ones), Croatia (71 per cent versus 89 per cent), Bulgaria (76 per cent versus 94 per cent), Portugal (66 per cent versus 82 per cent) and Greece (68 per cent versus 83 per cent). In other studies (Perugini and Pompei, 2016, 2017) we argued that this evidence could be explained by complementarities between formal education and informal skills that play a more important role in the group of tertiary educated workers. In other words, if temporary workers with higher formal education are not allowed to accumulate firm-specific human capital (due to their fixed-term contracts), the wage gap with respect to regular workers increases relatively more than for lower educated employees, who cannot exploit this complementarity. The evidence we add in the present work concerns the age profile of workers. From the last two columns of Table 4.2, we can deduce that in twenty-one out of twenty-eight EU countries the temp/perm wage gap is more severe within the group of older workers (aged 40–64). To this pool of countries belong those ones with the highest share of temporary workers (see Figures A4.2, A4.3 and A4.4 and their discussion) such as Cyprus (where the temp/perm gap for older workers is 46 per cent and 64 per cent for the younger ones), Spain (65 per cent versus 79 per cent) and Portugal (70 per cent versus 87 per cent). Of course, the larger is the gap for older workers with fixed-term contracts, the deeper is the penalty in terms of welfare for this category of employees. This could be a signal for the existence of a sort of trap of involuntary fixed-term contracts in which workers aged 40–64 might remain stuck. In the next section we analyse the temp/perm wage gap in a multivariate framework, i.e. controlling for all workers and job observable characteristics. After having quantified the size of the gap and shown that it is larger for older workers, we study the determinants of being a temporary worker after the age of 40.

3 Temporary/permanent wage gap for young and old workers

3.1 Econometric methods and empirical model

In order to estimate the baseline empirical model (for the whole sample, obtained pooling countries and years) for the drivers of individual wages, expressed as log hourly wages (*lhwage*), we rely on the human capital model as the theoretical basis for the earnings function (Becker, 1964; Mincer, 1958). We therefore assume that labour income increases first of all with accumulated formal (education) and informal (experience) skills. The latter is only partially approximated with age, as the work experience measure (PL 200 – number of years spent in paid work) in EU-SILC is not available for all countries and has many missing values. In order to measure the effect on wages of belonging to the pool of young or to the pool of the old workers, we also include a dummy variable *young* which is one if the worker is aged between 15 and 39 years, and zero otherwise. As a consequence, the variable age (and its square) captures the effect of experience within the two pools. Other explanatory variables are gender (*male*), marital status (*married*), health status (*health status*); urban/non-urban region of residence (*urban*); second job (*second job*); full-time job position (*full-time*); sector of employment (*sec*); occupation (*occ*); size of the firm (*firm size*). Information about occupations somehow helps control for differences in the intensity of routinary/no-routinary tasks that characterize jobs and shape the relative earnings patterns (Autor *et al.*, 2003). The variable of our main interest here is permanent/temporary employment status (coded as *temp*=1 if the contract is temporary and 0 otherwise); the coefficient of this dummy variable can therefore be interpreted as the (otherwise) unexplained wage gap (in per cent) due to the employment contract. The heterogeneity of the effects of being temporary in the two age groups (young and old workers) is measured by the coefficient of the interaction variable *temp*young*, which provides information about the significance and the size of the difference of the effects for young workers compared to the benchmark group, the old workers. The coefficient of the variable *temp* is therefore the temp/perm gap for old workers; the coefficient of the interaction (*temp*young*) is the difference in the gap between old and young workers.

Our baseline pooled (by country and by year) empirical model takes therefore the following form:

$$lhwage_{ik} = cons_{ik} + a_n X_{ik} + \beta_1 temp_{ik} + \beta_2 temp_{ik} \cdot young_{i,k} +$$
$$\tau east_k + u_k + \lambda_t + u_k \cdot \lambda_t + v_{ik} \tag{1}$$

where subscripts *i*, *k* and *t* denote individuals, countries and years, respectively; u_k denotes country fixed effects, λ_t year fixed effects and their interaction controls for country/year specific factors. The dummy variable *east* is 1 for the former communist EU members and zero otherwise. X_{ik} is the regressor matrix and a_n the vector of associated coefficients. The coefficients β_1 and β_2 measure the temporary/permanent wage gap for the benchmark group (old workers) and the difference for the group of young workers, respectively. v_{ik} is a mean-zero error term. The country and year specific estimates are obtained from equation 1 by restricting to zero all non-relevant fixed effects coefficients.

In all estimations we control for sample selection effects since, as it is well known, the selection of employees from the sample of working age individuals could be non-random and therefore produce biases in the estimation of the coefficients from the wage equations. To account for the selection effects we use a correction based on the Heckman two-stage method (Heckman, 1979), in which the first stage participation equation includes as regressor, besides the already described personal characteristics (gender, age, marital and health status, settlement and education), variables related to household structure that we were able to build considering the information available in EU-SILC. They refer to the household size and to the number of children (less than 3, 4–6 and 7–15 years old) and of elderly (65–74 and over 75 years old). The dependent variable of the selection equation is a binary variable which is one if the worker is an employee (and therefore earns a wage) and zero otherwise (inactive, unemployed, self-employed).

We also investigate the factors that increase/decrease the probability of staying in a temporary position in older stages of the working life. Ideally, the best alternative for this type of analysis would have been a longitudinal data set covering a period long enough to depict the transition/permanence of individuals from a temporary position in the earlier stages of the working life towards other job statuses as age proceeds; however, EU-SILC longitudinal data have a maximum length of four years, which is clearly not enough. We therefore decided to use the cross-section data sets and to estimate a probit model restricted to the sample to the older age group (40–64 years) and employing as the dependent variable the dummy *temp*. The probit model reads:

$$lhwage_{ik} = cons_{ik} + \alpha_n X_{ik} + \beta_1 temp_{ik} + \beta_2 temp_{ik} \cdot young_{i,k} +$$
$$\tau east_k + u_k + \lambda_1 + u_k \cdot \lambda_1 + \upsilon_{ik} \tag{2}$$

where symbols and variables correspond to those described in equation 1. However, since the variables related to occupations to a great extent include the information on the job position (being some occupations inherently temporary and some others inherently permanent) we decided not to include them from the set X_{ik}. As explained in Cameron and Trivedi (2010), the signs of the regression parameters in equation 2 can be interpreted as determining whether the probability of the dependent variable being 1 (i.e. staying temporary in older stages of working life) increases with the regressor. In order to measure the size of this (positive or negative) effect, we provide the marginal effects of the dummy variables on which we focus our attention (the levels of education attained) by keeping all other regressors at their mean value. Again, country and year specific estimates are obtained from equation 2 by restricting to zero all non-relevant country and country*year fixed effects coefficients. In order to account for sample selection we implement here a Heckman Probit Model, introduced for the first time by Van de Ven and Van Pragg (1981). The assumption implicit in the modelling strategy is that the primary "decision" of workers (older workers in our case) is whether to be employed as a dependent worker or not; only at a later stage, once he/she has decided to be an employee or not, will he/she seek a permanent position. Of course, the best alternative would again be to have longitudinal data covering long periods of time, but since only short panels of individuals are available in EU-SILC (maximum four years long), we opt here for a Heckman procedure. The first stage participation equation is therefore estimated using as the dependent variable a dummy that is one if the individual is a dependent worker and zero otherwise; the outcome equation estimates the impact of factors affecting the probability of being a temporary workers once the factors driving the selection into dependent employment are accounted for. As in the previous Heckman correction (wage equation), the selection equation includes among the regressor the explanatory variables of equation 2, plus the variables related to household size, the number of children (less than 3, 4–6 and 7–15 years old) and of elderly (65–74 and over 75 years old).

3.2 Results

Tables 4.3 and 4.4 and Figure 4.4 report the estimated coefficients for the model described in equation 1; although not displayed, all estimations include sector and occupation dummies. Those reported in Table 4.3, based on the EU-28 aggregate sample, also include country dummies; in addition, the pooled model includes year and country*year dummies. Results of the empirical model presented in Table 4.4, country by country, only include year dummies. In all estimations the correction for the sample selection is implemented.

A first remarkable piece of information emerging from the results is their overall strong stability and consistency with ex-ante expectations. Results in Table 4.3 show that the average (adjusted) wage gap between temporary and permanent workers is around 18 per cent. This figure is obtained as the average of the gap for old workers (coefficient of *temp*) and the one for younger ones (coefficient of *temp* + coefficient of *temp*young*). This is a remarkably lower

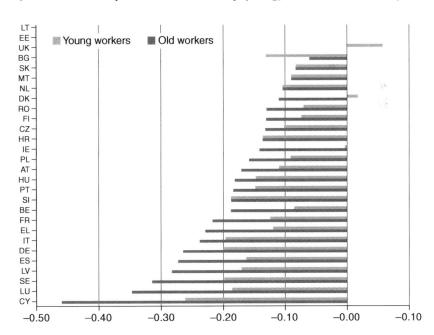

Figure 4.4 Adjusted temporary/permanent workers wage gap by age (estimated coefficients) (pooled 2010–2013).

Source: Our elaborations on EU-SILC data.

Table 4.3 Temporary jobs, age and hourly wages in EU-28 (2010–2013)

Dep. Var.: hwage	Pooled	2010	2011	2012	2013
Temp	-0.200***	-0.211***	-0.195***	-0.186***	-0.208***
	(0.003)	(0.005)	(0.005)	(0.005)	(0.005)
Temp*Young	0.042***	0.059***	0.040***	0.029***	0.040***
	(0.003)	(0.007)	(0.007)	(0.007)	(0.007)
Male	0.166***	0.169***	0.168***	0.164***	0.161***
	(0.001)	(0.003)	(0.002)	(0.002)	(0.002)
Married	0.024***	0.024***	0.021***	0.022***	0.027***
	(0.001)	(0.002)	(0.002)	(0.002)	(0.002)
Age	0.376***	0.340***	0.399***	0.370***	0.375***
	(0.010)	(0.021)	(0.019)	(0.019)	(0.019)
Age2	-0.036***	-0.032***	-0.038***	-0.035***	-0.035***
	(0.001)	(0.002)	(0.002)	(0.002)	(0.002)
Health status	-0.039***	-0.038***	-0.039***	-0.036***	-0.041***
	(0.001)	(0.002)	(0.002)	(0.002)	(0.002)
Young	-0.005**	-0.009**	-0.001	-0.006	-0.004
	(0.002)	(0.004)	(0.004)	(0.004)	(0.004)
Secondary Ed.	0.102***	0.096***	0.108***	0.098***	0.103***
	(0.002)	(0.004)	(0.004)	(0.004)	(0.004)
Tertiary Ed.	0.246***	0.247***	0.252***	0.241***	0.242***
	(0.003)	(0.006)	(0.005)	(0.006)	(0.005)

	(1)	(2)	(3)	(4)	(5)
Full-time	-0.036***	-0.034***	-0.037***	-0.049***	-0.039***
	(0.003)	(0.003)	(0.003)	(0.003)	(0.002)
Second Job	0.024	-0.057***	0.014	-0.010	-0.007
	(0.023)	(0.021)	(0.020)	(0.020)	(0.010)
Firm size (11–49)	0.095***	0.091***	0.089***	0.086***	0.090***
	(0.003)	(0.003)	(0.003)	(0.003)	(0.001)
Firm size (over 50)	0.188***	0.183***	0.179***	0.177***	0.182***
	(0.003)	(0.003)	(0.003)	(0.003)	(0.001)
Urban	0.034***	0.034***	0.037***	0.045***	0.037***
	(0.002)	(0.002)	(0.002)	(0.002)	(0.001)
East	-0.666***	-0.647***	-0.695***	-0.722***	-0.665***
	(0.007)	(0.007)	(0.007)	(0.008)	(0.007)
Constant	1.169***	1.129***	1.162***	1.295***	1.171***
	(0.049)	(0.049)	(0.048)	(0.049)	(0.025)
Mills (lambda)	0.054***	0.053***	0.071***	0.018*	0.051***
	(0.011)	(0.011)	(0.011)	(0.011)	(0.005)
Obs.	237,980	238,558	246,368	292,581	1,015,487
Censored Obs.	92,686	95,799	97,719	145,110	431,314
Uncensored Obs.	145,294	142,759	148,649	147,471	584,173

Notes

All estimations include: sector, occupation, country and year dummies. The Pooled model also includes country*year dummies; sample selection correction. Robust standard errors in parentheses. ***, ** and * denote significance at the 1, 5 and 10 per cent level, respectively.

Table 4.4 Temporary jobs, age and hourly wages in EU-28 countries (2010–2013)

Dep. Var.: hwage	AT	BE	CY	BG	CZ	DE	DK
Temp	-0.171***	-0.187***	-0.459***	-0.061***	-0.132***	-0.265***	-0.110***
Temp*Young	0.062**	0.102***	0.197***	-0.070***	0.031**	0.066***	0.128***
Obs.	25,595	27,301	25,431	26,884	39,111	50,232	18,830

	EE	EL	FI	ES	FR	HR	HU
Temp	0.006	-0.230***	-0.131***	-0.273***	-0.217***	-0.136***	-0.181***
Temp*Young	-0.083	0.111***	0.057***	0.110***	0.093***	0.021	0.034***
Obs.	26,311	31,094	37,034	54,303	55,311	26,698	50,290

	IE	IT	LU	LT	LV	MT	NL
Temp	-0.141***	-0.238***	-0.347***	0.019	-0.283***	-0.090***	-0.104***
Temp*Young	0.137***	0.042***	0.162***	0.019	0.112***	0.016	-0.011
Obs.	19,723	92,648	26,209	22,760	26,294	21,095	34,551

	PL	PT	SE	RO	SI	SK	UK
Temp	-0.184***	-0.158***	-0.314***	-0.130***	-0.187***	-0.082***	-0.013
Temp*Young	0.036**	0.067***	0.116***	0.060*	0.025	0.002	0.058**
Obs.	68,638	27,321	20,863	35,639	45,739	35,148	44,434

Notes
All estimations include: sector, occupation and year dummies; sample selection correction. Robust standard errors in parentheses. ***, ** and * denote significance at the 1, 5 and 10 per cent level, respectively.

average level compared to the raw gap observed in Table 4.2, first column, in which the gap was estimated at around 28 per cent. This difference reveals that, after adjusting for workers' and jobs characteristics, the "true" size of gap is smaller due to better characteristics of permanent workers. The latter are in fact better endowed with characteristics associated with higher wages, such as experience (approximated by the within subgroups age), and education. The average age for temporary workers is 38 years versus 43 for permanent ones. The share of fixed-term workers with primary and tertiary education is 21 and 26 per cent, respectively; the corresponding levels for permanent workers are 15 per cent and 33 per cent. Permanent workers are also relatively more employed in larger firms and in better-paid sectors and occupations.

The coefficients of the remaining explanatory variables largely correspond to ex-ante expectations and inform us that wages increase not linearly with age (the age variable has been divided by 10, so to have more readable coefficients), education, firm size and in urban areas; similarly, married individuals and men earn more than their counterparts (*ceteris paribus*). In our sample, full-time jobs are associated with lower hourly labour compensation compared to part-time ones; this might be due to the fact that in part-time jobs the reduction in monthly wage is not proportional to the reduction in hours worked. As a consequence, on an hourly basis, part-time positions are better remunerated. This outcome is in contrast with the literature on productivity/wage penalty for part-time workers, but consistent with alternative empirical evidence showing that the difference tends to disappear once the effects of self-selection into different segments of the labour market and personal and job characteristics are controlled for.

Our outcomes also show that the labour compensation for dependent work decreases as health status deteriorates as well as for those workers with a second job. The controls for occupations and sectors provide the expected hierarchy of coefficients (not reported for the sake of brevity, but available upon request). The dummy variable that identifies workers from Central and Eastern European countries has the expected negative, statistically significant coefficient.

As far as the focus of our analysis is concerned, results show that the temporary/permanent wage gap is systematically and statistically different between the two macro age groups identified (old and young workers). The evidence that older workers tend to suffer more than youngsters, in terms of wages, when holding a temporary position, supports the idea of entrapment adumbrated in Section 1. That means that on average in the whole sample, and in the majority of the EU-28 countries (seventeen out of twenty-eight), there is a relevant portion of involuntary temporary jobs that do not function as a stepping-stone to permanent employment but push workers into dead-end positions.

The temp/perm wage gap is on average (twenty-eight EU-countries and four years) 4 per cent lower for young than for old workers; the difference tends to decrease in the first three years of the period considered and seems to go up again in 2013. This main outcome can be interpreted in the light of the evidence (see, for example, Stancanelli, 2002 and Cabrales *et al.*, 2014) that temporary workers receive less training compared to permanent employees. Our results show that the effects of this weaker accumulation of knowledge and skills on wages are therefore more severe after 40. In other words, the higher wage gap for old temporary workers probably reflects differences in cognitive abilities that cannot accumulate in individuals with persistent and repeated fixed-term contracts and larger turnover rates. Again, these average figures (temporary/permanent wage gap for older workers, that is −20 per cent, and its greater magnitude compared to that for younger workers, −16 per cent) hide notable differences between EU-28 countries. Table 4.4 and Figure 4.4 present the size of the temp/perm wage gap for the two groups of workers at country level. In all countries but the United Kingdom, Estonia and Lithuania the gap is negative for both old and young workers; in the UK and Denmark being a temporary worker in the early stage of the working life does not mean earning less than the permanent counterparts; on the contrary, fixed-term contracts pay respectively 6 per cent and 2 per cent more. Another notable exception is Bulgaria, where the penalty associated with temporary employment is larger for young than for old workers. The difference between the two age groups is instead not statistically significant in Slovakia, Slovenia, the Netherlands, Malta, Croatia. In all remaining countries the perm/temp gap is negative for both age groups and systematically deeper for older workers. However, the size of the difference is rather heterogeneous: it ranges from the very high level of Ireland (the penalty for young temporary workers is about 2 per cent of the penalty for older ones), to the intermediate levels of Belgium (45 per cent), Greece (51 per cent), Luxembourg (53 per cent) and Romania (54 per cent), to the lowest levels of Portugal, Hungary and Italy (80 per cent, 81 per cent and 82 per cent, respectively).

The differences in labour market institutions highlighted by the literature and reported in Section 1, combined with the evidence reported in the descriptive analysis, help interpret some of these results. For example, the evidence for the UK and Denmark seems to perfectly match the results reported by Cabrales *et al.* (2014). Studying the association between temporary jobs, training and labour market institutions, these authors argued that where the dualism fuelled by asymmetries in the employment protection is negligible, as in the case of these two countries, temporary workers are better able to access training, hence suffering fewer wage penalties. On the other hand, it is likely that in countries where the wage gap for older workers is deeper than the average value (−20 per cent), a stronger labour market dualism has determined larger shares of temporary jobs within the cohort aged 40–64. This is especially the case for Cyprus, Spain and Greece, where large percentages of fixed-term contracts characterize the group of older workers with primary education (see Figure A4.2); but also for France, Sweden and Italy, that show above average shares of highly educated temporary workers aged 40–64 (see Figures A4.3 and A4.4 in the Appendix).

Based on the evidence that old workers suffer more due to holding temporary jobs, our next step is to study the workers' and job characteristics that increase or decrease the probability to stay in a temporary position in later stages of the working life. To this aim, we estimate the model described in equation 2, limited to the sample of old employees (40–64 years). The dependent variable of the probit (with Heckman correction) model is the dummy variable *temp*; the estimated coefficients (Table 4.5) indicate which characteristics increase (if positive) or decrease (if negative) the probability of holding a fixed-term contract. Results reveal that this probability is lower for older workers, for those married, in good health, holding a full-time job, being employed in larger firms and residing in urban areas. Similarly, higher levels of education significantly reduce the probability of being temporarily employed in the later stage of the working life. These outcomes depict a profile of a fully "entrapped" (old) worker (i.e. with all characteristics conducive to a fixed-term job) as one with a weak family structure, poor health conditions, low education, working in small firms, living in rural areas and having a part-time job. All these features are of course important; however, we focus now on the role of education. This dimension is crucial in terms of policy relevance and, as already explained, plays a crucial role in explaining the dynamics of (formal/informal) knowledge accumulation that is conducive to better jobs (Perugini and Pompei, 2016, 2017).

As we read at the bottom of Table 4.5 (marginal effects), having attained a higher level of education means decreasing the probability of being a temporary employee for workers over 40 years. On average (EU-28 and four years) workers with a secondary education, compared to those with the primary level, have approximately 3 per cent less probability to have a temporary job; the effect climbs to (−) 5 per cent for workers with tertiary education. Both effects are statistically significant and the difference in their size is also significant. The same results are obtained separating the sample for each year, although the size of the effect has some variability (for example the marginal effect of holding a tertiary education diploma ranges from −3.4 and −3.7 per cent in 2010 and 2012, to −5.7 per cent and −5.5 per cent in 2011 and 2013, respectively). This outcome could be explained by resorting to the latest business cycles and trends in the level of overall employment that materialized as a double-dip between 2010 and 2013 (European Commission, 2016a). It is plausible to hypothesize that during the years of downturns (2010 and 2012 plus first half of 2013) a falling overall labour market demand also decreased the probability of getting a permanent position for highly educated individuals.

Table 4.6 and Figure 4.5 report the size of the country specific marginal effects of secondary and tertiary education (compared to primary) on the estimated probability of being a temporary worker. Many interesting points emerge: first of all, in the large majority of countries (twenty-three out of twenty-eight) higher education levels are found to decrease the probability of being trapped into a temporary (and therefore lower wage) position for workers aged 40 or more. The few exceptions are represented by Sweden, Estonia and Demark on one side (no significant effects of higher education levels) and by UK and Ireland on the other. In UK, holding a tertiary education increases the probability of a temporary job (compared to primary and secondary); in Ireland, the probability increases for the secondary educated, while tertiary education does not provide any advantage/disadvantage compared to primary education.

Table 4.5 Older workers and temporary jobs in EU-28 (Heckman Probit, 2010–2013)

Dep. Var.: temp	Pooled	2010	2011	2012	2013
Male	0.012	-0.001	0.011	0.001	0.041***
	(0.008)	(0.017)	(0.015)	(0.015)	(0.015)
Married	-0.150***	-0.144***	-0.143***	-0.166***	-0.140***
	(0.007)	(0.015)	(0.015)	(0.015)	(0.015)
Age	-0.703***	-0.450	-1.023***	-0.447*	-0.747***
	(0.144)	(0.373)	(0.283)	(0.243)	(0.230)
Age2	0.055***	0.029	0.089***	0.028	0.060**
	(0.015)	(0.039)	(0.029)	(0.025)	(0.023)
Health status	0.056***	0.035**	0.067***	0.040***	0.079***
	(0.007)	(0.016)	(0.015)	(0.013)	(0.014)
Secondary Ed.	-0.209***	-0.196***	-0.233***	-0.159***	-0.240***
	(0.015)	(0.029)	(0.032)	(0.032)	(0.029)
Tertiary Ed.	-0.364***	-0.304***	-0.403***	-0.321***	-0.408***
	(0.019)	(0.040)	(0.037)	(0.039)	(0.035)
Full-time	-0.467***	-0.485***	-0.446***	-0.445***	-0.483***
	(0.010)	(0.020)	(0.019)	(0.020)	(0.019)
Second Job	0.819***	0.722***	0.807***	0.843***	0.924***
	(0.048)	(0.090)	(0.094)	(0.101)	(0.102)
Firm size (11–49)	-0.069***	-0.060***	-0.062***	-0.076***	-0.075***
	(0.009)	(0.018)	(0.018)	(0.018)	(0.018)

Firm size (over 50)	-0.181***	-0.160***	-0.181***	-0.192***	-0.189***
	(0.009)	(0.018)	(0.018)	(0.018)	(0.018)
Urban	-0.056***	-0.036**	-0.074***	-0.049***	-0.069***
	(0.008)	(0.016)	(0.017)	(0.016)	(0.017)
East	0.798***	0.585***	0.471***	0.626***	0.780***
	(0.056)	(0.057)	(0.064)	(0.056)	(0.061)
Constant	0.584	0.121	1.608**	0.032	0.679
	(0.365)	(0.918)	(0.732)	(0.625)	(0.596)
athrho	0.067	0.178*	-0.128	0.277**	-0.022
	(0.052)	(0.104)	(0.113)	(0.119)	(0.099)
LR test (indep. Eq.) rho=0 $\chi^2(1)$	1.690	2.910*	1.190	5.710**	0.05
Obs.	563,784	169,912	132,518	130,079	131,275
Censored Obs.	196,188	78,620	39,685	39,598	38,285
Uncensored Obs.	367,596	91,292	92,833	90,481	92,990
Marginal Effects					
Secondary Ed.	-0.026***	-0.022***	-0.033***	-0.018***	-0.032***
	(0.003)	(0.005)	(0.007)	(0.004)	(0.005)
Tertiary Ed.	-0.046***	-0.034***	-0.057***	-0.037***	-0.055***
	(0.004)	(0.007)	(0.009)	(0.006)	(0.007)
Test $\chi^2(1)$ – Diff. ME	*159.200****	*17.830****	*46.640****	*52.840****	*53.630****

Notes

All estimations include: sector, country and year dummies. The Pooled model also includes country*year dummies; sample selection correction. Robust standard errors in parentheses. ***, ** and * denote significance at the 1, 5 and 10 per cent level, respectively.

Table 4.6 Education and the probability of holding a temporary job for older workers in EU-28 countries (marginal effects, pooled 2010–2013)

Dep. Var.: temp	AT	BE	BG	CY	CZ	DE	DK
Secondary Ed.	-0.020***	-0.017***	-0.049***	-0.043***	-0.033***	-0.006	0.001
	(0.006)	(0.005)	(0.005)	(0.006)	(0.009)	(0.005)	(0.007)
Tertiary Ed.	-0.010	-0.038***	-0.070***	-0.064***	-0.047***	-0.016***	0.000
	(0.007)	(0.006)	(0.007)	(0.008)	(0.011)	(0.006)	(0.007)
Test chi2 (1) – Diff. ME	3.820*	15.460***	12.500***	10.350***	4.180**	11.540***	0.000

Dep. Var.: temp	EE	EL	ES	FI	FR	HR	HU
Secondary Ed.	-0.003	-0.077***	-0.040***	-0.006	-0.013***	-0.046***	-0.067***
	(0.004)	(0.013)	(0.006)	(0.009)	(0.005)	(0.009)	(0.005)
Tertiary Ed.	-0.002	-0.182***	-0.094***	-0.028***	-0.044***	-0.070***	-0.123***
	(0.004)	(0.016)	(0.006)	(0.009)	(0.005)	(0.012)	(0.007)
Test chi2 (1) – Diff. ME	0.260	56.100***	67.180***	14.220***	45.900***	5.610**	79.860***

Dep. Var.: temp	IE	IT	LT	LU	LV	MT	NL
Secondary Ed.	0.015*	-0.036***	-0.009	-0.023***	-0.018***	-0.014*	-0.022***
	(0.009)	(0.004)	(0.008)	(0.005)	(0.005)	(0.008)	(0.007)
Tertiary Ed.	0.005	-0.024***	-0.023***	-0.020***	-0.041***	0.012	-0.024***
	(0.009)	(0.005)	(0.008)	(0.006)	(0.007)	(0.008)	(0.007)
Test chi2 (1) – Diff. ME	1.500	5.730**	13.490***	0.280	24.200***	7.400**	0.120

Dep. Var.: temp	PL	PT	RO	SE	SI	SK	UK
Secondary Ed.	-0.090***	-0.029***	-0.009	0.016	-0.009	-0.034***	0.003
	(0.010)	(0.008)	(0.006)	(0.010)	(0.009)	(0.010)	(0.004)
Tertiary Ed.	-0.220***	-0.053***	-0.029***	0.003	-0.058***	-0.042***	0.015***
	(0.013)	(0.010)	(0.010)	(0.011)	(0.012)	(0.012)	(0.004)
Test chi2 (1) – Diff. ME	205.210***	4.560**	5.570**	4.160**	28.540***	1.870	15.360***

Notes
All estimations include: sector and year dummies; sample selection correction. Robust standard errors in parentheses. ***, ** and * denote significance at the 1, 5 and 10 per cent level, respectively.

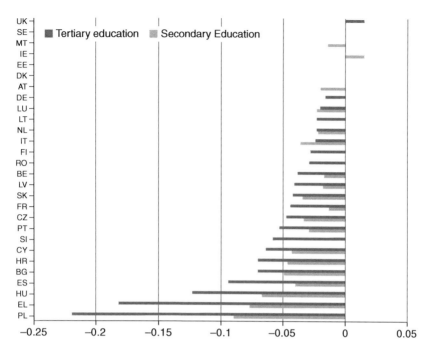

Figure 4.5 Education and the probability of holding a temporary job for older workers in
EU-28 countries (marginal effects, pooled 2010–2013).

Source: Our elaborations on EU-SILC data.

In the pool of the remaining twenty-three countries remarkable heterogeneities emerge: in Malta and Austria only secondary education is able to reduce the probability of holding a fixed-term contract, whereas the opposite holds for Germany, Latvia, Finland, Romania, Slovenia (only tertiary education helps). In the group of countries in which both (higher) levels of education reduce the probability of a temporary job for older workers, only in Italy is the effect of secondary education higher than tertiary education; in other countries (Luxembourg, the Slovak Republic and the Netherlands) the difference is not significant. In all remaining countries tertiary education means a lower probability of holding a temporary position not only compared to primary education, but also compared to secondary education (which is anyhow helpful). The range of the effects of tertiary education is quite wide and varies from a reduction of the estimated probability of a fixed-term contract of around 2 per cent (Germany, Luxembourg, Latvia, the Netherlands and Italy) to the highest levels of Poland (22 per cent), Greece (18 per cent), Hungary (12 per cent), Spain (9 per cent), Bulgaria and Croatia (7 per cent).

By combining the sectoral propensity to employ temporary workers and the different knowledge-intensity of industry, we could get to a tentative explanation of this evidence. First of all, we can assume that labour realloca-tions towards those knowledge intensity industries that employ less temporary workers improve the probability for highly educated people (especially if aged 40–64) to match high quality and regular jobs. According to Eurofound (2015a), the overall EU-28 temporary workers rate in 2012 in manufacturing is low (10.4 per cent) if compared to the one in service sectors such as Arts and Entertainment (21.4 per cent), Accommodation and Food (20.9 per cent) and Administrative and Support Services (18.9 per cent). At the same time, countries such as Poland, Greece and Hungary have experienced an increase of employment in Hi- and Medium-Hi-Tech sectors (European Commission, 2015); this could explain why high skills endowment in these countries remarkably increases the probability to attain a permanent job. In contrast, in countries such as Germany, the Netherlands, Italy, Spain and Bulgaria, employment in knowledge intensive industries remained stable, or slightly declined (European Commission, 2015). Our results suggest, for this group of countries, that a tertiary education is able to guarantee to older workers a much more limited advantage compared to their less educated peers, in terms of probability of escaping a temporary/low-pay job trap.

5 Discussion and final remarks

This chapter aimed at providing an up-to-date and comprehensive comparative perspective of both wage levels and determinants of temporary jobs compared to permanent positions, across the labour markets of the EU-28 countries and during the early post-crisis period (2010–2013). The main literature-based working hypothesis underlying the empirical analysis is that if temporary jobs are stepping stones to permanent and secure jobs, as part of the literature main-tains, we should find very low percentage of fixed-term contracts among older workers. This is because during their careers the bulk of temporary workers should be interested by a transition towards regular jobs. If this is the case, the temporary/permanent wage gap should narrow over the age profile of workers, since those older workers staying temporary should identify patterns in which the opportunity to accumulate experience and catch up with permanent workers pay has been possible and has been seized. This might be due to the truly tempo-rary nature of some jobs or to the preferences of some individuals oriented towards high risk/returns positions. Should the opposite hold (larger gap as age proceeds), a trap could emerge for involuntary temporary workers in later stages of the working life; in this case, it makes sense to investigate the determinants of being an old temporary worker.

In this context, we distinguished between workers aged 15–39 and those aged 40–64. The definition of young workers is larger compared to standard defini-tions (15–24 or 15–34) in order to take into account a reasonable time interval that individuals with tertiary education need to complete the transition from education to work. Both the descriptive statistics and the econometric estima-tions are designed to emphasize the role of different levels of formal skills endowments in shaping the wage gaps across the two age classes and in influencing the probabilities of being an old temporary worker.

We first of all provided aggregate (EU-28) and country-by-country evidence of the incidence of temporary jobs on total dependent employment and showed unadjusted and adjusted wage gaps between temporary and permanent jobs. Results coming from the descriptive statistics sketched out a pattern in which older temporary workers from the majority of EU countries (twenty-one out of twenty-eight) experienced, between 2010 and 2013, a more severe wage penalty with respect to younger temporary workers (the average unadjusted wage gap was –30 per cent versus –22 per cent, respectively). In this pool of countries fall both Western and Eastern EU members that show the highest percentages of older temporary workers, especially among individuals with primary and secondary education, and that literature labelled as economies with stabilized (Spain, Portugal, France, Italy) or emerging (Poland, Cyprus) dualism in their labour markets.

The econometric analysis confirmed that nineteen out of twenty-eight countries share a situation in which older temporary workers suffer a deeper wage penalty. Despite taking into account that all individual and social characteristics of workers notably reduces the overall wage gap, both the aggregate and the country-by-country profiles seem to suggest that a trap for temporary workers is pervasive across Europe.

In the second step of the empirical analysis we examined which individual, social and productive characteristics of workers aged 40–64 render holding a temporary job more likely. Outcomes reveal that a probable "entrapped worker" is one with a weak family structure, poor health conditions, low education, working in small firms, living in rural areas and having a part-time job. Especially the medium and high education levels have been found to be the characteristics that in twenty-three out of twenty-eight EU countries reduce for older workers the likelihood to fall into temporary job traps (the overall marginal effects are –5 per cent for tertiary and –3 per cent for secondary education).

The relatively low magnitude of these overall marginal effects and the large heterogeneity we have found across countries in the impact of tertiary education on the probability to be trapped, suggest that education policies alone would not be enough to alleviate the problem of temporary jobs as dead-ends. Indeed, by combining our country level results with other evidence found in literature (e.g. European Commission, 2015), we can say that only in countries that experienced important structural changes towards more knowledge intensive sectors, in the post-crisis years, holding a tertiary education remarkably reduces the probability of ending up in a temporary job in the later stages of the working life. For example, this is the case for Poland, Greece and Hungary, where for very different reasons the sectoral composition of labour shifted towards manufacturing sectors with low propensity to employ temporary workers. According to our results, attaining higher education in these countries decreases by about one-fifth the probability of being a temporary worker. In contrast, this marginal effect sinks to 4 per cent or 2 per cent for countries such as France, Italy and Germany, where the labour reallocation processes from manufacturing to temporary labour-intensive service sectors remained quantitatively important in the last years and seem strong enough to neutralize the positive effects of education in reducing the likelihood of being a temporary worker.

Appendix

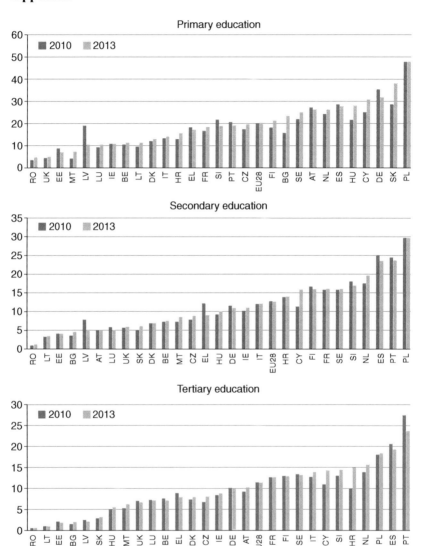

Figure A4.1 Temporary workers as percentage of total employees by educational attainment (2010 and 2013).

Source: Eurostat online database.

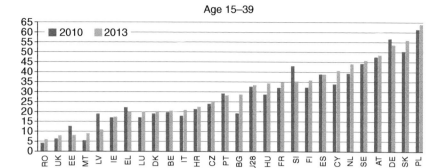

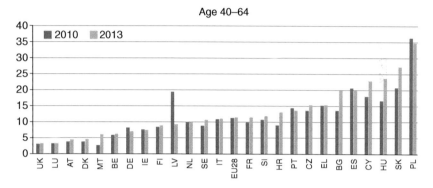

Figure A4.2 Temporary workers as percentage of total employees with primary education by age (2010 and 2013).

Source: Eurostat online database.

Age 15–39

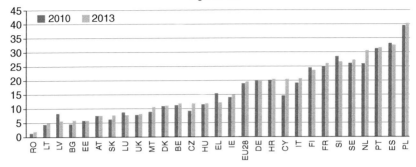

Age 40–64

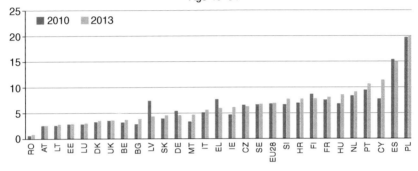

Figure A4.3 Temporary workers as percentage of total employees with secondary education by age (2010 and 2013).

Source: Eurostat online database.

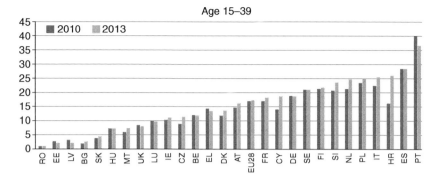

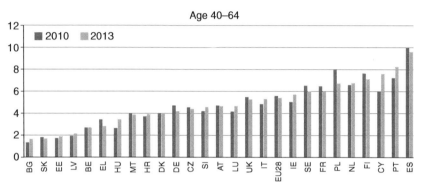

Figure A4.4 Temporary workers as percentage of total employees with tertiary education by age (2010 and 2013).

Source: Eurostat online database.

Notes

1 Occupations are classified into nine categories, corresponding to the major groups of the ISCO08 classification: 1. Managers, 2. Professionals, 3. Technicians and Associate Professionals, 4. Clerical Support Workers, 5. Services and Sales Workers, 6. Skilled Agricultural, Forestry and Fishery Workers, 7. Craft and Related Trade Workers, 8. Plant and Machine Operators and Assemblers, 9. Elementary Occupations. Workers in Armed Forces Occupations, consisting of a very limited number of individuals, have been aggregated into category 2. Industry breakdown has been limited to thirteen sectors, obtained as an aggregation of the NACE sections: 1. Agriculture (section A), 2. Industry (B-E), 3. Constructions (F), 4. Trade (G), 5. Transports (H), 6. Hotels and Restaurants (I), 7. Information and Communications (J), 8. Financial and Insurance Activities (K), 9. Real Estate, Professional and Administrative Activities (L-N), 10. Public Administration (O), 11. Education (P), 12. Health and Social Work Activities (Q), 13. Other services (R-U). Lastly, we consider three firm size classes: 0–10, 11–49, 50 and over employees.
2 In Perugini and Pompei (2015), a more detailed discussion upon structural differences between Central-Eastern and Western EU countries is analysed and discussed.

5 Living arrangements of young adults in Italy and Norway

The significance of gender, sociocultural background, work and money

Tindara Addabbo and Randi Kjeldstad

1 Introduction

This chapter analyses living arrangements among young Italian and Norwegian adults by gender. The starting point is the great difference between the two countries as regards the propensity of young adults to remain in their parents' home after compulsory schooling. Young Europeans leave their parents' home at different ages: Southern Europeans leave at the highest ages and, in Italy, postponement of leaving the nest is widespread and increasing, even compared to other Mediterranean countries. Young Nordic adults, including Norwegians, are the youngest leavers. They establish independent households at much younger ages, either on their own, or in cohabitation with a partner or friends.

Why is this the case, and who are the Italians and Norwegians who stay with their childhood family long into adulthood? And who are the ones who form independent households, either with or without a partner? What are the propensities in the two countries to stay with parents compared to living alone or with a partner, and what conditions and what characteristics are associated with the various propensities? In both countries, adult men stay longer at their parents' homes than adult women do. Why is that so? Are there reasons for believing that leaving the parents' home is related to dissimilarities in events and characteristics between women and men, between the two countries, and possibly even between Italian and Norwegian women and men? We examine these questions by means of a comparative data set (EU-SILC), containing demographic and standard-of-living information for both individuals and households in Italy and Norway. In contrast to studies in this field that explore residential *shifts*, we study the various residential *patterns* of young adults, giving a situational report on the year 2007. The year 2007 is chosen insofar as it was a time when the economic prospects and the labour market were relatively stable in both countries. Whereas most previous comparative analyses include a great number of countries, and hence are confined to rather general and often only slightly varying explanatory categories, we study two largely dissimilar countries. Italy and Norway may be considered European 'extremes' in this field. They differ significantly as regards demographic and labour market conditions and cultural norms relating to family and gender. This enables a relatively thorough and concrete examination of the residential and living conditions in early adulthood in the two countries.

2 Previous research

Macro studies show that the Norwegian and Italian national contexts differ significantly, both economically and culturally. Norway belongs to the *Social Democratic* regime (the Nordic or Scandinavian model), characterised by universal, citizen-based welfare transfers and services, comprehensive risk coverage, generous benefit levels and egalitarianism. Italy belongs to the Conservative regime (or the Corporatist, Southern-European or Mediterranean regime, according to more 'refined' regime classifications), characterised by strong corporative traits and familialism, where the family and private non-profit institutions play a crucial role in the provision of welfare services. In Italy, public services and transfers are mainly subsidiary, and the family has the ultimate responsibility for the welfare and social protection of its members (Esping-Andersen 1990, 1999; Ferrera, 1996; Kautto *et al.* 2001; Karamessini, 2008; Bertolini, 2011; Kvist *et al.*, 2012). On the national level, institutional differences result in different housing and household options for young adults and their next of kin. For example, Southern European welfare states, including Italy, are less prone to subsidising the everyday lives of students, whereas Nordic countries, including Norway, provide a relatively high level of welfare and student subsidies, making it easier for young adults to live on their own (Hellevik, 2005; Sandlie, 2011; OECD, 2012b). These differences in the state taking care of the youth are mirrored *inter alia* in the generosity of public student-support systems, where, according to OECD statistics (2012b), Norway belongs to the generous supporting countries and Italy to the less-developed supporting countries.

On the national level, long-term cultural differences interact with economic and political conditions and shape various contexts for young adults' living arrangements and household formation. These cultural traits are partly mutually reinforcing and partly shaped by the differences in institutional settings and policies between the two countries as regards young people's opportunities for education, independent accommodation, employment and self-support. Moreover, external factors such as the housing market and labour market reinforce the power parents have over their children (Schroeder, 2008). Differences in young adults' formation of independent households versus remaining in the parental home also reflect differences in the strength of intergenerational ties and in various norms for 'appropriate' life-course transitions as regards the timing of and reasons for leaving the parental home (Fauske, 1996; Oinonen, 2003; Clapham, 2005; Sandlie, 2011); Norway is characterised by relatively strong individualistic norms and Italy by strong familistic norms.

Whereas in the Southern European countries, adulthood and forming a household of one's own is usually associated with marriage and parenthood (Giuliano, 2007; Karamessini, 2008), young Nordic adults break away from the parental home for a great variety of reasons and form a household of their own long before the prospective of establishing a formal partnership (Oinonen, 2003; Sandlie, 2011). Today, young Norwegians usually enter their first partnership as cohabitants rather than as spouses, whereas cohabitation is still relatively rare in Italy. In fact, young Italian adults are among those least likely to cohabitate in Europe (Rosina and Fraboni, 2004; Schroeder, 2008). Rosina and Fraboni (2004) relate this to the strong family ties in Italy, and maintain that children in the Mediterranean area often avoid choices that openly clash with their parents' values. The level of satisfaction of parents in co-resident households with young adult children appears to be particularly high among Southern European families (Manacorda and Moretti, 2006). In the case of Italy, Manacorda and Moretti (2006) found a positive effect of parental income on children's co-residence, maintaining that Italian parents consider co-residence with their children as a "normal good" whose consumption increases with family income. In contrast, Hellevik (2005) and Brusdal and Berg (2011) emphasise the willingness of Norwegian parents who can afford it, to support their adult children's residential independence by helping them financially to set up a household on their own.

Traditions and norms for what is the 'right' time to form a household of one's own do not just differ between countries and regions; they also reflect the economic and social characteristics of individuals and families (Nilsson and Strandh, 1999; Stone *et al.*, 2011). Buchmann (1989) argues, however, that traditions are generally less significant now than before as regards how young adults live their lives, and that modern life courses are characterised by an increased differentiation in timing and type of living arrangements. At the same time, Oinonen (2003) finds that the erosion of significant family traditions is more evident in Northern than in Southern Europe. Today, Scandinavian household formation and household patterns are more related to when a person sees herself or himself as independent and self-supporting than to familial shifts (Arnett and Taber, 1994).

On the micro level, much research draws special attention to the occupational and economic situation of the person and his/her parents. Higher education can be positively related to both the desire and the economic ability to achieve residential autonomy, whereas low levels of education and difficulties entering the labour market are found to be negatively related to young people's exit from the parental household. This is true both in Southern European countries (Karamessini, 2008) and in Norway (Texmon, 1995). At the same time, Nordic and German data show that employment and attending university increase the likelihood of young adults living outside the parental home (Wagner and Huinink, 1991; Nilsson and Strandh, 1999). However, living at one's parents' home may also be seen as a strategy to achieve a better position later on in life while studying or searching for a better job (Saraceno, 2000, Giannelli and Monfardini, 2003b). The former correlation appears to be a Northern European phenomenon, while the latter is found more often in Southern Europe (Aassve *et al.*, 2002), reflecting the fact that Italian and Norwegian young adults face largely dissimilar housing options.

In both countries, high housing costs constitute a major barrier to establishing one's own first household outside the parental home. Indeed, Giannelli and Monfardini (2003b) and Modena and Rondinelli's (2011) Italian studies found a remarkable effect of the cost of housing in delaying young workers' decisions to leave the parental home, while Mencarini and Tanturri (2006) show the relevance of parental aid on Italian youth moving into their first home. At the same time, other European and Norwegian studies call attention to the fact that young adults, either in tertiary education or early in their job careers, largely opt for a slightly different housing market than older and more established people (Ford *et al.*, 2002; Sandlie, 2011). Although there has been an increase in young adult occupant owners in Norway over recent years, young households on average differ from older ones in that they start off as tenants, students often in multi-occupant households (Mulder and Hooimejer, 2002, Langsether and Sandlie, 2006); i.e. they seek dwellings outside the parents' home at manageable costs.

The timing of 'leaving the nest' is also closely linked to the national and local structure of the school systems. Italian universities and colleges are more spread across the various regions, leading to Italian youth having a lower incentive to move out than in the case of Norway, where tertiary educational institutions, particularly universities, are few and relatively centralised. Nordic studies (Texmon, 1995; Nilsson and Strandh, 1999; Sandlie, 2011) indicate that moving in connection with educational activities is relatively unstable, as students quite often move back 'home' for longer or shorter periods. It is characteristic of Norwegian students living in independent households to return to the parental home during summer and other long vacations. Enrolling in higher education may, however, lead to dissimilar living arrangements in different social contexts. Some may postpone leaving the parental home due to postponed economic self-support, whereas others leave home because the educational institution is located in another town (Sandlie, 2011). In general, the former applies to Italian and the latter to Norwegian young adults.

All over Europe, women leave the parental home earlier than men (Eurostat, 2009b). This is, of course, largely due to the fact that women marry or enter cohabitation at younger ages. Moreover, according to Chiuri and Del Boca (2010), young women's living arrangements appear to be more sensitive than young men's to environmental factors (the mortgage and labour markets) and to family structures. Aassve *et al.* (2001 and 2002) find work and employment to have an important positive impact, and unemployment to have a negative impact on young men leaving the parental home in Italy. For young women, however, they find that employment status has little or no impact. They explain this as due to Italian women being less reliant on work and their own income, and that finding a partner is a far more important factor. Likewise, Texmon (1995) indicates that young Norwegian men more often than women tend to take private economic conditions into consideration when deciding whether to move out or remain in the parental home. On the other hand, there is reason to believe that, despite significant changes in most countries towards less gender traditionalism, norms and customs are still gendered to a varying degree as regards what the 'right' timing of residential shifts is and what household type is socially acceptable for young women and men. Today, we assume that such possible gendered norms and customs may be somewhat less significant for Norwegian young adults than for Italians. Moreover, in taking into account gender differences in Italy, one has to consider the relevant difference between youth living in different areas of the country. Rosina and Rivellini (2004) have shown that daughters in particular are more exposed to family control, and Benassi and Novello (2007) have found that young adults have a higher likelihood of leaving the parental home because of marriage in Southern than in Central-Northern Italy.

3 Expected associations

Viewed in the light of the described cultural and (welfare) economic dissimilarities between Italy and Norway, we expect to find significant differences, not only as regards the living arrangements of young adults, but also where the relationship between individual characteristics, gender and living arrangements of young adults in the two countries is concerned. We expect to find the following associations:

I   Due to the wide-ranging dissimilarities in the institutional, cultural and economic conditions at the macro level in the two countries, we expect to find that, even after controlling for gender and a range of other important individual characteristics, the propensity to live with parents (and not in couples or alone) is still significantly higher for Italians than for Norwegians, while the corresponding propensity to live alone is higher among Norwegians.

II Due to the prevailing universal gendered life-course structuring, which involves women's earlier entrance into partnership(s), we expect to find that, after controlling for important individual characteristics, men still have a higher propensity to live in their parents' home, or alone, than women, whereas women have a higher propensity to live in a couple. We expect this to be the case for both Italians and Norwegians. Among Italians, however, we expect a particularly strong correlation between gender and the living with parents/living with a partner ratio (i.e. a higher relative propensity among men), whereas, among Norwegians, we expect a stronger analogous correlation between gender and the living alone/living with a partner ratio.

III At the individual level, we assume that economic activity/economic conditions and sociocultural background characteristics correlate significantly but differently as regards the living arrangements of young adults in the two countries. For instance, we expect that being a student or being unemployed (as compared to being in full-time employment) increases the probability of staying with parents in Italy and of staying alone in Norway. In the case of sociocultural background, like educational level, region and country of origin, we expect that low education increases the probability of living with parents in both countries, whereas being born in the country where they live, living in rural areas and in southern regions increases the probability (only) in Italy. We also assume that, in both countries, young adults with higher education tend to live in couples as opposed to living with parents/living alone.

4 Data and descriptives

We use EU-SILC data from 2007 on Italian and Norwegian women and men aged 20–39, excluding those in military service. The data include 13,290 Italians and 3,667 Norwegians, and provide comparable information on a broad spectrum of socio-economic determinants. We utilise information from the year 2007 instead of later years to avoid distorted comparability caused by the onset of the (southern) European economic crisis from 2008 onwards. The crisis hit the Italian labour market severely, particularly affecting the sphere of youth employment, whereas the Norwegian labour market has by and large been spared so far.

The dependent variable of our analysis is living arrangements, classified as:

- living in a couple;
- living with parents;
- living alone, i.e. either in a single or a multi-occupant household.

To account for the factors, in line with the literature surveyed in Section 2, expected to affect the probability of living in a certain type of arrangement, we control for age (since the likelihood of moving out and establishing a family or household of one's own increases with age in young adulthood) and for the number of children younger than 15 in the household,[1] and we include the following variables:

- sociocultural indicators (education, country of birth, area of residence – including also a dummy variable for the South of Italy);
- economic indicators: employment status (with reference also to the type of employment), gross earnings, social cash benefits (excluding unemployment benefit to avoid multicollinearity with unemployment status) and health status (chronic illness to account for the different welfare provision in case of illness by country).

Table A5.1 provides descriptive statistics on the composition of the Norwegian and Italian samples. More than four out of ten Italians live with their parents during the age span from twenty to forty years of age; the same is true for fewer than one out of ten Norwegians. The picture is almost the reverse as regards the proportions living 'alone'. The proportions living in couples are less dissimilar between the two countries, and in both countries, women live more frequently in couples, whereas men more frequently live with their parents or alone.

The figures show an almost identical age average of the groups in the sample. Norwegian young adults are more highly educated than Italians: one-third of Italian compared to one-fifth of Norwegian young adults are educated to primary level, and one-third of the Norwegians compared to only 15 per cent of the Italians have been through tertiary education. Women are more highly educated in both countries.

The great majority of the inhabitants of both countries are native-born and the gender differences as regards country of birth are negligible. The largest groups of foreign-born nationals in both Norway and Italy are from outside the EU. At the same time, more than eight out of ten Italians live in densely or intermediately populated areas. This is true for about six out of ten Norwegians, where three out of ten, against 15 per cent of Italians, live in sparsely populated areas. Hence, young adult Norwegians (like the average Norwegian population) are characterised by a more rural, sparsely populated residential pattern than Italians.

The majority of young adult women and men in both countries state that their main activity is paid work, men more often than women. Of these, the bulk are employees with permanent work contracts, more so in Norway than in Italy. Italian women have the lowest percentage of permanently employment (33 per cent) and Norwegian men the highest (60 per cent). Temporary work constitutes the main activity of approximately 10 per cent in both countries, least frequently among Norwegian men, whereas the proportion of self-employment is higher in Italy, particularly among Italian men (17 per cent compared with 10 per cent of Norwegian men). In both countries, men are more than twice as often self-employed than women.

Unemployment is generally low in Norway (3–4 per cent in recent years), and in 2007 young adult women were less often unemployed than young adult men were. The gender differences in young adult unemployment are smaller in Italy, but the total level is relatively high: two and a half times that of Norway. The inactivity level is approximately equal for Italian and Norwegian men; however, it is significantly higher among women in Italy, where almost one out of four young adult women state that they are mainly inactive. At the same time, one out of four young adult Norwegian women, against slightly over one out of ten Norwegian men, and Italian women and men, are mainly students.

Table A5.1 also presents the average annual individual earnings and social cash benefits in euro of young Norwegian and Italian adults, regardless of whether they are employed or not. It shows that the Norwegian levels are more than twice that of Italian women and men. Women's average work income amounts to barely 60 per cent of men's in both countries. Whereas the social benefit level is almost the same between Italian men and women, young adult Norwegian women receive one-third more in cash benefits than Norwegian men. The latter should be seen partly in light of the fact that women, and especially Norwegian women as shown in the table, more frequently live with children, and that Norwegian public social transfers are relatively generous to mothers/parents.

Finally, a tendency for women to report illness more frequently than men (Verbrugge, 1985) is shown in both countries. Somewhat surprisingly, however, Norwegian young adult women and men report significantly more chronic health problems than the Italians do. We interpret this mainly in conjunction with differences in the social cash benefits systems of the two countries, and the more generous regulations regarding sickness and disability benefits in Norway. Consequently, the economic incentives for having health problems acknowledged are stronger in Norway.

5 Analysis and results

To examine the association between individual variables and the various living arrangements, we estimate four multinomial logistic regression models for each country (Greene, 1993; Cameron and Trivedi, 2010) (Table 5.1). Living in a couple is used as a base category when compared to living in the parents' household or living alone. The regression results are presented with reference to a set of variables in the form of *relative risks* in Table 5.1. By and large, the figures corroborate our expectation (I) of a robustly higher propensity among Italians to live with parents and an equally higher propensity among Norwegians to live alone. Being Italian multiplies the relative likelihood of living with parents (as compared to living in a couple) by 17.6 and the relative likelihood of living alone by 0.6 (Model 4). The higher Italian propensity to live with parents increases slightly when differences in sociocultural background characteristics are taken into account (Model 2), whereas the higher Norwegian propensity to live alone decreases analogously due to both sociocultural background and individual economic characteristics (Models 2 and 3). The significance of the various sociocultural and economic factors that are included will be discussed further below.

Second (II), we assumed a robustly higher probability for young women, as compared to young men, to live in couples, and a higher probability for young men to live with parents or alone in both countries. The figures (Table 5.1, Model 4) corroborate our expectations and show an average female relative risk of living with parents that is half that of men (0.45), and a female relative risk of living alone that is three-quarters that of men (0.74), both as compared to living in a couple. As expected, the gendered pattern relates to both countries. We also predicted that in Italy, the significance of gender – i.e. men's higher propensity relative to women – would be most evident as regards living with parents, whereas for Norway, we predicted a stronger gender effect as regards living alone. The results are not consistent, however, with these predictions, since the national gender differences are not significant at the 5 per cent level. Instead, we found slightly opposite patterns to those expected, as women's relative risk of living with parents is 0.39 that of men among Norwegians and almost half (0.45) among Italians. The corresponding female-to-male risk of living alone is higher in Norway (0.84) than in Italy (0.74). The gender difference as regards living with parents increases in both countries when taking individual characteristics into consideration. Albeit subject to low statistical significance, this appears to be mainly due to economic characteristics (Model 3). This corroborates earlier studies, showing (Section 2) that poor work and income conditions serve to keep young men more than young women in the parental home. The same applies to living alone in Norway, as shown by the concurrent increased gender difference in the risk of living alone. On the other hand, the decreased gender difference in the risk of living alone in Italy *may* indicate that propitious work and income conditions encourage young women in particular to set up on their own. The Pseudo R^2s of Table 5.1 predominantly show that the four models are a better fit to the living arrangements of Italians than to those of Norwegian young adults.

Table 5.1 Multinomial logit estimation results. Relative risks of living with parents or alone versus living in a couple. Total for both countries and separately for each country, Models 1–4[1] showing estimates by country (A) and gender (A–C). All 20–39 years old, excluding those in military service. Standard errors in parenthesis

Variables	Model 1		Model 2		Model 3		Model 4	
	W/parents	Alone	W/parents	Alone	W/parents	Alone	W/parents	Alone
A) Italy + Norway								
Italy	16.1	0.49	19.6	0.56	15.6	0.54	17.64	0.61
	(1.46)	(0.04)	(1.87)	(0.04)	(1.7)	(0.05)	(1.98)	(0.05)
Female	0.52	0.71	0.51	0.71	0.47	0.74	0.45	0.74
	(0.04)	(0.05)	(0.04)	(0.05)	(0.03)	(0.06)	(0.03)	(0.06)
Pseudo R^2	0.37		0.39		0.39		0.41	
No. obs.	16.435							
B) Italy								
Female	0.52	0.68	0.51	0.68	0.48	0.74	0.45	0.74
	(0.04)	(0.06)	(0.04)	(0.06)	(0.04)	(0.07)	(0.04)	(0.07)
Pseudo R^2	0.36		0.38		0.38		0.40	
No. obs.	12.861							
C) Norway								
Female	0.42	0.93	0.47	0.96	0.36	0.80	0.39	0.84
	(0.05)	(0.09)	(0.06)	(0.1)	(0.05)	(0.09)	(0.06)	(0.09)
Pseudo R^2	0.26		0.27		0.28		0.29	
No. obs.	3.574							

Notes
1 Model 1 includes country and gender, plus controls; Model 2 includes country, gender, sociocultural indicators, plus controls; Model 3 includes country, gender, economic indicators, plus controls; Model 4 includes all independent variables, plus controls, cf. Table 5.2.

To examine our third expected outcome (III), we estimated the relative risk of the various living arrangements of the sample in total and of Italians, Norwegians, and Italian and Norwegian women and men separately, based on multinomial analyses including all independent variables (Table 5.2).

Among the individual sociocultural indicators included (variables 3–9, Table 5.2), geographical affiliation appears to be the most significant. As expected, *not being native-born* largely decreases the relative risk of living with parents and increases the risk of living alone, most clearly when born outside the EU and among those living in Italy. Living arrangements are also partly correlated to the population characteristics of the person's area of residence. As expected, *not living in rural areas* decreases the likelihood of living with parents in Italy. The more significant correlations with these geographical characteristics in the Italian case – in addition to significant *Italian Central-Northern vs Southern regional differences* in the risk of living with parents – reveal the crucial importance of local cultural norms and the individual and family expectations with regard to the living arrangements of young adults in Italy. These traits appear to be largely independent of human capital and the economic status of the persons involved. Besides country of birth, the single most significant sociocultural background factor in the Norwegian case is *educational level* (tertiary as against primary education), which implies a significantly lower likelihood of the highly educated living with parents. This is partly in line with our expectations, that the highly educated prefer a more 'modern' life, independent of their parents. However, when we look at men and women separately, we find that these expected correlations are only evident for Norwegian men and not for Norwegian women or Italian women or men. This is somewhat surprising. In the Italian case, it may be due to the relatively poorer prospects of Italian youth, also among the more highly educated, when entering the labour market. Furthermore, the corresponding lack for all groups of a significant effect of higher education on the risk of living alone indicates that higher education per se is not a crucial factor in young adults' choice of living arrangements in the two countries.

Turning to the work and money indicators (variables 10–16 plus 17, Table 5.2), as expected, we find that they correlate quite differently with the two types of living arrangements in Italy and Norway. Also as expected, with the exception of a slightly positive correlation for Norwegian women, *being a student* (as opposed to being in permanent employment) correlates by far the most positively to living with parents in Italy. The most striking difference between the two countries is shown to be among young male students: the relative risk of Norwegian male students living with their parents is insignificantly negative, whereas the corresponding risk of Italian male students is twenty-eight times that of living in a couple. The risk of living alone is positively correlated, however, with being a student in both countries and for both sexes.

Being *temporarily employed* increases the risk of living with parents in Italy and, at a lower level of significance, of living alone in Norway. We largely find the same pattern for both sexes. This probably means that being in temporary and not permanent employment implies a reduced propensity to marry or to live

Table 5.2 Multinomial logit estimation results. Relative risks of living with parents or living alone versus living in a couple. Total for both countries and separately for each country. All 20–39 years old excluding those in military service. Standard errors in parenthesis

Variables	Both countries All W/parents	Both countries All Alone	Both countries Women W/parents	Both countries Women Alone	Both countries Men W/parents	Both countries Men Alone	Italy All W/parents	Italy All Alone	Italy Women W/parents	Italy Women Alone	Italy Men W/parents	Italy Men Alone	Norway All W/parents	Norway All Alone	Norway Women W/parents	Norway Women Alone	Norway Men W/parents	Norway Men Alone
1 Italy	17.64*** (1.980)	0.61*** (0.055)	27.52*** (4.671)	0.69*** (0.087)	14.36*** (2.243)	0.65*** (0.087)												
2 Female	0.45*** (0.033)	0.74*** (0.062)					0.45*** (0.036)	0.74*** (0.072)					0.39*** (0.055)	0.84* (0.090)				
3 High school	1.02 (0.084)	0.96 (0.090)	0.98 (0.123)	0.92 (0.122)	0.98 (0.117)	0.92 (0.128)	1.01 (0.088)	0.91 (0.095)	0.96 (0.126)	0.88 (0.132)	0.95 (0.123)	0.85 (0.131)	1.06 (0.169)	1.18 (0.168)	1.72* (0.473)	1.19 (0.239)	0.86 (0.186)	1.24 (0.256)
4 Tertiary	1.20* (0.128)	1.08 (0.125)	1.13 (0.167)	0.82 (0.128)	1.17 (0.193)	1.23 (0.223)	1.28** (0.147)	1.11 (0.150)	1.14 (0.178)	0.80 (0.147)	1.31 (0.242)	1.35 (0.289)	0.54*** (0.114)	0.83 (0.123)	1.11 (0.365)	0.95 (0.186)	0.37*** (0.110)	0.72 (0.157)
5 EU-born	0.34*** (0.096)	1.08 (0.271)	0.14*** (0.056)	1.17 (0.374)	0.68 (0.279)	1.19 (0.465)	0.34*** (0.103)	1.09 (0.337)	0.15*** (0.060)	1.20 (0.479)	0.70 (0.322)	1.22 (0.601)	0.33** (0.184)	1.22 (0.339)	0.00*** (0.000)	1.32 (0.464)	0.37 (0.224)	0.99 (0.426)
6 Born in other countries	0.18*** (0.028)	1.69*** (0.228)	0.17*** (0.039)	1.38* (0.257)	0.20*** (0.047)	2.29*** (0.495)	0.18*** (0.031)	1.74*** (0.259)	0.19*** (0.045)	1.51** (0.314)	0.20*** (0.050)	2.24*** (0.522)	0.70 (0.208)	1.16 (0.222)	1.24 (0.527)	0.86 (0.229)	0.70 (0.291)	1.74* (0.506)
7 Intermed. popul. area	0.68*** (0.061)	0.65*** (0.067)	0.76** (0.100)	0.73** (0.103)	0.61*** (0.078)	0.57*** (0.087)	0.69*** (0.066)	0.63*** (0.074)	0.79* (0.109)	0.74* (0.123)	0.61*** (0.084)	0.55*** (0.093)	1.23 (0.248)	0.90 (0.155)	1.93** (0.603)	0.82 (0.198)	1.11 (0.302)	1.00 (0.252)
8 Densely popul. area	0.90 (0.080)	1.06 (0.106)	1.07 (0.136)	1.23 (0.164)	0.76** (0.099)	0.89 (0.137)	0.94 (0.091)	1.08 (0.130)	1.13 (0.153)	1.30 (0.215)	0.80 (0.115)	0.90 (0.163)	0.75* (0.115)	1.04 (0.123)	1.19 (0.287)	1.13 (0.180)	0.59** (0.124)	0.95 (0.175)
9 Italy South							1.24** (0.106)	0.90 (0.097)	1.53*** (0.187)	1.12 (0.170)	1.11 (0.141)	0.81 (0.126)						
10 Temporary work	1.44*** (0.171)	1.12 (0.152)	1.44** (0.217)	1.20 (0.194)	1.41* (0.268)	1.04 (0.236)	1.43*** (0.179)	1.09 (0.167)	1.40** (0.221)	1.15 (0.213)	1.43* (0.288)	1.01 (0.256)	0.90 (0.257)	1.68** (0.353)	1.72 (0.650)	1.84** (0.470)	0.56 (0.232)	1.57 (0.525)
11 Self-employed	1.05 (0.111)	1.22* (0.145)	0.90 (0.165)	1.30 (0.250)	1.18 (0.162)	1.30 (0.205)	1.03 (0.114)	1.20 (0.151)	0.89 (0.164)	1.25 (0.258)	1.18 (0.168)	1.28 (0.218)	1.75* (0.583)	1.42* (0.290)	2.60 (1.602)	0.98 (0.412)	1.78 (0.688)	2.00** (0.572)

	(1)	(2)	(3)	(4)	(5)	(6)	(7)	(8)	(9)	(10)	(11)	(12)	(13)	(14)	(15)	(16)	(17)	(18)
12 Unemployed	3.17*** (0.458)	1.83*** (0.334)	2.38*** (0.458)	1.44 (0.337)	5.45*** (1.188)	3.45*** (0.971)	3.12*** (0.483)	1.92*** (0.390)	2.27*** (0.466)	1.47 (0.375)	5.37*** (1.254)	3.56*** (1.113)	2.14** (0.816)	3.24*** (1.048)	1.86 (1.050)	2.06 (0.969)	3.59* (2.505)	6.87*** (4.509)
13 Student	6.86*** (1.198)	4.58*** (0.857)	5.91*** (1.296)	4.41*** (0.994)	11.21*** (3.142)	8.00*** (2.537)	9.24*** (2.111)	6.10*** (1.611)	6.52*** (1.718)	4.97*** (1.579)	27.57*** (12.807)	18.79*** (9.494)	1.31 (0.269)	2.61*** (0.488)	1.97** (0.565)	3.67*** (0.811)	0.79 (0.234)	1.79** (0.484)
14 Inactive	0.92 (0.122)	0.59*** (0.094)	0.60*** (0.107)	0.48*** (0.092)	4.33*** (1.301)	2.14** (0.746)	0.89 (0.123)	0.59*** (0.108)	0.54*** (0.100)	0.46*** (0.103)	4.29*** (1.383)	2.12* (0.824)	0.97 (0.298)	1.68* (0.468)	0.53 (0.310)	1.56 (0.487)	1.77 (0.951)	2.23 (1.236)
15 Earnings	0.98*** (0.003)	1.00 (0.002)	0.99* (0.006)	1.02*** (0.004)	0.98*** (0.004)	1.00 (0.003)	0.99*** (0.003)	1.01 (0.003)	1.00 (0.006)	1.03*** (0.005)	0.98*** (0.004)	1.00 (0.004)	0.98*** (0.005)	1.00 (0.002)	1.00 (0.010)	1.01 (0.004)	0.98*** (0.006)	1.00 (0.003)
16 Soc. cash benefits	1.02 (0.013)	1.02** (0.011)	1.04** (0.018)	1.04** (0.014)	0.99 (0.019)	1.01 (0.014)	1.01 (0.014)	1.02 (0.014)	1.04* (0.019)	1.02 (0.020)	0.99 (0.023)	1.00 (0.027)	1.04** (0.017)	1.01 (0.013)	1.06* (0.039)	1.02 (0.015)	1.02 (0.022)	1.00 (0.021)
17 Chronically ill	1.64*** (0.213)	1.59*** (0.229)	1.52** (0.256)	1.51** (0.265)	1.61** (0.343)	1.68*** (0.235)	1.68*** (0.235)	1.38* (0.247)	1.58** (0.283)	1.36 (0.297)	1.61** (0.379)	1.36 (0.421)	0.53** (0.149)	2.34*** (0.357)	0.42** (0.161)	2.05*** (0.408)	0.61 (0.248)	2.82*** (0.745)
18 Children 0 to 14	0.04*** (0.003)	0.05*** (0.005)	0.06*** (0.007)	0.12*** (0.014)	0.03*** (0.003)	0.01*** (0.002)	0.04*** (0.003)	0.05*** (0.005)	0.06*** (0.007)	0.11*** (0.014)	0.03*** (0.003)	0.01*** (0.003)	0.23*** (0.039)	0.08*** (0.010)	0.39*** (0.117)	0.21*** (0.035)	0.20*** (0.044)	0.02*** (0.005)
19 Age	0.81*** (0.006)	0.97*** (0.008)	0.82*** (0.009)	0.99 (0.011)	0.80*** (0.009)	0.94*** (0.012)	0.81*** (0.007)	0.97*** (0.010)	0.82*** (0.009)	0.99 (0.013)	0.80*** (0.010)	0.94*** (0.014)	0.77*** (0.018)	0.99 (0.011)	0.70*** (0.036)	0.98 (0.016)	0.79*** (0.021)	0.98 (0.015)
Constant	179.7*** (44.39)	4.2*** (1.22)	33.3*** (11.51)	1.1 (0.44)	489.9*** (179.77)	14.2*** (6.14)	2,797.3*** (785.82)	3.0*** (1.10)	715.1*** (273.99)	0.7 (0.36)	7,383.1*** (3,190.29)	13.8*** (7.49)	876.5*** (485.74)	2.3*** (0.83)	1,001.7*** (1,123.06)	1.3 (0.65)	1,009.0*** (684.64)	4.1*** (2.10)
Observations	16 435	16 435	8 312	8 312	8 123	8 123	12 861	12 861	6 537	6 537	6 324	6 324	3 574	3 574	1 775	1 775	1 799	1 799
Pseudo R²	0.406	0.406	0.386	0.386	0.436	0.436	0.404	0.404	0.387	0.387	0.431	0.431	0.286	0.286	0.223	0.223	0.372	0.372

Notes
*** p<0.01, ** p<0.05, * p<0.1.

with a partner in both countries. The same is largely the case for being *unemployed*. Although *self-employed* Norwegian men exhibit a slightly reduced risk of being partnered, self-employment predominantly appears to be an unimportant predictor of household patterns. Being *inactive* (neither a student nor in the workforce) implies dissimilar living arrangements for women and men in the two countries, as it decreases the risk of women and increases the risk of men living with their parents in both countries, although only significantly so for Italian women and men. For men in both countries and for Norwegian women, inactivity increases the risk of living alone, though only significantly for Italian men. For Italian women, however, inactivity is negatively associated with the risk of living alone. The significantly reduced risk of living with parents or alone as opposed to living in a couple, which is particularly evident for Italian women, clearly indicates that Italian women, more than Norwegian women and more than men of both nationalities, tend to be provided for by a partner in marriage.

As expected, high *earnings* reduce the risk of living with parents in both countries, although slightly more so for men than for women, and only increase the risk of living alone (as compared to in a couple) for Italian women. For women in both countries, receiving *social cash benefits* slightly increases the relative risk of living with parents. In addition, we included *health status* as an economic indicator, since being chronically ill triggers more generous welfare services and payments in Norway than in Italy. As expected, we find that chronic illness slightly decreases the likelihood of young Norwegian adults, both women and men (not significantly for men though) living in the parental home, and that it increases the likelihood of young Italians, both women and men, living in the parental home. In both countries, however, chronically ill persons more often live alone than with a partner. This applies particularly to Norwegian women and men, where the relative risk of the chronically ill living alone is between two and three times higher than for those without a chronic illness. Finally, the effects of the two control variables, *age* and *small children in the household*, appear to be as expected. Increasing age implies moving out of the parental home, and children in the household implies living in a couple.

6 Conclusions

The present analysis compares the living arrangements of young adult women and men in Norway and Italy, i.e. two countries with largely dissimilar contextual characteristics, such as welfare state provision, labour markets and housing policies, as well as cultural and normative conditions. In order to examine individual sociocultural and economic factors related to the observed differences in living arrangements, we estimated multinomial logit models by using a comparable data set (EU-SILC), collected in a non-economic crisis year (2007) in both countries. We found a significantly higher propensity to live in the parental home in Italy, and to live in a separate household – either alone or with other singles in a multi-occupant household – in Norway, and (as expected) dissimilar correlations between individual characteristics and young adults' living arrangements in the two countries. In general, the propensity of young adults to live with parents and not in a couple appears to be more sensitive to individual character-istics in Italy than in Norway. This applies to both sociocultural and economic characteristics. The gendered correlation between economic and labour market status and living arrangements among young Italians is most clearly shown by the significance of the *inactive* status of Italian women and men, since being inactive, i.e. neither employed, unemployed nor a student, correlates strongly and positively to living with parents for men and to living in a couple for women. The former are most probably provided for by parents, while the latter most probably by a husband.

Whereas the inclination to stay in the parental home relates more strongly to individual economic factors in Italy than in Norway, the inclination to live in a separate household in Norway also relates partly to the same factors. This means that marrying or starting a family with a partner and possibly children in young adulthood is largely related to having a secure and well-established position in the labour market in both countries. The only option for those with a marginal labour market position and poor economic prospects is, in Italy, to stay with parents and, in Norway, to live alone or with others living 'alone'. This picture should be supplemented, however, by the strong macro-economic, social and cultural dissimilarities between the two countries. The generally less propitious labour market prospects in Italy, even in an economically unproblematic year on average (2007), most probably implies more uncertain economic prospects for young adult Italians than for Norwegians. This is reflected, for example, in the Norwegian figures for the chronically ill, who find themselves able to establish a household of their own due to welfare state provisions in the form of transfers, services and housing. Hence, moving out of the parental home involves a signifi-cantly higher economic risk for young adult Italians than for young adult Norwe-gians. The higher dependence of the Italian youth on the economic risk in their living arrangements, with the deep negative impact of the great recession (par-ticularly on youth employment prospects in Italy), may lead to a further delay in their leaving parental households, with depressing effects on fertility rates and the autonomy of young adults from their families of origin.

Appendix

Table A5.1 Descriptive statistics by gender and country (those in military service are excluded)

Country		Italy		Norway	
Gender		Men	Women	Men	Women
Household affiliation	With parents	50.2	37.4	11.3	5.8
	In a couple	35.4	51.3	47.5	60.1
	Alone	14.4	11.3	41.1	34.1
Education	Primary	35.1	30.8	22.6	19.1
	High school	51.1	52.0	50.1	41.1
	Tertiary	13.8	17.2	27.3	39.9
Country of birth	Native	90.4	89.4	88.7	88.4
	EU	1.4	1.5	3.6	3.5
	Other	8.3	9.1	7.7	8.0
Area of residence	Sparsely pop.	16.6	15.8	29.4	29.6
	Intermed. pop.	40.9	40.7	15.3	14.6
	Densely pop.	42.5	43.6	55.2	55.9
Region (only for Italy)	Central-Northern	63.1	62.4		
	Southern	36.9	37.6		
Main activity	Perm. employed	46.7	33.5	60.0	47.8
	Temp. employed	10.8	11.0	7.2	10.7
	Self-employed	17.3	7.8	9.5	4.1
	Unemployed	9.4	10.0	5.0	2.8
	Student	11.3	13.7	14.0	24.3
	Inactive	4.4	24.0	4.3	10.4
Earnings	Mean	18,172	10,215	37,142	21,897
Soc. cash benefits	Mean	675	612	1,533	2,052
Health status	Chron. ill	6.5	8.7	12.6	13.0
Children <15 in household	Yes	30.3	45.5	35.0	53.9
Age	Mean age	30.5	30.6	30.1	30.2
Number of observations		6,529	6,749	1,834	1,794

Acknowledgements

Funding by the Research Council of Norway and by the Italian Ministry of University and Research are gratefully acknowledged. Previous versions of this paper have been presented at the workshop 'Gender and partnership dynamics' by Statistics Norway/The Research Council of Norway, Program for Gender Research, and at the Italian National Conference of Labour Economics. We thank the participants to the conferences and an anonymous referee for their stimulating comments. Usual disclaimers apply.

Note

1 Due to data restrictions, we cannot identify the person's actual relationship to the child(ren), whether he or she is the biological parent or not. Nevertheless, with this constraint in mind, we believe that controlling for children contributes to a more focused analysis of the economic vs sociocultural influence on the living arrangements of young adults.

6 Youth unemployment and the transition from school to work in Germany and Greece

Hans Dietrich, Annie Tubadji, Brigitte Schels,
Anette Haas, Ioanna Tsoka, Vasilis Angelis and
Katerina Dimaki

1 Introduction[1]

Since the Great Recession, the total number of young unemployed individuals increased across the European Union (EU28) from 4.2 million in 2008 to 5.6 million in 2013. The corresponding youth unemployment rate increased from 15.6 per cent in 2008 to 23.3 per cent in 2013. The political debate referred to this development as threatening to the entire young generation of this period, resulting in a "lost generation" (O'Higgins 2012). "It is the fall in demand for labour that is the culprit" stated Bell and Blanchflower (2010:13), an analysis that is commonly shared. Scarpetta *et al.* (2010) argue that in times of recession, job offers become scarce and competition among jobseekers is fierce. Using data about former periods of economic crisis, Choudhry Tanveer *et al.* (2012:87) find cumulative crisis effects on youth unemployment. Economic downturns typically affect young people more than others on the labour market (Jimeno and Rodríguez-Palenzuela 2002). However, the Great Recession and its long-lasting effects, especially in Mediterranean countries, indicate a strong correlation between youth unemployment and adult unemployment (Dietrich and Möller 2016). With respect to the variety of the European countries, however, the Great Recession created severe differences in the quality and quantity in youth unemployment across European countries (Dietrich 2013).

The orthodox explanation of unemployment draws attention to labour market institutions. Layard *et al.* (2005) and Bell and Blanchflower (2010:11) state that the validity of the empirical results supporting this view has been called into question. The increases in unemployment are not due to decreases in labour market flexibility, nor has friction in the market increased; rather, there has been a collapse in the demand for labour because product demand has fallen, according to Bell and Blanchflower (2010:13). However, there is a body of literature that draws a connection between institutional reform and the rise of unemployment. Bernal-Verdugo *et al.* find that "improvements in labour market flexibility have a statistically and significant negative impact on unemployment outcomes (overall unemployment, youth unemployment and long-term unemployment)" (Bernal-Verdugo *et al.* 2012:10). Noelke (2015:480) states that while the effects of job security provisions are inconsistent across specifications, there is suggestive evidence that deregulating temporary contracts at high levels of job security provisions has significantly increased youth unemployment rates. Along these lines, Noelke (2015) identifies a negative interaction effect between employment protection and youth employment rates. From a more general perspective, Boeri and Jimeno argue that the divergence in European countries derives from interactions between the "magnitude of the macroeconomic shocks, nature (financial vs. real) of these shocks, and labour market institutions conditioning firms' adjustment to those shocks" (Boeri and Jimeno 2016:33).

Aside from labour market institutions, the educational system is relevant in regard to youth unemployment. As Bell and Blanchflower (2010:5) state, for all age groups and countries, unemployment rates are higher for the least educated. The structure of the educational system and the related mechanism of selectivity shape school-to-work transitions (Bol and van de Werfthorst 2013) and the occurrence and duration of youth unemployment. Furthermore, the flexibility of the educational system could affect individuals' flexibility of becoming or remaining unemployed. One possible response to rising unemployment on the part of the youth has been to return to full-time education (Blanchflower and Freeman 2000). However, that option is limited due to institutional-based access limitations and individuals' assets. Additionally, families' socio-economic background limits individuals' educational choices (Goldthorpe 1996). Especially for the lowest educated, both the family background and the educational system offer fewer options to return to education.

Based on this rich theoretical and empirical background, the chapter explores the effect of the Great Recession on individuals' unemployment experiences under the control of individual characteristics, country-specific institutional settings and the country-specific variation of additional macro factors such as demographic factors.

We employ the school-to-work-transition (StWT) model as a heuristic to structure models on adolescents' risk of being unemployed within their initial years on the labour market. Attention is paid to the institutional differences in both countries and their possible direct and indirect effects on becoming unemployed. We assume that country-specific institutions shape both the patterns of school-to-work transitions in general and the experience of youth unemployment in detail in Greece and Germany. Educational and labour market-related institutions will be addressed via explanatory variables representing the educational system, countries' employment protection legislation and public employment services.

To address country-specific institutions, we limit the number of possible countries to two extreme cases, Germany and Greece. Germany and Greece differ not only in terms of the development at the macro level but also due to several core institutions, which constitute the countries' StWT-process. These countries not only differ due to the quality and quantity of the emergence of unemployment but also with respect to the institutions of the educational system and the labour market as well as time-varying opportunity sets (business cycle and demography). The observation window of this study ranges from 2004 to

2013. This period includes the year of pre-recession and the Great Recession, which lasted at least until 2013 in Greece; Germany only experienced a short recession period (2009/2010) and since then a long recovery episode. Thus, the data design captures a systematic variation of time-sensitive factors, such as the already mentioned business cycle and demographic effects and their interaction with institutional and individual factors.

The remainder of the chapter has the following components. Section 2 sketches the theoretical and empirical background of the school-to-work-transition, which will be applied in an attempt to analyse an individual's risk of becoming unemployed in Greece and Germany comparatively from 2004 to 2013. Section 3 introduces the data we use, the operationalization of our key variables and the estimation strategy. Section 4 reports the empirical results, and Section 5 offers some concluding remarks that may lead, among others, to improved policy and decision making in both countries.

2 Theoretical and empirical background

What is the reason for higher unemployment risks among youth? There are several perspectives that support the hypothesis that the first labour market entrants have an above-average unemployment risk. In the following section, we introduce the school-to-work heuristic as a framework to combine individual- and firm-based decisions, institutional arrangements and time-varying macro-factors.

2.1 The school-to-work transition model as a heuristic framework

The StWT model is better classified as a heuristic than as a modern theory, which is typically tailored for empirical tests. However, the StWT model delivers a structured view on an individual's transition(s) from school to work, framing individuals' action or decisions with a social background and embedded in a country-specific setting of organizational, institutional, cultural and time-specific factors. Thus, the StWT model could be helpful for generating analytical research questions. In contrast to pathway oriented attempts (Raffe 2003; Iannelli and Raffe 2007; Schneider and Tieben 2011), where country-specific patterns of individual transitions within the context of countries' institutions are typified – which are typically stylized as naïve two- or three-step models (general education to vocational training to work) – we favour a more elaborated heuristic based on a life course approach (Mayer 2009). From a life course perspective, an individual's transition from school to work is split up into a succession of single status episodes. These status episodes may be episodes of secondary and tertiary education, vocational training, temporary or other forms of atypical jobs, military or voluntary service, participation in training and labour market schemes, job searches, unemployment episodes or other activities, including leisure time, taking care of family members and children or institutionalized episodes (Dietrich 2003:85). These episodes are typically of a temporary nature. The destination of these transitions is integration into the labour market – whatever this means from an individual or country-specific perspective (Ryan 2001). Obtaining a decent job (Russell and O'Connell 2001) is defined as the destination of individuals' StWT in the early life period.

Based on this framework, unemployment is a competing risk to alternative outcomes at any stage of the school-to-work transition. From an empirical perspective, individual characteristics such as gender, level of education, social background of family – such as social class, family and household formation – or socio-cultural background – measured by nationality, migration background or ethnicity – influence not only the outcomes from education and entry into employment but also the risk of becoming unemployed at the next transition.

From both a theoretical and empirical perspective, episodes of unemployment are to be interpreted differently or may fulfil different functions within the school-to-work transition process. From a neo-classical perspective, unemployment episodes are interpreted as voluntary search time for a new career. Given time-fixed entry dates for schools, apprenticeship training or military service, episodes of unemployment may serve as waiting time. From a life course perspective, episodes of unemployment may serve as periods of vocational (re)-orientation or career planning. Thus, unemployment periods can be interpreted as the intended or unintended result of individual action in more or less market-organized matching processes embedded in specific institutions settings (Dietrich 2013).

Empirical research has identified country-specific patterns of school-to-work-transition that are mainly shaped by country-specific institutions (Ryan 2001; Müller and Gangl 2003). The structure of general and vocational education, training and life-long learning vary across countries. In particular countries, institutions of higher education and vocational training structure the school-to-work transition prominently. Labour market entry positions are organized in a country-specific way, based on the respective social and labour laws. The same is true for country-specific instruments of the labour market policy for young people. Fostered by the European Youth Guaranty Programme (European Commission 2016b), most European member states have developed guidance and counseling opportunities and supporting schemes for young people, such as additional education, qualification or training and employment schemes, to assist young people into the labour market. However, the design of the labour market policy for young people and the implemented instruments (also called youth programmes in the following; comp: ILO 2015) vary remarkably between countries. Compared to adults' unemployment risk, the period of youth is shaped by a sequence of transitions from school to work. Each transition is connected with unemployment risks, which typically led to higher unemployment risks than that of adults.

2.2 Action based factors

First-time entrants into the labour market have little or no work experience and, beyond casual or holiday work, typically no firm tenure. An important exception here are apprentices, who are qualified by firm-based training (see Section 2.2).

From a human capital perspective, labour market entrants have not been able to accumulate occupational and firm-specific human capital. By contrast, experienced workers have already profited from longer on-the-job training and hence are typically more valuable to the firm (Pastore 2015a). As a result, young workers have lower productivity levels. Although young workers are also paid lower wages, the pay differential might not fully compensate for the productivity gap (Blau and Kahn 1992). This might be especially true in case of a more egalitarian or a relatively rigid wage structure.

From a signal-theory perspective (Altonji 1995; Borjas 2010:262ff), firms are not able to estimate LM entrants' potential productivity: school certificates vary across schools and regions and work only as weak signals. References from former employers are typically not applicable at that point of life. Thus, potential employers are less confident and prefer more experienced workers or reduce the entrants' wages and job security, e.g. by approbation time or forms of temporary work.

This is in line with a third argument, which derives from the Insider-Outsider theory (see, for instance, Lindbeck and Snower 2001). Young workers as entrants in the labour market are typically in an outsider position. Insiders know that they are valuable to the firm and that there is limited competition from outsiders. The incumbent workforce disposes of some market power because of the existence of initial training costs and layoff restrictions. As the Insider-Outsider theory has shown, insiders are therefore able to enforce higher wages. This results in a lower level of employment at the cost of the outsiders. This also implies that the stability of jobs for prime-age workers may have elevated the unemployment of young workers. In a similar way, it can be argued that in times of economic slackness, insiders have little interest in making wage concessions that could save the jobs of labour market entrants or the non-regular workforce.

Fourth, with regard to substantial lay-offs in times of severe recession, inverse seniority matters (see Kalleberg and Sorensen 1979: Baron *et al*. 1986: Bell and Blanchflower 2011:2). The last in–first out argument, which favours senior workers, is widely supported by empirical evidence (Choudhry Tanveer *et al*. 2012: 83; ILO 2015). Reagan (1992) argues that while experienced workers perform a dual task (aside from performing tasks, they are also engaged in training new and typically younger workers), they are compensated with job security. As a consequence, a last in–first out principle is established, typically at the expense of younger workers. Regulations within so-called "social compensation plans" (*Sozialpläne*) also give prime-age workers' needs more priority for family and other reasons. As a result, the younger workforce serves as a buffer stock in times of economic crisis.

From a search theory perspective (Holzer 1988; Krueger and Mueller 2016), young people are distinct from senior workers because they are less attached to the labour market. Additionally, the reservation wage might be more unrealistic because young people remain longer in the reservation period to enter a better starting position and because search strategies are less developed and may be supported by professional guidance. These factors tend to prolong the search time. In line with this argument, job-shopping arguments (Franz 1981) are relevant. At the beginning of their careers, workers are often still seeking better job opportunities and matches. Therefore, job mobility in general is higher for young workers. Because job mobility typically comes with shorter or longer spells of joblessness, this yields higher aggregate age-specific unemployment rates for the young.

Based on these theoretical arguments, one can derive two main hypotheses: (i) the youth unemployment rate should be higher than the prime-age rate; (ii) compared to overall joblessness, youth unemployment should be more sensitive to the business cycle.

While most economics theories are demand-side oriented, from a sociological perspective, supply-side oriented models of educational choice are suggested (Boudon 1974; Bourdieu and Passeron 1990). Following Boudon (1974), educational decisions reflect both the process of familial socialization, which leads to class-related school performance, and class-related familial decisions on educational choice. Especially in the education system, school performance and educational choice are assumed to be key factors for educational attainment and the precondition for successful labour market entry and an ongoing labour market career. Economic, social and cultural capital define the assets for social reproduction and, from a choice perspective, the risk set, which are causal for educational success (Bourdieu and Passeron 1990). Empirical tests support the model-specific assumptions (see Breen and Yaish 2006; Stocké 2007).

2.3 Educational system in Germany and Greece

From a school-to-work-transition perspective, the educational system affects the transition from school to work in a multifold way. Due to the degree of differentiation (specificity and selectivity) and standardization (van de Werfthoft and Mijs 2010), the educational system delivers both certificates and signals of different quality to the labour market. As mentioned in the context of signal theoretical considerations, educational systems tend to deliver only imperfect information regarding (expected) productivity and trainability of the school graduates. Thus, the duration or level of education and the distinction between general and vocational degrees are employed as typical indicators of school performance and acquired sets of skills. Due to the standard model of human capital theory, years of education or the level of the degree cause wage differences. Later, years of education or the level of degree influence both individuals' job search and employment stability. Aside from the years/level of education, the distinction between general education-oriented tracks versus vocational-oriented tracks have gained attention in recent years (Gangl 2003; Forster *et al.* 2016; Hanushek *et al.* 2017). Graduates from general educational tracks need more search time on average but are also more flexible with respect to occupational choice. In contrast, graduates from vocational tracks need less search time to realize a job match but are typically limited with regard to the choice of occupation or sector. The distinction between firm-based and school-based vocational education is discussed contradictorily in the literature (Hanushek *et al.* 2017). Retention is a fundamental element of firm-based vocational training, which allows smoother transitions from training to work in contrast to school-based training. On the contrary, less specialized graduates appear to be more flexible later in their job careers.

The educational institutions in Greece and Germany differ substantially and refer to two different educational regimes. The German educational regime is characterized by an early and strict school tracking, in line with the strict stratified ranking of educational tracks and degrees. Further in the German system, there is a distinct general and consecutive vocationally oriented educational setting. The German educational regime is influenced by apprenticeship training, which sees participation from approximately two-thirds of an age cohort. German apprenticeship training is characterized by highly standardized and recognized vocational degrees. However, most recently, Germany has been experiencing a second wave of expansion of university education. Several processes should be mentioned here that contribute to the reshaping of educational distribution in Germany: i) more students enrol in academic tracks at the secondary level of general education (Gymnasium); ii) a larger share of upper-secondary graduates (Abiturienten) opt for academic study instead of an apprenticeship training; iii) the duration of education from an academic gymnasium was reduced from nine to eight years of schooling; and iv) university reform in Germany (in line with the so-called Bologna process) introduced bachelor degrees as a first degree and offered an early option to graduate from university programmes. These elements lead to a higher share of young people below 25 both attending tertiary-level education and graduating at a younger age. Table 6.1 indicates an increasing share of tertiary-level students of all students in Germany since the late 2000s.[2]

Compared to the German educational regime, the Greek educational regime is less stratified, where school tracking starts rather late at age 15 when compulsory schooling ends. Within the non-compulsory upper-secondary years, students can decide between a three-year course at an academic upper-secondary Lykeia (GEL) in preparation for university study, a three-year course at an upper-secondary vocational Lykeia (EPAL), a two-year course at a vocational school (EPAS) or a two-year course at a vocational training institute (IEK) (see Ioannidou and Stavrou 2013). Due to educational reforms in 2013, the EPAS was assumed to become obsolete.[3] Because vocational education and training is less recognized, the academic track is favoured. Empirical findings correspond with the general description (see Table 6.1). As Table 6.1 indicates, the share of students in tertiary courses in Greece is almost twice as high as in Germany. However, the overall rate of tertiary students in Greece decreases slightly while more or less steadily increasing in Germany (Table 6.1). However, in both countries, acceptance into vocational and academic tracks and acceptance within the two tracks is performance based.

Similar findings are shown with regard to educational degrees in Germany and Greece in young people below the age of 25. Here, the figures are split

Table 6.1 Educational level attended (in a reference period of four weeks) in Germany and Greece 2004–2013

Year	2004	2005	2006	2007	2008	2009	2010	2011	2012	2013	Total
Germany											
Low	30.87	30.78	30.99	28.83	27.91	28.2	28.94	27.82	27.44	26.53	28.9
Medium	48.05	49.93	48.2	50.87	47.62	48.9	46.62	46.97	45.84	44.98	47.8
High	21.08	19.29	20.8	20.31	24.47	22.9	24.44	25.21	26.72	28.48	23.3
Greece											
Low	5.42	4.27	4.35	4.7	4.16	5.04	5.53	5.17	4.15	3.9	4.67
Medium	52.21	49.22	50.64	52.25	53.16	46.4	50.01	53.5	54.21	54.53	51.6
High	42.37	46.51	45.01	43.05	42.68	48.5	44.46	41.32	41.64	41.57	43.7

Source: EUROSTAT-LFS scientific use file 2013; own calculations.

Note
Base: all students, for coding of educational level see note 2.

between students and non-students. Table 6.2 shows only a margin of students in both countries that are still studying and have already attended a first tertiary programme before the age of 25. However, in Germany this figure is increasing due to the Bologna Reform.

Table 6.2 confirms the expected country differences with higher levels of graduates from vocational training at the secondary level in Germany with regard to apprenticeship training. However, in Greece, a significant number of young people are entering the labour market with a medium level of education.

The German version of firm-based apprenticeship training enables the training firm to observe individuals' productivity and work behaviour during the training period. Later, the trainees accumulate occupational and firm-specific experience while training. Finally, apprenticeship graduates have already passed a firm-specific selection process. Thus, especially at the medium level of education, graduates from apprenticeship training programmes in Germany should show a smoother transition from training to work compared to school-to-work-based transitions in Greece.

At the tertiary level of education, the share of labour market entrants in Greece is still approximately twice as high compared to Germany, even if the share of tertiary-level graduates entering the labour market has increased in both countries. Until now, there have been no significant indicators for over-education at the academic level for either country (OECD 2014b). Hence, the human capital argument is favoured. Additionally, the higher the human capital of graduates is, the lower the unemployment risk is. However, because the Bologna Reform has affected the upgrading of education in both countries, this process prolongs the average duration that individuals spend on education and reduces the probability of becoming established on the labour market within the youth stage (below the age of 25).

Table 6.2 Highest educational level (already) attained – students and non-students – Germany and Greece 2004–2013

Year	2004	2005	2006	2007	2008	2009	2010	2011	2012	2013	Total
Germany											
Students											
Low	73.3	74.3	72.8	73.4	68.8	70.7	69.5	56.3	55.0	52.9	67.7
Medium	26.0	25.1	26.7	26.3	30.3	28.2	29.1	41.2	42.2	44.3	31.0
High	0.7	0.7	0.6	0.4	0.9	1.1	1.4	2.4	2.7	2.8	1.3
Non-students											
Low	27.3	31.4	30.0	32.3	27.8	26.3	25.9	27.7	26.5	26.1	28.2
Medium	67.3	64.0	65.2	63.6	66.9	69.8	67.4	65.9	65.6	65.6	66.1
High	5.4	4.7	4.8	4.1	5.3	3.9	6.7	6.3	8.0	8.4	5.7
Greece											
Students											
Low	51.6	47.1	49.6	50.9	50.6	50.7	52.0	53.2	53.1	52.5	51.1
Medium	47.2	51.9	49.1	47.9	48.3	48.3	47.1	46.0	46.1	46.5	47.9
High	1.2	1.0	1.4	1.1	1.0	1.0	0.9	0.8	0.9	0.9	1.0
Non-students											
Low	30.8	34.0	34.7	32.7	33.1	33.6	30.9	30.5	27.1	24.7	31.5
Medium	60.0	57.8	53.2	54.3	53.6	54.0	56.3	55.0	57.4	58.6	56.2
High	10.2	8.1	12.2	13.1	13.4	12.5	12.9	14.5	15.5	16.7	12.4

Source: EUROSTAT-LFS scientific use file 2013; own calculations.

Note
For coding of educational level see note 2.

2.4 Labour market institutions in Germany and Greece

As described above, the educational system delivers country-specific signals regarding school performance, trainability and expected productivity, which generally support the search activity of individuals and the matching process. Especially in the case of labour market, entrants' employers must use signals from the educational system because there are no labour market-based signals available for that group of people.

With respect to labour market institutions, there is a rich body of literature that characterizes the openness or tightness of labour market access in general and for young people specifically. At its core, the most relevant instruments are derived from employment protection legislation and internal, external and wage flexibility. Fixed-term contracts, temporary work agency employment, casual contracts and contract forms creating dependent self-employment as non-regular work contracts – in contrast to permanent work contracts – "are still disproportionately held by younger, less-educated and lower-skilled workers and are not a voluntary choice for most employees" (OECD 2014a:142). Even if non-regular work contracts function as stepping stones into a permanent position (Scherer 2004; McGinnity *et al.* 2005; Bruno *et al.* 2014b; Pastore 2015a), due to the European findings, less than 50 per cent of temporary contract holders will be employed on a permanent contract after three years (OECD 2014a:143).

Intern versus extern flexibility

The metaphor of intern versus extern flexibility describes the mechanism of adaption that firms typically apply when labour is to be reduced or expanded. Following Kalleberg (2003), firms have two options to adapt labour to firms' current demand: i) numeric or external flexibility – adopting the number of employees to the new demand for labour and keeping the volume per worker more or less constant; and ii) functional or internal flexibility – adopting the work time and keeping the volume of workers more or less constant. Typically, the second strategy is more pronounced in the corporate and social democratic welfare models in Europe because the status of workers is protected by labour laws and work council agreements, while the first strategy is the dominant strategy in the liberal countries, e.g. in the US or UK. During the crisis, the "German job miracle" is supposed to be supported by super flexible adaption of working hours, creating "zero-hour" contracts supplemented by state-based wage subsidies and training (Möller 2010). To the contrary, "zero-hour" contracts without state support create extreme forms of non-regular employment. "For example, in the United Kingdom, zero-hour on-call contracts are possible, in which the worker remains available for work but the employer does not guarantee any minimum amount of work in a given month" (OECD 2014a: 146).

Typically, a low level of firing labour is in line with low levels of re-employment of labour; thus, in more liberal countries, the labour market is responding rather directly to business cycle effects, while the conservative or social democratic model requires more time for adaption in both directions. However, outsiders, such as new labour market entrants, appear to be more disadvantaged by the second model.

Temporary contracts

Typically, Germany is reported to be a country with high shares of temporary contracts at the youth stage (OECD 2012a:3). However, when correcting for apprenticeship training, which is typically reported as a specific form of temporary contract, the figures decrease significantly. Thus, the volume of temporary contracts in Germany and Greece do not differ significantly from an overall perspective. However, between 2004 and 2013, the trend in the two countries differs. Employing LFS data from 2001/2012, on average, 85.6 per cent of all employees in Germany and 89.2 per cent in Greece have permanent contracts, while 14.4 per cent in Germany and 10.8 per cent in Greece have temporary contracts (Figure 6.1).

Agency work represents a specific form of temporary work. However, the figures are still rather low both in Germany and Greece. Overall, 2.8 per cent of all employees in Germany work for a temp agency on a temporary or permanent contract; the corresponding Greece figure is 0.4 per cent (OECD 2014a: Table 4.1). Thus, agency work is not considered in the empirical section.

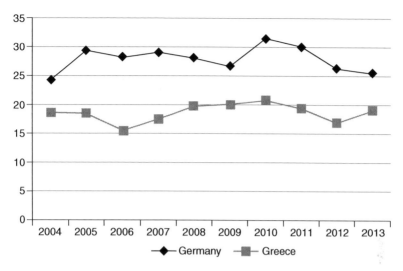

Figure 6.1 Temporary contracts for 15–24-year-old workers (not including apprentices) – 2004–2013.

Source: EUROSTAT-LFS scientific use file 2013; own calculations.

Part-time work

With respect to working hours, on average, 16 per cent of young people who are employed work part-time in Germany and 9 per cent in Greece; however, while the rate has been decreasing over the last several years in Germany, the rate in Greece has increased. Thus, increasing labour demand will reduce part-time work, while in times of unemployment, it can serve as a buffer (Figure 6.2).

Self-employment

The majority of young people in Greece and Germany work as dependent employees. While approximately 95 per cent of all young people in Germany are dependent employees, a significant proportion (22–28 per cent) of the young work force in Greece is stated as self-employed or family helpers. During the Great Recession, the share of young people not covered by a dependent work contract notably increased in Greece, while in Germany, no corresponding Recession effect is observable (Figure 6.3).

PES: guidance and counseling

Public employment services (PES) could play a significant role with regard to the school-to-work transition process of young people. There are several fields of action: PES is able to employ the country-specific instruments of passive and active labour market policies such as guidance and counselling, unemployment benefits and labour market schemes. Scharle and Weber (2011) reviewed the literature on European PES and conclude that there has been little systematic evaluation on the guidance and counselling effect of PES in Europe.

PES could support occupational aspirations and decisions and foster individuals' placement in the labour market, especially for young people without

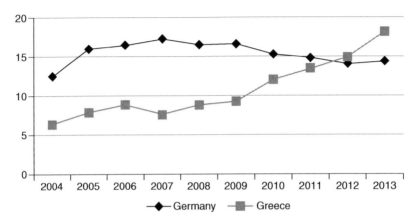

Figure 6.2 Part-time employment in Germany and Greece – 15–24 years old (not including apprentices) – 2004–2013.

Source: EUROSTAT-LFS scientific use file 2013; own calculations.

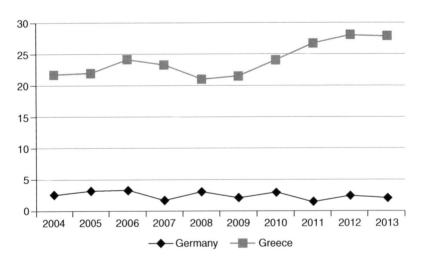

Figure 6.3 Not dependently employed: 15–24 years old (not including apprentices) – 2004–2013.

Source: EUROSTAT-LFS scientific use file 2013; own calculations.

labour market experience. With regard to the later function typically the registration as job seeker or unemployed is required. Finally, PES is the prevailing structure if individuals wish to access unemployment benefits. However, these support systems are, institutionally and structurally, essentially different in Greece and in Germany.

Launov and Waelde (2016) explored recent labour market reforms in Germany. They find a weak effect of unemployment benefit reduction on the re-employment probability (5 per cent) but a more substantial (20 per cent) reform effect of enhanced effectiveness of PES. However, they did not control for age-specific effects.

From an StW perspective, we focus on two aspects: first, how much young people employ the services of PES at all. Here, becoming registered with PES is used as a first rough proxy. The second aspect is to what intensity PES as a formal search channel is used compared to friends and relatives as informal search channels.

In a first step, the share of young people who are identified as unemployed[4] is reported and are registered as unemployed at PES. While an average of 84 per cent of all young unemployed individuals (below 25 years of age) are registered in Germany, only 51 per cent of all young unemployed individuals in Greece are registered (Figure 6.4). However, within the observation period, the share of registered unemployed individuals in Germany is decreasing notably, while in Greece, this share is increasing in a non-linear way.

Because not every unemployed person receives benefits, in the next step, we focus on the share of benefit recipients out of all young unemployed individuals. Again, the share of benefit recipients among all young unemployed people varies

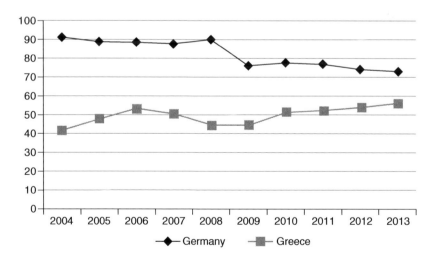

Figure 6.4 Share of unemployed registered individuals at PES – 15–24 years old – 2004–2013.

Source: EUROSTAT-LFS scientific use file 2013; own calculations.

remarkably across both countries and time. The share of registered unemployed youth among all unemployed youth is significantly higher in Germany compared to Greece. The share of young benefit recipients is decreasing in Germany over time, while in Greece, this share stagnated at a low level (approximately 5 per cent) (Figure 6.5).

Search channels

Since 2004, the registration rate of young unemployed people at PES and the share of benefit recipients among young unemployed individuals have decreased in Germany, but young unemployed people have also reduced their propensity to use PES as a channel for job searches. In 2004, 96 per cent of all young unemployed people below the age of 25 employed PES as a search channel, but only 66 per cent did so in 2013 in Germany. A rising share of graduates from tertiary-level education, which appears to be less connected to PES, may drive the composition effect here. In the same time period, job searching through friends and relatives gained importance as a search channel. While 28 per cent of subjectively unemployed individuals mentioned friends and relatives as a search channel in 2004, approximately 40 per cent of all job-seeking young people below the age of 25 mentioned friends and relatives as a search channel in 2013.

In Greece, we observe a different pattern. Between 2004 and 2013, PES gained importance as a search channel; however, albeit at a much lower level compared to Germany. At the same time, the importance of friends and relatives for job search was growing, and started already at a high level in 2004 (89 per cent) and 94 per cent in 2013.

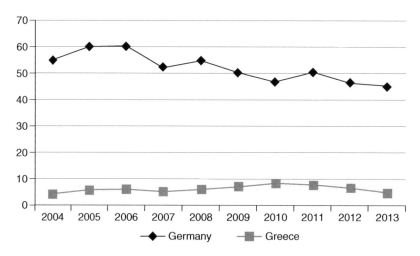

Figure 6.5 Share of unemployed receiving unemployment benefits – 15–24 years old – 2004–2013.

Source: EUROSTAT-LFS scientific use file 2013; own calculations.

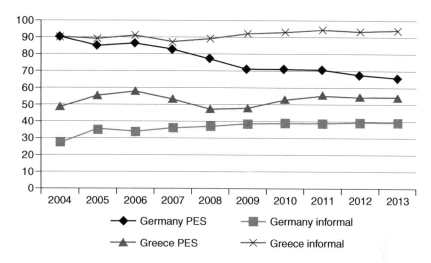

Figure 6.6 Job search channels of young unemployed individuals (four weeks before the interview) – 15–24 years old – 2004–2013.

Source: EUROSTAT-LFS scientific use file 2013; own calculations.

2.4 Time-varying opportunity sets in Germany and Greece

From a cross-country perspective, a choice-based explanation of school-to-work transitions framed by institutional settings that deliver opportunities (Kerckhoff 1995) is favoured. Additionally, time-varying opportunity sets, such as the business cycle or demographic factors, are to be considered intervening factors, especially with regard to cross-country comparisons of country-specific institutions, and institution-based mechanisms are to be considered. Furthermore, institutions may interact with time-varying factors, such as the business cycle, in a country-specific way. According to Boeri and Jimeno, the interactions of institutions with the magnitude and nature of the shocks from the Great Recession and the Eurozone debt crisis are to be considered (Boeri and Jimeno 2016:32).

Time-varying opportunity sets – especially the business cycle and economic growth on one side and population effects such as the variation of cohort size over time caused by fertility, migration or mortality – are to be considered time- and cohort-specific opportunity sets. Furthermore, time-specific factors such as demand-side (business cycle) and supply-side factors (cohort-specific birth rates, migration and life expectancy) affect individuals' entry probability. Independent from other factors, the literature introduced the business cycle as a key factor for the overall level of young people becoming unemployed. Germany and Greece differ distinctly by the shape that the business cycle took in the aftermath of the Great Recession, while at the zenith of the Recession, the business cycle moved similarly (Figure 6.7).

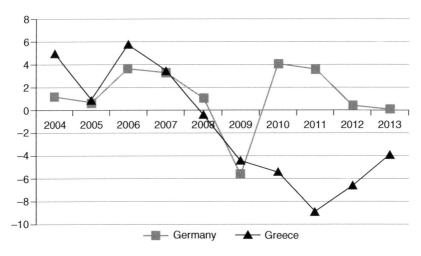

Figure 6.7 Real growth rate (GDP change) – Germany and Greece – 2004–2013.
Source: EUROSTAT-LFS scientific use file 2013; own calculations.

The demographic factor

With regard to the demographic factor in general, an increasing youth population is reducing individuals' labour market perspectives and increasing competition within the youth population and vice versa. In the case of Germany, we observe a non-linear decrease of the youth population from 9.8 million in 2004 to 9.1 million in 2013 (−7 percentage points). This reduction was mostly caused by the post-unification fertility effect in the New German Länder. The youth labour market participation rate (share of work force of the youth population) remained more or less stable over this observation window (approximately 50 per cent) in Germany; the correlation is negative but not very strong (−0.65). In the Greek case, the youth population decreased more pronouncedly from 1.4 million in 2004 to 1.1 million in 2013 (−20 percentage points). For the same period, the labour market participation rate decreased remarkably from 2004 to 2008, which is more or less constant from 2008 to 2010, and reduced again from 2011 to 2013. The correlation is positive and strong (0.91).

3 Data and methods

3.1 LFS data and population of analysis

The European Labour Force Survey (LFS) data from wave 2004 to wave 2013 are employed to analyse youth unemployment in Germany and Greece. The Germany labour force survey is conducted as a household survey and is identified by a two-step sampling procedure (regions, blocks and dwelling units, plus

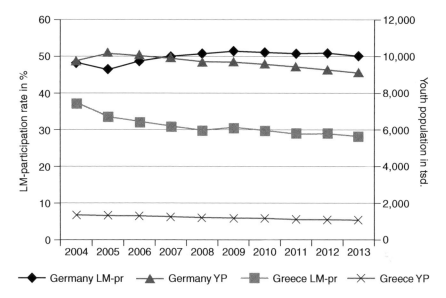

Figure 6.8 Youth population size and youth LM participation rate – Germany and Greece – 2004–2013.

Source: EUROSTAT-LFS scientific use file 2013; own calculations.

Notes
LM-pr=labour market participation rate; YP=youth population.

institutional households), where each household is included for four consecutive years in the survey. Survey participation in Germany is mandatory, and the attrition rate is close to 100 per cent. Fifty-six per cent of the annual interviews are performed as personal interviews; a significant share of interviews is conducted as proxy interviews, where a household member is delivering information for a third person.

In the Greek case, the survey is conducted as a household survey. Households are identified by a two-step sampling procedure (regions and blocks and dwelling units, without institutional households), where households are included in the survey for six consecutive quarters. Survey participation is moderate (response rate 2013: 76 per cent, Eurostat 2014b: 19). Between 2004 and 2013, the average share of proxy interviews for Greece is 60 per cent, with a significant proxy effect for underreporting unemployment.

Age is a factor that is dealt with in a manner of immense disparity, both as definitional and as registered results and performance with regard to youth. Some definitions of youth regard the age category from 15 to 25 years of age as the youth population. Other definitions are derived both from practical work (such as social policy or youth work) and theory (e.g. youth sociology or life course research), which suggest a relaxed definition of youth. Here, the age limit is set less strictly; even people aged 32 and even 35 could be included in the youth category. Furthermore, country-specific differences are to be considered (see Dietrich 2013 for a detailed presentation of the definitional discrepancies with regard to age and youth unemployment). Most importantly, however, depending on the age category taken into consideration, the results obtained regarding youth unemployment are quite different due to the myriad personal characteristics that differ among the different "youth" age groups in terms of experience, educational level, etc., which leads both to different employment benefits and different unemployment period lengths (see Dietrich 2013 for a detailed analysis for all EU countries).

In contrast to the standard literature on youth unemployment, there is no strict age definition (below 25 years of age); instead, a dynamic definition derived from a StWT-perspective is applied. In the following section, the first five years of individuals' potential years on the labour market are used for analysis.

3.2 Variables

As a dependent variable, the unemployment rate within the first five years of being on the labour market is calculated. Figure 6.9 contrasts the newly cal-culated unemployment rate of people who have been on the labour market for up to five years (5yUR) with the classical young peoples' (below 25 years of age) unemployment rate (YUR). As Figure 6.9 indicates, for both Germany and Greece, there are almost no observable differences between the youth unemployment rate and the unemployment rate of young people below the

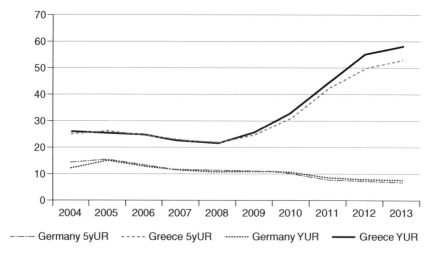

Figure 6.9 Unemployment rate of young people below 25 years of age (YUR) versus people who have spent their first five years on the labour market (5yUR) – Germany and Greece 2004–2013.

Source: EUROSTAT-LFS scientific use file 2013; own calculations.

age of 35 who have spent up to five years on the labour market before the Great Recession. However, differences emerge in the crisis years, especially in Greece.

At the macro level, GDP growth as the percentage of the weighted difference of the GDP from two consecutive years[5] is employed to control for the business cycle. Additionally, the GDP-growth in its one-year-lagged form is included to address the cumulative effect of the business cycle on unemployment. The growth of the youth population is applied as the weighted difference of the youth population from two consecutive years. Control for institutional effects, shares in temporary employment, part-time work or search strategies are included.

At the micro level, there are two variables of interest: the highest educational level individuals have attained and individuals' years on the labour market. Years on the labour market is applied as a proxy for potential labour market experience.

Gender, migration background, marital status and urban status are employed as controls. As an additional control, a proxy variable is included that indicates whether the data derive from personal interviews or third-party interviews regarding the person of interest (tables of descriptive variables are presented in the Appendix, Table A6.1 for Germany and Table A6.2 for Greece).

3.3 Estimation strategy

The chapter follows a two-step estimation strategy of modelling year-country models at the micro level in the first step to identify individual effects over time within the two countries of interest. In a second step, country models are estimated covering the whole observation window, where macro variables will be included stepwise.

The specification of the first step logit of interest can be stated as follows:

$$\text{Logit}(Y_{1/0} \mid X_i = x_i) = \beta_0 + \beta_1 X_1 + \cdots + \beta_n X_n,$$

where Y is the individual labour market status in the year of observation that has a binary outcome: employed and unemployed in year t; and $X_{1...n}$ represent the time-varying characteristics of respondents, especially potential years on the labour market since graduation and highest level of education attained. As controls, gender, citizenship, marital status and urban status of place of residence are included.

In a second step, business cycle information and the growth of the youth population are included. Additionally, time-varying institutional variables are included in separate models to avoid collinearity:[6] share of part-time employment, share of temporary employment (not including apprenticeship training), self-employment rate in the youth stage, share of young people using PES and informal search channels.

The average marginal effects of these estimations are obtained for the purposes of comparison.

4 Determinants of youth unemployment in the years of crisis – a comparative analysis

Our analysis first considers the two countries of interest – Greece and Germany – separately, analysing them on the basis of the same type of empirical model. In the first state, the effect of individual factors on the risk of being unemployed is modelled year by year. In the next step, macro variables are introduced, and finally, in a stepwise process, a set of variables controlling for institutional effects is used. Generally, for both countries, the used model (1) behaves in a statistically stable way with the hypothesized explanatory variables showing high level of significance.

4.1 Individual factors and the risk of being unemployed within the school-to-work transition – micro models for Germany and Greece

It is common in both countries that – in line with our theoretical expectations – education has a dramatic effect on the risk of being unemployed. More importantly, this effect even holds in strong recessions. However, in recession years, the effect of education weakened to a certain degree. Graph 6.1 compares the effect of Greece and Germany (for more details, see Table A6.3 for Germany and Table A6.4 for Greece). In Germany, the level of education is distinct, especially between low-qualified individuals at the one hand and medium or higher qualified individuals on the other hand, and with less variation over time, we observe a distinction in Greece between lower- and medium-side qualification on the one side, tertiary education on the other side and severe variation over time. These findings indicate a less clear distinction between lower- and medium-level educational degrees in Greece compared to Germany, where the medium level of educational degrees is characterized by apprenticeship training degrees.

In line with our theoretical assumptions regarding the StWT process and related arguments, such as the job-search theory or job-shopping within the first five years on the labour market, which capture the labour market entry process, the risk of being unemployed decreases year by year.

Graph 6.2 compares the entry process for the first five years on the labour market in Germany and Greece.

Third, individual characteristics identifying the mechanism of segregation or even discrimination indicate stronger effects in times of unemployment when the competition becomes more severe (Biddle and Hamermesh 2013; Baert *et al.* 2015). As Tables A6.3 and A6.4 indicate, the group-specific unemployment risk of females or migrants decreases, with an overall reduction of unemployment in Germany, while in the case of Greece, these groups experienced a decreasing risk of unemployment when the overall unemployment increased.

As a special case, the proxy problem is mentioned here. In proxy interviews, household members report for other household members. From a social

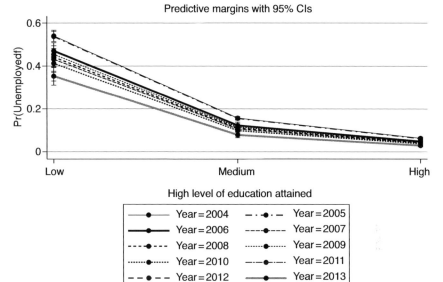

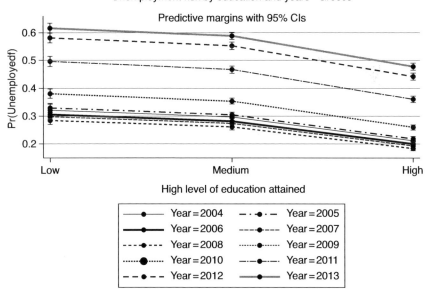

Graph 6.1 Unemployment risk by education and years – Germany and Greece.

Source: EUROSTAT-LFS scientific use file 2013; own calculations.

Note
For coding of educational level see note 2.

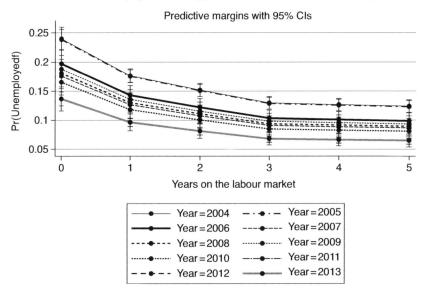

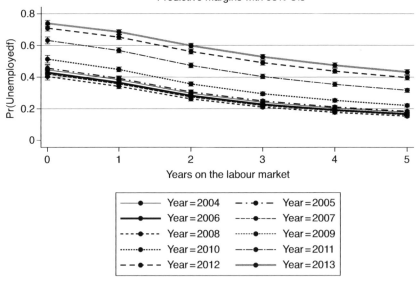

Graph 6.2 Unemployment risk by years on the labour market – Germany and Greece

Source: EUROSTAT-LFS scientific use file 2013; own calculations.

theory, it could be expected that individuals might be reluctant to report household members' unemployment or job search activity (Blair *et al.* 1991). In the German case, we found no significant effect of the proxy variable for any wave; in the Greek case, the proxy variable becomes significant in almost all waves. However, excluding proxy interviews, the R^2 increased, but the direction of the coefficient remains. Thus, the results for the whole sample are reported.

4.2 Country-specific models for Germany and Greece combining micro and macro perspectives

In the second step, macro variables are considered. Due to our theoretical motivation, the business cycle is of key interest. To control for the cumulative effect of downturns or upturns, the lagged GDP growth is also included. As shown in Tables A6.5 and A6.6, the GDP effect and the lagged effect indicate a strong non-linear effect for Greece, while for Germany, the effect appears to be rather weak.

As a second factor, which directly affects individuals' opportunity structure, the cohort size of young people is introduced in the estimates. A change in the cohort size of the youth population is strongly positive and is correlated with unemployment in both Germany and Greece. This indicates that a declining number of young people in the years around the Great Recession is associated with a reduction of the unemployment risk in the first years of labour market entry. However, the causal structure is not clearly identified by the model.

Based on the introducing indicator for institutional settings at the country level, such as the share of young people working in temporary contracts (excluding apprenticeship training contracts) or part-time contracts or the self-employment rate of young people, the results indicate factor-specific associations of the type of contracts with individuals' risk of being unemployed in the first years of the labour market entry. In both countries, part-time work and self-employment are positively associated with unemployment in the years of transition. To the contrary, the share of temporary contracts is associated negatively with unemployment at the beginning of individuals' employment careers. The effects of searches at the beginning of the employment career appears to be country-specific. In Germany, employing the PES as a search channel is positively associated with unemployment. In times of high unemployment, labour market entrants show a higher propensity to employ PES with their job search, while the job search channel of "asking friends" is negatively correlated with unemployment. In the Greek case, neither search channel is correlated with individuals' unemployment risk upon labour market entry.

5 Discussion and conclusions

In summary, the current chapter presents a descriptive analysis and logistic regression models with average marginal effects presented for Greece and

Germany. Based on the extensive micro-level data sets of the Eurostat Labour Force Survey, the analysis explores young people's unemployment risk in Germany and Greece. In contrast to the literature, where unemployment in the youth stage (below the age of 25) is used, here, individuals' first five years on the labour market are addressed. The chosen attempt follows the school-to-work-framework. With regard to youth unemployment, an age-based approach is connected with severe limitations. Graduates from higher education in particular experience only a short or even no labour market experience in the statistical youth age below 25. The approach applied here relaxes the age limitation and observes each individual for the first five potential years on the labour market. This approach identifies similarities and dissimilarities regarding the unemployment risk for graduates from all levels of education. All educational groups show a high risk of unemployment in the first year of the labour market entry; however, the speed of recovery is correlated with the level of educational degree. Academics in Greece and both upper-secondary (apprenticeship)-trained individuals and academics in Germany are more quickly integrated into the labour market and appear to be better protected from unemployment compared to respectively lower qualified individuals in each country. These findings may also reflect differences within the educational systems in Germany and Greece. In Germany, upper-secondary education and especially apprenticeship training prepares individuals well for the labour market; however, the corresponding level of education in Greece is less market oriented. The analysis indicates a strong distinction between lower- and upper-secondary education in Germany, while in Greece, secondary-level degrees appear to be devalued in terms of labour market relevance.

This pattern holds for the whole observation window, even in the years of recession. In the years of recession, however, different amplitude and timing are seen. Thus, the analyses identify systematic time-dependent processes of integration into the labour market for both Germany and Greece.

Country-specific differences are connected with the specific extent to which both countries were affected by the Great Recession and its consequences. While in the German case, the Great Recession shows a sharp but short decrease in GDP growth, which scarcely affected the youth unemployment rate, in the Greek case, the Great Recession caused a severe and long-lasting economic downturn and a dramatic increase in youth unemployment until the end of the observation window in 2013. However, in both countries, episodes of an above-average risk of youth unemployment are associated with higher shares of part-time employment and self-employment.

In Germany, the supportive function of PES is especially employed in years of economic downturn, but we did not observe a similar pattern for Greece. This finding might be explained by the weakness of the Greek PES in general.

Appendix

Table A6.1 Descriptive statistics – Germany 2004–2013

Year	2004	2005	2006	2007	2008	2009	2010	2011	2012	2013
Dependent variable										
Unemployed	14.49	15.78	13.16	11.98	11.39	11.46	10.36	8.15	7.47	7.33
Explanatory variables										
GDP		0.7	3.7	3.3	1.1	−5.6	4.1	3.6	0.4	0.1
GDP lagged		1.2	0.7	3.7	3.3	1.1	−5.6	4.1	3.6	0.4
Youth population growth		4.20	−1.51	−0.90	−2.06	−0.22	−1.61	−1.41	−1.78	−1.61
Job search channel: friends		35.3	33.79	36.02	37.09	38.72	38.78	38.73	39.42	39.34
Potential years on LM										
0	5.87	10.22	11.24	12.08	11.23	10.61	11.12	10.34	9.59	9.26
1	21.21	19.04	19.19	19.02	19.32	20.4	18.21	19.61	19.5	20.01
2	18.71	18.79	20.15	18.28	19.96	19.61	19.16	17.66	19.37	19.04
3	18.84	17.18	17.2	17.05	16.88	16.58	17.6	19.01	17.79	18.02
4	17.83	17.72	17.41	18.6	15.88	18.59	17.1	16.74	17.54	16.98
5	17.53	17.05	14.81	14.97	16.74	14.21	16.81	16.64	16.22	16.7
High degree attained										
Low	6.04	7.99	8.77	9.91	7.8	6.6	7.49	7.13	6.01	5.6
Medium	61.47	61.22	60.82	58.15	58.25	59.87	58.72	57.61	55.63	55.03
High	32.49	30.79	30.41	31.94	33.95	33.52	33.79	35.26	38.35	39.37
Female	46.49	45.38	47.25	47.05	46.84	47.89	46.31	47.42	46.74	46.76
Single	83.88	83.31	84.96	84.74	82.44	84.79	84.6	85.05	83.94	83.93
German citizen	92.22	91.5	93.48	94.01	92.06	92.78	91.56	90.03	90.87	90.4
Urbanity										
Densely populated area	50.37	51.87	52.11	52.1	54.02	52.78	56.92	52.69	42.96	43.17
Intermediate area	30.5	30.2	32.61	33.04	32.75	34.65	30.23	33.81	37.28	37.41
Thinly populated area	19.13	17.93	15.28	14.87	13.23	12.57	12.85	13.5	19.76	19.42
Self-reported	63.21	65.1	65.51	62.5	65.04	66.18	64.27	66.85	67.62	68.47
N (unweighted)	11,105	20,294	2,210	2,119	2,166	2,123	2,109	2,182	21,406	20,639

Table A6.2 Descriptive statistics – Greece 2004–2013

Year	2004	2005	2006	2007	2008	2009	2010	2011	2012	2013
Dependent variable										
Unemployed	25.43	26.26	24.5	22.99	21.78	24.87	31.22	42.19	49.95	53.3
Explanatory variables										
GDP	5	0.9	5.8	3.5	−0.4	−4.4	−5.4	−8.9	−6.6	−3.9
GDP lagged	6.6	5	0.9	5.8	3.5	−0.4	−4.4	−5.4	−8.9	−6.6
Youth population growth	−2.12	−2.52	−2.44	−2.51	−3.04	−2.81	−2.47	−2.45	−1.91	−1.68
Search channel: friends	89.96	89	91.03	86.8	88.88	92.03	93.07	94.35	93.48	93.9
Potential years on LM										
0	0.15	2.78	3.56	3.43	3.82	3.93	3.54	4.18	3.53	4.42
1	16.99	12.66	15.28	13.42	12.63	13.5	14.09	14.06	14.75	14.32
2	18.08	17.11	18.21	19	17.73	16.32	16.74	18.91	19.03	17.86
3	18.66	22.28	18.7	20.41	20.99	19.48	19.65	20.37	21.52	21.38
4	22.62	20.92	23.04	20.17	22.48	22.05	22.23	20.92	20.7	19.2
5	23.51	24.25	21.2	23.58	22.35	24.71	23.76	21.55	20.47	22.82
High degree attained										
Low	6.32	6.2	10.21	8.38	9.57	8.21	6.98	7.31	6.43	6.02
Medium	55.73	54.78	45.28	41.87	38.84	39.84	39.74	37.08	36.46	36.62
High	37.95	39.02	44.51	49.75	51.58	51.95	53.28	55.61	57.11	57.36
Female	53.68	53.93	53.29	53.1	52.9	54.54	54.48	53.25	53.59	51.02
Single	86.53	90.34	92.02	92.74	92.73	91.64	91.75	92.26	92.05	92.94
German citizen	95.79	94.95	95.34	95.34	94.73	94.14	94.27	94.84	94.64	94.51
Urbanity										
Densely populated area	75.51	74.55	72.79	75.23	75.13	42.15	46.72	47.67	47.24	44.21
Intermediate area	10.21	10.89	11.66	11.27	10.8	10.38	14.05	12.84	28.13	29.54
Thinly populated area	14.28	14.56	15.55	13.5	14.07	47.47	39.23	39.48	24.63	26.26
Self-reported	36.44	33.58	33.78	34.33	32.57	32.81	32.34	33.34	35.91	35.44
N (unweighted)	3,161	11,400	10,506	9,838	9,516	9,918	10,039	8,833	8,159	8,299

Table A6.3 Individual characteristics – Germany – annual models (AME – logit models) – 2004–2013

	2004	2005	2006	2007	2008	2009	2010	2011	2012	2013
Potential years on LM (ref=0)	0	0	0	0	0	0	0	0	0	0
	(.)	(.)	(.)	(.)	(.)	(.)	(.)	(.)	(.)	(.)
1	-0.0880***	-0.0695***	-0.0358	-0.0272	-0.0974**	-0.0583	-0.0457	-0.0454	-0.0193*	-0.0429***
	(-4.59)	(-6.08)	(-1.19)	(-1.02)	(-3.21)	(-1.91)	(-1.58)	(-1.60)	(-2.36)	(-4.92)
2	-0.138***	-0.100***	-0.0506	-0.0483	-0.0791*	-0.0704**	-0.0910**	-0.0544	-0.0417***	-0.0579***
	(-7.28)	(-8.97)	(-1.68)	(-1.86)	(-2.55)	(-2.34)	(-3.27)	(-1.88)	(-5.29)	(-6.82)
3	-0.146***	-0.127***	-0.0762*	-0.0535*	-0.118***	-0.0741**	-0.0997***	-0.0859**	-0.0529***	-0.0649***
	(-7.73)	(-11.45)	(-2.55)	(-2.05)	(-3.85)	(-2.42)	(-3.62)	(-3.16)	(-6.81)	(-7.72)
4	-0.151***	-0.134***	-0.0796**	-0.0764***	-0.0917**	-0.101***	-0.0858***	-0.0875***	-0.0434***	-0.0681***
	(-7.96)	(-12.15)	(-2.67)	(-2.98)	(-2.90)	(-3.40)	(-3.00)	(-3.23)	(-5.51)	(-8.05)
5	-0.155***	-0.140***	-0.0867**	-0.0633*	-0.111***	-0.111***	-0.0915***	-0.0653*	-0.0545***	-0.0617***
	(-8.18)	(-12.62)	(-2.84)	(-2.33)	(-3.57)	(-3.69)	(-3.25)	(-2.35)	(-6.88)	(-7.16)
High degree attained (Ref=low)	0	0	0	0	0	0	0	0	0	0
	(.)	(.)	(.)	(.)	(.)	(.)	(.)	(.)	(.)	(.)
Medium	-0.298***	-0.352***	-0.300***	-0.380***	-0.311***	-0.366***	-0.352***	-0.269***	-0.330***	-0.283***
	(-14.08)	(-25.13)	(-7.80)	(-10.16)	(-7.15)	(-8.38)	(-8.38)	(-6.27)	(-21.48)	(-18.09)
High	-0.398***	-0.446***	-0.385***	-0.449***	-0.374***	-0.423***	-0.411***	-0.326***	-0.373***	-0.327***
	(-18.80)	(-31.39)	(-9.93)	(-12.14)	(-8.59)	(-9.59)	(-9.77)	(-7.75)	(-24.29)	(-20.97)
Female	-0.0425***	-0.0224***	-0.0186	-0.00747	0.00254	-0.0213	-0.0137	-0.0241*	-0.00434	-0.00608
	(-6.28)	(-4.33)	(-1.33)	(-0.56)	(0.18)	(-1.57)	(-1.05)	(-1.97)	(-1.23)	(-1.69)
German citizen	-0.0200	-0.0366***	-0.0691**	0.0326	-0.0559*	-0.0290	-0.00763	0.00702	-0.0280***	-0.0113
	(-1.45)	(-3.43)	(-2.61)	(1.14)	(-2.21)	(-0.96)	(-0.34)	(0.32)	(-4.54)	(-1.74)
Single	0.0229*	-0.00170	-0.00140	-0.0173	0.0140	0.0273	0.0371	0.0204	0.0214***	0.000977
	(2.16)	(-0.20)	(-0.07)	(-0.86)	(0.68)	(1.13)	(1.51)	(0.94)	(3.43)	(0.17)
Urbanity (Ref= Densely populated area)	0	0	0	0	0	0	0	0	0	0
	(.)	(.)	(.)	(.)	(.)	(.)	(.)	(.)	(.)	(.)
Intermediate area	-0.0239**	-0.0287***	-0.0123	-0.0412**	-0.0303*	-0.0219	-0.0229	-0.0332**	-0.0162***	-0.0212***
	(-3.15)	(-5.01)	(-0.78)	(-2.82)	(-2.08)	(-1.50)	(-1.62)	(-2.67)	(-3.96)	(-5.01)
Thinly populated area	-0.000523	0.00733	0.00235	-0.0215	0.0148	-0.0238	-0.0399*	-0.00186	-0.0277***	-0.0075***
	(-0.06)	(0.99)	(0.12)	(-1.11)	(0.64)	(-1.07)	(-2.18)	(-0.09)	(-6.03)	(-5.59)
Self-reported	-0.0101	-0.000496	0.00824	-0.00673	0.00915	0.0165	0.0165	0.00551	0.00167	-0.00376
	(-1.46)	(-0.09)	(0.55)	(-0.49)	(0.63)	(1.10)	(1.19)	(0.42)	(0.44)	(-0.98)
N	11,105	20,294	2,210	2,119	2,166	2,123	2,109	2,182	21,406	20,639

Notes
t statistics in parentheses.
* p < 0.05, ** p < 0.01, *** p < 0.001.

Table A6.4 Individual characteristics – Greece – annual models (AME – logit models) – 2004–2013

	2004	2005	2006	2007	2008	2009	2010	2011	2012	2013
Potential years on LM (ref=0)	0	0	0	0	0	0	0	0	0	0
	(.)	(.)	(.)	(.)	(.)	(.)	(.)	(.)	(.)	(.)
1	0.220	-0.0973**	0.0369	-0.131***	-0.0254	-0.119***	-0.142***	-0.0473	-0.0608	-0.00231
	(1.55)	(-2.93)	(1.19)	(-3.95)	(-0.85)	(-3.93)	(-4.53)	(-1.52)	(-1.73)	(-0.07)
2	0.112	-0.135***	-0.0725*	-0.188***	-0.124***	-0.187***	-0.216***	-0.198***	-0.0857*	-0.143***
	(0.79)	(-4.16)	(-2.41)	(-5.90)	(-4.33)	(-6.31)	(-7.06)	(-6.53)	(-2.51)	(-4.44)
3	0.109	-0.238***	-0.0916*	-0.255***	-0.206***	-0.276***	-0.293***	-0.281***	-0.188***	-0.125***
	(0.77)	(-7.51)	(-3.07)	(-8.13)	(-7.43)	(-9.59)	(-9.72)	(-9.40)	(-5.52)	(-3.97)
4	0.0591	-0.295***	-0.152***	-0.276***	-0.212***	-0.290***	-0.368***	-0.282***	-0.249***	-0.182***
	(0.42)	(-9.32)	(-5.19)	(-8.86)	(-7.64)	(-10.13)	(-12.45)	(-9.49)	(-7.42)	(-5.68)
5	0.00859	-0.329***	-0.171***	-0.302***	-0.268***	-0.321***	-0.380***	-0.329***	-0.220***	-0.234***
	(0.06)	(-10.51)	(-5.83)	(-9.77)	(-9.81)	(-11.34)	(-12.90)	(-11.26)	(-6.46)	(-7.52)
High degree attained (Ref=low)	0	0	0	0	0	0	0	0	0	0
	(.)	(.)	(.)	(.)	(.)	(.)	(.)	(.)	(.)	(.)
Medium	0.00383	-0.00253	-0.0350*	-0.0132	-0.0477**	-0.0508**	-0.0872***	-0.0607**	0.0256	-0.0142
	(0.10)	(-0.12)	(-2.12)	(-0.74)	(-2.73)	(-2.75)	(-4.27)	(-2.65)	(1.04)	(-0.59)
High	-0.0724	-0.0753***	-0.113***	-0.0589***	-0.119***	-0.120***	-0.161***	-0.141***	-0.129***	-0.175***
	(-1.75)	(-3.36)	(-6.83)	(-3.26)	(-6.76)	(-6.43)	(-7.77)	(-6.02)	(-5.21)	(-7.13)
Female	0.113***	0.104***	0.108***	0.0923***	0.0722***	0.0802***	0.0899***	0.0648***	0.0742***	0.0786***
	(6.75)	(11.76)	(11.63)	(9.83)	(7.91)	(8.55)	(8.98)	(5.46)	(5.89)	(6.45)
German citizen	0.0883	0.113***	0.0375	0.00792	0.0777***	0.0942***	0.0173	-0.00123	-0.0422	-0.0857**
	(1.77)	(4.52)	(1.56)	(0.35)	(3.50)	(4.48)	(0.84)	(-0.05)	(-1.45)	(-3.12)
Single	0.0500	0.0478**	0.0469*	0.0723***	0.0777***	0.0241	0.0302	0.0761***	0.0857***	0.0583*
	(1.78)	(2.85)	(2.44)	(3.60)	(3.98)	(1.40)	(1.69)	(3.56)	(3.66)	(2.38)
Urbanity (Ref= Densely populated area)	0	0	0	0	0	0	0	0	0	0
	(.)	(.)	(.)	(.)	(.)	(.)	(.)	(.)	(.)	(.)
Intermediate area	0.0387	0.0395**	0.0424***	0.0318*	-0.00311	-0.00745	-0.00184	-0.00108	0.0660***	-0.0269
	(1.55)	(3.04)	(3.30)	(2.37)	(-0.24)	(-0.48)	(-0.12)	(-0.05)	(4.33)	(-1.86)
Thinly populated area	0.0508*	0.0414***	0.0225	0.0281*	0.0144	0.0388***	0.0433***	0.0471***	0.0938***	0.0513***
	(2.30)	(3.59)	(1.96)	(2.24)	(1.20)	(3.87)	(4.07)	(3.77)	(6.37)	(3.49)
Self-reported	-0.0382*	-0.0128	-0.0304***	-0.0190*	-0.0322***	-0.0426***	-0.0532***	-0.0666***	-0.0615***	-0.0718***
	(-2.15)	(-1.34)	(-3.15)	(-1.97)	(-3.33)	(-4.25)	(-4.94)	(-5.33)	(-4.75)	(-5.75)
N	3,161	11,400	10,506	9,838	9,516	9,918	10,039	8,833	8,159	8,299

Notes

t statistics in parentheses.

* $p < 0.05$, ** $p < 0.01$, *** $p < 0.001$.

Table A6.5 Individual, institutional and macro characteristics – Germany – (AME – logit models) – 2004–2013

	Individual	GDP	GDP+pop	Individual-GDP-pop	+temp	+part-time	+self-employed	+PES	+friends
Years on labour market									
0	0			0	0	0	0	0	0
	(.)			(.)	(.)	(.)	(.)	(.)	(.)
1	-0.0494***			-0.0495***	-0.0494***	-0.0480***	-0.0494***	-0.0481***	-0.0485***
	(-5.85)			(-5.85)	(-5.85)	(-5.69)	(-5.85)	(-5.71)	(-5.74)
2	-0.0655***			-0.0655***	-0.0654***	-0.0641***	-0.0657***	-0.0644***	-0.0648***
	(-7.79)			(-7.78)	(-7.77)	(-7.63)	(-7.82)	(-7.66)	(-7.70)
3	-0.0839***			-0.0838***	-0.0838***	-0.0819***	-0.0835***	-0.0819***	-0.0823***
	(-10.13)			(-10.11)	(-10.11)	(-9.90)	(-10.08)	(-9.88)	(-9.92)
4	-0.0850***			-0.0853***	-0.0852***	-0.0839***	-0.0852***	-0.0840***	-0.0843***
	(-10.25)			(-10.28)	(-10.28)	(-10.15)	(-10.28)	(-10.15)	(-10.17)
5	-0.0874***			-0.0876***	-0.0876***	-0.0855***	-0.0875***	-0.0856***	-0.0860***
	(-10.40)			(-10.42)	(-10.42)	(-10.20)	(-10.42)	(-10.18)	(-10.22)
Edu level: low	0			0	0	0	0	0	0
	(.)			(.)	(.)	(.)	(.)	(.)	(.)
Medium	-0.329***			-0.328***	-0.328***	-0.323***	-0.328***	-0.323***	-0.324***
	(-26.84)			(-26.75)	(-26.78)	(-26.61)	(-26.73)	(-26.52)	(-26.52)
High	-0.395***			-0.393***	-0.393***	-0.387***	-0.392***	-0.387***	-0.388***
	(-32.23)			(-32.06)	(-32.13)	(-31.99)	(-32.01)	(-31.83)	(-31.82)
Self-reported	0.00500			0.00516	0.00527	0.00581	0.00510	0.00550	0.00526
	(1.25)			(1.29)	(1.32)	(1.46)	(1.28)	(1.38)	(1.32)
GDP growth		-0.000309	0.00113	0.0000945	-0.000545	0.000211	-0.000449	-0.00299**	-0.00257**
		(-0.39)	(1.38)	(0.12)	(-0.49)	(0.29)	(-0.54)	(-3.23)	(-2.83)
GDP growth lagged		-0.00103	-0.000794	-0.000837	-0.000560	-0.00143	0.000698	-0.00217**	-0.00186**
		(-1.42)	(-1.05)	(-1.12)	(-0.71)	(-1.90)	(0.84)	(-2.71)	(-2.32)
Youth population growth			0.00922***	0.00801***	0.00759***	0.00693***	0.00614***	0.00268***	0.00406***
			(20.81)	(17.33)	(10.87)	(13.26)	(8.52)	(2.73)	(4.86)
Share: temporary contracts					0.00154				
					(1.00)				
Share: part-time contracts						0.0124***			
						(6.86)			
Share: self-employment							0.0172***		
							(4.25)		
Share: search channel: PES								0.00249***	
								(6.71)	
Search channel: friends									-0.00820***
									(-6.18)
N	75,248	75,248	75,248	75,248	75,248	75,248	75,248	75,248	75,248

Notes

t statistics in parentheses.

* $p < 0.05$, ** $p < 0.01$, *** $p < 0.001$.

Table A6.6 Individual, institutional and macro characteristics – Greece – (AME – logit models) – 2004–2013

	Individual	GDP	GDP–pop	Individual-GDP-pop	+temp	+part-time	+self-employed	+PES	+friends
Years on labour market									
0	0 (.)			0 (.)	0 (.)	0 (.)	0 (.)	0 (.)	0 (.)
1	-0.0651*** (-5.88)			-0.0653*** (-6.04)	-0.0655*** (-6.06)	-0.0641*** (-5.93)	-0.0652*** (-6.03)	-0.0653*** (-6.04)	-0.0653*** (-6.04)
2	-0.150*** (-13.88)			-0.148*** (-14.06)	-0.149*** (-14.09)	-0.147*** (-13.95)	-0.148*** (-14.08)	-0.148*** (-14.06)	-0.148*** (-14.06)
3	-0.215*** (-20.28)			-0.216*** (-20.81)	-0.216*** (-20.81)	-0.215*** (-20.71)	-0.215*** (-20.76)	-0.216*** (-20.81)	-0.216*** (-20.81)
4	-0.262*** (-24.85)			-0.257*** (-24.94)	-0.257*** (-24.94)	-0.255*** (-24.82)	-0.256*** (-24.90)	-0.257*** (-24.94)	-0.257*** (-24.94)
5	-0.288*** (-27.56)			-0.285*** (-27.94)	-0.285*** (-27.92)	-0.284*** (-27.85)	-0.284*** (-27.87)	-0.285*** (-27.95)	-0.285*** (-27.95)
Edu level: low	0 (.)			0 (.)	0 (.)	0 (.)	0 (.)	0 (.)	0 (.)
Medium	-0.0140* (-2.05)			-0.0310*** (-4.67)	-0.0308*** (-4.63)	-0.0301*** (-4.54)	-0.0298*** (-4.48)	-0.0311*** (-4.68)	-0.0310*** (-4.67)
High	-0.0832*** (-11.97)			-0.122*** (-18.08)	-0.122*** (-17.99)	-0.123*** (-18.07)	-0.121*** (-17.92)	-0.122*** (-18.07)	-0.122*** (-18.07)
Self-reported	-0.0371*** (-9.83)			-0.0419*** (-11.43)	-0.0421*** (-11.46)	-0.0418*** (-11.40)	-0.0420*** (-11.45)	-0.0419*** (-11.43)	-0.0419*** (-11.43)
GDP growth		0.00175** (3.06)	-0.00991*** (-13.47)	-0.0102*** (-14.42)	-0.0122*** (-12.64)	-0.00802*** (-10.41)	-0.0101*** (-14.37)	-0.0103*** (-13.46)	-0.0102*** (-14.43)
GDP growth lagged		-0.0207*** (-38.50)	-0.00145 (-1.67)	-0.000670 (-0.80)	0.000418 (0.47)	0.00206* (2.16)	0.00227* (2.38)	-0.000650 (-0.77)	-0.000764 (-0.54)
Youth population growth			0.198*** (26.82)	0.207*** (28.64)	0.203*** (27.50)	0.150*** (14.40)	0.156*** (14.25)	0.206*** (26.36)	0.207*** (26.61)
Share: temporary contracts					-0.00518** (-2.99)				
Share: part-time contracts						0.0117*** (7.08)			
Share: self-employment							0.0132*** (6.46)		
Share: search channel: PES								0.000118 (0.17)	
Search channel: friends									-0.000187 (-0.09)
N	86,508	86,508	86,508	86,508	86,508	86,508	86,508	86,508	86,508

Notes
Controls: gender, citizenship, and urbanity; robust standard errors; weighted data.
T statistics in parentheses, * $p < 0.05$, ** $p < 0.01$, *** $p < 0.001$.

Notes

1 This chapter has been supported by travelling grants from DAAD and IKY.
2 In the following, the educational levels represent collapsed ISCED (UNESCO 2013) codes (low indicates ISCED codes of 0 to 2 and includes lower secondary degrees as the highest degree; medium indicates ISCED codes of 3 to 4, including upper secondary degrees; high indicates ISCED codes of 5 and higher, including tertiary degrees) (see Eurostat 2014a).
3 See https://webgate.ec.europa.eu/fpfis/mwikis/eurydice/index.php/Greece:Secondary_ and_Post-Secondary_Non-Tertiary_Education.
4 Unemployed people, in the case of LFS, are respondents who are not working but are searching for work, while respondents without a job and are not searching for work are classified as inactive.
5 Source: Eurostat (Table tec00115).
6 See Blanchard and Wolfers (2000) for the interaction of shocks and institutions and Sachs and Smolny (2014) for collinearity and possible reversed causality problems in greater detail.

7 Unemployed and NEET youth

Well-being in a gender perspective – the case of Italy and Spain

Tindara Addabbo, Paula Rodríguez-Modroño and Lina Gálvez-Muñoz

1 Introduction

Labour market vulnerability among young people is one of the most scarring effects of the Great Recession, especially in Europe. In fact, several analyses of the group popularly known as millennials show that they are at risk of becoming the first-ever generation to register lower lifetime earnings or lower levels of home ownership than their predecessors (Gardiner 2016), making them a deeply pessimistic generation (Economic Innovation Group 2016).

Even though, at the European Union (EU) level, the situation has improved since 2014, in 2013 over 5.5 million young Europeans aged 15–24 were still unemployed, this being the highest level of youth unemployment ever recorded in the history of the EU (Eurofound 2016). During the crisis, 17 EU member states reached their highest-ever levels of youth unemployment (Eurofound 2014). Despite the significantly high youth unemployment data and its multiple scarring effects, the recent economic crisis has proved how unemployment is not the best indicator for showing youth labour market vulnerability and social exclusion, or to what extent Europe is facing 'a lost generation'. The NEET concept (young people not in employment, education or training) has become widely used at research and policy levels in order to fully understand multifaceted youth labour market vulnerability, as well as young people's economic opportunities or risk of social exclusion in the crisis and post-crisis contexts, as characterized by the effects of the IT revolution, globalization and austerity policies. The probability of being socially excluded is higher the longer the duration of the NEET experience. And the persistence in the NEET status is more likely to occur among youth coming from more disadvantaged backgrounds and with lower educational levels (Carcillo *et al.* 2015). Also before the crisis, youth leaving school earlier were found to be trapped at the margins of the labour market (OECD 2010, 2016).

While young people have been particularly hit by the crisis compared to the overall working-age population in all European countries (Dolado 2015), there are important differences at a national, regional and local level, as well as specific problems faced by the different population groups. In fact, one of the main criticisms levelled at the NEET concept is the heterogeneity of the population that it captures (Eurofound 2016). In order to improve our knowledge of the behaviour and reactions of this population in relation to youth policies, its heterogeneity makes it necessary to disaggregate the available data at country and regional level by personal characteristics such as, for instance, gender differences. This is precisely what the present analysis has aimed to do.

Several studies on youth labour market participation during and after the crisis have defined different clusters of countries. The Eurofound study (2016, 42–46), by grouping countries on the basis of similar NEET characteristics, identifies three clusters. The first one is composed of Nordic, Western and continental countries (plus Malta) and is characterized by 'low NEET rates with a low share of long-term unemployed and discouraged workers. Countries in this cluster are characterized by a well-functioning Youth Guarantee and strongly developed dual educational systems, and are neo-liberal economies.' The second cluster is made up of Mediterranean countries plus Ireland, having

> a high share of NEETs and a considerable share of long-term unemployed and discouraged workers. This cluster is composed of countries that have been hit very hard by the economic crisis or that have traditionally had problems ensuring smooth school-to-work transitions.

The third cluster groups together Eastern EU member states, which, despite their heterogeneity, are characterized by high percentages of NEETs due to family responsibilities, having a higher share of NEET women.

Dolado (2015, 6–9) studies youth unemployment in a smaller group of European countries – which includes some non-EU member states and excludes Eastern European countries – and classifies them into three clusters. The first group (Austria, Germany and Switzerland) is defined as successful in keeping youth unemployment low 'mostly because of their efficient use of vocational training and programs targeted at disadvantaged youth'. The second group (France, UK and Sweden) is considered less successful, mainly due to 'employment protection and minimum wages, plus a partly dysfunctional education system'. And, finally, the third group (Greece, Italy, Spain and Portugal) is the one most hardly hit by the crisis and showing the highest youth unemployment rates, because of labour market segmentation, 'lack of aggregate demand, and poor vocational training among the main reasons'.

In both classifications, Spain and Italy appear among the worst performers, as regards both youth unemployment rates and, especially, NEET percentages – they are actually the champions of this indicator. However, both countries show important differences concerning, for instance, the youth-adult unemployment gap or NEET participation by gender. They have also suffered different institutional reforms during the crisis years.

Similarities and differences between the two countries can shed light when analyzing young people's labour vulnerability in the short run, but also in the long run, the implication of such vulnerability in life satisfaction and happiness, and the differences by gender. Latest election polls and results and the rising of populism point to an important generational break and to the difficult social inclusion of young people, very much related with depressing economic opportunities and decreasing life satisfaction (Gardiner 2016).

Recent studies have revealed the links between economic crises and many stress-related manifestations, involving high risks to well-being and the quality of life, since unemployed people show low levels of self-esteem with strong effects on life satisfaction and happiness (Paul and Moser 2009; Gili *et al.* 2013; Urbanos-Garrido and López-Valcárcel 2015), including long-term effects (McKee-Ryan *et al.* 2005).

These long-term effects can lead to path dependence at an individual level. As analysed by Addabbo *et al.* (2015), this path dependence at individual level can also be combined with path dependence at national level (Anxo *et al.* 2010). In fact, at the national level, the increase of precarious jobs and non-employment among young people implies high costs for society related to the waste of youth human capital. Growth prospects are thereby reduced, also because of the risk of brain drain. The risk of poverty increases, as well as income inequalities within and across generations, while budget costs related to low fiscal revenues and high social expenditures increase (Plantenga *et al.* 2013; Addabbo *et al.* 2015).

As a matter of fact, youth unemployment and high NEET numbers relate to complex issues of labour and economic performance, but also to individual and collective well-being and to deep cultural and social changes in our societies. This work aims at contributing to clarifying this complex problem by analysing the factors that increase the risk of being NEET in Spain and Italy and its costs in terms of life satisfaction, meaning of life and financial satisfaction by gender.

The structure of the work is as follows. Section 2 includes a brief review of the literature on NEETs, youth unemployment and well-being. Section 3 examines the impact of the recent global crisis on youth unemployment and NEET rates in Spain and Italy. Section 4 presents the data and methodology. The econometric results are summarized in Section 5. Section 6 presents the conclusions and discusses some policy implications.

2 Literature review

Young people have been negatively affected to a greater extent than other populations by the recent crisis. This is related to the greater sensitivity of youth unemployment to cyclical conditions, given the lower qualifications, less experience and weaker work contracts among young workers (Brada *et al.* 2014; Choudhry Tanveer *et al.* 2012). According to recent empirical studies, the protracted recession or stagnation that has characterized this global financial and economic crisis, especially within the Eurozone, has been particularly detrimental to young people (Choudhry Tanveer *et al.* 2012).

In addition to the greater impact of the crisis on young unemployment rates (YUR) as compared to adult unemployment rates, further evidence concerns the persistence of unemployment over time and the increasing extent of long-term unemployment. Young people are not only more vulnerable to the effects of a crisis than adults are, but also these effects are likely to be more long-lasting for the young (O'Higgins 2012; Plantenga *et al*. 2013).

Youth are more exposed to the risk of being unemployed with substantially higher unemployment rates in the two countries selected for the applied analysis, and they are more likely to find themselves inactive. Thus, under bad cyclical conditions, the 'discouraged worker hypothesis' explains why YUR may not increase: to a great extent because of temporarily falling participation rates. Some young people may decide to remain in, or even return to, education during recessions (Kelly *et al*. 2014); however, in other cases, the outcome is worse, because they join the NEET group. Bruno *et al*. (2014c) find that NEET rates are persistent and that the persistence increases during periods of crisis, although with differentiated gender compositions. Research shows that the share of NEETs increases with age and decreases as educational level rises, although Southern European and Mediterranean countries such as Spain or Italy tend to have a large proportion of well-educated NEETs as a result of the crisis. Research findings also show that young women are more likely to become NEETs (Eurofound 2016; OECD 2016). Women's specialization in care explains why they are more likely to become NEETs, although not all countries have a larger percentage of women among their NEETs, as the Spanish case will show.

Regarding life satisfaction, there is plenty of evidence showing that being unable to find a job is strongly and negatively correlated with a range of well-being measures and reduces happiness. Akerlof and Shiller (2009) consider unemployment as a terrible thing, because a persons without a job not only lose their income but often as well the sense that they are fulfilling the duties expected from a human being. Employment is generally seen as the most important means of obtaining adequate economic resources, which are essential for material well-being, and full participation in today's society. In addition, work meets important psychological needs in societies where employment is the norm, since it is central to individual identity, social roles and social status (Extremera and Rey 2016).

The European Social Survey for 2002–2009 analyses unemployed workers in all 21 participating European countries and shows a life satisfaction gap between unemployed and employed workers ranging from a low of 0.5 points to a high of around 2.5 points. The study by Winkelmann (2014), which used the German socio-economic panel and allows tracking the same individual over time, reveals how, when people are re-employed, life satisfaction does not reach its early pre-unemployment level. The potential and felt scarcities and worries associated with unemployment are manifold, including less social contact, less social recognition, less money, a less structured day, less control of one's life and less certainty about what the future will bring. In addition, the pressure of psychological scarcity derived from unemployment can result in bad decision-making, as it reduces mental bandwidth. Although ineffective job search could arise from a combination of factors, and not only from a sense of psychological scarcity, the unhappiest unemployed people might also be the least employable individuals (Winkelmann 2014). One spell of unemployment may be followed by poorer subsequent employment patterns and increased risk of further periods of unemployment (Lakey 2001).

This is very important when studying young unemployed people, especially in a crisis and post-crisis context, since the massive cohort of unemployed young people faces a very different labour market.

> Developments such as the IT revolution and globalization have changed the context of the European labour market. At the same time, an enhanced level of wealth and well-being and a shift towards post-materialistic societies have affected attitudes, perceptions and behaviours within European societies, including among young people.
>
> (Eurofound 2016, 5)

The impact of unemployment on well-being and health can be modified by socio-economic status, income and degree of financial anxiety, as well as by individual factors such as gender and family status, age, education, social capital, social support, previous job satisfaction and reason for job loss, duration out of work and desire and expectancy of re-employment, plus regional deprivation and local unemployment rates. In fact, for a minority of people (5–10 per cent) unemployment can lead to improved health and well-being (Extremera and Rey 2016).

The literature also shows how important the social norm is: where unemployment is more uncommon, it is a more stigmatizing experience (Hall and Nayyar 2015). Winkelmann (2014) includes plenty of evidence supporting the hypothesis that the evaluative component of well-being depends on the degree in which one conforms to or deviates from the norms of the social group one associates with. In fact, for this author, the finding that unemployed women tend to report greater life-satisfaction than unemployed men can also be viewed as a social norm effect, particularly in more tradition-oriented societies where men are seen as the breadwinners of the household. Most evidence supporting the basic concept that work is beneficial for health and well-being is actually on men. This is consistent with time use studies showing how women increase the time devoted to household and care work much more than men when they become unemployed (Giménez-Nadal and Molina 2014).

Despite the important bulk of literature linking work and happiness (Waddell and Burton 2006; Hall and Nayyar 2015) and, more specifically, economic crises and well-being effects for unemployed people (Jahoda 1982; Winkelmann and Winkelmann 1998; Lucas *et al.* 2004; McKee-Ryan *et al.* 2005; Wanberg 2012) in the countries studied in this chapter (Gili *et al.* 2013; Urbanos-Garrido and López-Valcárcel 2015; Extremera and Rey 2016), there are not many related to youth and the NEET group.

Alfieri *et al.* (2015a) use the Youth Report Survey carried out in 2011 by the Toniolo Institute in Italy on a sample of 9,087 young Italians aged 18–29. They define NEET as 'only young people who have been outside educational, work, or training spheres for at least six months' (Alfieri *et al.* 2015a, 314). NEETs represent 15 per cent of the sample. These authors' analysis of the determinants of NEET status reveals the protective effect played by parents' higher education. Interestingly, these authors show that higher parental intrusiveness is associated with a higher likelihood that young women will become NEET. They do find, only for men, a negative effect of individual autonomy on the probability of being NEET and a negative effect of parents' support on the probability that both young men and young women will be NEET, the effect being higher for young men. Alfieri *et al.* (2015b) are also concerned with the effects that being a NEET in Italy (according to the Youth Report Survey) has on civic participation, measured by participation in voluntary activities or political groups; they show that NEETs have a lower degree of participation.

Focusing again on the differences between NEET and non-NEET youth, the analysis performed by Nardi *et al.* (2015) on a reduced sample of 111 NEETs and 117 non-NEETs aged 16–23 in Italy did not show relevant differences by NEET status on health or psychological problems.

The study by Bynner and Parsons (2002) on British longitudinal data detects a negative effect of NEET status on labour market inclusion for men and psychological costs for young women and reflects, together with lower education, different determinants by gender. Living in the inner city, for men, and lower parental interest in girls' education, for women, are associated with a higher likelihood of being NEET.

Therefore, notwithstanding the high and persistent presence of youth unemployment and NEET status, the studies on the determinants and the effects of being NEET are still limited, especially in relation to the discussion on the effects that being NEET has on subjective measures of individual well-being.

3 Youth unemployment and NEETs in Spain and Italy

The deterioration of the labour market for young people in Spain and Italy has been particularly severe. According to Eurostat Labour Force Survey data, total employment among those aged under 29 collapsed during the recession, falling by 2,545,000 jobs (−52 per cent) in Spain and 1,137,000 jobs (−30 per cent) in Italy between 2007 and 2014. While the unemployment rates for the population aged 15–74 increased from 8.2 per cent in 2007 to 24.5 per cent in 2014 in Spain, and from 6.1 per cent in 2007 to 12.7 per cent in 2014 in Italy, the Spanish youth (15–24) unemployment rate increased from 18.1 per cent in 2007 to a high of 53.2 per cent in 2014, and the Italian rose from 20.4 per cent in 2007 to 42.7 per cent in 2014. The ratio between youth and total unemployment rates in Spain is a little above 2, the same as in the EU-28; but in Italy the ratio is over 3.

Youth unemployment rates in Spain and Italy are double the average youth unemployment rate in Europe: respectively 48.3 per cent and 40.3 per cent, as compared to 20.4 per cent in 2015. However, the gap between youth and adult unemployment is larger in Italy than in Spain. This might be a consequence of greater general labour market deterioration in the Spanish case, although some authors explain the divergence by pointing to the differentiated labour market institutions.[1]

In any case, it is important to be careful when interpreting unemployment among young people, given that they may choose to remain in education rather than entering the labour market at a time of recession. This can be observed by focusing on the labour force participation rate, which has steadily fallen from 47.9 per cent in Spain and 30.8 per cent in Italy in 2007 to just 34.7 and 26.2 per cent, respectively, in 2015. The fall in participation among the younger age groups during the crisis may be explained, in the first place, by a return to education and, second, by the increasing outward migration. The participation rate of young people in education and training over the total population aged 15–24 has increased in Spain from 59 per cent in 2007 to 72 per cent in 2015, while it rose from 63 per cent to 65 per cent in Italy. Also the number of early leavers from education and training as a percentage of the total 18–24 population has dropped, from 31.7 per cent in Spain and 19.6 per cent in Italy in 2008 to, respectively, 20 and 14.7 per cent in 2015.

An alternative measure of unemployment among young people is the unemployment ratio, which not only takes into account the size of the young labour force, but the young population (active and inactive) as a whole. It provides a more accurate reflection of the unemployment situation among young people because the size of the young labour force does not trigger effects in the youth unemployment ratio, contrary to what happens with the unemployment rate. The unemployment ratio is, by definition, always smaller than the unemployment rate. The unemployment ratio for 15–24 year-olds increased sharply from 8.7 per cent in Spain and 6.3 per cent in Italy in 2007 to 19 per cent in 2014 in Spain and 11.6 per cent in 2014 in Italy. In 2015, the unemployment ratios in Spain and Italy stood, respectively, at 16.8 and 10.6 per cent for the 15–24 age group and at 24.3 and 15.1 per cent for the 25–29 age group, compared to the EU-28 average of 8.4 per cent and 10.2 per cent for each age group (Table 7.1).

Female unemployment rates are usually higher than male rates in the EU, particularly in Southern Europe, though there is clearly a tendency towards convergence of youth unemployment rates by gender. However, women still present lower unemployment ratios.

Three trends raise particular concerns in relation to young unemployed people. First, the growth in the unemployment rate of youth without formal education, which rose from 20.4 per cent of unemployed people aged 15–24 in 2007 to 61.2 per cent in 2014, in the case of Spain, and from 22.6 per cent in 2007 to 48.8 per cent in 2014 in that of Italy.

Second, the percentage of youth in a long-term unemployment situation, which increased from 10.1 per cent in Spain and 41.1 per cent in Italy in 2007 to, respectively, 40.5 per cent and 59.7 per cent in 2014. Long-term unemployment for young people has serious implications, because it prevents the accumulation of work experience, producing negative effects on lifetime income, career opportunities and unemployment incidence in later life, the so-called 'scarring effects' of youth unemployment.

Third, the rising number of young people not in employment, education or training (NEETs aged 15–29), which has grown from 12.8 per cent in 2007 to 20.7 per

Table 7.1 Youth unemployment rates and ratios by sex and age (%)

| | Unemployment rates | | | | | | Unemployment ratios | | | | | |
| | Females | | | Males | | | Females | | | Males | | |
	EU-28	Spain	Italy	EU-28	Spain	Italy	EU-28	Spain	Italy	EU-28	Spain	Italy
15–19 year-olds												
2007	20.5	35.9	37.4	19.7	23.9	27.9	4.5	7.1	3.1	5.1	6.7	3.8
2015	23.8	70.7	66.1	25.4	64.7	57.1	4.5	7.3	3.5	5.3	8.4	4.9
20–24 year-olds												
2007	14.3	18.1	20.6	13.6	12.4	16.2	8.3	11.3	8.6	9.3	9.0	9.3
2015	18.2	43.9	39.5	21.0	48.6	38.8	10.4	23.9	14.6	12.9	26.6	18.3
25–29 year-olds												
2007	9.3	10.7	12.7	8.1	7.5	8.6	7.1	8.8	8.0	7.2	6.8	6.9
2015	12.3	28.1	24.1	12.5	28.9	21.1	9.5	23.3	14.5	11.0	25.4	15.7
30–34 year-olds												
2007	7.8	9.6	8.8	5.9	5.6	5.3						
2015	10.2	23.2	15.9	9.1	20.3	12.7						

Source: Eurostat, LFS [lfsa_urgan] [yth_empl_140].

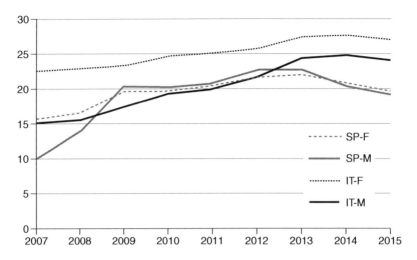

Figure 7.1 Young people (15–29 year-olds) neither in employment nor in education or training by sex (NEET rates) in Spain and Italy.

Source: Eurostat, LFS [yth_empl_150].

cent in 2014 for Spain, and from 18.8 per cent in 2007 to 26.2 per cent in 2014 for Italy. These values are among the highest in Europe, together with those of Greece, Cyprus, Bulgaria and Croatia. The growth of the NEET group is an even greater problem for society than overall unemployment, as it creates the risk of a 'lost generation'. Many authors argue that the size of the 'youth left behind' group can be better proxied by the NEET indicator than by the youth unemployment rate (Scarpetta *et al.* 2010; O'Higgins 2011) since it shows better the lack of alternatives to employment, even if the NEET group is a heterogeneous one.[2]

The estimated average age of young people leaving the parental household by sex was already high in these countries prior to the crisis, and has continued rising slightly, from 28.4 in 2007 to 29.1 in 2015 for Spain and from 29.8 to 30.1 in Italy between those same years.

As the study by Bell and Blanchflower (2015) shows, when young people have jobs, they tend to be underemployed. Youngsters are faced with a double whammy, because their job is more likely to be temporary than permanent and to have shorter hours than they would like. The increase in the share of 15–24 year-olds in temporary employment between 2008 and 2015 is especially marked in Spain, where it rose from 59 per cent to 70.4 per cent, while it augmented from 43.4 per cent to 57 per cent in Italy. The share of involuntary part-time employment as percentage of total part-time employment increased from 32.7 per cent to 54.3 per cent in Spain and from 52.6 per cent to 84.7 per cent in Italy. This chapter also analyses changes in youth's well-being since 2000 using data from the Eurobarometer Survey. Its authors find that the happiness level of the

15–24 age group fell the most in those countries most hardly hit by high youth unemployment: Portugal (−0.27 pts), Spain (−0.21 pts), Greece (−0.21 pts) and Italy (−0.13 pts). Especially sharp is the fall in happiness for those aged 25–29 in Spain (−0.21 pts) and Italy (−0.16 pts).

4 Model and data

The two countries chosen for the present study are characterized by a high likelihood of youth being jobless and living with their parents. The aim of this work is to analyse the factors that increase the risk of being a NEET for youth in the two countries and its costs in terms of lower life satisfaction, financial satisfaction and happiness.

For these purposes, the 2013 EU-SILC cross-section has been used, since it allows gathering individual and household information on variables that can affect individual satisfaction and employment status.

To measure the effect of each variable on the probability of being NEET, a probit model has been estimated (equation 1):

$$Y = \Phi(X\beta + \varepsilon) \tag{1}$$

where Y is a dummy variable taking the value of 1 if the individual is NEET and 0 otherwise; X are individual, household and context variables affecting the NEET status; β measures the effect of each variable included in the model on being NEET; and ε is the error term. The variables considered include the person's age and education level, the equivalized household income and different living arrangements, considering living as a couple as the reference situation: living with parent/s, alone, as a couple with the parents, as a lone parent or other arrangements. The marginal effects have then been computed at the mean values of the continuous variables and as the dummy variables included in the model take the value 1.

To measure the effect of the different factors on life satisfaction, the overall meaning of life and satisfaction with the financial situation, a regression model has been estimated:

$$Y = \beta_0 + \beta_1 X_1 + \beta_2 X_2 + \ldots + \varepsilon \equiv X\beta + \varepsilon \tag{2}$$

where Y is the level of satisfaction, X are individual, household and context variables affecting it, β measures the effect of each variable on life satisfaction and ε is the error term.

In the regressions, dummy variables have been added to capture whether the youth are students, NEETs, have part-time jobs or a fixed-term contract, are self-employed, chronically ill or with disability. The probit model and regressions include data on unemployment for 2013 from the Italian and Spanish labour force surveys. A dummy variable for medium unemployment regions, which in Italy correspond to the centre of the country and in Spain to Asturias, Catalonia, the Balearic Islands, Galicia, Castilla-Leon and Aragon, has also been included, as well as another one for high unemployment regions, i.e. Southern Italy and the following Spanish regions: Andalusia, Ceuta and Melilla, Extremadura, the Canary Islands, Castilla La Mancha, Murcia and Valencia.

Before presenting the results of the estimation on the probability of being NEET in the two countries and on the effect that being NEET has on subjective measures of well-being as life satisfaction, the overall meaning of life and satisfaction with the financial situation, a few descriptions of the sample analysed and of the living arrangements by gender and NEET condition in the two countries are here provided. As shown on Tables 7.2a and 7.2b, NEET women have a much higher likelihood of living as a couple than non-NEET women in the same age group and gender, showing the persistence of the traditional gender division of labour and the continuity of female specialization in unpaid care work at the household. The majority of NEET males are living with their parents; only a few live as a couple – more in Spain than in Italy – or alone. The distribution by gender of the different living arrangements is more similar for non-NEETs than for NEETs in both countries.

The estimation of the determinants of being NEET has been carried out by using the observable set of variables EU-SILC, which, according to the literature, can have an effect on the NEET status. However, it is important to warn about

Table 7.2a NEETs' living arrangements by gender – Italy and Spain, 15–34 age group

Living arrangement	Italy		Spain	
	M	W	M	W
With parent/s	78.8	37.0	65.6	42
As a couple	11.1	56.3	18.4	50.3
Outside the family	2.6	1.9	6.9	4
Alone	7.4	2.6	8.6	2.1
As a lone parent	0.2	2.2	0.5	1.7
Total	100	100	100	100

Source: Selection of Eurostat metadata from EU-SILC 2013.

Table 7.2b Not NEETs' living arrangements by gender – Italy and Spain, 15–34 age group

Living arrangement	Italy		Spain	
	M	W	M	W
With parent/s	59.4	57.1	65.6	62.7
As a couple	25.8	28.5	23.2	27.5
Outside family	2.4	2.6	4.9	3.8
Alone	12.3	9.3	6.1	5.4
Lone parent	0.1	2.4	0.2	0.6
Total	100	100	100	100

Source: Selection of Eurostat metadata from EU-SILC 2013.

the non-availability in the surveys of other variables that, in the literature, turned out to affect youth's NEET status significantly. For instance, it is not possible to observe the degree of parental intrusiveness in their children's lives or their degree of support, which in other studies have proved to be significantly associated to the children's NEET status (Bynner and Parsons 2002; Pemberton 2008; Alfieri *et al.* 2015a).

5 Results

In Italy, the probability of being NEET when in the 15–24 age group increases with age and is lower for the more educated ones (Table 7.3a). Young men are

Table 7.3a Probit model on the probability of being NEET. Marginal effects evaluated at the means – Italy, 15–34 age group

Variables	All	Men	Women
Woman	0.0911***		
	(8.04)		
Age	0.105***	0.0792***	0.110***
	(10.54)	(6.04)	(7.51)
Age squared	−0.00201***	−0.00149***	−0.00210***
	(−10.05)	(−5.56)	(−7.32)
Secondary education	−0.0574	−0.0769*	−0.0386
	(−1.51)	(−1.93)	(−0.66)
High school diploma	−0.113***	−0.108***	−0.119**
	(−3.00)	(−2.79)	(−2.04)
Tertiary education	−0.194***	−0.175***	−0.191***
	(−4.73)	(−3.90)	(−3.07)
Living with parents	−0.0212	0.204***	−0.177***
	(−1.29)	(8.88)	(−7.95)
Living alone	−0.171***	0.0642*	−0.345***
	(−6.21)	(1.86)	(−8.14)
Lone parent	−0.122***	−0.113**	−0.164***
	(−4.08)	(−2.53)	(−4.00)
Living as a couple with parents	0.017	0.0791	0.033
	(0.33)	(1.16)	(0.36)
Other living arrangements	−0.0429	0.150***	−0.152***
	(−1.11)	(3.10)	(−2.64)
Equiv. Household Income	−0.00000805***	−0.00000876***	−0.00000755***
	(−5.93)	(−6.68)	(−3.75)
Centre	0.0534***	0.0423**	0.0538**
	(3.32)	(1.99)	(2.45)
South	0.116***	0.0799***	0.151***
	(7.54)	(4.38)	(6.81)
N	9116	4552	4564
pseudo R^2	0.12	0.13	0.17

Source: Own elaboration on IT-SILC 2013.

Notes
t statistics in parentheses, * $p < 0.10$, ** $p < 0.05$, *** $p < 0.01$.

more likely to be NEET if they live with their parents (the probability of being NEET increases by 20 per cent for men if they still live with their family). On the other hand, living with parents decreases the probability of being NEET among young women with respect to the reference type of living arrangement: living as a couple. Actually this is consistent with the larger share of NEET women in Italy living with their partner as housewives. With respect to the reference living arrangement, living alone increases the probability of being NEET for men and decreases it for women. On the other hand, as a lone parent the probability of being NEET decreases for both men and women. Other living arrangements increase the probability of being NEET for men and decrease it for women.

A high equivalized household income decreases the probability of being NEET; however, the effect is rather negligible. This effect can be related to the parents' higher level of education (a positive effect found in the literature; for instance, in Italy, by Alfieri *et al.* 2015a); this can determine a higher level of household income for those youth still living with the family. If women live in the south of Italy, their probability of being NEET increases by 15 per cent, whereas for men living in the same area, the probability rises by 8 per cent. With respect to living in the north of Italy, living in the centre increases the probability of being NEET by about 4–5 per cent for both men and women.

In Spain, the probability of being NEET in the 15–34 age group increases with age and is much lower for the more educated ones, in both cases to a greater extent for women than for men (Table 7.3b). The probability of being NEET decreases by 25 per cent for women with a high school diploma (a sensibly higher effect than among Italian youth) or university degree, and by 20–21 per cent for men.

Regarding the living arrangements, the probability of being NEET increases by 17 per cent for men if they still live with their families, while it decreases by 4 per cent for young women living with their families, a much lower effect for Spanish women than for Italian women. With respect to the reference living arrangement – living as a couple – living alone decreases the probability of being NEET for women, again to a lower extent than for Italian women. If a lone parent, the probability of being NEET decreases for both men and women; however, the effect is not statistically significant. Other living statuses increase the probability of being NEET for men. A high equivalized household income decreases the probability of being NEET, though the effect is rather negligible. In contrast with Italy, the labour market context does not seem to affect the probability of being NEET among Spanish youth.

Life satisfaction

The data on the average level of life satisfaction show that Italy's achievement is low with respect to the EU-28 average (Table 7.4). Though Spanish levels are also lower than the European average, the gap is small.

Both in Italy and Spain being a woman increases the level of life satisfaction (Table 7.5). Women's higher life satisfaction, however, can be the outcome of a

Table 7.3b Probit model on the probability of being NEET. Marginal effects evaluated at the means – Spain, 15–34 age group

Variables	All	Men	Women
Woman	0.0316**		
	(2.28)		
Age	0.182***	0.141***	0.203***
	(12.12)	(7.10)	(9.41)
Age squared	–0.00314***	–0.00234***	–0.00353***
	(–10.68)	(–6.01)	(–8.44)
Secondary education	–0.0796***	–0.0447	–0.106***
	(–3.23)	(–1.39)	(–2.93)
High school diploma	–0.244***	–0.216***	–0.256***
	(–9.76)	(–6.59)	(–6.97)
Tertiary education	–0.233***	–0.204***	–0.250***
	(–8.36)	(–5.48)	(–6.12)
Living with parents	0.0445**	0.169***	–0.0394
	(2.25)	(5.90)	(–1.47)
Living alone	–0.0826**	0.0661	–0.236***
	(–2.11)	(1.30)	(–4.11)
Lone parent	–0.0790*	–0.112	–0.0578
	(–1.71)	(–1.44)	(–1.07)
Living as a couple with parents	0.114	0.204	0.0609
	(1.63)	(1.46)	(0.84)
Other living arrangements	0.00101	0.119**	–0.0730
	(0.03)	(2.43)	(–1.47)
Equiv. Household Income	–0.0000106***	–0.0000109***	–0.0000104***
	(–9.03)	(–7.02)	(–6.01)
Medium unemployment regions	0.00411	0.00135	0.00543
	(0.19)	(0.05)	(0.18)
High unemployment regions	0.0249	0.00796	0.0313
	(1.20)	(0.28)	(1.06)
N	6,064	3,079	2,985
pseudo R^2	0.14	0.14	0.17

Source: Own elaboration on ES-SILC 2013.

Notes
t statistics in parentheses, * $p < 0.10$, ** $p < 0.05$, *** $p < 0.01$.

Table 7.4 Average level of life satisfaction

	Italy		Spain		EU-28	
	M	F	M	F	M	F
16–24	7.0	7.2	7.4	7.5	7.5	7.6
25–34	6.7	6.9	7.0	7.2	7.2	7.3
16 and over	6.7	6.7	6.9	6.9	7.1	7.0

Source: Selection of Eurostat metadata from EU-SILC 2013.

Table 7.5 Life satisfaction – Italy and Spain, 15–34 age group

Variables	Italy			Spain		
	All	Men	Women	All	Men	Women
Woman	0.0593***			0.0355**		
	(0.0177)			(0.0154)		
Age	-0.0191	-0.00978	-0.0341	-0.0302	-0.0477	-0.0197
	(0.0260)	(0.0450)	(0.0281)	(0.0258)	(0.0344)	(0.0350)
Age squared	0.000307	0.000163	0.000557	0.000360	0.000603	-6.79e-05
	(0.000458)	(0.000800)	(0.000492)	(0.000461)	(0.000620)	(0.000608)
Chronically ill	-0.0298	-0.000750	-0.0520	-0.0578**	0.0118	-0.102***
	(0.0292)	(0.0512)	(0.0337)	(0.0230)	(0.0317)	(0.0308)
Secondary educ.	0.033	0.039	0.0271	0.0215	0.0420	-0.0280
	(0.0646)	(0.0737)	(0.109)	(0.0443)	(0.0624)	(0.0391)
High school dip.	0.123**	0.132**	0,112	0.0284	0.0443	-0.0182
	(0.0603)	(0.0629)	(0.107)	(0.0434)	(0.0613)	(0.0391)
Tertiary educ.	0.139**	0.125*	0.15	0.0454	0.0797	-0.00985
	(0.0605)	(0.0640)	(0.107)	(0.0460)	(0.0656)	(0.0412)
Equiv. H. Income	1.88e-06***	1.42e-06*	2.15e-06*	4.59e-06***	5.00e-06***	3.98e-06***
	(7.13e-07)	(8.03e-07)	(1.24e-06)	(7.86e-07)	(1.14e-06)	(1.04e-06)
Medium unemployment regions	0.00769	0.0286	-0.00810	-0.000384	-0.0128	0.00336
	(0.0239)	(0.0404)	(0.0253)	(0.0201)	(0.0312)	(0.0210)
High unemployment regions	-0.0472**	-0.0274	-0.0625***	0.0450**	0.0633*	0.0189
	(0.0210)	(0.0349)	(0.0226)	(0.0205)	(0.0329)	(0.0194)
NEET	-0.128***	-0.205***	-0.0803***	-0.164***	-0.180***	-0.147***
	(0.0316)	(0.0639)	(0.0261)	(0.0217)	(0.0351)	(0.0235)
Student	-0.00371	0.0187	-0.00648	0.0206	0.0129	0.0411
	(0.0484)	(0.0670)	(0.0638)	(0.0231)	(0.0351)	(0.0305)

	(1)	(2)	(3)	(4)	(5)	(6)
Part-time contr.	-0.0236	-0.0361	-0.00779	-0.0558**	-0.0826*	-0.0298
	(0.0237)	(0.0608)	(0.0238)	(0.0253)	(0.0467)	(0.0223)
Temporary contr.	-0.0295	-0.0521	-0.0191	-0.0846***	-0.118***	-0.0528***
	(0.0254)	(0.0514)	(0.0219)	(0.0163)	(0.0262)	(0.0174)
Self-employed	-0.280	-0.281	-0.286	-0.0530	-0.128	-0.00865
	(0.207)	(0.298)	(0.197)	(0.0649)	(0.157)	(0.0614)
Disabled	-0.585	0.0954	-1.841***	-0.320	-0.690***	0.277***
	(0.674)	(0.0775)	(0.0481)	(0.249)	(0.233)	(0.0748)
Living with parents	-0.0983***	-0.0573	-0.119***	-0.0898***	-0.0721***	-0.104***
	(0.0289)	(0.0465)	(0.0363)	(0.0178)	(0.0258)	(0.0227)
Living alone	-0.113***	-0.0737**	-0.143***	-0.112**	-0.130**	-0.0812**
	(0.0221)	(0.0320)	(0.0291)	(0.0438)	(0.0643)	(0.0343)
Lone parent	-0.101**	-0.210*	-0.0848**	-0.0606	0.267***	-0.163**
	(0.0408)	(0.115)	(0.0425)	(0.0753)	(0.0785)	(0.0768)
As a couple with parents	-0.00604	-0.00721	0.024	-0.170**	0.0236	-0.259**
	(0.0725)	(0.108)	(0.0577)	(0.0859)	(0.0630)	(0.108)
Other living arr.	-0.127***	-0.0566	-0.167***	-0.111***	-0.0646	-0.152***
	(0.0343)	(0.0470)	(0.0463)	(0.0364)	(0.0519)	(0.0499)
Constant	2.143***	1.985***	2.421***	2.525***	2.800***	2.160***
	(0.370)	(0.623)	(0.414)	(0.345)	(0.449)	(0.500)
Observations	2,289	1,047	1,242	3,194	1,627	1,567
R-squared	0.12	0.11	0.15	0.17	0.21	0.17

Source: Own elaboration from IT-SILC and ES-SILC 2013.

Notes
Robust standard errors in parentheses, * p<0.1, ** p<0.05, *** p<0.01.

greater adaptation to adverse living conditions, as outlined in the literature (Sen 1999). In Italy, higher educational levels have a positive effect on young men's life satisfaction, whereas they do not appear to affect young women's level of life satisfaction. In Spain, higher educational levels do not affect youth's level of life satisfaction. A higher equivalized household income positively contributes to life satisfaction though to a negligible degree.

NEET status has a negative effect on life satisfaction. Being NEET decreases by 20.5 per cent young men's life satisfaction and by 8 per cent young women's life satisfaction in Italy, while in Spain the reduction amounts to 18 per cent for young men and 14.7 per cent for young women. Note the even larger effect of being NEET on youth's satisfaction regarding their financial situation (Table 7.7).

Unlike in Italy, in Spain young people with a temporary contract present lower life satisfaction levels: –12 percentage points for men and –5 percentage points for women. A part-time contract is negatively related to life satisfaction for men but not for women, maybe because it is more common among female workers or because women in that age group are more likely than men to work part-time in order to achieve a better work-life balance and this could positively affect their life satisfaction. Note that this effect is not present for Italian youth.

Being disabled in Italy decreases women's life satisfaction but has no impact on men's. In Spain, being chronically ill affects women negatively, while being disabled decreases men's life satisfaction but has a positive impact on women's.

As for the living arrangements, when compared to the reference situation of living as a couple, Italian women show a lower degree of life satisfaction when living with their parents than men do (this seems consistent with Giannelli and Monfardini's analysis (2003b) on youth's living arrangements in Italy, with living with parents being more likely to be felt as a cage by women and as a nest by young men). Living alone or as lone parents reduces life satisfaction for both men and women, with a larger effect of living alone on women and of being a lone parent on men.

Spanish women show a lower degree of life satisfaction than men when living with their parents, either as a couple with parents or without their partner. Living alone reduces life satisfaction for both men and women, while being a lone parent increases life satisfaction for men and decreases it for women.

Meaning of life

The meaning of life variable refers to the respondent's opinion/feelings regarding the value and purpose of life, important life goals and, for some, spirituality. NEET status does not affect women's overall meaning of life in Italy, only men's, while in Spain it affects negatively both men's and women's overall meaning of life (Table 7.6).

Living with parents in Italy has a negative effect on the overall meaning of life only for young women. In Spain, the negative effect is similar for men and women. Living alone has a negative impact for both females and males in Italy, the same as being self-employed. Italian youth living in regions with high unemployment rates like the south show a significantly lower level regarding the meaning of life than Spanish youth do in the same situation. On the other hand, in Spain, the effect on the overall meaning of life is positive when youth live in areas characterized by high employment rates. Youth with a tertiary education level in Italy show a higher level of overall meaning of life, whereas in Spain the effect is not significant.

Satisfaction with financial situation

Tertiary education has a positive effect on youth's satisfaction with their financial situation (Table 7.7). NEET status has, on the contrary, a strong negative effect on it. Being NEET decreases by 23 per cent young men's satisfaction with their financial situation and by 20 per cent young women's satisfaction. Note that being NEET has a much higher negative effect on men's financial satisfaction in Italy than it does in Spain, and a lower effect on women in Italy than on women in Spain (being NEET decreases satisfaction with the financial situation by 43 per cent if men and by 11 per cent if women). Also young men with temporary or part-time contracts present lower satisfaction levels in relation to their financial situations. In Italy, this can be observed only for women in cases of temporary contracts (their satisfaction with the financial situation decreases by 7 per cent) and for men with part-time jobs (whose satisfaction with their financial situation decreases by 13 per cent).

6 Conclusions

This study focuses on a particularly weak group within the working-age population that represents a significant share in Italy and Spain: those youth who are neither in employment nor in education or training. A first focus was set on the variables affecting the probability of being NEET in the two countries. Being NEET in Italy and Spain is more likely for older individuals in the analysed age group, a higher educational level protects against the risk of being NEET and there are gender differences with regards to living arrangements, since women are more likely to be NEET and live as a couple, whereas men are more likely to be NEET while living with their parents, living alone or in other living arrangements. High regional unemployment rates affect the likelihood of being NEET only in Italy, and especially for women.

The observed association between NEET status and living arrangements in Italy and Spain imply a greater role of the family of origin in sustaining the NEET status for men and a higher share of NEETs living as a couple for young women. If, consistently with the literature, a higher household income (positively related for those living with parents with the parents' educational level, as found in the literature) decreases the likelihood of being NEET, adverse labour market conditions increase that probability, especially for young women.

Table 7.6 Overall meaning of life – Italy and Spain, 15–34 age group

Variables	Italy			Spain		
	All	Men	Women	All	Men	Women
Woman	0.0466*** (0.0174)			0.0466*** (0.0165)		
Age	0.016 (0.0184)	0.00805 (0.0285)	0.011 (0.0247)	-0.0196 (0.0172)	-0.0427* (0.0243)	0.00335 (0.0241)
Age squared	-0.000341 (0.000340)	-0.000222 (0.000530)	-0.000224 (0.000452)	0.000228 (0.000309)	0.000609 (0.000438)	-0.000139 (0.000430)
Chronically ill	-0.0128 (0.0354)	-0.0284 (0.0569)	0.00241 (0.0430)	-0.00851 (0.0159)	0.00973 (0.0259)	-0.0191 (0.0182)
Secondary education	0.09 (0.0895)	0.175 (0.137)	-0.0259 (0.0723)	0.0136 (0.0218)	0.0159 (0.0268)	0.00174 (0.0376)
High school diploma	0.160* (0.0851)	0.234* (0.130)	0.06 (0.0637)	0.0189 (0.0229)	-0.000810 (0.0304)	0.0359 (0.0369)
Tertiary education	0.191** (0.0848)	0.249* (0.129)	0.105* (0.0635)	0.0119 (0.0254)	-0.0126 (0.0342)	0.0380 (0.0366)
Equiv. H. Income	-3.40e-07 (8.78e-07)	-4.70e-07 (1.26e-06)	-3.36e-07 (9.91e-07)	1.78e-06** (7.05e-07)	2.68e-06** (1.15e-06)	8.61e-07 (7.27e-07)
Medium unemployment regions	0.00750 (0.0158)	0.1798611 (0.0234)	-0.00673 (0.0221)	0.0429* (0.0242)	0.0613 (0.0376)	0.0214 (0.0192)
High unemployment regions	-0.0657*** (0.0197)	-0.0577* (0.0296)	-0.0703*** (0.0257)	0.114*** (0.0249)	0.145*** (0.0387)	0.0756*** (0.0191)
NEET	-0.0762*** (0.0280)	-0.131*** (0.0479)	-0.0398 (0.0260)	-0.0717*** (0.0142)	-0.0943*** (0.0216)	-0.0493*** (0.0177)
Student	-0.00984 (0.0447)	-0.0958 (0.0778)	0.06 (0.0490)	0.0200 (0.0207)	0.0301 (0.0300)	0.0200 (0.0284)

	(1)	(2)	(3)	(4)	(5)
Part-time contract	-0.0109	0.00221	-0.0388	-0.0911	0.00732
	(0.0228)	(0.0259)	(0.0322)	(0.0625)	(0.0173)
Temporary contract	-0.0116	0.017	-0.0462***	-0.0713***	-0.0137
	(0.0236)	(0.0240)	(0.0156)	(0.0225)	(0.0156)
Self-employed	-0.140***	-0.125*	0.00163	-0.0651	0.0264
	(0.0396)	(0.0687)	(0.0773)	(0.208)	(0.0534)
Disabled	-0.462	-1.012*	-0.315*	-0.582***	0.170***
	(0.387)	(0.530)	(0.182)	(0.171)	(0.0590)
Living with parents	-0.0654***	-0.0986***	-0.0691***	-0.0569**	-0.0787***
	(0.0233)	(0.0377)	(0.0170)	(0.0265)	(0.0175)
Living alone	-0.0969***	-0.0922***	-0.0243	-0.00569	-0.0495*
	(0.0213)	(0.0282)	(0.0253)	(0.0373)	(0.0262)
Lone parent	-0.0276	0.016	0.0176	0.143***	-0.0238
	(0.0466)	(0.0397)	(0.0620)	(0.0524)	(0.0705)
As a couple with parents	0.07	0.123**	-0.0743	0.0675	-0.133**
	(0.0597)	(0.0592)	(0.0525)	(0.0774)	(0.0538)
Other living arr.	-0.120***	-0.152***	-0.0776***	-0.0717*	-0.0742*
	(0.0370)	(0.0477)	(0.0295)	(0.0434)	(0.0409)
Constant	1.727***	1.906***	2.349***	2.686***	2.045***
	(0.254)	(0.333)	(0.240)	(0.331)	(0.342)
Observations	2,292	1,244	3,198	1,627	1,571
R-squared	0.09	0.09	0.10	0.14	0.07

Source: Own elaboration from IT-SILC and ES-SILC 2013.

Notes
Robust standard errors in parentheses, * $p<0.1$, ** $p<0.05$, *** $p<0.01$.

Table 7.7 Satisfaction with financial situation – Italy and Spain, 15–34 age group

Variables	Italy			Spain		
	All	Men	Women	All	Men	Women
Woman	0.0457*			0.0236		
	(0.0237)			(0.0180)		
Age	-0.0358	0.00735	-0.0793**	-0.0659**	-0.105**	0.000737
	(0.0245)	(0.0334)	(0.0360)	(0.0323)	(0.0415)	(0.0471)
Age squared	0.000544	-0.000273	0.00136**	0.00108*	0.00170**	-2.03e-05
	(0.000450)	(0.000627)	(0.000652)	(0.000578)	(0.000755)	(0.000827)
Chronically ill	-0.0300	-0.0295	-0.0432	-0.0637**	-0.0362	-0.0745**
	(0.0335)	(0.0429)	(0.0469)	(0.0291)	(0.0457)	(0.0366)
Secondary educ.	0.09	0.075	0.11	-0.00451	-0.00339	0.00383
	(0.0906)	(0.108)	(0.133)	(0.0524)	(0.0644)	(0.0855)
High school dip.	0.175**	0.13	0.259**	0.0646	0.0305	0.123
	(0.0874)	(0.105)	(0.124)	(0.0521)	(0.0644)	(0.0840)
Tertiary educ.	0.234***	0.183*	0.337***	0.118**	0.0914	0.166**
	(0.0882)	(0.106)	(0.126)	(0.0531)	(0.0676)	(0.0832)
Equiv. H. Income	5.91e-06***	6.00e-06***	5.19e-06***	1.08e-05***	1.03e-05***	1.17e-05***
	(9.40e-07)	(1.32e-06)	(1.54e-06)	(1.02e-06)	(1.43e-06)	(1.33e-06)
Medium unemployment regions	-0.0230	0.038	-0.0799**	0.0520**	0.0239	0.0714**
	(0.0260)	(0.0361)	(0.0364)	(0.0238)	(0.0317)	(0.0325)
High unemployment regions	-0.0424	-0.0131	-0.0712*	0.0668***	0.0471	0.0836***
	(0.0267)	(0.0355)	(0.0381)	(0.0240)	(0.0319)	(0.0321)
NEET	-0.229***	-0.431***	-0.110***	-0.219***	-0.227***	-0.200***
	(0.0380)	(0.0667)	(0.0415)	(0.0255)	(0.0361)	(0.0347)
Student	-0.103*	-0.157**	-0.0586	0.00214	-0.0373	0.0606
	(0.0607)	(0.0737)	(0.0820)	(0.0329)	(0.0485)	(0.0461)

Part-time contract	-0.0706** (0.0339)	-0.127* (0.0741)	-0.0289 (0.0379)	-0.0700** (0.0280)	-0.131*** (0.0484)	-0.0103 (0.0285)
Temporary contr.	-0.0436 (0.0273)	-0.00873 (0.0455)	-0.0716** (0.0324)	-0.0690*** (0.0210)	-0.105*** (0.0311)	-0.0300 (0.0257)
Self-employed	-0.331 (0.326)	-0.430 (0.395)	0.07 (0.102)	-0.0699 (0.0936)	0.00491 (0.196)	-0.0850 (0.108)
Disabled	-0.345*** (0.0511)	-0.447*** (0.0669)		-0.167 (0.230)	-0.482** (0.218)	0.394** (0.157)
Living with parents	0.03 (0.0299)	0.135*** (0.0429)	-0.0287 (0.0446)	-0.00387 (0.0216)	0.000686 (0.0319)	-0.0136 (0.0272)
Living alone	-0.0587** (0.0292)	-0.0292 (0.0376)	-0.0597 (0.0456)	-0.0798* (0.0464)	-0.111* (0.0643)	-0.0381 (0.0564)
Lone parent	-0.208*** (0.0647)	-0.163 (0.155)	-0.209*** (0.0740)	-0.220 (0.208)	-0.0102 (0.178)	-0.258 (0.245)
As a couple with parents	-0.0373 (0.118)	0,054	-0.0537 (0.222)	-0.167* (0.0868)	-0.0784 (0.117)	-0.210** (0.106)
Other living arr.	-0.183** (0.0903)	-0.218 (0.139)	-0.0665 (0.0961)	-0.0317 (0.0514)	-0.0157 (0.0672)	-0.0514 (0.0786)
Constant	2.101*** (0.338)	1.547*** (0.438)	2.643*** (0.511)	2.544*** (0.436)	3.221*** (0.554)	1.465*** (0.656)
Observations	2,217	1,016	1,201	3,121	1,592	1,529
R-squared	0.15	0.22	0.15	0.23	0.23	0.25

Source: Own elaboration from IT-SILC and ES-SILC 2013.

Notes

Robust standard errors in parentheses, * p<0.1, ** p<0.05, *** p<0.01.

The high persistence of NEET rates, as well as of young unemployment rates, and the smaller response to changes in the GDP of southern European regions suggests that, even when the economy recovers, many years will elapse in those countries before the situation of young people can improve. Actually, youth unemployment rates appear to reduce more slowly in those countries where the overall unemployment rate has not fallen (OECD 2016). This study shows the high cost of the effect of the NEET status on subjective measures of well-being, in terms of reduced life satisfaction, lowered satisfaction with the financial situation and a negative impact on the overall meaning of life. These costs can be associated with the negative psychological effects of being NEET found in the literature (Bynner and Parsons 2002), and can contribute to social exclusion, as well as to future poor labour market performance and decreased possibility in job finding (Winkelmann 2014), but also to disturbing election results (Gardiner 2016), affecting Europe's democratic health.

The risk of a 'lost generation' highlights the need to adopt effective active and passive labour policies and adequate school-to-work transition institutions, including education, placement and training plans, to minimize the increase in the number of young people losing effective contact with the labour market and permanently damaging their employment prospects. In economies undertaking structural changes, for example from construction and manufacturing to services, specific labour market programmes are important to enable youth to acquire the skills and competencies required in these new sectors (Hutengs and Stadtmann 2014; Kelly *et al.* 2014).

We thank an anonymous referee for his/her comments and suggestions on a previous version of this Chapter.

Funding acknowledgements

This work was supported by Programa Estatal de Investigación, Desarrollo e Innovación, Retos (project no. CSO2014–58378-R).

Notes

1 Following Dolado (2015), the Italian large unemployment gap between young and adult people is due to its dual labour market, resulting from the deregulation of temporary contracts in the late 1990s; to a specific institution of the Italian labour market, the Cassa Integrazione Guadagni, which provides income support to permanent workers who are laid off, implying they are not counted as unemployed in the official statistics; to the pension reform of 2012, which increased the pension age hindering the substitution of older workers with young ones in the short run; and, finally, to a weak dual voluntary training system leading to a high increase of NEETs. On the contrary, the gap between young and adult people in Spain is at almost the same level as the OECD average (García-Pérez and Vall Castello 2015).
2 The Eurofound study (2016) proposes a disaggregation of the NEET population into the following seven subgroups: re-entrants in labour market or education; short-term unemployed; long-term unemployed; discouraged workers; people with disability; young people with family responsibilities; and other NEETs for whom it is not possible to infer reasons for their NEET status.

8 Job satisfaction among young Russian workers

Francesco Bartolucci, Aleksandra Bashina, Giovanni S. F. Bruno, Olga Demidova and Marcello Signorelli

1 Introduction

The economic literature includes a wide range of analysis of the determinants and features of job satisfaction, but research dealing with young people remains scarce, and mainly focused on developed countries (for example, Bruno *et al.* 2013 examines job-satisfaction among young Italian workers based on survey data). This chapter analyses job satisfaction among young Russian workers.

Job satisfaction among Russian workers has been studied in papers such as Linz (2003) and Linz and Semykina (2012), both based on cross-sectional data, and Senik (2004), based on panel data. Frijters *et al.* (2006), focuses on life satisfaction in Russia. All these studies pool workers of any age in the data, maintaining constant marginal effects across young and adult workers.

The data used in this chapter have been collected for four items, the first of which regards general job satisfaction; the other three items concern specific aspects of job satisfaction, with regard to working conditions, earnings and opportunities for professional growth. The corresponding response variables are divided into five ordered categories, from "completely unsatisfied" to "completely satisfied". The longitudinal data set (2006–2010/2011) also contains personal information about the respondents as covariates: gender, age, marital status, number of children, educational level and working leave. In order to analyse such data, a fixed-effect ordered logit estimator is employed (Das and Van Soest 1999; Ferrer-i-Carbonell and Frijters 2004; Baetschmann *et al.* 2015).

The chapter is structured as follows. The next section presents a survey of the existing estimation strategies in job satisfaction literature. Section 3 outlines the theoretical framework, while the data set is described in Section 4, and the following section is dedicated to highlighting the key research question, with a discussion of the factors that (potentially) influence job satisfaction. Section 6 presents the econometric model, and the results are summarized in Section 7. The closing remarks are presented in the final section.

2 Existing estimation methods

A non-structural approach to the analysis of job satisfaction may be based on linear projections of the declared satisfaction scores. For example, in order to assess the short- and long-term well-being effects of changes in working conditions, Hanglberger (2011) uses the Least Squares Dummy Variables estimator (LSDV) on the BHPS data set. Chadi and Hetschko (2013) apply OLS methods, checked for robustness by propensity score matching estimators, to German survey data (GSOEP).

For the purposes of this chapter it was decided to follow a structural approach, which recognizes that a family of possibly heterogeneous individual utility functions exists, underlying the declared satisfaction scores and, as such, is more suitable for a causal analysis. This brings into play non-linear panel data methods for the estimation of latent regression models, along with the well-known incidental parameter problem, which warns of using individual indicators to accommodate latent heterogeneity in panel data models with small clusters of individuals.

The following is a list of the most common solutions to the incidental parameter problem in panel-data literature. One may estimate the latent regression model by a random effect (RE) ordered probit with the individual components modelled à la Mundlak, through a linear combination of regressors in group means (Wooldridge 2010). Senik (2004) applies this method to the 1994–2000 waves of the RLMS data to investigate the impact of income distribution on job satisfaction among Russian workers. The same method is applied by Salvatori (2010) to the ECHP data to estimate the impact of labour market policies on the well-being of permanent and temporary European workers.

A convenient estimation strategy, related to the RE ordered probit à la Mundlak, is based on a fixed effect (FE) extension of the linear approach to ordered response models described in Van Praag and Ferrer-i-Carbonell (2004) and (2006), also known as probit OLS (POLS). Papers using FE POLS as the main estimator include Green and Leeves (2011) on Australian data, Bruno *et al.* (2014a) on Italian survey data regarding young workers, and Pagán (2013) on the SHARE data for 11 European countries. RE POLS can always be implemented as an alternative to FE POLS. Indeed, Van Praag and Ferrer-i-Carbonell (2004) advocate the use of the former for two reasons: 1) if valid, it is more efficient and 2) it can identify effects of time-constant variables, such as gender. It must be considered, however, that RE POLS is less robust than FE POLS to correlated individual effects. In addition, if the time constant variable of interest is qualitative with a limited number of categories, such as gender, its impact can be assessed at the most general level, on the entire set of coefficients, carrying out separate FE estimators on the subsamples corresponding to each category (see Bruno *et al.* 2014b). Van Praag and Ferrer-i-Carbonell (2006) show that ordered probit and POLS estimates are almost identical up to a proportionality coefficient. Bruno *et al.* (2014c) demonstrate that the probit analogous of the FE POLS is the RE Ordered Probit à la Mundlak.

All the foregoing methods share the disadvantage of modelling the unobserved individual heterogeneity through group means, which is restrictive in non-linear models. Two popular panel-data methods that obviate this problem are both based on the Chamberlain conditional logit estimator, where the individual effects are conditioned out in the log-likelihood function: the fixed-effect ordered logit minimum distance estimator by Das and Van Soest (1999), and its popular variant by Ferrer-i-Carbonell and Frijters (2004). Recent applications of the latter estimator include Böckerman *et al.* (2011) on linked-employer-employee Finnish data, and de Graaf-Zijl (2012) on Dutch data. However, Baetschmann *et al.* (2015) demonstrate that the various ways through which Ferrer-i-Carbonell and Frijter's method has been implemented lead to inconsistent estimators. They therefore rectify the method in order to make it consistent and computationally simpler. For these reasons it was decided to base the econometric strategy on the estimator by Baetschmann *et al.* (2015). Among a number of studies applying this estimator, Buddelmeyer *et al.* (2013) applied it to Australian data.

3 The theoretical model

Job disamenities are important factors in the evaluation of job satisfaction. This section outlines the effects that can be identified in a job satisfaction model incorporating job disamenities as latent variables.

Let $u = U(w, D, Z, \mu_u)$ denote the utility function of an employee, where w, D and Z are, respectively, the wage, the $k_D \times 1$ vector of job disamenities and the $k_Z \times 1$ vector of the employee's observed characteristics, $\mu_u = \alpha + \varepsilon$ is a latent variable comprising a zero-mean, uncorrelated, idiosyncratic component, ε, and a possibly correlated latent heterogeneity component, α. The utility function is increasing in the wage and decreasing in job disamenities, that is $\partial_w U > 0$ and $\partial_D U < 0$.

The theory of compensating wage differentials predicts that disamenity increases are compensated by higher wages, and thus postulates the existence of a relationship between market wages and job disamenities, known as the hedonic wage equation, $w = w(D, X, \mu_w)$, where $\partial_D w > 0$, X is a vector of wage determinants that may partly overlap with z and μ_w is a latent heterogeneity component. The hedonic wage equation represents the combinations of job disamenities and wages offered by firms to workers. In competitive markets it is an envelope of zero profit conditions. Given the hedonic wage equation, workers maximize their utility functions sorting into the jobs with the desired amount of disamenities. More formally, plugging the wage equation into the utility function gives

$$u = U\left[w(D, X, \mu_w), D, Z, \mu_u\right]$$

and if job disamenities are optimally chosen by the workers, this provides the system of k_D equations

$$\partial_w U \cdot \partial_D w + \partial_D U = 0. \tag{1}$$

Böckerman *et al.* (2011) show that, with a linear utility function and a linear wage equation, the constraints implied by the foregoing system make D disappear from the reduced form utility function incorporating $w(D, X, \mu_w)$.

$$U[w(D, X, \mu_w), D, Z, \mu_u] \equiv U^*(D, X, Z, \mu_w, \mu_u).$$

In fact, if $u = \beta_0 + \beta_w w + \beta_Z' Z + \beta_D' D + \mu_u$ and $w = \lambda_0 + \lambda_X' X + \lambda_D' D + \mu_w$, then

$$
\begin{aligned}
u &= \beta_0 + (\beta_w \lambda_D' + \beta_D')D + \beta_w \lambda_X' X + \beta_Z' Z + \beta_w \mu_w + \mu_u \\
&= \beta_0 + \beta_w \lambda_X' X + \beta_Z' Z + \beta_w \mu_w + \mu_u,
\end{aligned}
\tag{2}
$$

where the second equality follows from Equation (1). Based on Equation (2), Böckerman *et al.* (2011) argue that if compensating wage differentials are at work, and job disamenities are observed, the D variables are redundant in a satisfaction regression excluding the wage and including X and Z. Their approach does not require that the wage variable be included in the regression, and as such dispenses with accommodating the endogeneity of wages, stemming from the correlation of w and μ_w. It is not possible to replicate the test by Böckerman *et al.* (2011) as job disamenities are latent in this specification. Nonetheless, a test corresponding with Böckerman *et al.*'s can be applied in this case. To elaborate, Equation (2) has the strong implication that u and (w, D) are mean independent conditional on X, Z and μ_w, which is operational in a panel framework if it is assumed that μ_w is time-constant. Indeed, Equation (2) establishes that, in the presence of compensating wage differentials, the wage is redundant in a job satisfaction regression excluding job disamenities and including X and Z along with fixed effects absorbing α and $\beta_w \mu_w$, which can be easily tested with a job satisfaction model which includes the wage as an explanatory variable. However, if wage differentials are not related to job disamenities, one can expect to estimate a significantly positive wage effect, $\partial_w U$. If wage differentials only partially compensate for job disamenities, then the estimated wage effect can be affected by an attenuation bias, due to the positive correlation between w and D and $\partial_D U < 0$ (for a similar approach see also Lalive 2002 and Clark 2006).

4 Characteristics of the database and descriptive statistics

This analysis is based on the results of the Russian Longitudinal Monitoring Survey (the RLMS) – a household-based survey designed to measure individual and household economic well-being. The survey is conducted by the National Research University Higher School of Economics and ZAO "Demoscope", together with the Carolina Population Center (University of North Carolina) and the Institute of Sociology RAS. The questionnaire contains different modules of questions regarding individual and household characteristics. It should also be mentioned that the sets of questions differ from wave to wave. However, this chapter only makes use of information that is collected in each round of the survey. Individual data are used regarding young people from the 15th, 16th, 17th, 18th and 19th waves of the survey. These waves were conducted in 2006, 2007, 2008, 2009 and the end of 2010 – beginning of 2011 years, respectively.[1] Although the target number of respondents is constant for every wave, the set of respondents differs from wave to wave: some of them move to another address, or refuse to participate in further rounds, and vanish from the set of respondents. For the purposes of this survey "young people" is taken to mean persons aged between 16 and 26 during the 19th wave of the survey. The age was fixed at the time of last wave in order to keep respondents "young" until the end of the examined time period. This clearly limits the number of observations that can be used for analysis (see Table A8.1 in Appendix). This type of limitation is however inevitable if the data are to be kept homogeneous.

The sample consists of 1,938 observations after observations with missing data have been removed. Four types of variables are used as characteristics of job satisfaction: satisfaction about the job as a whole, working conditions, earnings and opportunities for professional growth. These variables are divided into categories, ranging in value from "completely unsatisfied" to "completely satisfied", corresponding respectively to the lowest and highest value of the dependent variable. The respondent's personal characteristics are used as covariates: age, gender, marital status, number of children, educational level and working leave (as for their distribution, see Table A8.2 in the Appendix). The conditional scores for each item given the covariate are presented as additional descriptive statistics (Table 8.1). It should be noted that one of the most relevant factors affecting all items regards wages (expressed in ppp). If individuals on wages inferior or superior with respect to the median threshold (near 10,000 in ppp) are distinguished, this results in significant higher values of the conditional scores for those with higher wages. In addition, it can be observed that the lowest level of satisfaction is recorded with regard to earnings (item 3) and (while better) opportunities for professional growth (item 4). As for most of the other covariates, the conditional scores of job satisfaction (for each item) are quite similar (with slightly higher values for "single", "male", persons not "on leave", with a "higher educational level" and living in "capitals"), while the values are the highest in the absence of children, and decline in accordance with the number of children (especially with a number of children higher than 1).

5 Key research question and factors affecting job satisfaction

As anticipated by the theoretical model presented in Section 3, the key research question is to test the validity of the theory of compensating wage differentials and, more generally, to investigate the role of wage levels in determining job satisfaction.

Three factors influencing levels of job satisfaction are identified: job characteristics, the personal characteristics of the respondent, and external factors, including family characteristics and type of residence. A discussion follows regarding the assumptions about the role of these factors, starting with arguably the most important, job characteristics. The main idea in this case is that better working conditions lead to a higher level of satisfaction. As previously mentioned, wage level is the most important factor in this situation, and a higher wage leads to a higher level of satisfaction, in the case of rejection of the main hypothesis as stated in Section 3. A negative influence is to be expected with regard to the length of the working week: people are happier when they work

Table 8.1 Conditional score for each item given the covariates

Covariate	Modality	Item			
		1	*2*	*3*	*4*
marital status	single	2.583	2.581	1.878	2.075
	together	2.567	2.514	1.740	2.001
children	0	2.606	2.604	1.860	2.084
	1	2.519	2.446	1.711	1.935
	>1	2.373	2.190	1.532	1.889
educational level	lower	2.512	2.397	1.833	2.010
	base	2.557	2.512	1.781	2.002
	high	2.665	2.743	1.877	2.156
gender	male	2.601	2.534	1.875	2.083
	female	2.551	2.560	1.750	1.995
age	<=23	2.528	2.524	1.775	2.025
age.high	>23	2.632	2.577	1.851	2.053
working status	on leave	2.437	2.408	1.751	1.953
	working	2.586	2.559	1.814	2.044
hours	<=40	2.614	2.631	1.777	2.100
	>40	2.523	2.437	1.851	1.954
wages (ppp)	<= 10,000	2.408	2.416	1.495	1.832
	>10,000	2.751	2.687	2.141	2.254
living	capital	2.615	2.613	1.882	2.058
	city	2.571	2.570	1.740	2.065
	other	2.501	2.396	1.743	1.967
year	2006	2.459	2.433	1.607	1.889
	2007	2.537	2.447	1.791	2.021
	2008	2.529	2.529	1.885	1.967
	2009	2.557	2.607	1.798	2.074
	2010	2.633	2.576	1.826	2.081
Overall		2.575	2.548	1.809	2.037

Legend
Item 1=general job satisfaction; item 2=satisfaction concerning working conditions; item 3=satisfaction concerning earnings; item 4=satisfaction concerning opportunities for professional growth.

Note
All items range from 0 (completely unsatisfied) to 4 (completely satisfied). The score is the weighted average of the numbers from 0 to 4 with weights equal to the conditional frequencies given each covariate configuration.

less, especially young people, who need more time for education and socializing. However, taking into account the fact that the length of the working week is usually fixed for an employee, an insignificant influence can be observed on the level of satisfaction, due to the low variability of this characteristic in the sample. It is also useful to take into account the working status of the respondent (i.e. whether the respondent works or is on leave) in order to verify potential different effects on satisfaction.

Another group of characteristics influencing job satisfaction includes the personal profile of the respondent. The same job might result in different levels of satisfaction for different people. Three types of personal characteristics are discussed in this chapter: the age of the respondent, his/her education and gender. For age, the assumption of non-linear dependence is quite usual. Regarding this research, we assume that the influence is linear because of the fact that all respondents in the sample are young – the maximal difference in age between respondents is 11 years. In this situation a linear approximation can provide reliable results, help to avoid problems of multicollinearity and reduce the number of estimated parameters. Another important characteristic is the educational level of the respondent. On the one hand, expectations from work are lower for respondents with less formal education, while their dissatisfaction with work and life in general can be higher, due to limited career options. However, it should also be noted that better educated young people might be less satisfied due to overeducation (or bad matching). Three groups of respondents are identified: subjects with graduate and postgraduate qualifications, subjects who have attended secondary and secondary professional education, and those with a lower educational level. The possible influence of the respondent's gender should also be taken into account. It can be argued that the same factors can influence the satisfaction level of women and men in different ways.

The third group of factors concerns the external characteristics of the respondent's life. The first part of this set of factors consists of family characteristics, including marital status, and the presence of children in the family. One might suppose that married people with children have a higher level of needs, and as a result want more from work; consequently, the job satisfaction level for these respondents would be lower. However, the presence of (a higher number of) children may increase job satisfaction in terms of the higher perceived utility of having a job (and income that can also be used to provide for children), in comparison to being unemployed (a condition that can have a dramatic effect, especially if the subject has children).[2] The final factor employed in the analysis regards the respondent's place of residence. It is to be expected that people living in big cities will be more satisfied with their job, as they have more opportunities to find suitable work than people living in smaller villages.

6 The econometric model

An econometric model was considered in which each observed ordinal response is seen as a discretized version of a certain type of satisfaction conceived as a continuous latent variable depending on fixed effects (for the unobserved heterogeneity) and the covariates. In particular, for each response variable $j = 1, \ldots, J$, the latent variable for subject $i = 1, \ldots, n$ at occasion $t = 1, \ldots, T$ satisfies the model:

$$y_{ijt}^* = \alpha_{ij} + x_{it}'\beta_j + \varepsilon_{ijt}, \ i = 1,\ldots,n, \ j = 1,\ldots,J, \ t = 1,\ldots T,$$

where ε_{ijt} are independent random error terms with standard logistic distribution.

The ordinal observed variables y_{ijt} are obtained by discretizing the latent variables according to a series of cutpoints $\tau_0, \ldots, \tau_{c-1}$ where c is the number of ordered response categories, from 0 to $c-1$; therefore:

$$
y_{ijt} = f(x) = \begin{cases} 0, & -\infty < y^*_{ijt} \leq \tau_1, \\ \quad \vdots \\ c-1, & \tau_{c-1} \leq y^*_{ijt} < \infty. \end{cases}
$$

In order to estimate the model the method described in Baetschmann *et al.* (2015) is adopted, based on maximizing a log-likelihood function taking into account all the possible dichotomizations of the response variables. In particular, for dichotomization d, with $d = 1, \ldots, c-1$, every response variable y_{ijt} is transformed in the binary variable $z^{(d)}_{ijt} = 1\{y_{ijt} \geq d\}$, where $1\{\cdot\}$ denotes the indicator function equal to 1 if its argument is true and to 0 otherwise. It is easy to prove that the above assumptions imply the following logit model on these dichotomized variables:

$$
\log \frac{p(z^{(d)}_{ijt} = 1 \mid \alpha_{ij}, x_{it})}{p(z^{(d)}_{ijt} = 0 \mid \alpha_{ij}, x_{it})} = \alpha_{ij} + x'_{it}\beta_j.
$$

Therefore, with reference to each response variable j, with $j = 1, \ldots, J$, the log-likelihood that is maximized to estimate the parameter vector β_j has the following expression:

$$
l(\beta_j) = \sum_{d=1}^{c-1} l^{(d)}(\beta_J),
$$

where $l^{(d)}(\beta_j)$ is the conditional log-likelihood based on the above logistic model for the dichotomized variables $z^{(d)}_{ijt}$. Standard errors may be computed as usual by a sandwich formula.

The estimator based on the maximization of $l(\beta_j)$ has desirable properties. In particular, it is consistent for β_j even if the unit specific effects α_{ij} are generated from a distribution correlated with the covariates. Moreover, as opposed to a random-effects approach, such a distribution need not be specified. On the other hand, as with any other fixed-effects approach, the estimation approach adopted here does not allow for the estimation of the effect of time-fixed covariates or covariates (e.g. age) which are collinear with time dummies when these are included; the approach may also lack efficiency with respect to a random-effects approach.

7 Econometric results

The results for the overall sample are presented first, followed by separate analyses differentiated by the gender, place of residence and age of the respondents.

This section concludes with an interpretation of the results as tests of compensating wage differentials, in the light of Section 3.

With regard to the overall sample (Table 8.2), the wage appears to be the most important covariate, as this significantly (and positively) affects the responses to all four questions. Satisfaction with respect to earnings is also significantly (negatively) affected by the last time dummy; a possible explanation involves the lag in the impact of the financial crisis and "great recession" on a perceived reduction in job security and in terms of higher uncertainty about future earnings prospects.

As for the separate analysis for gender (Table 8.3), the pattern is interestingly different: for women the only significant covariate is wages, which positively affects the opinion about job satisfaction with respect to any of the four aspects. A possible explanation relates to the "unpaid work" that is mainly done by women and produces a higher opportunity cost of "paid work", with consequently higher job satisfaction determined by higher wage levels. As for men, the situation is more complex and less clear. For men, having a partner has a negative effect on their degree of satisfaction with respect to opportunities for professional growth; this can also be explained by the fact that married people might have less geographical mobility to search for better career opportunities. Having a higher education has a negative effect on opinions about job satisfaction with respect to earnings, perhaps due to overeducation[3] (or bad matching) phenomena. Finally, job satisfaction with respect to earnings is affected positively by wage levels, and negatively by the time dummy for the year 2009.

Distinguishing young people living in capitals, in cities or in other situations (mainly rural areas), offers a diversified picture (Table 8.4). With regard to subjects living in capitals, the covariate of wages (in ppp) has a significant positive role for all types of satisfaction (but with respect to working conditions); in other terms, higher job satisfaction for those living in capitals is strongly related to higher wage levels (in ppp). In addition, educational level has a certain importance in affecting job satisfaction among better-educated subjects; in particular, a tertiary level of education negatively affects job satisfaction with respect to jobs in general and earnings.[4] As for subjects living in capitals, no covariate appears to have a significant effect on perceived job satisfaction with regard to working conditions; on the contrary, for subjects living in cities, this latter item is affected significantly and negatively by marital status and hours of work, and positively by base educational level.[5] Finally, with regard to subjects living in "other places with respect to capitals and cities", it is worth noting the significant and positive effect of wages for two items (the second and third), again confirming the key role of wage levels in affecting job satisfaction. In addition, the third item, concerning satisfaction with respect to earnings, is significantly and negatively affected by the time dummies (2007–2010), likely due to a structural decline in the prospects of rural areas with respect to capitals and cities, also as a consequence of the

Table 8.2 Parameter estimates for the overall sample

Covariate	General job satisfaction			Working conditions			Earnings			Opportunities for growth		
	est.	s.e.	p-value	est.	s.e.	p-value	est.	s.e.	p-value	est.	s.e.	p-value
marital.together	-0.087	0.178	0.623	-0.063	0.177	0.723	-0.208	0.171	0.223	-0.264	0.182	0.148
n.children	-0.061	0.207	0.767	0.071	0.204	0.729	0.188	0.188	0.316	0.223	0.189	0.239
education.base	-0.028	0.270	0.917	0.253	0.292	0.387	-0.206	0.302	0.494	-0.076	0.266	0.776
education.higher	0.073	0.370	0.843	0.462	0.395	0.242	-0.325	0.393	0.409	-0.213	0.358	0.551
work.leave	-0.172	0.257	0.503	-0.044	0.251	0.861	0.315	0.250	0.208	0.046	0.226	0.839
hours	0.005	0.010	0.608	-0.003	0.009	0.741	0.006	0.009	0.494	0.005	0.009	0.590
wages	*0.035*	*0.012*	*0.004*	*0.032*	*0.011*	*0.004*	*0.080*	*0.017*	*0.000*	*0.030*	*0.011*	*0.007*
2007	-0.047	0.181	0.794	-0.127	0.178	0.475	0.026	0.173	0.881	0.106	0.161	0.510
2008	-0.037	0.183	0.839	0.028	0.186	0.879	0.089	0.188	0.635	-0.121	0.171	0.478
2009	-0.056	0.184	0.763	0.071	0.183	0.698	-0.231	0.196	0.239	0.122	0.181	0.502
2010	-0.033	0.203	0.871	-0.182	0.205	0.375	*-0.459*	*0.215*	*0.033*	0.007	0.199	0.971

Note
In "bold and italic" significant at 5%.

Table 8.3 Separate parameter estimates for men and women

Covariate	General job satisfaction			Working conditions			Earnings			Opportunities for growth		
	est.	s.e.	p-value	est.	s.e.	p-value	est.	s.e.	p-value	est.	s.e.	p-value
Men												
marital.together	-0.093	0.265	0.727	-0.137	0.285	0.629	-0.283	0.264	0.283	**-0.525**	**0.281**	**0.062**
n.children	-0.090	0.249	0.717	0.128	0.256	0.616	0.233	0.255	0.361	0.171	0.253	0.499
education.base	-0.211	0.385	0.583	0.257	0.377	0.495	-0.610	0.372	0.101	-0.136	0.327	0.677
education.higher	-0.118	0.614	0.847	0.569	0.660	0.388	*-1.300*	*0.548*	*0.018*	-0.708	0.555	0.202
work.leave	-0.517	0.899	0.565	0.217	0.610	0.722	0.073	1.091	0.947	-1.672	1.400	0.232
hours	-0.004	0.014	0.778	0.000	0.015	0.989	0.000	0.014	0.980	0.002	0.014	0.899
wages	0.014	0.019	0.456	0.004	0.017	0.802	*0.072*	*0.020*	*0.000*	0.025	0.019	0.183
2007	0.091	0.272	0.737	0.073	0.257	0.777	-0.019	0.238	0.936	-0.010	0.251	0.968
2008	0.203	0.279	0.467	0.342	0.278	0.219	0.057	0.265	0.829	0.004	0.269	0.987
2009	0.106	0.277	0.703	0.187	0.269	0.488	**-0.521**	**0.277**	**0.060**	0.238	0.274	0.387
2010	0.238	0.307	0.439	-0.012	0.302	0.970	-0.450	0.303	0.137	0.089	0.307	0.772
Women												
marital.together	-0.075	0.242	0.758	-0.047	0.223	0.833	-0.156	0.226	0.490	-0.089	0.253	0.726
n.children	-0.003	0.364	0.994	0.126	0.351	0.720	0.186	0.294	0.526	0.337	0.324	0.298
education.base	0.213	0.356	0.549	0.410	0.451	0.363	0.752	0.489	0.124	-0.103	0.427	0.809
education.higher	0.323	0.469	0.490	0.511	0.548	0.351	0.789	0.583	0.176	-0.100	0.516	0.847
work.leave	-0.160	0.306	0.601	-0.038	0.303	0.900	0.303	0.284	0.285	0.068	0.273	0.803
hours	0.012	0.013	0.360	-0.005	0.012	0.698	0.012	0.012	0.321	0.008	0.013	0.519
wages	*0.051*	*0.017*	*0.003*	*0.059*	*0.017*	*0.001*	*0.090*	*0.029*	*0.002*	*0.037*	*0.015*	*0.016*
2007	-0.161	0.244	0.510	-0.310	0.246	0.208	0.028	0.250	0.912	0.198	0.215	0.357
2008	-0.217	0.247	0.380	-0.230	0.252	0.361	0.081	0.270	0.763	-0.232	0.227	0.306
2009	-0.184	0.252	0.466	-0.021	0.251	0.933	-0.018	0.275	0.949	0.034	0.250	0.891
2010	-0.222	0.272	0.414	-0.291	0.277	0.293	-0.490	0.307	0.111	-0.053	0.274	0.846

Note
In "bold" significant at 10%, in "bold and italic" significant at 5%.

Table 8.4 Separate analysis for capital/city/other

Covariate	General job satisfaction			Working conditions			Earnings			Opportunities for growth		
	est.	s.e.	p-value	est.	s.e.	p-value	est.	s.e.	p-value	est.	s.e.	p-value
Capital												
marital.together	0.230	0.273	0.398	0.240	0.281	0.392	-0.125	0.248	0.613	-0.049	0.264	0.854
n.children	-0.080	0.294	0.784	0.076	0.334	0.821	0.150	0.279	0.590	0.206	0.281	0.465
education.base	-0.677	0.406	0.095	-0.476	0.441	0.281	-0.952	0.386	0.014	-0.407	0.364	0.263
education.higher	-0.559	0.482	0.246	-0.104	0.537	0.846	-1.232	0.497	0.013	-0.533	0.458	0.244
work.leave	-0.049	0.387	0.900	0.088	0.400	0.826	0.410	0.329	0.213	-0.039	0.319	0.902
hours	0.007	0.014	0.592	0.004	0.012	0.757	0.006	0.012	0.630	0.004	0.012	0.775
wages	0.029	0.015	0.051	0.020	0.014	0.159	0.066	0.016	0.000	0.028	0.014	0.054
2007	0.255	0.272	0.350	-0.062	0.252	0.804	0.344	0.240	0.152	0.559	0.224	0.013
2008	0.166	0.262	0.525	0.181	0.278	0.515	0.390	0.265	0.141	0.191	0.245	0.434
2009	0.013	0.268	0.962	-0.007	0.272	0.978	-0.081	0.264	0.758	0.310	0.265	0.243
2010	0.079	0.297	0.791	-0.325	0.313	0.298	-0.126	0.298	0.673	0.158	0.291	0.586
City												
marital.together	-0.418	0.333	0.210	-0.684	0.343	0.046	-0.306	0.360	0.394	-0.552	0.399	0.167
n.children	0.110	0.408	0.787	0.238	0.349	0.496	0.167	0.334	0.617	0.497	0.352	0.158
education.base	0.349	0.449	0.437	0.760	0.420	0.071	0.431	0.526	0.413	0.356	0.522	0.495
education.higher	0.547	0.716	0.445	0.706	0.764	0.355	0.695	0.751	0.355	0.164	0.715	0.819
work.leave	0.240	0.523	0.646	0.150	0.449	0.738	0.177	0.576	0.758	0.745	0.537	0.165
hours	-0.012	0.023	0.595	-0.048	0.024	0.049	0.004	0.020	0.859	-0.024	0.020	0.224

wages	0.048	0.030	0.104	0.024	0.025	0.344	0.059	0.048	0.217	0.041	0.029	0.167
2007	-0.319	0.345	0.355	0.201	0.370	0.586	0.381	0.357	0.286	-0.212	0.335	0.526
2008	-0.546	0.375	0.145	-0.150	0.393	0.703	0.292	0.410	0.477	-0.489	0.370	0.187
2009	-0.564	0.362	0.119	0.125	0.389	0.747	-0.038	0.426	0.928	-0.447	0.376	0.234
2010	**-0.675**	**0.393**	**0.085**	0.168	0.391	0.669	-0.548	0.478	0.251	-0.335	0.420	0.425
Other												
marital.together	-0.290	0.340	0.393	0.085	0.317	0.788	-0.127	0.365	0.728	-0.300	0.327	0.360
n.children	-0.137	0.450	0.760	-0.168	0.381	0.659	0.382	0.459	0.405	-0.058	0.392	0.883
edu.base	1.075	0.842	0.202	1.188	0.883	0.178	0.302	0.660	0.647	0.424	0.558	0.448
edu.higher	1.102	1.158	0.341	1.201	1.101	0.275	0.411	1.046	0.695	0.518	1.174	0.659
work.leave	**-0.861**	**0.453**	**0.057**	-0.451	0.455	0.321	0.445	0.490	0.363	-0.293	0.408	0.472
hours	0.019	0.018	0.299	0.019	0.018	0.294	0.023	0.017	0.162	***0.043***	***0.020***	***0.036***
wages	0.027	0.033	0.418	***0.063***	***0.030***	***0.036***	***0.153***	***0.030***	***0.000***	0.023	0.030	0.435
2007	-0.381	0.358	0.287	**-0.599**	**0.359**	**0.095**	***-0.936***	***0.333***	***0.005***	-0.470	0.310	0.130
2008	0.004	0.371	0.991	-0.135	0.347	0.696	***-0.858***	***0.342***	***0.012***	-0.390	0.341	0.253
2009	0.238	0.378	0.529	0.052	0.351	0.882	***-1.018***	***0.379***	***0.007***	0.314	0.348	0.366
2010	0.303	0.400	0.450	-0.320	0.394	0.416	***-1.241***	***0.404***	***0.002***	-0.020	0.367	0.957

Note
In "bold" significant at 10%, in "bold and italic" significant at 5%.

Table 8.5 Separate analysis for younger and older subjects

Covariate	General job satisfaction			Working conditions			Earnings			Opportunities for growth		
	est.	s.e.	p-value	est.	s.e.	p-value	est.	s.e.	p-value	est.	s.e.	p-value
Younger												
marital.together	**-0.516**	**0.275**	**0.061**	-0.200	0.289	0.488	*-0.664*	*0.276*	*0.016*	-0.294	0.302	0.331
n.children	*0.720*	*0.334*	*0.031*	**0.624**	**0.363**	**0.086**	*0.781*	*0.317*	*0.014*	*0.797*	*0.305*	*0.009*
education.base	-0.225	0.368	0.541	-0.168	0.357	0.637	-0.107	0.412	0.795	-0.196	0.358	0.584
education.higher	-0.065	0.561	0.907	-0.086	0.608	0.888	-0.842	0.585	0.150	-0.557	0.526	0.289
work.leave	**-0.702**	**0.386**	**0.069**	-0.255	0.387	0.511	0.311	0.415	0.453	-0.340	0.333	0.308
hours	0.000	0.015	0.976	-0.006	0.014	0.654	0.003	0.013	0.827	0.006	0.013	0.606
wages	*0.059*	*0.019*	*0.002*	*0.055*	*0.018*	*0.002*	*0.142*	*0.022*	*0.000*	*0.064*	*0.020*	*0.001*
2007	-0.128	0.218	0.556	-0.271	0.226	0.230	-0.132	0.213	0.537	0.132	0.199	0.506
2008	-0.133	0.252	0.597	-0.215	0.246	0.383	-0.288	0.233	0.217	-0.279	0.239	0.244
2009	-0.234	0.261	0.370	-0.390	0.262	0.136	*-0.657*	*0.261*	*0.012*	-0.088	0.258	0.733
2010	-0.157	0.314	0.618	-0.506	0.313	0.106	*-1.114*	*0.304*	*0.000*	-0.247	0.303	0.414
Older												
marital.together	0.025	0.387	0.949	-0.116	0.424	0.784	0.408	0.312	0.191	-0.288	0.320	0.369
n.children	**-0.744**	**0.427**	**0.081**	-0.418	0.411	0.310	-0.060	0.321	0.852	-0.060	0.356	0.867
education.base	0.417	0.668	0.532	0.961	0.655	0.142	-0.064	0.613	0.917	0.118	0.497	0.812
education.higher	*1.469*	*0.803*	*0.068*	*3.000*	*0.888*	*0.001*	0.490	0.800	0.541	0.260	0.720	0.718
work.leave	-0.081	0.414	0.845	0.267	0.375	0.476	0.432	0.405	0.286	0.334	0.381	0.380
hours	0.008	0.021	0.698	**0.035**	**0.020**	**0.087**	0.015	0.018	0.419	0.002	0.017	0.892
wages	0.014	0.019	0.468	0.028	0.019	0.125	0.049	0.032	0.124	0.015	0.016	0.372
2007	1.595	1.955	0.414	0.555	2.119	0.794	0.140	2.240	0.950	*0.853*	*0.260*	*0.001*
2008	1.631	1.952	0.403	0.577	2.099	0.783	0.429	2.247	0.849	*0.741*	*0.263*	*0.005*
2009	1.496	1.950	0.443	0.500	2.121	0.814	0.013	2.247	0.996	*0.838*	*0.272*	*0.002*
2010	1.477	1.956	0.450	0.081	2.132	0.970	-0.230	2.252	0.918	*0.760*	*0.289*	*0.009*

Note
In "bold" significant at 10%, in "bold and italic" significant at 5%.

varied geographical and sectoral impact of the international financial crisis and the consequent "great recession".

Finally, individuals that are at most 23 years old at the last interview can be considered separately from other subjects.[6] The results highlight that job satisfaction among younger subjects is much more sensitive to wages; a possible explanation relates to the higher opportunity cost of younger individuals, due to a higher potential investment in schooling and other educational or training activities. Interestingly, the wage is never significant for older subjects, which supports fully compensating wage differentials for this category of workers (this issue will be discussed at the end of this section). In addition, marital status ("together") negatively affects younger respondents, possibly due to consequent lower geographical mobility. As for the covariate "number of children", it should be noted that, while it does not have a significant effect on overall sample, it has a significant effect on the sample of younger people; in particular, the presence of (a higher number of) children positively affects job satisfaction (with respect to all items) in the case of younger workers; as already mentioned in Section 5, a possible explanation refers to the comparative higher perceived value/utility (and satisfaction) of having a job and a labour income (with respect to being unemployed) when it crucially permits a better life and education for children. However, for "older" workers satisfaction with the job in general is negatively affected by the presence of children, highlighting the need for a more in-depth investigation.[7] In addition, for younger people to be in "work leave" negatively affects the satisfaction with the job in general; while for older respondents satisfaction with working conditions is positively affected by the working hours. As for this latter group the positive and significant effect of having a tertiary education on job satisfaction should be mentioned, with respect to the job in general and with respect to working conditions.[8] Finally, 2009–2010 dummy variables negatively affect satisfaction among younger subjects with respect to earnings, while for older respondents all time dummies have a positive effect on job satisfaction with respect to opportunities for professional growth.

The results can now be interpreted in the light of the discussion in Section 3. For all but one of the samples considered, there is at least one response variable for which the estimated wage effect turns out to be significantly positive. This finding is at odds with wage differentials fully compensating for latent workplace disamenities. Partially compensating wage differentials could in fact obscure even larger pure wage effects. An interesting exception regards the older subjects in the sample, for whom wage differentials have no explanatory power for differentials in job satisfaction, however this variable is defined. This appears to support the theory of compensating wage differentials for the more experienced subjects in the Russian youth labour market.

8 Final remarks

This chapter has estimated ordered logit models of job satisfaction with individual fixed effects for a panel data of young Russian workers, carrying out separate analyses for the general job satisfaction variable and three variables regarding specific aspects of job satisfaction. A number of sub-samples have also been considered along with the overall sample.

The wage plays a prominent role as an explanatory variable in the model specifications. Indeed, for all but one sample considered, there is at least one job satisfaction variable with a significantly positive wage effect. This result can be interpreted as a failure of the theory of compensating wage differentials in the Russian youth labour market. Interestingly, compensating wage differentials only appear to be at work among the older subjects; the estimates also show strong gender and location effects. This chapter is a first attempt to investigate job satisfaction among Russian youth, and a more in-depth analysis would appear to be necessary.[9] However, a number of general and specific policy implications already emerge as a result of this analysis. In particular, one general policy implication regards the opportunity to improve and extend the definition of the policy objectives regarding the (youth) labour market, by including performance indicators regarding several dimensions of job quality and job satisfaction, in addition to traditional performance indexes (employment/unemployment and NEET rates). In addition, these results could also favour a better definition of specific policy interventions and public services for young people in general and, in particular, for some specific segments, such as young women, young people with children, and those living outside capitals and cities.

Appendix

Table A8.1 Frequency of each interview configuration: 1 for interviewed in a certain year, 0 otherwise

2006	2007	2008	2009	2010	Frequency
0	0	0	0	1	902
0	0	0	1	0	54
0	0	1	0	0	53
0	1	0	0	0	18
1	0	0	0	0	17
Total with 1 interview					1,044
0	0	0	1	1	160
0	0	1	0	1	49
0	0	1	1	0	33
0	1	0	0	1	24
0	1	0	1	0	9
0	1	1	0	0	14
1	0	0	0	1	8
1	0	0	1	0	4
1	0	1	0	0	12
1	1	0	0	0	10
Total with 2 interviews					323
0	0	1	1	1	155
0	1	0	1	1	28
0	1	1	0	1	25
0	1	1	1	0	25
1	0	0	1	1	9
1	0	1	0	1	5
1	0	1	1	0	13
1	1	0	0	1	9
1	1	0	1	0	13
1	1	1	0	0	7
Total with 3 interviews					289
0	1	1	1	1	84
1	0	1	1	1	28
1	1	0	1	1	10
1	1	1	0	1	26
1	1	1	1	0	21
Total with 4 interviews					169
1	1	1	1	1	113
Total with 5 interviews					113
Total					1,938

Table A8.2 Distribution of the covariates

Covariate	Modality/ indicator	2006	2007	2008	2009	2010	Overall
marital status	single	0.626	0.567	0.557	0.474	0.443	0.498
	together	0.374	0.433	0.443	0.526	0.557	0.502
children	yes	0.180	0.227	0.285	0.319	0.345	0.303
n.children	mean	0.193	0.243	0.311	0.345	0.397	0.338
	s.d.	0.428	0.465	0.516	0.531	0.592	0.545
n.minors	mean	0.193	0.241	0.306	0.336	0.391	0.332
	s.d	0.428	0.464	0.511	0.526	0.590	0.542
education	lower	0.151	0.154	0.151	0.133	0.116	0.133
	base	0.748	0.709	0.674	0.639	0.604	0.647
	higher	0.102	0.138	0.175	0.228	0.280	0.221
gender	male	0.462	0.456	0.462	0.469	0.494	0.476
	female	0.538	0.544	0.538	0.531	0.506	0.524
age	mean	21.223	21.872	22.342	23.287	24.001	23.101
	s.d.	1.621	1.807	2.114	2.133	2.364	2.364
working status	on leave	0.052	0.067	0.075	0.074	0.077	0.073
	working	0.948	0.933	0.925	0.926	0.923	0.927
hours	mean	41.377	41.555	41.124	41.241	41.817	41.516
	s.d.	7.748	7.424	8.426	7.817	7.207	7.625
wages	means	6.321	8.413	11.005	11.381	13.407	11.440
	s.d.	4.439	4.867	7.639	7.022	8.344	7.690
living	capital	0.475	0.450	0.486	0.490	0.490	0.483
	city	0.249	0.261	0.270	0.278	0.272	0.270
	other	0.275	0.289	0.244	0.232	0.238	0.247
n. obs.		**305**	**436**	**663**	**759**	**1,635**	**3,798**

Notes

1 Data collected during earlier waves of the survey is not used due to problem of sample exhaustion.
2 Clearly country-specific conditions could also play a key role. What follows is some basic information about regulations in Russia, and the system of support for families with children: (i) every healthy man aged 18–27 years should undergo military service; men with two children are exempt from military service; (ii) Russian women caring for a baby (for up to three years) cannot be fired; after the birth of her second child, the family receives what is known as "maternity capital", which can be used, for example, to improve housing conditions. Some of these conditions might explain the positive effect the number of children could have on job satisfaction, especially among younger people. At the same time they may be less important for "older" people, where the presence of a higher number of children may strongly limit career growth, without the possibility of availing of benefits to compensate for missed career opportunities.
3 It consists of graduates that find a job for which their degree is neither necessary nor useful.
4 This can be partly explained by the existence of "bad matching" (or overeducation) and a consequent inadequate return for the individual (and family) investment in tertiary education.
5 In addition, the significant negative effect of the 2010 time dummy shows the impact of the crisis on job satisfaction with respect to work in general for young people living in cities.

6 It should be considered that in Russia 17–18 is the age when people finish secondary school, and 22–23 is the age when some young people receive a master degree. Obviously, there is heterogeneity, and while some young people also work during their tertiary educational period, others look for and find a job only after completing their education.

7 As mentioned in a previous note, the Russian system of support for families with children could play a key role. Results can also be found for different specifications of the econometric model, e.g. distinguishing younger and older respondents according to gender. All results are available upon request.

8 This result, partly contrasting with previous results on the overall sample, shows a positive role – for this older group – of investment in higher education, also in terms of job satisfaction (but excluding satisfaction with respect to earnings and opportunities for professional growth).

9 For example, this research could be extended along two directions: (i) by relaxing the assumption of strictly exogenous wages and (ii) by including measures of job disamenities in the analysis.

9 The school-to-work transition in the Latin Rim

The case of Italy

Francesco Pastore

Introduction

The immediate impact of what the Nobel Prize winner Paul Krugman has referred to as a twenty-first-century version of the Great Depression has been to make existing weaknesses in Italy's school-to-work transition system worse, adding further cause for concern. In fact, the crisis has dramatically increased both the absolute and relative disadvantage of young people as compared to adults, which was however already high before the crisis.

This chapter starts from setting out the main effects the current recession has had on youth labour market outcomes over the past decade, to proceed with an in-depth analysis of the long-term weaknesses of the Italian school-to-work transition system. In fact, beyond the outcomes of recent years, young Italians have always had to face one of the toughest school-to-work transition paths in the world. The main argument of this chapter is, in fact, that youth unemployment is the consequence of disorganized school-to-work transitions. They can be seen as two sides of the same coin. In turn, the difficulties young people encounter in achieving *smooth* transitions and the ensuing long-term unemployment depend not so much on insufficient labour market flexibility, as on the failure of the education and training systems to deal with and overcome what appears to be undoubtedly the principal handicap of the young, the one that sets them apart from adults: namely, their lack of generic, but even more so job specific work experience.

A school-to-work transition regime denotes the set of institutions and rules that govern and supervise the passage from school to adulthood. They include the degree of regulation and flexibility of the labour market, but also the degree of flexibility of the educational and training system. Typically, the state also provides placement services to help young people find a job more easily. The household is also part of the transition, by providing, for instance, financial support during the entire transition and hence also a cushion against the risk of unemployment. The role assigned to each institution within a regime is different from one country to the other and, based on such differences, it is possible to identify different regimes (Ryan, 2001; O'Higgins, 2001; Hammer, 2003; Pastore, 2015a).

On a national scale, in fact, the indicators of absolute and relative disadvantage of the young tend to form clusters of countries that share similar characteristics, rather than arranging themselves in an orderly line. Different school-to-work transition *regimes* can therefore be said to characterize more or less homogeneous groups of nations. These *regimes* tend to overlap those of the welfare state: a) "Continental European"; b) "Scandinavian"; c) "Liberal"; d) "Mediterranean European"; e) "Post-communist"; f) "Asian". The first three regimes are the traditional ones in Esping-Andersen's definition (1990).

The Italian regime belongs to the Mediterranean European group that also includes France, Greece, Portugal and Spain. In these countries, each institution that takes part in the transition process, namely the family, enterprises, the market, educational and professional training systems, employment agencies and labour legislation, plays a very similar role.

Over the past 20 years there has also been a similar evolution in legislation that has witnessed the gradual reform of employment contract regulations. This reform has brought greater flexibility and diversity to work contracts and a radical overhaul of education systems as outlined by the so-called Bologna Process, begun within the wider context of the Lisbon Agenda and continued under that of Europe 2020.

The analysis will also allow discussing the conditions for a successful implementation of the European Youth Guarantee in Italy. In principle, the programme should be able to affect the frictional and mismatch components of unemployment, if not the Keynesian and neoclassical ones, as also the experience of Scandinavian countries suggests. However, this requires an in-depth transformation of the entire school-to-work transition system, involving not only public employment services, but also educational and training systems. To tackle the Keynesian and neoclassical components, instead, it is vital to rethink the European austerity and reduce the labour wedge.

2 Facts that characterize the Italian scenario

The current dramatic youth condition is the result of great depression, but also before the crisis exploded, Italy experienced a high youth unemployment rate. This suggests that the new situation is simply exacerbating long-term difficulties.

2.1 The impact of the Great Depression

Italy differs very little from other Southern EU countries with regard to the way the youth unemployment rate (YUR) has evolved during the current recession. Figure 9.1 shows the trend in the YUR and in the adult unemployment rate (AUR) by gender between 1993 and 2012. Not surprisingly, the young have been the worst hit by the recent recession. The weakness of young people during any economic recession is a well-known fact in the literature due to the tendency of firms to apply the so-called "LIFO (last-in-first-out) principle" to their decisions concerning dismissals. The YUR increased from 24 per cent in 2007 to around 32 per cent in 2011 and 35.3 per cent in 2012. In Italy, the financial crisis hit hard the real sector only from the end of 2011.

What is new when we compare the current economic crisis to that of 1991, is that the LIFO principle has tended to become stronger as a result of the widespread use of temporary employment contracts over the past 15 years. In fact, Figure 9.1 illustrates increased fluctuation in the YUR since 1997 when, for the first time, the Treu Law began to liberalize the use of short-term contracts. While the late 1990s and early 2000s witnessed a reduction in the YUR, mainly on account of the widespread use of short-term contracts, at the start of the economic crisis in 2008, the YUR soared, quickly reaching, by the year 2011, the mid-1990s level.

By comparison, the AUR has remained much more stable over the entire period. The recent two-tier reforms have, in some ways, further reduced fluctuation in the AUR, since pressures on the business cycle have been transferred to the YUR.

Interestingly, in the period under consideration, we can observe a slight decrease in gender differences in unemployment rates both for the young and for adults. The gender gap in the YUR goes down from 9.3 per cent in 1993 to 3.8 per cent in 2012. This complex phenomenon, which has already been reported in other countries, is mainly the result of a growing educational gap in favour of women.

The YUR is an index of absolute disadvantage that expresses how the youth labour market problem is affected by the business cycle. It does not enable us, however, to understand whether the disadvantage of young people in the labour market is higher or lower than that of adults. The aim of Figure 9.2 is to show how the YUR/AUR ratio has evolved by gender from 1993 to the present day. It

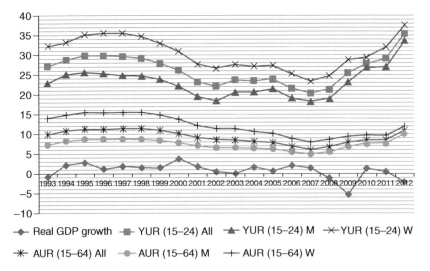

Figure 9.1 Recent evolution in YUR (15–24 years), AUR (15–64 years) and real GDP growth.

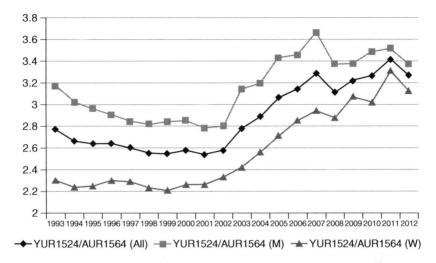

Figure 9.2 Recent evolution in the YUR (15–24 years) and AUR (25–54 years) ratio.

clearly indicates that not only has the mean value remained very high by EU standards (about 2), but the relative disadvantage of young people has escalated even more dramatically as a result of the two-tier reforms implemented in the early 2000s.

Interestingly, in 2012, the youth to adult unemployment ratio has fallen because also the AUR has increased. As Newell and Pastore (1999) note, the depth of the recession can be measured from the involvement of the adults: when firms close down, rather than marginally reducing their workforce, mass dismissals become conspicuous and also the adults experience unemployment.

An interesting way of assessing the impact of the crisis on the young is to examine the YUR in relation to the level of education of the unemployed. Figure 9.3 does this and shows that the crisis has not had the same effect on all categories of workers. In fact, the worst affected groups are those whose education did not go beyond the compulsory level. The absolute position of young people with a secondary high school diploma has also worsened. Only for young people in possession of a university degree has there been a decrease in the unemployment rate. Based on unreported outcomes by gender, the reduction in the unemployment rate of young people holding a university degree depends particularly on women. Other educational groups seem to exhibit similar evolutions across genders.

2.2 Long-term facts

The facts we are reporting with regard to the current Great Depression are actually the result of structural problems. More than 60 per cent of the unemployed

204   *F. Pastore*

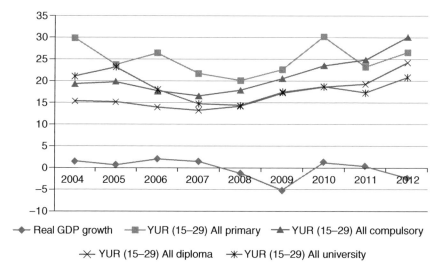

Figure 9.3 YUR (15–29 years) by educational level.

in Italy belong to the category of *new entrants* (workers who are entering the labour market for the first time). Despite a greater proliferation of temporary, casual and short-term jobs, in 2010, 26.1 per cent of the unemployed admitted to a complete lack of work experience.

The above-mentioned ratio of the YUR (15–24 years) to the AUR (25–54 years) is just over 2 in the European Union (EU), whereas the corresponding figure for Italy is close to 4 (Figure 9.4).

The share of long-term youth unemployment (more than 12 months) is much higher in Italy than in other European countries. This is a rather unusual phenomenon compared to elsewhere. As Clark and Summers (1982) have pointed out, the duration of youth unemployment is usually lower than the mean on account of the tendency of the young to change frequently from one situation to another on the labour market. Young people seek the *best job-worker match*, but before finding it, they often follow winding paths that lead them to experiment with a variety of labour market conditions. This search tends to interrupt the mean duration of their periods of unemployment.

What causes even greater concern on the Italian scene is the period of transition from school to permanent employment. According to an estimate made by Quintini *et al.* (2007, table 2), it is the highest among OECD countries. This period of transition which was 62.4 months (5.2 years) in 1995, reached 70.5 months in 2000, and fell to 51.3 months in 2005 when temporary jobs became more available. During the same period of time, the EU average was 30 months, i.e. less than half.

How can these differences be explained? They depend on a number of different factors:

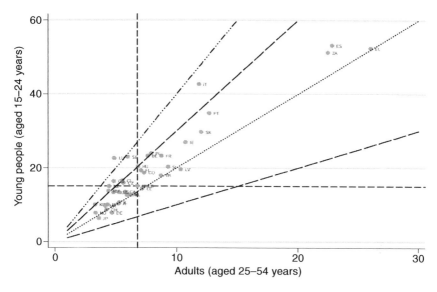

Figure 9.4 Youth and adult unemployment rate in OECD countries (2014).

Source: Own processing of OECD data.

a   the excessively rigid education system, particularly in the tertiary stage, that results in very late entry to the labour market;

b   the low level of both secondary and tertiary education;

c   insufficient contact between the world of education and the labour market, that prevents young people from gaining work experience;

d   the lack of an adequate vocational training system;

e   the lack of intermediation between demand and supply of qualifications.

As in the other so-called Latin Rim countries, gender differences among the young favour men. This is the opposite of what occurs in Northern and East European countries. For example, Figure 9.5 shows that in Italy, as in Greece, and a limited number of other traditionally Catholic countries such as Chile, Portugal, Poland and Belgium, the gap clearly goes against young women.

According to Eurostat data (2009), Italy is near the bottom of the EU table for the number of young university graduates. In fact, in 2011, in the population aged between 25 and 34, only 27 out of every hundred had a university degree. This figure has risen in the past decade, but remains below the European mean of 30 per cent, while countries such as France, Spain, Denmark, Sweden and the United Kingdom have reached a total of 40 per cent.

This is surprising as 75 per cent of Italian students (one of the highest percentages in OECD countries) obtain a secondary high school diploma that gives access to university. Why then do only a small percentage of students obtain a

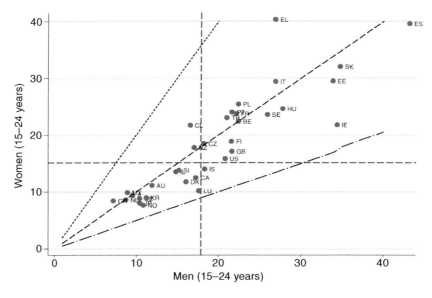

Figure 9.5 Gender gap in youth unemployment rates (2010).

Source: Own processing of OECD data.

degree? Difficulties seem to arise at the time of enrolling for university. In fact, only just over 70 per cent of those who *could* enrol actually sign up for a university course (OECD, 2009, A2.2).

This initial "creaming off" of students precedes a subsequent "selection" during the course of university studies. Italy is the leader among OECD countries for the number of students who drop out: in 2006, approximately 55 per cent of students dropped out without even obtaining the three-year degree qualification, a percentage that is considerably higher than the average 31 per cent (OECD, 2008, chart A4.1).

Another problem is the excessive duration of university studies (*fuoricorsismo – many students fail to finish their degree courses in the prescribed time*). This diminishes the incentive to invest in education.

Moreover, Eurostat (2009a) claims that in Italy, the probability of obtaining a degree is still closely linked to family social background. The offspring of better educated citizens have a seven-fold greater chance of obtaining a degree compared to their peers from poorer backgrounds. In the United Kingdom, this probability is two-fold, while in France and Spain it is 2.5 times higher. It is easy to imagine the negative consequences for young Italians caused by static social mobility (Caroleo and Pastore, 2012).

In addition to a low standard of education, it is important to underline the significant *mismatch* of human capital generated by disparity in demand (technical) and supply (humanistic). The mismatch often results in *over-education*: because of the lack of demand for their particular type of qualification, young people are forced to accept jobs intended for candidates with lower qualifications. McGuinness and Sloane (2010, table 3.6) report that in Italy the percentage of graduates employed in posts meant for secondary high school diploma holders, is one of the highest (23 per cent for first-time hiring) in the EU countries in their sample. With a total of 13 per cent of overeducated five years after graduation, Italy is the third lowest country in terms of performance, just marginally ahead of Spain and the United Kingdom.

3 Theoretical framework

This section provides a general theoretical framework useful when thinking of cross-country differences in the youth unemployment problem and the role of different policy instruments to help young people have a smooth school-to-work transition (for a detailed definition of the concept of transition system, see Raffe, 2008). The main reason for young people moving between different labour market statuses is their lower level of human capital and, therefore, productivity compared to adults, which *ceteris paribus* makes employers prefer adults. As also Becker (1962) noted, human capital has three general components: education, generic work experience and job-specific work experience. Generic work experience includes the ability to cope with the functional distribution of tasks within an organization, to respect deadlines and the internal hierarchy of an organization. All these skills can be learned in any type of job and are easily transferred from one job to another. Job specific work experience comprises specific skills that can only be gained and used in a given type of job. They include the ability to carry out specific types of task, such as, in rural areas, harvesting, feeding livestock.

This type of reasoning helps solve a typical puzzle of youth labour markets. With ever increasing educational attainment worldwide, the educational level of the younger generation is almost always greater than the old generation. Despite this, young people still have lower chances of finding employment. Why is that? The likely explanation is their lack of the other two components of human capital, generic and job specific work experience. That is, that behind the youth unemployment problem, there is a "youth experience gap".

Aiming to fill this gap, young people move in and out of employment in search of a best job-worker match, but if not found quickly, they tend to become unemployed or have inactivity while searching for a better job. During employment, some young people become aware of their gaps in education or training and, consequently, return to school (Clark and Summers, 1982 and the entire NBER volume edited by Freeman and Wise, 1982).

Youth unemployment is clearly related to the hardship involved in accumulating work experience. In the neo-liberalist view (see, for instance, OECD, 1994), causes of youth unemployment, especially the long spells experienced by many young people, can be found in past unemployment experiences, reducing their chances of finding gainful employment. In this stream of economic thought

(Blanchard and Diamond, 1994), unemployment causes a process of deskilling from the supply side: since the unemployed cannot use their skills because they are unemployed, they have lower productivity. On the demand side, employers see unemployment as a stigma: a sign of lack of skills and motivation. Lowering the share of long-term unemployment and reducing the average period would be an important policy target for neo-liberalists.

The OECD (1994) and Krugman (1994), among others, suggested that by rendering the labour market more flexible through legalizing and encouraging part-time and fixed-term contracts, the policy-makers will provide a simple and effective solution to young people's problem of work experience, enabling them to find the job they desire. There are two ways to make this happen. First, easily accessible fixed-term contracts would provide young people with more opportunities to gain the work experience they need and learn different working methods and tasks through short periods of employment. Second, increasing the degree of turnover in the labour market shortens the average duration of unemployment.

It should now be clear why, within this framework, labour market flexibility and low entry wages are the best solution to ease school-to-work transition. These solutions to the youth experience gap also have the merit of being low cost, since they automatically exist in the labour market. This is an important aspect of such a policy and helps understand its appeal in a time of increasingly stringent budget constrains for many governments worldwide.

Two arguments cast doubt on this solution to youth unemployment, suggesting that it is too simplistic and in need of amendments. The first is based on the empirical finding that only the least skilled and least motivated fall into long-term unemployment, therefore, there would be no lower job finding rate for them; instead the causal link would go in the opposite direction. Less skilled individuals would experience greater difficulty in finding gainful employment and, as a consequence, also longer unemployment spells (Heckman and Borjas, 1980; Heckman and Singer, 1984).

The policy implications of this reasoning are important. Training programmes finely tuned to the least skilled and motivated groups would be the best policy option to reduce youth unemployment. They would be more effective than increasing labour market flexibility. There is no guarantee that labour market flexibility would help the least skilled and least motivated and it is more likely it would only help those who are better educated and more motivated.

The second argument, for which Becker (1962) provides the theoretical basis, criticizes the effectiveness of labour market flexibility to actually help young people increase their human capital to the level of adults with similar education. The reasoning is that fixed-term contracts only generate sufficient incentive to invest in the formation of generic work experience. They do not allow young people to increase other skills specific to a given type of job due to their short time horizon. Why should employers and employees invest in the accumulation of skills specific only to a given type of job if the contract is temporary?

It is a common occurrence in countries with increased flexibility in youth labour markets that short-term contracts fail to provide young people with specific work experience. This type of market failure should be addressed by providing incentives to prolong short-term contracts or, specific programmes of on-the-job training aimed at enabling young people to accumulate job specific work experience.

In addition, from a more practical point of view, there is increasing empirical evidence to support the view that fixed-term contracts create precariousness of income for many young people experiencing frequent interruptions to their career. Too many temporary workers end up in dead-end jobs that they hoped would be a stepping stone to decent work (Bentolila and Dolado, 1994; Berton *et al.*, 2011).

The above arguments help understand why, in many of the countries, increasing flexibility of labour market entry – the so-called two-tier reforms – has reduced youth unemployment only to a small extent, while generating work precariousness (Blanchard and Landier, 2002; Bentolila *et al.*, 2012b). Fixed-term contracts alone cannot fill the youth experience gap.

Moreover, as ILO (2004) and Cazes and Nesporova (2007), among others, note, the experience of flexibility has shown that what its advocates usually consider its main advantage, namely its supposed universality is, in fact, one of its major shortcomings. Labour market flexibility is not the best solution for every country and confirms the wisdom that there are no such policy interventions that fit any country or economic condition. Labour market flexibility alone proves too often to be ineffective. It is a good instrument in particular types of labour market conditions where, for instance, there is also a high average level of educational attainment, where it goes together with flexibility in the market for goods and financial services.

These arguments also explain why labour market flexibility is only one of the policy instruments adopted in any country to help young people fill in the youth experience gap. Efficient educational and training systems, passive income support schemes on a contractual basis, fiscal incentives for employers, who are willing to hire long-term unemployed, prove to be no less important instruments (see, among others, Hennan *et al.*, 1996; Ryan, 2001; O'Higgins, 2001; Hammer, 2003; Raffe, 2008).

It is certainly difficult to find policies concordant with the institutional framework of any country. However, comparison of different countries' outcomes in addressing the problem of school-to-work transition suggests that youth unemployment is lower where:

- educational systems are more flexible;
- educational systems follow a dual (as opposed to a sequential) principle, which means that young people are provided training while at school and not after school;
- where labour market flexibility is coupled with high educational attainment;
- where Active Labor Market Policy (ALMP) is fine-tuned to the needs of the weakest groups and targeting and evaluation of training programmes are

implemented in a systematic way to discard the least effective and develop the most effective;
- where households do not bear all the cost of youth unemployment.

The educational system is more flexible if it foresees few or no obstacles to young people moving from one curriculum to another, does not impose constraints to access a given type of education and requires a reasonable number of years to attain a diploma. The educational systems that are more flexible and provide training, together with general education, appear to be more inclusive and feature lower dropout rates.

To sum up, labour market flexibility is not the one-size-fit-all solution to every problem young people encounter during their school-to-work transition. Labor market institutions are also very important. In particular, in the case of young people, the educational and training systems play a no less important role than the degree of labour market flexibility.

4 The evolution of labour market rules

4.1 A brief historical digression

At the beginning of the 1990s, there were two important reasons for increasing labour market flexibility. The first was related to Italy's unusual position within the international division of labour. Although it is an advanced country, it continues to produce a significant share of GDP in the traditional manufacturing sector. This encourages industries to request greater labour flexibility, since price competition can be important in traditional sectors.[1]

The second reason concerned the high degree of labour market rigidity, especially if we compare it with the United States, but also in relation to other European countries. In the early 1990s, many observers considered Italy to be one of the most rigid countries in what was already an inflexible Europe. Salary indexation had widened the gap between internal and European inflation to values above zero. The CIG (*Cassa Integrazione e Guadagni* – Redundancy and Earnings Fund) was believed to have made the closure of enterprises and collective dismissals both difficult and costly. Some observers argued that individual dismissals were also considerably impeded by art. 18 of the Workers' Statute that prohibits dismissal without a "just cause", a generic term which, according to prevailing case law, tribunals always interpret in favour of workers.

To obtain wage flexibility, salaries needed to be linked to work productivity instead of inflation. This issue was tackled in a series of large-scale political and social clashes in the decade between the 1984 St. Valentine Referendum and the 1993 Protocol Agreement. The latter led to *institutional indexation*, i.e. an agreement between unions, management and the government with regard to planned inflation. The institutional nature of the agreement meant that if real inflation rose above planned inflation, the trade unions had to wait until the subsequent national labour contract had been signed before they could recover the loss of purchasing power they had suffered. This mechanism led to an immediate dampening of inflation, but every time real inflation exceeded the programmed rate, it also involved an inevitable loss of wage purchasing power for the entire period between one contract and another. Moreover, the duration of collective labour contracts was prolonged, so that in the following period, real wages actually sustained substantial losses, often falling below growth in labour productivity, and therefore curbing growth in internal consumption (see also Pastore, 2010; Tronti, 2010).

Starting with the 1997 Treu Law that legalized the use of so-called atypical employment, a number of measures have succeeded in introducing greater numerical flexibility, especially for temporary work and coordinated and continuous collaboration (the so-called *co.co.co*). However, some aspects of this law, which were designed to prevent temporary work being used in a "non-standard" way, have never been put into practice. Furthermore, no insurance provisions have been brought into effect to cover the loss of income during periods of unemployment.

The following period witnessed new legislative provisions, such as the Maroni Law of 2003, for achieving numerical flexibility, rather than for protecting temporary workers. On the one hand, as many labour law experts claim, this law enabled employers to avoid their obligation of stipulating permanent contracts. At the same time, though, the law did introduce a more restrictive regulation with regard to co.co.co.s (now called co.co.pro.s). Unlike under the Treu Package, employers were obliged to make contracts official, thus granting workers some important juridical and economic rights. Nevertheless, the eagerly awaited conversion of co.co.pro.s to permanent employment contracts rarely occurred and many young people continued to work under a form of semi-dependent employment contract for years and years.

Overall, the aforementioned legislative measures diverge significantly from the 1970s Workers' Statute. Nevertheless, the strongest supporters of flexibility have criticized both the Treu Package and Biagi's Law for not reducing the costs of dismissal.

A new labour reform was implemented in 2012. The main aim of the so-called "Fornero Law", named after Elsa Fornero, the Minister of Labour who proposed it, was to eliminate some of the disadvantages young people encounter in entering the labour market. According to a number of observers, young people were meeting serious and increasing hardship in finding permanent employment on account of the two-tier reforms implemented previously. The Fornero Law aimed to improve young people's chances of accessing permanent work in two ways: first by lowering the cost of permanent employment, mainly through the removal of restrictions imposed by art. 18 of the 1970 Workers Statute on the decision of firms to dismiss employees; and second, by increasing the cost of temporary work by granting workers social security rights that were not foreseen under the Treu (1997) and Maroni (2003) reforms.

4.2 An attempt at measuring the degree of labour flexibility in Italy

Has flexibility increased, and to what extent? Close observation of the way in which the OECD synthetic indicator of degree of employment protection has evolved (Figure 9.6), clearly reveals that Italy is an emblematic example of reforms at the margin. At the end of the 1980s, with a score of 3.6, Italy almost topped the table for the most rigid labour market in European countries. Since then, however, it has witnessed the largest reduction in this indicator which, in 2003, dropped to 1.9, closer to the minimum 0.7 level recorded in the UK than to the maximum of 3.5 reported for Portugal. This reduction was related to the relaxing of restrictions on temporary employment (in fact the relative rigidity indicator fell by 60 per cent), whereas protection for regular employment remained the same.

Before the Treu reform, the share of atypical employment was considerably below the EU mean, especially for temporary work. In 2010, despite the impact of the economic crisis that predictably led to a decrease in atypical employment in particular, the gap between the Italian figure and the European mean was all but filled, above all for women. The incidence of female part-time employment was also within the European mean. In Italy part-time employment is principally a female phenomenon (Table 9.1).

Despite all the debates, and possibly on account of methodological difficulties in calculating flow data, there are still few indices to measure numerical flexibility on the labour market. Table 9.2 describes the annual rate of *job finding* as a percentage of the total number of unemployed, and *job separations* as a percentage of the total number of employed, in a range of countries.

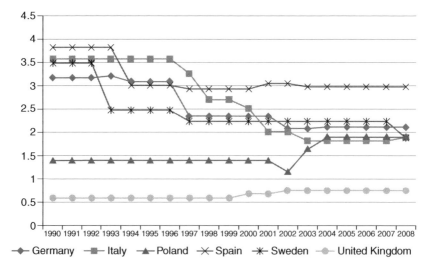

Figure 9.6 Rigidity of legislation for employment protection (1990–2008).

Source: Own processing of OECD data.

The table highlights the fact that in Italy there has been a gradual but significant increase in the *turnover* rate, especially with regard to the *job finding* (almost tripled from 13.1 per cent to about 30 per cent), while the percentage of job separation has remained roughly unchanged, except in the last years of the crisis. In the same period, the duration of unemployment fell from 7.6 to roughly 3 years.

This confirms that the reforms have had a significant impact on the degree of flexibility, at least the numeric component, and, for quite some time, on the unemployment rate that fell from 11 per cent to 8 per cent before the crisis, mainly due to workers finding atypical jobs rather than permanent employment.

Table 9.1 Atypical work in Italy and in the EU-15 (1990–2010)

% of wage employment	Year	Italy			EU-15		
		Total	Men	Women	Total	Men	Women
Part-time work	1990	9.8	4.0	19.9	14.0	4.1	28.0
	1998	12.6	5.1	24.5	16.5	5.6	30.3
	2000	13.6	5.8	25.2	16.9	5.8	30.6
	2003	13.1	4.8	31.6	18.5	7.1	31.4
	2008	16.9	5.6	31.6	18.5	7.1	31.4
	2010	17.5	5.9	32.2	19.5	7.7	32.3
Temporary work	1990	5.2	3.9	7.6	10.6	9.9	11.6
	1998	8.5	7.4	10.2	12.0	11.8	12.2
	2000	10.1	8.8	12.2	12.6	12.3	12.9
	2003	9.9	8.2	12.2	13.4	12.8	14.1
	2008	13.3	11.6	15.6	14.6	13.7	15.8
	2010	12.8	11.4	14.5	15.1	14.7	15.6

Source: OECD.

Note
Measures with harmonized definition.

Table 9.2 Job finding and job separation rates for different countries and different years

Country	Job finding	Job separation
United States, 1992–1993	65.9	2.8
Poland, regions with low unemployment1994–2005	36.3	2.5
Poland, regions with high unemployment 1994–2005	31.5	4.4
Russia, 1994–1995	40.8	3.7
Italy, 1994–1995	13.1	1.6
Italy, 2001–2002	20.3	1.5
Italy, 2007–2008	33.5	1.6
Italia, 2008–2009	28.3	2.3
Italia, 2009–2010	26.9	2.3

Source: for Poland, Newell and Pastore (2006, tables 6 and 7); for Russia and the United States, cf. Boeri and Terrell (2002); for Italy, years 1994–1995 and 2001–2002, cf. Ansari *et al.* (2014) for the following years own elaboration on the ISTAT longitudinal file.

Italian labour flexibility is still below that of the United States and ex-communist countries. However, it is worth considering whether the latter are examples to be followed: the US offers few guarantees of stable employment, while post-communist countries are undergoing a dramatic, albeit historically unique, process of structural change.

A number of studies point to the existence of a *causal* effect of temporary employment on the probability of finding permanent employment. In a quasi-experimental context, Ichino *et al.* (2008) reported a positive net impact of 19 per cent in Tuscany and 11 per cent in Sicily, where the effect was, however, only slightly significant when compared to a gross effect of 31 per cent and 23 per cent, respectively. In other words, say in Tuscany, the share of temporary workers who find permanent employment after a year is 31 per cent, a value 19 per cent higher than that of individuals with similar characteristics (education, work experience and others), but unemployed. This means that holding a temporary contract implies a higher probability of finding a permanent job than being unemployed. Using INPS data, Berton *et al.* (2011) confirmed that temporary employment could act as a port of entry for permanent employment, but that it could also become a trap. In fact, they found that temporary contracts tended to persist in the same firm, probably because enterprises benefited from a reduction in employment costs.

It is too early to assess the impact of the Fornero Law, but the expected results of the implemented measures on permanent employment may be over-optimistic, as art. 18 applies only to a small number of firms: over 90 per cent of firms have fewer than 10 employees, while about 46 per cent of employment is in firms with 9 or fewer employees and about 50 per cent in firms with 15 or fewer employees.

In its monitoring report on implementation of the law, ISFOL (2013) shows that the law had a negligible impact on permanent work, while it strongly reduced the number of temporary contracts, especially co.co.pro. In the logic of the difference-in-difference approach to evaluation, Boeri (2013) shows that in Veneto, there is no statistically significant difference between individual dismissals in firms with fewer and firms with more than 15 employees, the only ones affected by the reform. Instead, in the second half of 2012, co.co.pro. experienced an anomalous reduction as compared to both temporary and permanent contracts.

The very nature of wage flexibility makes it difficult to measure it in an unequivocal way. A synthetic measurement can be obtained by the speed with which real wages return to their equilibrium level, as determined by the dynamics of labour productivity. According to an estimate made by Pastore (2010), the 1993 income policy agreements caused the speed at which real wages readjusted to their long-term value, based on labour productivity, to increase from 46 per cent to 79 per cent. In other words, after 1993, only 20 per cent of the gap of any given year between real wages and labour productivity is left to later years. Increased wage flexibility also resulted in the share of dependent employment income undergoing a dramatic reduction (−11 per cent of GDP) from the mid-1990s onwards (Figure 9.7).

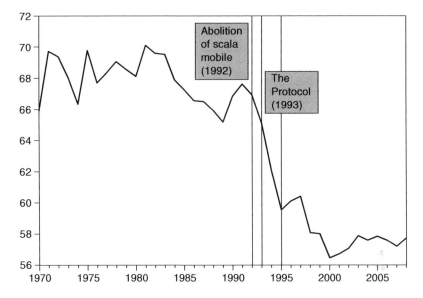

Figure 9.7 Share of GDP allocated to dependent employment income (1970–2008).

Source: Quoted in Pastore (2010, figure 3).

However, while numeric and wage flexibility have been dramatically reduced, instead, the cost of labour has remained still very high as a consequence of the high wedge between gross and net wage. The components due to income taxes, social security and unemployment insurance make the wedge equal about 120 per cent of the net wage.

To sum up this assessment exercise, labour market flexibility has advanced in different directions bringing Italy closer to the European mean. However, the Italian labour market still has not reached the type of conditions that characterize the most flexible Anglo-Saxon countries.

5 The education and vocational training system

Although the Italian labour market is becoming more and more flexible, as noted previously, the education system still presents numerous inefficiencies. How can we explain the difficulty young people – especially those from poorer backgrounds – encounter in getting a proper education? The answer involves factors that concern both demand and supply.

5.1 Demand-side explanations

First of all, we must point to the low demand for human capital in a production system characterized by limited technological innovation. This leads to poor returns for educational qualifications. Naticchioni *et al.* (2008) demonstrated that over the period 1993 through 2004 economic returns for degree and secondary high school qualifications (already low compared to those in advanced economies), have lost considerable ground with regard to humanistic and professional degrees, although this is not the case for degrees in scientific subjects. The salary premium for secondary high school has fallen by at least 30 per cent in all salary distribution quantiles.

The decline in economic returns for education in Italy becomes all the more surprising if we compare it to the strong increase in returns witnessed in other developed countries, be they Anglo-Saxon or Northern European. In fact, in these countries, technological innovation is thought to have led to disproportionate economic returns for the most highly qualified. This would indicate that Italy is moving along what some refer to as the *low road to development*. Another possible explanation emphasizes the role of income policy in producing a curb on wages.

5.2 Supply-side explanations

If education brings fewer economic returns than elsewhere, why do young Italians continue to enrol *en masse* at university? ISTAT figures indicate that between the academic years 1999–2000 and 2003–2004, the number of students matriculating rose from 286,893 to 353,199. A significant increase (+12 per cent) occurred following the introduction of the "3 + 2 years" Zecchino reform.

This indicates that a provision for reducing the unduly prolonged duration of university studies had been eagerly awaited and also that the procedure for producing human capital was inefficient. As Bratti *et al.* (2008) point out, tertiary education reform have led to a far greater increase in the number of university enrolments than in the number of graduates.

The reason for the failure in implementing the "3 + 2 reform" lies in the limited democracy of the reforming process. The government essentially decided the reform with little debate within the universities. That has prevented university lecturers, students and parents from absorbing the positive elements of the reforms that seem, in fact, to be perfectly in keeping with the Lisbon and Bologna agendas.

The reforms have not succeeded in eliminating a contradiction that is inherent in a system that initially allows nearly all holders of a secondary high school diploma to enter university (following the 1969 reform), but then induces most of them to drop out, possibly after wasting many years (Aina *et al.*, 2013).

Human capital theory may help to explain the poor supply of first-class qualifications. Educational choices are influenced by the prospect of better future net remuneration. Not only does education pay less in Italy compared to other countries, it also costs more. While direct expenditure (university fees, books, lodgings) is the same, indirect costs (no earnings on the part of the student for the prolonged period needed to obtain a degree and complete the transition from university to employment) are a burden on the family budget. Let us compare

Italy and the United States (Figure 9.8). The earnings curve is steeper in the United States: the return for each year of education is approximately 18.4 per cent as compared to the 6.7 per cent in Italy. The other difference concerns the indirect cost of education. In the United States, the earnings curve commences around the age of 22–23 years, when students get a degree (21 years) and find employment (almost immediately). In Italy, the same curve starts further over to the right, since the mean graduation age is 27–28 years, and young people enter their first job at roughly 30 years of age. Since the retirement age is the same, Italian graduates fail to make the best use of the complementary relationship between education and work experience, merely because of delayed entry to the labour market.

But why do university studies last so long? The most obvious answer is that the aim is to kill many birds with a single stone by making it difficult to obtain a degree. Since anyone with a secondary high school diploma can enter university, there is no proper entry selection, except for the more remunerative faculties (e.g. School of Medicine). Selection therefore occurs in the course of university study, slowing down even those students who would have been capable of graduating on time. Moreover, because of lack of funding, there is a limited choice of courses, and attendance is low.

Furthermore, courses focus mainly on the theoretical aspects of a subject. Little attention is given to practical applications, thus preventing young students from learning the problem-solving skills that are extremely useful for the world of work. In addition, there are few links between the education system and the labour market. This is evident not only in the lack of apprenticeships, stages and other company training schemes that are typical of other education systems based on the dual principle, but also in the absence of links during the

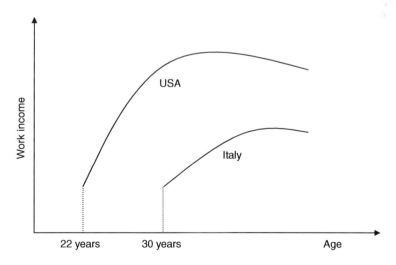

Figure 9.8 Earnings curve. A comparison of Italy and the United States.

post-graduation period. In fact *job placement* activities are virtually non-existent. All this means that it takes many years to get a degree, and that the transition period to a permanent job is more than brief.

5.3   The "class-oriented" education system

The discouraging effect of the low returns and high costs of education is influenced by social class background: the poorer a student is, the lower his cultural background, the higher the direct (effort, motivation) and indirect (time) costs of getting an education, the lower the economic returns for education. The offspring of professionals graduate earlier not only on account of their above-average cultural background, but also because of the better prospects of future earnings. These prospects give them a greater incentive to overcome the obstacles that lead out of the difficult transition tunnel towards a stable and satisfying job.

A study by Hertz *et al.* (2007) shows that Italy has one of the lowest social mobility rates in the world, below that of countries such as the US where university fees are much higher. Checchi *et al.* (1999) were perhaps the first to report this paradox in a very interesting comparison with the United States where selective entry mechanisms based on merit and family income are highly developed. Cappellari (2004) found that there is a strong association between the type of secondary high school attended, family background and previous school performance.

Checchi and Flabbi (2010) point out that in Germany, an early tracking system determines, at the age of ten, whether a child will become an apprentice or attend an academic high school (gymnasium), the latter being the only route of entry to university. In Italy, decisions concerning the choice of a secondary high school are taken at the age of 14, and all secondary high school diplomas give access to university. In theory, family background should influence this choice more in Germany than in Italy, but in practice the opposite occurs, probably because parental choice is not necessarily linked to a child's school performance, whereas German parents must accept a mandatory rule.

About ten years after the Bologna Declaration and subsequent university reforms, it is essential to assess the results in terms of levels of education and disparity. Cappellari and Lucifora (2009) claim that the Bologna Process has not succeeded in significantly modifying the Italian education system that is biased to favour inequalities. Following the reform, students who attained their high school diploma had a 15 per cent better chance of enrolling for university than students who were otherwise their peers. This increase was found principally among those who had a better school performance and a poorer family background. The authors interpreted this result as indicating that the most talented students from under-privileged families encounter impediments when choosing the best educational path. They also found that the reform has had a slightly negative impact on the university dropout rate.

Nevertheless, there is now clear empirical evidence that in the past decade, there has been only a moderate increase in the percentage of graduates coming from families with a poor social background and/or educational level (see also the annual AlmaLaurea reports).

6 The European Youth Guarantee

The EU Parliament and the other EU institutions have agreed with the national governments of all EU members the implementation of the European Youth Guarantee (EYG), a programme which essentially implies the (moral, if not legal) "obligation" for each member country to provide young people with a job, training or educational opportunity within three months from the beginning of their unemployment spell. The EYG is clearly inspired by the Scandinavian experience and has already been recently implemented in Germany, Austria, The Netherlands and Poland.

The first condition to implement the EYG in Italy is one of *administrative capacity*. The EYG needs the good functioning of the Public Employment Services (PES). What is the condition of the PES in Italy? Since 1991, the state sector has lost a monopoly control over labour intermediation, also for low skill jobs, which it had maintained from 1970. This did not help increase the share of the unemployed who found a job, though, just the opposite. Since 1997, when the Treu Law allowed private agencies to contend the activity of job placement to the PES for temporary contracts, things have not changed much. The afore-mentioned Maroni Law of 2003, which strongly encouraged the cooperation between public and private agencies, was not much more successful. Against the expectations of experts and policy-makers, the share of jobs placed through the PES has remained stubbornly low (just above 3 per cent). This compares to about 7.7 per cent in the UK and 13 per cent in Germany. A possible explanation of the inefficiency of PES is the lack of available resources, both financial and human. Just to make a quick comparison: in Italy, there are 150.1 unemployed for every staff of the PES; the comparable number for the UK is about 24.2 and in Germany about 48.6. In addition, the current legislation does not help much in as much as it assigns to PES eminently bureaucratic tasks (Cicciomessere and Sorcioni, 2007; Giubileo, 2011; Pastore, 2013).

In a period of dramatically reducing opportunities in the public sector, with the share of jobs offered falling down from about 29.5 per cent in the mid-1990s to about 8.6 per cent in the late 2000s, the percentage of young people who are seeking jobs through their network of family and friends has dramatically increased from 24.4 per cent in the mid-1990s to about 35.3 per cent in the late 2000s. In the meantime, private agencies of temporary work have increased their market share up to 5 per cent in the late 2000s (Mandrone, 2011).

The EYG will be useful in the case of Italy if it implies that public and private employment services will play a role in the labour market. In order for this to happen, though, it is necessary that the PES be endowed with sufficient human and financial resources, while being cleaned from bureaucratic burdens which could be assigned to private call centers thus paying a lower cost (Giubileo, 2011).

Second, if the EYG means providing young people with employment or, at least, training opportunities, then there are only a few training programmes implemented at a regional level, whose impact is negligible. The current Italian organization of the entire system is confusing: according to the 1995 constitutional reform, the state is in charge of the education system, regions are in charge of the training system and provinces (counties) are in charge of the PES.

Implementation of the EYG would need to restructure the way regional bodies manage training programmes. They should be properly targeted and the effectiveness of any intervention should be assessed with sound evaluation studies. More importantly, it is necessary to think of some interaction with the educational system.

The third problem is one of fine-tuning the EYG to the needs of those who can benefit more from it, which implies also coordinating the scheme with the existing policy tools, such as the new apprenticeship law. It is inspired by the German system, but with an important difference: it is a post-school, post-university programme for young people up to the age of 29 years. This means giving up an important aspect of the German model, namely the duality principle, which allows young people to develop their competences and skills when they are still in education. Nonetheless, in the Italian labour market vacuum, allowing some form of interrelation between the training system and the labour market is in principle an important novelty. Another novelty is that also university graduates can be apprentices. The German type of professional universities could be an alternative for those young people who find it hard to get a university degree (Cappellari and Leonardi, 2013).

7 Conclusions

This chapter has examined the Italian school-to-work transition regime, which is a typical example of the European Mediterranean system where the presence of the State is marginal compared to the central role played by the family. The latter has to bear the costs of the difficult transition period young people undergo on their way to stable employment.

In the past two decades, there have been reforms designed, on the one hand, to make the labour market more flexible, and, on the other, to make both secondary and tertiary education more inclusive. A number of different indicators point to an increase in wage, functional and numerical flexibility. These changes in the labour market have opened the way to lower unemployment, but have not succeeded in altering the overall school-to-work transition period that remains one of the longest in the world. This also explains why in Italy, as in other Latin Rim countries, the disadvantage of the young compared to adults is still severe.

The education system is one of the factors that can be further exploited, once labour market flexibility has been achieved. The "3 + 2" university reform aimed to give more young people the opportunity to undertake tertiary studies in a country where the mean level of education is one of the lowest in the EU.

However, more than ten years after its introduction, it seems clear that this reform has only partially produced the expected results. In fact:

a   there has been only a small increase in the percentage of graduates;
b   the university dropout percentage is still very high;
c   nearly all the graduates with a three-year degree sign up for the specialist degree course, thus contributing to increasing rather than reducing the mean duration of university studies;
d   it has not been possible to introduce some elements of the dual principle, choosing instead to shift the problem downstream to the labour market and rely on temporary employment.

In connection with this last and vital point, there have been only a few positive innovations such as the Moratti school reform and the so-called "Testo Unico" on Apprenticeships passed in September 2011. The government is changing this shortcoming in the education system in various ways. A recent measure enables young undergraduates who have reached the final year of their degree course to start practical training. Much more could and should be done, but the roadmap that has recently been adopted is undoubtedly the right one.

These conclusions naturally pose a series of questions for *policy-makers*, since the 2001 university reform has not yet reduced the cost (indirect) of education and this often proves to be an insurmountable obstacle, especially for the weaker social classes, regardless of individual ability. What can be done to ensure equal access to university?

Clearly, expenditure on scholarships and university equipment and facilities is still insufficient. In fact, recent university reforms have not envisaged any additional costs. Therefore, as a first step, this tendency needs to be inverted. Moreover, the 2001 reform should be adjusted so as to introduce measures that would drastically reduce the mean duration of university studies without impinging on the standard of quality.

Furthermore, to reduce the school-to-work transition period, private practice and many goods and services markets should be liberalized, and efficient vocational training and careers guidance systems should be developed. There are various ways of building closer links between the education system and the world of work. Germany has a dual model, in Japan schools and universities place qualified students directly in firms and there is also the Anglo-Saxon *job placement* model where both young people and individual firms play important roles. It is absolutely vital that Italy opts for one of these possible alternatives and does not leave the situation unchanged.

Note

1 Price competition which is typical of traditional manufacturing markets that function in a very similar way to those of perfect competition, is considered here to be in contrast with competition for capacity of product innovation, typical of markets characterized by imperfect or monopolistic competition.

10 Assessing the stability of employment among young people in Ireland after the Great Recession

Elish Kelly, Seamus McGuinness and Adele Whelan

1 Introduction

It is well documented that the Great 2008–2009 Recession had severe negative effects on countries' labour markets, particularly those economies that were worst affected by the crisis. Ireland was one such country where its unemployment rate increased from 4.6 per cent in 2004 to 15 per cent in 2012, while its employment rate fell from 65.9 per cent to 58.8 per cent over the same time period (see Table 10.1).

The negative impact that these labour market changes had on Ireland's population has been studied in detail, with the research indicating that the negative effects have not been evenly spread across the population (Barrett and Kelly, 2012; Kingston *et al.*, 2013; Russell *et al.*, 2014; Kelly *et al.*, 2014; Kelly *et al.*, 2015). At the same time, it is recognised that young people in particular were badly affected by the recession: research by Kelly *et al.* (2014) and Kelly and McGuinness (2015) illustrate this. One of the main reasons why youths were so badly affected is because they tend to be concentrated in cyclically sensitive industries, particularly, in the Irish case, the construction sector. Kelly *et al.* (2014) and Kelly and McGuinness (2015) also show that one of the most vulnerable groups were young people with low levels of educational attainment.

Table 10.1 Irish labour force statistics: 2004–2015

	2004	2005	2006	2007	2008	2009	2010	2011	2012	2013	2014	2015	2016
Unemployment rate %[1]	4.6	4.8	4.7	4.8	5.8	12.3	13.9	14.6	15.0	13.9	11.9	9.8	8.6
Participation rate %[2]	60.5	62.1	63.2	64.1	63.7	62.5	61.1	60.5	60.1	60.5	60.0	60.2	60.6
Employment rate %[3]	65.9	67.5	68.5	69.1	67.9	62.2	60.0	59.2	58.8	60.2	61.3	63.1	64.7

Source: Quarterly National Household Survey Q2, Central Statistics Office.

Notes
1 Based on persons aged 15–74;
2 Based on persons aged 15 and over;
3 Based on persons aged 15–64.

The Irish economy turned the corner on the economic crisis in 2012 with Gross National Product (GNP) growing by 1.6 per cent (Duffy *et al.*, 2015). The labour market also started to improve towards the end of that year with the unemployment rate falling to 13.8 per cent and the numbers in employment starting to grow again for the first time since the start of 2008 (see Figure 10.1). Unemployment has continued to fall since this time period – the rate stood at 6.7 per cent in quarter 4 2016, while employment has continued to increase. The rate was 65.6 per cent in quarter 4 2016, which is the highest that the country's employment rate has been since the end of 2008.[1]

The improvement that has taken place in the labour market has received a lot of attention, particularly in terms of the growth in employment being a "green shoots" indicator of economic recovery. Since employment growth commenced again in quarter 4 2012, 199,200 additional jobs have been created: as of quarter 4 2016, there were 2,048,100 people in employment, which is an increase of 10.8 per cent between then and quarter 4 2012. This appears to be a good news story, but very little is known about the quality of the jobs that have been created since the recovery, particularly among young people, and how this varies by educational attainment. Are the jobs that newly qualified young people are entering permanent or temporary in nature?

The OECD (2014) argue that labour market performance should be assessed not just in terms of an increase in job numbers but also by the quality of jobs on offer. They found that temporary employment is strongly associated with poor job quality, specifically in terms of lower pay, higher levels of job insecurity and higher job strain. Eichhorst and Tobsch (2014), on the other hand, offer a different perspective on temporary work and other atypical employment arrangements. They argue that the growth in non-standard forms of employment in Germany have contributed to job growth and assisted the country to withstand the Great Recession as unemployment did not increase over the period and the numbers in work did not decline either. Eichhorst and Tobsch (2014) conclude

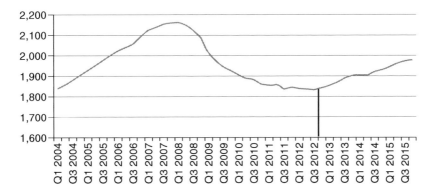

Figure 10.1 Numbers in employment: 2004–2015.

Source: Derived using Quarterly National Household Survey (QNHS) data.

that the growth in temporary, part-time and other atypical forms of employment in Germany is complementing the standard employment segment of the German labour market and that job quality is not declining, in general, as a result of the growth in atypical working arrangements. While flexible labour markets increase an economy's capacity to adjust, a study on temporary jobs in Ireland has shown that fixed term and casual contracts are associated with lower earnings, less training and lower autonomy (Layte *et al.*, 2008). In a more recent piece of research, the OECD (2015a) indicate that "traditional" permanent, full-time work is increasingly being replaced with non-traditional working arrangements, such as part-time and temporary work. They argue that such atypical working arrangements can create job opportunities for some people who would otherwise be out of work, and that the growth in these non-standard forms of employment also reflects the needs of some workers as well as the movement away from manufacturing dominated economic growth to services and knowledge work. At the same time, however, the OECD (2015a) highlights some issues that are emerging with the growth in atypical employment arrangements; in particular, that these non-standard forms of employment may be adding to inequality and poverty, especially among low-educated workers, females and young people. As a result of this, the OECD argues that governments need to make sure that part-time and temporary work are stepping-stones to better employment and not an end in themselves.

In order to provide further context, using data from the quarterly EU Labour Force Surveys (EU-LFS), we examine the pattern of temporary contracts for all employees over the period 2003–2012 for Ireland, the EU-14[2] and the EU-28 (Figure 10.2). In Ireland, the share of temporary contracts has grown steadily since 2006, rising from 4 per cent to just over 10 per cent. The share of temporary contracts was found to be quite static over the entire period for the EU-28 and EU-14 with higher average rates, than those observed in Ireland, of around 11 per cent and 13 per cent respectively. Therefore, while the shares of temporary contracts for all employees in Ireland have changed significantly over this period, the levels are not disproportionate when compared to other EU countries.

Given the growth in atypical forms of employment, this chapter examines the issue of job quality for newly qualified young people since the Great Recession, particularly in terms of identifying if such individuals have faced an increased likelihood of temporary employment between 2006 and 2012. We begin by initially examining the descriptive evidence on temporary versus permanent employment among newly qualified young people since the Great Recession. We then go on to assess the extent to which the marginal impact of various credentials on the likelihood of temporary employment compared to permanent has changed over the 2006–2012 time period.

2   Data

The analysis presented in this chapter is based on individual-level data from Ireland's Labour Force Survey, which is known as the Quarterly National

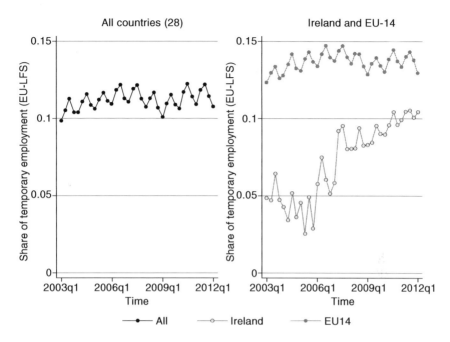

Figure 10.2 Share of temporary contracts among all employees.

Source: EU Labour Force Survey.

Note
The EU-14 includes Austria, Belgium, Germany, Denmark, Spain, Finland, France, Greece, Italy, Luxemburg, Netherlands, Portugal, Sweden, and the United Kingdom.

Household Survey (QNHS),[3] for Quarter 2 (Q2) 2006 and 2012. In particular, we focus on young people aged between 15 and 25 who entered employment[4] subsequent to obtaining a formal qualification[5] in the previous 12 months. The data are weighted to ensure that the results are representative of the population being studied.

3 Descriptive results

Descriptive information on both the incidence and characteristics of temporary employment amongst newly qualified youth for 2006 and 2012 is reported in Tables 10.2 and 10.3. It is clear that temporary employment became much more common over the period accounting for 44 per cent of employment in 2012 relative to just below 31 per cent in 2006 (Table 10.2). The rapid rise in the incidence of temporary employment amongst the cohort was also associated with compositional changes (Table 10.3).

The 2006 and 2012 period saw increased exposure to temporary employment among both youth age cohorts, those aged 15–19 and 20–25. The increase in

Table 10.2 The proportion of permanent and temporary contracts among newly qualified young people[1]: 2006 and 2012 (per cent)

	2006 Q2	2012 Q2
Contract Type:		
Permanent	69.2	56.0
Temporary	30.8	44.0
Total:	74,419	41,589

Source: Derived using Quarterly National Household Survey data.

Note
1 Based on young people aged 15–25 years of age.

relative exposure was highest among 20–25 year olds, with the share of workers in this age group employed on temporary contracts almost doubling over the period. In terms of gender, the 2006–2012 period saw a decline in the lower relative exposure of males, with over 40 per cent of both genders in temporary employment in 2012 (Table 10.3). Finally, in terms of education,[6] the proportion of newly qualified graduates on temporary contracts increased from 23 to 38 per cent over the period, with the corresponding figures for medium qualified workers rising from 30 to almost 50 per cent (Table 10.3). The proportion of new entrants with low levels of education in temporary employment also rose from 58 to 68 per cent over the period.

Table 10.3 Personal characteristics of young newly qualified temporary contract employees[1]: 2006 and 2012 (per cent)

	2006 (Q2)	2012 (Q2)
Age:		
15–19	43.5	54.7
20–25	21.6	39.5
Gender:		
Male	26.7	41.4
Female	34.5	45.7
Educational Attainment:		
Low	58.0	68.2
Medium	30.2	49.3
High	23.3	38.0
Total	74,419	41,589

Source: Derived using Quarterly National Household Survey data.

Note
1 Based on young people aged 15–25 years of age.

4 Econometric results

In terms of the econometrics analysis, we begin by estimating a basic model with a 2012 time dummy to assess the average change in temporary employment risk amongst young people over the period, before moving to a complete specification that controls for factors such as, gender, age, nationality, educational attainment, location and sector (Table 10.4). Specification 1, in Table 10.4, indicates that the average risk of temporary employment among young new entrants increased by 13 percentage points between 2006 and 2012 with the marginal impact of the time variable falling to between 10 and 11 per cent when other control variables are included in the model.

Table 10.4 Probit model of temporary employment contracts for newly qualified young people

	Year	*Full specification: students excluded*	*Full specification: students included*
Year (Ref: 2006)			
Year 2012	0.132***	0.100***	0.114***
	(0.025)	(0.027)	(0.028)
Gender (Ref: Female)			
Male		−0.033	−0.019
		(0.026)	(0.027)
Age (Ref: 20–25)			
Age 15–19		0.123***	0.075*
		(0.039)	(0.039)
Nationality (Ref: Non-Irish)			
Irish		−0.041	−0.063
		(0.041)	(0.043)
Educational Attainment (Ref: Low)			
Medium		−0.117***	−0.040
		(0.037)	(0.039)
High		−0.123**	−0.039
		(0.053)	(0.055)
Job Type (Ref: Full-Time)			
Part-time		0.270***	0.124***
		(0.029)	(0.035)
Self-Defined Economic Status (Ref: Non-Student)			
Student			0.327***
			(0.037)
Location (Ref: Dublin)			
Border		0.027	0.046
		(0.047)	(0.049)
Midlands		0.084	0.093*
		(0.054)	(0.055)
West		0.105**	0.079*
		(0.047)	(0.046)

continued

Table 10.4 Continued

	Year	Full specification: students excluded	Full specification: students included
Location (Ref: Dublin)			
Mid-East		−0.014	−0.010
		(0.042)	(0.043)
Mid-West		0.151***	0.168***
		(0.049)	(0.051)
South-East		−0.029	−0.007
		(0.044)	(0.045)
South-West		0.097***	0.113***
		(0.037)	(0.039)
Sector (Ref: Industry)			
Agriculture, Forestry and Fishing		0.020	0.024
		(0.129)	(0.116)
Construction		−0.201***	−0.196***
		(0.041)	(0.041)
Wholesale and Retail		−0.116**	−0.134***
		(0.048)	(0.048)
Transportation and Storage		−0.145**	−0.141*
		(0.071)	(0.075)
Accommodation and Food Storage		−0.054	−0.073
		(0.053)	(0.052)
Information and Communication		−0.027	−0.046
		(0.083)	(0.084)
Financial, Insurance and Real Estate		−0.153***	−0.147**
		(0.059)	(0.059)
Professional, Scientific and Technical		−0.096	−0.096
		(0.059)	(0.059)
Administrative and Support Services		−0.017	−0.032
		(0.081)	(0.078)
Public Administration and Defence		−0.027	−0.052
		(0.094)	(0.088)
Education		0.298***	0.328***
		(0.077)	(0.073)
Health and Social Work		−0.122**	−0.103*
		(0.053)	(0.054)
Creative, Arts and Entertainment		−0.034	−0.049
		(0.074)	(0.075)
Other Services		−0.033	0.018
		(0.070)	(0.074)
Sector Unknown		0.115	0.196
		(0.201)	(0.205)
Observations	1,973	1,973	1,973
Pseudo R-squared	0.0133	0.148	0.185

Notes

Robust standard errors in parentheses; *** p<0.01, ** p<0.05, * p<0.1.

1 The comparison group is newly qualified young people aged 15–25 that obtained a permanent contract.

When individual level controls are included in the model (specification 2) the results from the pooled 2006–2012 model indicate that temporary employment risk is highest among young people aged 15–19, those with low levels of educational attainment, employed part-time, domiciled in some areas outside of Ireland's capital city Dublin and employed in sectors such as Education and Industry (Table 10.4).

The first two columns of Table 10.5 allow us to assess the change in the role of personal characteristics in exposing newly qualified youth to temporary employment risk over the 2006–2012 period. The models suggest that, over the period, the level of risk associated with belonging to the 15–19 age group or having a medium or high level of educational attainment (relative to low level accreditation) became statistically insignificant. The results suggest that as the incidence of temporary employment increased it became common across all groups irrespective of age, gender, education or region. The influence of being employed part-time on contractual status remained relatively stable, with part-time workers approximately 27 percentage points more likely to be on temporary contracts in both periods.

With respect to sectors, some changes have become apparent with employment in certain sectors, such as Wholesale and Retail and Transportation and Storage, being associated with a lower likelihood of temporary employment for young new entrants in 2012 relative to 2006. However, in both periods, the Education and Industry sectors were associated with the highest temporary employment risk among this cohort.

In our analysis, we use the ILO economic status classification, which is based on individuals being assigned a labour market status (unemployment, employment and inactivity) based on well-defined group of questions, which are used in many international Labour Force Surveys. Under the ILO measurement, individuals still participating in education will be classified as inactive. However, the Irish Labour Force Survey (i.e. the QHNS) data contain a self-defined principal economic status variable and, while ILO-defined inactive were excluded from our sample, when we add the self-defined student variable in our estimated models we find that this impacts our results, suggesting some discrepancies between the two economic status measurement approaches (the ILO and self-defined measure). The student variable is highly significant and indicates that student status raised the likelihood of temporary employment by almost 40 percentage points in 2006 and 28 percentage points in 2012. After the inclusion of this additional control, we find the part-time coefficient becomes insignificant in 2006 and falls from 28 to 18 per cent in 2012, suggesting that many of those self-identifying as students were also employed on a part-time basis in both waves.

Table 10.5 Probit model of temporary employment contracts for newly qualified young people

	Full specification: no student control		Full specification: student control	
	2006	*2012*	*2006*	*2012*
Gender (Ref: Female)				
Male	−0.028	−0.030	−0.027	−0.001
	(0.029)	(0.051)	(0.030)	(0.051)
Age (Ref: 20–25)				
Age 15–19	0.187***	0.028	0.149***	−0.027
	(0.043)	(0.074)	(0.044)	(0.077)
Nationality (Ref: Non-Irish)				
Irish	−0.057	−0.025	−0.090*	−0.051
	(0.051)	(0.070)	(0.053)	(0.074)
Educational Attainment (Ref: Low)				
Medium	−0.099***	−0.088	−0.022	0.015
	(0.037)	(0.104)	(0.039)	(0.109)
High	−0.029	−0.192	0.052	−0.084
	(0.057)	(0.124)	(0.058)	(0.130)
Job Type (Ref: Full-time)				
Part-time	0.271***	0.279***	0.058	0.183***
	(0.034)	(0.052)	(0.042)	(0.059)
Self-Defined Economic Status (Ref: Non-Student)				
Student			0.397***	0.276***
			(0.044)	(0.064)

Location (Ref: Dublin)

	(1)	(2)	(3)	(4)
Border	0.090*	−0.077	0.112**	−0.063
	(0.051)	(0.092)	(0.054)	(0.094)
Midlands	0.164**	−0.020	0.147**	0.008
	(0.064)	(0.095)	(0.063)	(0.099)
West	0.095*	0.104	0.044	0.101
	(0.056)	(0.086)	(0.050)	(0.088)
Mid-East	0.063	−0.114	0.101*	−0.139*
	(0.049)	(0.076)	(0.054)	(0.074)
Mid-West	0.249***	−0.044	0.277***	−0.041
	(0.055)	(0.094)	(0.056)	(0.099)
South-East	−0.053	−0.021	−0.048	0.007
	(0.046)	(0.081)	(0.047)	(0.084)
South-West	0.160***	−0.017	0.193***	−0.018
	(0.044)	(0.068)	(0.046)	(0.069)

Sector (Ref: Industry)

	(1)	(2)	(3)	(4)
Agriculture, Forestry and Fishing	0.080	−0.076	0.116	−0.113
	(0.157)	(0.221)	(0.141)	(0.187)
Construction	−0.129**	−0.330***	−0.130***	−0.326***
	(0.050)	(0.091)	(0.047)	(0.097)
Wholesale and Retail	−0.031	−0.231***	−0.053	−0.244***
	(0.057)	(0.089)	(0.055)	(0.090)
Transportation and Storage	−0.029	−0.363***	0.003	−0.383***
	(0.096)	(0.084)	(0.106)	(0.069)

Sector (Ref: Industry)

	(1)	(2)	(3)	(4)
Accommodation and Food Storage	0.046	−0.182**	0.009	−0.188**
	(0.068)	(0.092)	(0.064)	(0.092)
Information and Communication	0.062	−0.132	0.060	−0.179
	(0.100)	(0.164)	(0.100)	(0.160)

continued

Table 10.5 Continued

	Full specification: no student control		Full specification: student control	
	2006	2012	2006	2012
Financial, Insurance and Real Estate	-0.157***	-0.002	-0.146**	-0.012
	(0.059)	(0.162)	(0.060)	(0.163)
Professional, Scientific and Technical	-0.027	-0.199*	-0.025	-0.199*
	(0.070)	(0.111)	(0.069)	(0.113)
Administrative and Support Services	0.045	-0.093	0.033	-0.112
	(0.093)	(0.153)	(0.093)	(0.145)
Public Administration and Defence	0.056	-0.207	0.020	-0.236
	(0.108)	(0.196)	(0.103)	(0.169)
Education	0.350***	0.242**	0.359***	0.292***
	(0.096)	(0.121)	(0.097)	(0.113)
Health and Social Work	-0.060	-0.187*	-0.053	-0.161
	(0.064)	(0.098)	(0.065)	(0.103)
Creative, Arts and Entertainment	-0.062	0.073	-0.078	0.061
	(0.074)	(0.174)	(0.072)	(0.180)
Other Services	-0.062	0.006	-0.011	0.061
	(0.075)	(0.131)	(0.081)	(0.133)
Sector Unknown	0.185		0.296	
	(0.205)		(0.216)	
Observations	1,434	539	1,434	539
Pseudo R-squared	0.179	0.121	0.231	0.147

Notes
Robust standard errors in parentheses; *** p<0.01, ** p<0.05, * p<0.1.
1 The comparison group is newly qualified young people aged 15–25 that obtained a permanent contract.

4 Summary and conclusions

In keeping with the experience of many developed economies, the evidence suggests that labour market deregulation in the form of increased temporary and part-time working has become a more prominent feature of the Irish labour market in recent years. Focussing on the period 2006–2012, which captures pre- and post-recession points, we find that among newly qualified youth the proportions employed on temporary contracts increased from 31 to 44 per cent over the period. Whilst in the past, temporary employment status has traditionally been associated with workers who were very young, poorly educated and working part-time, our evidence suggests that the rise in the incidence of temporary employment has resulted in it becoming almost mainstreamed to the extent that almost no particular group is the most susceptible. In particular, between 2006 and 2012 we observed the elimination of the contractual disadvantage experienced by those aged 15–19 and young workers located in some areas outside of Dublin. Nevertheless, a number of factors are associated with substantial risk, in particular, student status and being employed in sectors such as Education and Industry substantially raising the probability of non-permanent employment both pre- and post-recession. Finally, from a policy perspective a particularly worrying aspect of the analysis is that obtaining a third-level qualification did not provide a buffer against temporary employment status for young new entrants into the Irish labour market in either time period.

Notes

1 www.cso.ie/en/qnhs/releasesandpublications/qnhspostcensusofpopulation2011/.
2 The EU-14 refers to the EU-15 without Ireland, i.e. Austria, Belgium, Germany, Denmark, Spain, Finland, France, Greece, Italy, Luxemburg, Netherlands, Portugal, Sweden and the United Kingdom.
3 The QNHS is compiled by the Central Statistics Office (CSO).
4 Employees only with public sector job creation scheme workers excluded.
5 Formal educational qualifications refer to lower secondary, upper secondary, post-secondary and tertiary levels.
6 Educational attainment that is classified as "low" refers to primary and lower secondary levels; "medium" refers to upper secondary and post-secondary levels; while "high" refers to those with third level qualifications.

Bibliography

Aassve, A., Billari, F. C. and Ongaro, F. (2001). The Impact of Income and Employment Status on Leaving Home: Evidence from the Italian ECHP Sample. *MPIDR Working Paper* n. 2000–012, revised 21 June 2001.

Aassve, A., Billari, F. C., Mazzuco, S. and Ongaro, F. (2002). Leaving Home: A Comparative Analysis of ECHP Data. *Journal of European Social Policy* 12: 259–275.

Acemoglu, D. and Autor, D. (2012). What Does Human Capital Do? A Review of Goldin and Katz. *Journal of Economic Literature* 50(2): 426–463.

Addabbo, T. and Solinas, G. (2012). Non-standard Employment and Quality of Work: Toward New Forms of Measurement. In Addabbo, T. and Solinas, G. (eds), *Non-standard Employment and Quality of Work: The Case of Italy*. AIEL Series in Labour Economics, Heidelberg: Springer Verlag.

Addabbo, T., Rodríguez-Modroño, P. and Gálvez, L. (2015). Young People Living as Couples: How Women's Labour Supply is Adapting to the Crisis. Spain as a Case Study. *Economic Systems* 39(1): 27–42.

Ai, C. and Norton, E. (2003). Interaction Terms in Logit and Probit Models. *Economics Letters* 80(1): 123–129.

Aina, C., Baici, E., Casalone, G. and Pastore, F. (2013). Il fuoricorsismo fra falsi miti e realtà. *Economia & Lavoro* XLVII(1): 147–154.

Akerlof, G. A. and Shiller, R. J. (2009). *Animal Spirits*. Princeton, NJ: Princeton University Press.

Alfieri, S., Rosina, A., Sironi, E., Marta, E. and Marzana, D. (2015a). Young Italian NEETs (Not in Employment, Education, or Training) and the Influence of Their Family Background. *Europe's Journal of Psychology* 11(2): 311–322.

Alfieri, S., Rosina, A., Sironi, E., Marta, E. and Marzana, D. (2015b). Who Are Italian 'NEETS'? Trust in Institutions, Political Engagement, Willingness to Be Activated and Attitudes toward the Future in a Group at Risk for Social Exclusion. *Rivista Internazionale Di Scienze Sociali* 123(3): 285–306.

Allen, J. and van der Velden, R. (2001). Educational Mismatches versus Skill Mismatches: Effects on Wages, Job Satisfaction and On-the-job Search. *Oxford Economic Papers* 53(3): 434–452.

Altavilla, C. and Caroleo, F. E. (2013). Asymmetric Effects of National-based Active Labour Market Policies. *Regional Studies* 47(9): 1482–1506.

Altonji, J. G. (1995). The Effects of High School Curriculum on Education and Labor Market Outcomes. *The Journal of Human Resources* 30(3): 409–438.

Ansari, M. R., Mussida, C. and Pastore, F. (2014). Note on Lilien and Modified Lilien Index *Stata Journal* 14(2): 398–406.

Antonczyk, D., Fitzenberger, B. and Sommerfeld, K. (2010). Rising Wage Inequality, the Decline of Collective Bargaining, and the Gender Wage Gap. *Labour Economics* 17(5): 835–847.

Anxo, D., Bosch, G. and Rubery, J. (2010). Shaping the Life Course: A European Perspective. In Anxo, D., Bosch, G. and Rubery, J. (eds), *The Welfare State and Life Transitions: A European Perspective*. Cheltenham: Edward Elgar: 1–77.

Arak, P., Lewandoski, P. and Zacowiewcki, P. (2014). Dual Labour Market in Poland: Proposals for Overcoming the Deadlock. *IBS Policy Papers* n. 01/2014.

Arnett, J. J. and Taber, S. (1994). When Does Adolescence End?. *Journal of Youth and Adolescence* 23: 517–537.

Autor, D., Levy, F. and Murnane, R. (2003). The Skill Content of Recent Technological Change: An Empirical Investigation. *Quarterly Journal of Economics* 118(4): 1279–1333.

Baert, S., Cockx, B., Gheyle, N. and Vandamm, C. (2015). Is There Less Discrimination in Occupations Where Recruitment is Difficult?. *ILR Review* 68(3): 467–500.

Baetschmann, G., Staub, K. and Winkelmann, R. (2011). Consistent Estimation of the Fixed Effects Ordered Logit Model. *IZA Discussion Paper* n. 5443.

Baetschmann, G., Staub, K. E. and Winkelmann, R. (2015). Consistent Estimation of the Fixed Effects Ordered Logit Model. *Journal of the Royal Statistical Society: Series A (Statistics in Society)* 178(3): 685–703.

Bakas, D. and Papapetrou, E. (2014). Unemployment in Greece: Evidence from Greek Regions Using Panel Unit Root Tests. *The Quarterly Review of Economics and Finance* 54(4): 551–562.

Bandeen-Roche, K., Miglioretti, D. L., Zeger, S. L. and Rathouz, P. J. (1997). Latent Variable Regression for Multiple Discrete Outcomes. *Journal of the American Statistical Association* 92(440): 1375–1386.

Banerji, A., Lin, H. and Saksonovs, S. (2015). Youth Unemployment in Advanced Europe: Okun's Law and Beyond. *IMF Working Paper* n. 15/5.

Barbieri, P. and Scherer, S. (2009). Labour Market Flexibilization and Its Consequences in Italy. *European Sociological Review* 25(6): 677–692.

Bardasi, E. and Francesconi, M. (2004). The Impact of Atypical Employment on Individual Wellbeing: Evidence from a Panel of British Workers. *Social Science and Medicine* 58(9): 1671–1688.

Baron, J. N., Davis-Blake, A. and Bielby, W. T. (1986). The Structure of Opportunity: How Promotion Ladders Vary Within and Among Organizations. *Administrative Science Quarterly* 31(2): 248–273.

Barrett, A. and Kelly, E. (2012). The Impact of Ireland's Recession on the Labour Market Outcomes of Its Immigrants. *European Journal of Population* 28(1): 91–111.

Bartolucci, F., Bacci, S. and Gnaldi, M. (2012). MultiLCIRT: Multidimensional Latent Class Item Response Theory Models, R package version 2.0.

Bartolucci, F., Farcomeni, A. and Pennoni, F. (2012). *Latent Markov Models for Longitudinal Data*. London: Chapman and Hall/CRC.

Bartolucci, F., Choudhry Tanveer, M., Marelli, E. and Signorelli, M. (2015). Financial Crises and Unemployment in Developed and Developing Countries. Paper presented at the *56th Annual Meeting of the Italian Economic Association*, Naples, October 2015.

Bassanini, A. and Duval, R. (2006a). Employment Patterns in OECD Countries: Reassessing the Role of Policies and Institutions. *OECD Social, Employment and Migration Working Papers* n. 35.

Bassanini, A. and Duval, R. (2006b). The Determinants of Unemployment Across OECD Countries. *OECD Economic Studies* 42(1): 7–86.

Bassanini, A., Nunziata, L. and Venn, D. (2009). Job Protection Legislation and Productivity Growth in OECD Countries. *Economic Policy* 24(58): 349–402.

Becker, G. S. (1962). Investment in Human Capital: A Theoretical Analysis. *The Journal of Political Economy* 70(5): 9–49.

Becker, G. S. (1964). *Human Capital: A Theoretical and Empirical Analysis with Special Reference to Education.* New York: Columbia University Press.

Bell, D. N. F. and Blanchflower, D. G. (2009). What Should Be Done About Rising Unemployment in the UK?. *IZA Discussion Papers* n. 4040.

Bell, D. N. F. and Blanchflower, D. G. (2010). Youth Unemployment: Deja Vu?. *Stirling Economics Discussion Paper* n. 2010-04.

Bell, D. N. F. and Blanchflower, D. G. (2011). Youth Unemployment in Europe and the United States. *Nordic Economic Policy Review* 1: 11–37.

Bell, D. N. F. and Blanchflower, D. G. (2015). Youth Unemployment in Greece: Measuring the Challenge. *IZA Journal of European Labor Studies* 4(1).

Benassi, D. and Novello, D. (2007). L'evoluzione dei modelli di uscita dalla famiglia d'origine. Uno studio in cinque aree urbane italiane. *La Rivista delle Politiche Sociali, Italian Journal of Social Policy* 4(3): 73–93.

Bentolila, S. and Dolado, J. J. (1994). Labour Flexibility and Wages: Lessons from Spain. *Economic Policy* 9(18): 53–99.

Bentolila, S., Cahuc, P., Dolado, J. J. and Le Barbanchon, T. (2012a). Two-tier Labour Markets in the Great Recession: France versus Spain. *The Economic Journal* 122(562): F155–F187.

Bentolila, S., Dolado, J. J. and Jimeno, J. F. (2012b). Reforming an Insider-Outsider Labor Market: The Spanish Experience. *IZA Journal of European Labor Studies* 1(4).

Berloffa, G., Modena, F. and Villa, P. (2015). Changing Labour Market Opportunities for Young People in Italy and the Role of the Family of Origin. *Bank of Italy, Temi di discussione* n. 998.

Bernal-Verdugo, L. E., Furceri, D. and Guillaume, D. M. (2012). Crises, Labor Market Policy, and Unemployment. *International Monetary Fund Working Paper* n. 65.

Bertolini, S. (2011). The Heterogeneity of the Impact of Labour Market Flexibilization on the Transition to Adult Life in Italy: When Do Young People Leave the Nest?. In Blossfeld, H. P., Hofacker, D. and Bertolini, S. (eds), *Youth on Globalised Labour Markets: Rising Uncertainty & Its Effects on Early Employment & Family Lives in Europe.* Opladen and Farmington Hills: Barbara Budrich Publishers: 163–187.

Berton, F. and Garibaldi, P. (2012). Workers and Firms Sorting into Temporary Jobs. *The Economic Journal* 122(562): F125–F154.

Berton, F., Richiardi, M. and Sacchi, S. (2009). *Flex-insecurity. Perchè in Italia la flessibilità diventa precarietà.* Bologna: Il Mulino.

Berton, F., Devicienti, F. and Pacelli, L. (2011). Are Temporary Jobs a Port of Entry into Permanent Employment? Evidence from Matched Employer-Employee Data. *International Journal of Manpower* 32(8): 879–899.

Biagi, F. and Lucifora, C. (2008). Demographic and Education Effects on Unemployment in Europe. *Labour Economics* 15(5): 1076–1101.

Biddle, J. E. and Hamermesh, D. S. (2013). Wage Discrimination Over the Business Cycle. *IZA Journal of Labor Policy* 2: 1–19.

Blair, J., Menon, G. and Bickart, B. (1991). Measurement Effects in Self vs. Proxy Response to Survey Questions: An Information – Processing Perspective. In Biemer, P. P. *et al.* (eds), *Measurement Errors in Surveys.* New York: Wiley: 145–166.

Blanchard, O. J. and Diamond, P. (1994). Ranking, Unemployment Duration, and Wages. *Review of Economic Studies* 61(3): 417–434.

Blanchard, O. J. and Landier, A. (2002). The Perverse Effects of Partial Labour Market Reforms: Fixed-Term Contracts in France. *Economic Journal* 112(480): F214–F244.

Blanchard, O. J. and Wolfers, J. (2000). The Role of Shocks and Institutions in the Rise of European Unemployment: The Aggregate Evidence. *The Economic Journal* 110(462): Conference Papers C1–C33.

Blanchflower, D. G. (2000). Self-employment in OECD Countries. *Labour Economics* 7(5): 471–505.

Blanchflower, D. G. and Freeman, R. B. (2000). The Declining Economic Status of Young Workers in OECD Countries. In Blanchflower, D. G. and Freeman, R. B. (eds), *Youth Employment and Joblessness in Advanced Countries.* Chicago: University of Chicago Press: 19–56.

Blanchflower, D. G. and Oswald, A. J. (1999). Well-being, Insecurity and the Decline of American Job Satisfaction. Paper presented at the *Cornell University Conference*, May 1999, Dartmouth College, *mimeo.*

Blau, F. D. and Kahn, L. M. (1992). The Gender Earnings Gap: Learning from International Comparisons. *The American Economic Review* 82(2): 533–538.

Blöndal, S., Field, S. and Girouard, N. (2002). Investment in Human Capital Through Upper-secondary and Tertiary Education. *OECD Economic Studies* 1: 41–89.

Bloom, N. and Van Reenen, J. (2010). Why Do Management Practices Differ Across Firms and Countries?. *Journal of Economic Perspective* 24(1): 203–224.

Bloom, N., Bond, S. R. and Van Reenen, J. (2001). The Dynamics of Investment Under Uncertainty. *Institute for Fiscal Studies Working Paper* n. 01/05.

Blundell, R. and Bond, S. (1998). Initial Conditions and Moment Restrictions in Dynamic Panel Data Models. *Journal of Econometrics* 87: 115–143.

Böckerman, P., Ilmakunnas, P. and Johansson, E. (2011). Job Security and Employee Well-being: Evidence from Matched Survey and Register Data. *Labour Economics* 18(4): 547–554.

Boeri, T. (2011). Institutional Reforms and Dualism in European Labor Markets. In Card, O. and Ashenfelter, O. (eds), *Handbook of Labor Economics.* Volume 4, Part B, Chap. 13, Amsterdam: Elsevier: 1173–1236.

Boeri, T. (2013). Licenziamenti e legge Fornero. www.lavoce.info.

Boeri, T. and Garibaldi, P. (2007). Two Tier Reforms of Employment Protection: A Honeymoon Effect?. *The Economic Journal* 117(521): 357–385.

Boeri, T. and Jimeno, J. F. (2016). Learning from the Great Divergence in Unemployment in Europe During the Crisis. *Labour Economics* 41(C): 32–46.

Boeri, T. and Terrell, K. (2002). Institutional determinants of labor reallocation in transition. *Journal of Economic Perspective* 16(1): 51–76.

Bol, T. and van de Werfhorst, H. G. (2013). Educational Systems and the Trade-off Between Labor Market Allocation and Equality of Educational Opportunity. *Comparative Education Review* 57(2): 285–308.

Bollen, K., Guilkey, D. and Mroz, T. (1995). Binary Outcomes and Endogenous Explanatory Variables: Tests and Solutions with an Application to the Demand for Contraceptive Use in Tunisia. *Demography* 32(1): 111–131.

Booth, A. L., Francesconi, M. and Frank, J. (2002). Temporary Jobs: Stepping Stones or Dead Ends?. *Economic Journal* 112(480): F189–F213.

Borjas, G. J. (2010). *Labor Economics.* Boston, MA: McGraw-Hill/Irwin.

Boudon, R. (1974). *Education, Opportunity, and Social Inequality. Changing Prospects in Western Society.* New York: Wiley.

Bourdieu, P. (1986). The Forms of Capital. In Richardson, J. (ed.), *Handbook of Theory and Research for the Sociology of Education.* Westport, CT: Greenwood: 241–258.

Bourdieu, P. and Passeron, J.-C. (1990). *Reproduction in Education, Society and Culture.* London: Sage Publications.

Brada, J. C., Marelli, E. and Signorelli, M. (2014). Introduction: Young People and the Labor Market: Key Determinants and New Evidence. *Comparative Economic Studies* 56(4): 556–566.

Bradley, D. E. and Roberts, J. A. (2004). Self-Employment and Job Satisfaction: Investigating the Role of Self-efficacy, Depression, and Seniority. *Journal of Small Business Management* 42(1): 37–58.

Brandolini, A., Rosolia, A. and Torrini, R. (2010). The Distribution of Employees' Labour Earnings in the EU: Data, Concepts and First Results. *ECINEQ Working Paper* n. 198.

Bratti, M., Checchi, D. and de Blasio, G. (2008). Does the Expansion of Higher Education Increase the Equality of Educational Opportunities? Evidence from Italy. *Labour* 22(special issue): 53–88.

Breen, R. and Yaish, M. (2006). Testing the Breen-Goldthorpe Model of Educational Decision Making. In Morgan, S. L., Grusky, D. B. and Fields, G. S. (eds), *Mobility and Inequality.* Stanford, CA: Stanford University Press: 232–258.

Bruno, G. S. F., Caroleo, F. E. and Dessy, O. (2013). Stepping Stones Versus Dead End Jobs: Exits from Temporary Contracts in Italy After the 2003 Reform. *Rivista Internazionale di Scienze Sociali* 1: 31–60.

Bruno, G. S. F., Caroleo, F. E. and Dessy, O. (2014a). Temporary Contracts and Young Workers' Job Satisfaction in Italy. In Malo, M. A. and Sciulli, D. (eds), *Disadvantaged Workers: Empirical Evidence and Labour Policies.* AIEL Series in Labour Economics, Heidelberg: Springer Verlag: 95–120.

Bruno, G. S. F., Choudhry Tanveer, M., Marelli, E. and Signorelli, M. (2014b). Youth Unemployment: Key Determinants and the Impact of Crises. In Malo, M. A. and Sciulli, D. (eds), *Disadvantaged Workers: Empirical Evidence and Labour Policies.* AIEL Series in Labour Economics, Heidelberg: Springer Verlag: 121–148.

Bruno, G. S. F., Marelli, E. and Signorelli, M. (2014c). The Rise of NEET and Youth Unemployment in EU Regions After the Crisis. *Comparative Economic Studies* 56(4): 592–615.

Bruno, G. S. F., Choudhry Tanveer, M., Marelli, E. and. Signorelli, M (2016a). The Short- and Long-run Impact of Financial Crises on Youth Unemployment in OECD Countries. *Applied Economics Online*: 1–24.

Bruno, G. S. F., Marelli, E. and Signorelli, M. (2016b). The Regional Impact of the Crisis on Young People in Different EU Countries. In Coppola, G. and O'Higgins, S. N. (eds), *Youth and the Crisis.* Oxford: Routledge: 249–271.

Brusdal, R. and Berg, L. (2011). Unge voksne og lånefinansiert forbruk. Statens institutt for forbruksforskning (SIFO), *Oppdragsrapport* n. 2011/4.

Bryan, M. and Jenkins, S. P. (2013). Regression Analysis of Country Effects Using Multilevel Data: A Cautionary Tale. *IZA Discussion Papers* n. 7583.

Brzinsky-Fay, C. (2007). Lost in Transition? Labour Market Entry Sequences of School Leavers in Europe. *European Sociological Review* 23(4): 409–422.

Brzinsky-Fay, C. and Solga, H. (2016). Compressed, Postponed, or Disadvantaged? School-to-work Transition Patterns and Early Occupational Attainment in West Germany. *Research in Social Stratification and Mobility* 46(part A): 21–36.

Buchmann, M. (1989). *The Script of Life in Modern Society: Entry into Adulthood in a Changing World.* Chicago: The University of Chicago Press.

Buchmann, M. and Kriesi, I. (2011). Transition to Adulthood in Europe. *Annual Review of Sociology* 37: 481–503.

Buddelmeyer, H., McVicar, D. and Wooden, M. (2013). Non-Standard 'Contingent' Employment and Job Satisfaction: A Panel Data Analysis. *Melbourne Institute Working Paper* n. 29/13.

Buechel, F. (2002). Successful Apprenticeship-to-Work Transitions: On the Long-Term Change in Significance of the German School-Leaving Certificate. *IZA Discussion Paper* n. 425.

Burdett, K. and Mortensen, D. (1998). Wage Differentials, Employer Size, and Unemployment. *International Economic Review* 39(2): 257–273.

Bynner, J. and Parsons, S. (2002). Social Exclusion and the Transition from School to Work: The Case of Young People Not in Education, Employment, or Training (NEET). *Journal of Vocational Behavior* 60(2): 289–309.

Cabrales, A., Dolado, J. J. and Mora, R. (2014). Dual Labour Markets and (Lack of) On-the-job Training: PIAAC Evidence from Spain and Other EU Countries. *CEPR Discussion Paper* n. 10246.

Cahuc, P., Carcillo, S., Rinne, U. and Zimmermann, K. F. (2013). Youth Unemployment in Old Europe: The Polar Cases of France and Germany. *IZA Journal of European Labor Studies* 2(18): 1–23.

Caliendo, M. and Schmidl, R. (2016). Youth Unemployment and Active Labor Market Policies in Europe. *IZA Journal of Labor Policy* 5(1).

Caliendo, M., Künn, S. and Schmidl, R. (2011). Fighting Youth Unemployment: The Effects of Active Labor Market Policies. *IZA Discussion Paper* n. 6222.

Cameron, A. C. and Trivedi, P. K. (2005). *Microeconometrics*. Cambridge: Cambridge University Press.

Cameron, A. C. and Trivedi, P. K. (2010). *Microeconometrics Using Stata*. College Station, TX: Stata Press.

Caporale, G. M. and Gil-Alana, L. A. (2012). Persistence in Youth Unemployment. *CESifo Working Paper: Labour Markets* n. 3961.

Caporale, G. M. and Gil-Alana, L. A. (2014). Youth Unemployment in Europe: Persistence and Macroeconomic Determinants. *Comparative Economic Studies* 56(4): 581–591.

Cappellari, L. (2004). The Effects of High School Choices on Academic Performance and Early Labour Market Outcomes. *Royal Economic Society Annual Conference*, Royal Economic Society.

Cappellari, L. and Leonardi, M. (2013). A favore di un Sistema di 'vocational tertiary education' in Italia. In Dell'Aringa, C. and Treu, T. (eds), *Giovani senza futuro*. Bologna: Il Mulino.

Cappellari, L. and Lucifora, C. (2009). The 'Bologna Process' and College Enrollment Decisions. *Labour Economics* 16(6): 639–647.

Cappellari, L., Dell'Aringa, C. and Leonardi, M. (2012). Temporary Employment, Job Flows and Productivity: A Tale of Two Reforms. *The Economic Journal* 122(562): F188–F215.

Carcillo, S., Fernández, R., Königs, S. and Minea, A. (2015). NEET Youth in the Aftermath of the Crisis: Challenges and Policies. *OECD Social, Employment and Migration Working Papers* n. 164.

Card, D. (1999). The Causal Effect of Education on Earnings. In Ashenfelter, O. and Card, D. (eds), *Handbook of Labour Economics*. Amsterdam: Elsevier Science: 1801–1862.

Caroleo, F. E. (2012). The Hard Access to the Labour Market of Youth Leaving School: What Policy Choices?. *MPRA – Munich Personal RePEc Archive Paper* n. 37645.

Caroleo, F. E. and Pastore, F. (2007). The Youth Experience Gap: Explaining Differences Across EU Countries. *Università di Perugia, Quaderni del Dipartimento di Economia, Finanza e Statistica* n. 41.

Caroleo, F. E. and Pastore, F. (2009). Le cause del(l'in)successo lavorativo dei giovani. *Economia & Lavoro* 3: 107–131.

Caroleo, F. E. and Pastore, F. (2012). Talking About the Pigou Paradox. Socio-Educational Background and Educational Outcomes of AlmaLaurea. *International Journal of Manpower* 33(1): 27–50.

Caroleo, F. E. and Pastore, F. (2016). Overeducation: A Disease of the School-to-work Transition System. In Coppola, G. and O'Higgins, N. S. (eds), *Youth and the Crisis Unemployment, Education and Health in Europe*. London: Routledge: 36–56.

Caroleo, F. E., Ciociano, E. and Destefanis, S. (2017). Youth Labour-Market Performance, Institutions and VET Systems: A Cross-Country Analysis. *Italian Economic Journal* 3(1): 39–69.

Cazes, S. and Nesporova, A. (2007). *Flexicurity: A Relevant Approach in Central and Eastern Europe*. Geneva: International Labour Office.

Cazes, S. and Tonin, M. (2010). Employment Protection Legislation and Job Stability: A European Cross-country Analysis. *International Labor Review* 149(3): 261–285.

Cazes, S., Verick, S. and Al-Hussami, F. (2011). Diverging Trends in Unemployment in the United States and Europe: Evidence from Okun's Law and the Global Financial Crisis. *ILO Employment Working Papers* n.106.

Cazes, S., Malo, M. A. and Khatiwada, S. (2012). Employment Protection and Industrial Relations: Recent Trends and Labour Market Impact. In ILO. *World of Work Report 2012: Better Jobs for a Better Economy*. Geneva: International Labour Office: Chapter 2.

Cedefop (2008). *Terminology of European Education and Training Policy: A Selection of 100 Key Terms*. European Centre for the Development of Vocational Training. Luxembourg: Office for Official Publications of the European Communities.

Chadi, A. and Hetschko, C. (2013). Flexibilization Without Hesitation? Temporary Contracts and Workers' Satisfaction. *IAAEU Discussion Paper* n. 04/2013.

Checchi, D. and Flabbi, L. (2010). Intergenerational Mobility and Schooling Decisions in Germany and Italy: The Impact of Secondary School Tracks. *Rivista di Politica Economica* 3: 7–57.

Checchi, D., Ichino, A. and Rustichini, A. (1999). More Equal but Less Mobile? Education Financing and Intergenerational Mobility in Italy and in the USA. *Journal of Public Economics* 74(3): 351–393.

Chiuri, M. C. and Del Boca, D. (2010). Home-leaving Decisions of Daughters and Sons. *Review of Economics of the Household* 8(3): 393–408.

Choudhry Tanveer, M., Marelli, E. and Signorelli, M. (2012). Youth Unemployment Rate and Impact of Financial Crises. *International Journal of Manpower* 33(1): 76–95.

Choudhry Tanveer, M., Marelli, E. and Signorelli, M. (2013). Youth and the Total Unemployment Rate: The Impact of Policies and Institutions. *Rivista internazionale di Scienze Sociali* 121(1): 63–86.

Cicciomessere, R. and Sorcioni, M. (2007). *La collaborazione fra gli operatori pubblici e privati*. Roma: Italia Lavoro.

Cingano, F., Leonardi, M., Messina, J. and Pica, G. (2010). Employment Protection and Investment. *Economic Policy* 25(61): 117–163.

Clapham, D. (2005). *The Meaning of Housing*. Cambridge: Polity Press.

Clark, A. E. (1996). Job Satisfaction in Britain. *British Journal of Industrial Relations* 34(2): 189–217.

Clark, A. E. (1997). Job Satisfaction and Gender: Why Are Women So Happy at Work. *Labour Economics* 4(4): 189–217.

Clark, A. E. (2006). Looking for Labour Market Rents with Subjective Data. *DELTA*, mimeo.

Clark, A. E. and Oswald, A. J. (1996). Satisfaction and Comparison Income. *Journal of Public Economics* 69(1): 57–81.

Clark, A. E., Oswald, A. J. and Warr, P. (1996). Is Job Satisfaction U-shaped in Age?. *Journal of Occupational and Organizational Psychology* 60(1): 57–81.

Clark, K. B. and Summers, L. H. (1982). The Dynamics of Youth Unemployment. In Freeman, R. and Wise, D. (eds), *The Youth Labour Market Problem: Its Nature, Causes and Consequences*. Chicago: University of Chicago Press: 199–234.

Comi, S. and Grasseni, M. (2012). Are Temporary Workers Discriminated Against? Evidence from Europe. *The Manchester School* 80(1): 28–50.

Da Silva, A. D. and Turrini, A. (2015). Precarious and Less Well-paid? Wage Differences Between Permanent and Fixed-term Contracts across the EU Countries. European Commission, *European Economy, Economic Papers* n. 544.

Das, M. and Van Soest, A. (1999). A Panel Data Model for Subjective Information on Household Income Growth. *Journal of Economic Behavior and Organization* 40(4): 409–426.

Daveri, F. (2004). Delayed IT Usage: Is It Really the Drag on European Productivity?. *CESifo Economic Studies* 50(3): 397–421.

Daveri, F. and Mascotto, A. (2006). The IT Revolution Across the United States. *Review of Income and Wealth* 52(4): 569–602.

Daveri, F. and Parisi, M. L. (2015). Experience, Innovation and Productivity. Empirical Evidence from Italy's Slowdown. *ILR Review* 68(4): 889–915.

de Graaf-Zijl, M. (2012). Job Satisfaction and Contingent Employment. *De Economist* 160: 197–218.

de Graaf-Zijl, M., van den Berg, G. J. and Heyma, A. (2011). Stepping Stones for the Unemployed: The Effect of Temporary Jobs on the Duration until (Regular) Work. *Journal of Population Economics* 24(1): 107–139.

de la Fuente, A. and Doménech, R. (2012). Educational Attainment in the OECD, 1960–2010, version 3.0. *Barcelona GSE Working Paper* n. 658.

de la Fuente, A. and Doménech, R. (2015). Educational Attainment in the OECD, 1960–2010. Updated Series and a Comparison with Other Sources. *Economics of Education Review* 48: 56–74.

De Lange, M., Gesthuizen, M. and Wolbers, M. H. (2014). Youth Labour Market Integration Across Europe: The Impact of Cyclical, Structural, and Institutional Characteristics. *European Societies* 16(2): 194–212.

Demidova, O., Marelli, E. and Signorelli, M. (2013). Spatial Effects on the Youth Unemployment Rate: The Case of Eastern and Western Russian Regions. *Eastern European Economics* 51(5): 94–124.

Demidova, O., Marelli, E. and Signorelli, M. (2015). Youth Labour Market Performances in the Russian and Italian Regions. *Economic Systems* 39(1): 43–58.

Dempster, A. P., Laird, N. M. and Rubin, D. B. (1977). Maximum Likelihood from Incomplete Data Via the EM Algorithm (With Discussion). *Journal of the Royal Statistical Society* 39(1): 1–38.

Desjardins, R. and Rubenson, K. (2011). An Analysis of Skill Mismatch Using Direct Measures of Skills. *OECD Education Working Papers* n. 63.

Destefanis, S. and Mastromatteo, G. (2010). Labour Market Performance in the OECD: Some Recent Cross-country Evidence. *International Journal of Manpower* 31(7) 713–731.

Destefanis, S. and Mastromatteo, G. (2012). Assessing the Reassessment: A Panel Analysis of the Lisbon Strategy. *Economics Letters* 115(2): 148–151.

Destefanis, S. and Mastromatteo, G. (2015). The OECD Beveridge Curve: Technological Progress, Globalisation and Institutional Factors. *Eurasian Business Review* 5(1): 151–172.

Di Giorgio, C. and Giannini, M. (2012). A Comparison of the Beveridge Curve Dynamics in Italy and USA. *Empirical Economics* 43(3): 945–983.

Dietrich, H. (2003). Scheme Participation and Employment Outcome of Young Unemployed: Empirical Findings from Nine European Countries. In Hammer, T. (ed.), *Youth Unemployment and Social Exclusion in Europe: A Comparative Study*. Bristol: The Policy Press: 83–108.

Dietrich, H. (2012). Youth Unemployment in Europe: Theoretical Considerations and Empirical Findings. *Friedrich Ebert Stiftung Study*.

Dietrich, H. (2013). Youth Unemployment in the Period 2001–2010 and the European Crisis – Looking at the Empirical Evidence. *Transfer: European Review of Labour and Research* 19(3): 305–324.

Dietrich, H. and Möller, J. (2016). Youth Unemployment in Europe: Business Cycle and Institutional Effects. *International Economics and Economic Policy* 13(1): 5–25.

Dolado, J. J. (ed.) (2015). *No Country for Young People? Youth Labour Market Problems in Europe*. London: CEPR Press.

Dolton, P., Makepeace, G. and Treble, J. (1994). The Youth Training Scheme and the School-to-Work Transition. *Oxford Economic Papers*, New Series 46(4): 629–657.

Duffy, D., McQuinn, K., Morley, C. and Foley, D. (2015). *Quarterly Economic Commentary: Winter 2015*. Dublin: Economic and Social Research Institute.

Dustmann, C., Ludsteck, J. and Schönberg, U. (2009). Revisiting the German Wage Structure. *The Quarterly Journal of Economics* 124(2): 843–881.

Economic Innovation Group (2016). *The Millennial Economy*. Washington, DC: Economic Innovation Group.

Eichhorst, W. (2016). Promoting Youth Employment in Europe: Evidence-based Policy Lessons. *IZA Policy Paper* n. 119.

Eichhorst, W. and Tobsch, V. (2014). Not So Standard Anymore? Employment Duality in Germany. *IZA Discussion Paper* n. 8155.

Eichhorst, W., Hinte, H. and Rinne, U. (2013). Youth Unemployment in Europe: What to Do about It?. *IZA Policy Paper* n. 65.

Eichhorst, W., Rodríguez-Planas, N., Schmidl, R. and Zimmermann, K. F. (2015). A Roadmap to Vocational Education and Training Systems Around the World. *Industrial and Labor Relations Review* 68(2): 314–337.

Elder, S. (2009). *ILO School-to-work Transition Survey: A Methodological Guide*. Geneva: International Labour Office.

Elder, S. and Matsumoto, M. (2010). Characterizing the School-to-work Transitions of Young Men and Women: Evidence from the ILO School-to-work Transition Survey. *ILO Employment Working Paper* n. 51.

Escudero, V. (2015). Are Active Labour Market Policies Effective in Activating and Integrating Low-skilled Individuals? An International Comparison. *ILO Research Department Working Paper* n. 3.

Esping-Andersen, G. (1990). *The Three Worlds of Welfare Capitalism*. Cambridge: Polity Press.

Esping-Andersen, G. (1999). *Social Foundations of Postindustrial Economies*. Oxford: Oxford University Press.

Estevez-Abe, M., Iversen, T. and Soskice, D. (2001). Social Protection and the Formation of Skills: A Reinterpretation of the Welfare State. In Hall, P. A. and Soskice, D. (eds),

Varieties of Capitalism: The Institutional Foundations of Comparative Advantage, Vol. 145, Oxford: Oxford University Press: 145–183.

Eurofound (2007). *Job Satisfaction and Labour Market Mobility.* Luxembourg: Publications Office of the European Union.

Eurofound (2012). *Trends in Job Quality in Europe.* Luxembourg: Publications Office of the European Union.

Eurofound (2013a). *Employment Polarisation and Job Quality in the Crisis: European Jobs Monitor 2013.* Luxembourg: Publications Office of the European Union.

Eurofound (2013b). *Young People and Temporary Employment in Europe.* Luxembourg: Publications Office of the European Union.

Eurofound (2014). *Mapping Youth Transitions in Europe.* Luxembourg: Publications Office of the European Union.

Eurofound (2015a). *Recent Developments in Temporary Employment: Employment Growth, Wages and Transitions.* Luxembourg: Publications Office of the European Union.

Eurofound (2015b). *Recent Developments in the Distribution of Wages in Europe.* Luxembourg: Publications Office of the European Union.

Eurofound (2016). *Exploring the Diversity of NEET.* Luxembourg: Publications Office of the European Union.

European Central Bank (2012). Euro Area Labour Markets and the Crisis. *Structural Issues Report.*

European Commission (2001). *Employment in Europe.* Employment and social affairs directorate. Luxembourg: Office for Official Publications of the European Union.

European Commission (2007). *Toward Common Principles of Flexicurity: More and Better Jobs Through Flexibility and Security.* Luxembourg: Office for Official Publications of the European Communities.

European Commission (2010). *Employment in Europe 2010.* Brussels: Directorate-General for Employment, Social Affairs and Equal Opportunities.

European Commission (2013). *Labour Market Developments in Europe 2013.* European Economy series 6/2013.

European Commission (2015). *EU Structural Change 2015.* Luxembourg: Publications Office of the European Union.

European Commission (2016a). *Employment in Europe 2016.* Brussels: Directorate-General for Employment, Social Affairs and Equal Opportunities.

European Commission (2016b). *The Youth Guarantee and Youth Employment Initiative Three Years On.* Strasbourg: EU COM(2016) 646 final.

Eurostat (2009a). 30% of 25–34 Year-olds in the EU27 Are Graduates from Higher Education. *Eurostat News Release* n. 58.

Eurostat (2009b). *Youth in Europe: A Statistical Portrait.* Brussels: European Commission.

Eurostat (2014a). EU Labour Force Survey Database – User Guide. Version December 2014. (mimeo). http://ec.europa.eu/eurostat/documents/1978984/6037342/EULFS-Database-UserGuide.pdf.

Eurostat (2014b). Labour Force Surveys in the EU, Candidate and EFTA Countries. Main Characteristics of National Surveys, 2013. Luxembourg: European Union.

Extremera, N. and Rey, L. (2016). Attenuating the Negative Impact of Unemployment: The Interactive Effects of Perceived Emotional Intelligence and Well-Being on Suicide Risk. *PLoS ONE* 11(9).

Fauske, H. (1996). Livsløp og etablering. In Øia, T. (ed.), *Ung på 90-tallet. En antologi.* Oslo: Cappelen Akademisk Forlag.

Ferrera, M. (1996). The 'Southern' Model of Welfare in Social Europe. *Journal of European Social Policy* 6(1): 17–37.

Ferrer-i-Carbonell, A. and Frijters, P. (2004). How Important is Methodology for the Estimates of the Determinants of Happiness?. *The Economic Journal* 114(497): 641–659.

Ford, J., Rugg, J. and Burrows, R. (2002). Conceptualising the Contemporary Role of Housing in the Transition to Adult Life in England. *Urban Studies* 39(13): 2455–2467.

Forster, A. G., Bol, T. and van de Werfhorst, H. G. (2016). Vocational Education and Employment Over the Life Cycle. *Sociological Science* 3: 473–494.

Franz, W. (1981). Zur Dauer der Jugendarbeitslosigkeit: Theoretische Überlegungen, empirische Resultate und wirtschaftspolitische Implikationen. *Mitt Arbeitsmarkt Berufsforschung* n. 14.

Freeman, R. (1978). Job Satisfaction as an Economic Variable. *American Economic Review* 68(2): 135–141.

Freeman, R. and Wise, D. (eds). (1982). *The Youth Labor Market Problem: Its Nature, Causes and Consequences*. Chicago: University of Chicago Press.

Frijters, P., Geishecker, I., Haisken-DeNew, J. P. and Shields, M. A. (2006). Can the Large Swings in Russian Satisfaction Be Explained by Ups and Downs in Real Income?. *Scandinavian Journal of Economics* 108(3): 433–458.

Gangl, M. (2003). *Unemployment Dynamics in the United States and West Germany*. Heidelberg: Physika Verlag.

Gangl, M. (2004). Institutions and the Structure of Labour Market Matching in the United States and West Germany. *European Sociological Review* 20(3): 171–187.

García-Pérez, J. I. and Vall Castello, J. (2015). Youth Unemployment in Spain: More Issues than Just High Unemployment. In Dolado, J. J. (ed.), *No Country for Young People? Youth Labour Market Problems in Europe*. London: CEPR Press: 117–128.

Gardiner, L. (2016). *Stagnation Generation: The Case for Renewing the Intergenerational Contract*. Resolution Foundation, Intergenerational Commission Report.

Garloff, A., Pohl, C. and Schanne, N. (2013). Do Small Labor Market Entry Cohorts Reduce Unemployment?. *Demographic Research* 29(4): 379–406.

Gebel, M. (2009). Fixed-term Contracts at Labour Market Entry in West Germany: Implications for Job Search and First Job Quality. *European Sociological Review* 25(6): 661–675.

Gebel, M. (2013). Is a Temporary Job Better than Unemployment? A Cross-country Comparison Based on British, German, and Swiss Panel Data. *Schmollers Jahrbuch* 133(2): 143–155.

Ghoshray, A., Ordóñez, J. and Sala, H. (2016). Euro, Crisis and Unemployment: Youth Patterns, Youth Policies?. Universitat autònoma de Barcelona, Facultat d'Economia i Empresa, *Departament d'Economia Aplicada Document de Traball* n. 16/09.

Giannelli, G. C. and Monfardini, C. (2003a). Joint Decisions on Household Membership and Human Capital Accumulation of Youths: The Role of Expected Earnings and Labor Market Rationing. *Journal of Population Economics* 16(2): 265–285.

Giannelli, G. C. and Monfardini, C. (2003b). Young People Living with Their Parents: The Gender Impact of Co-residence on Labour Supply and Unpaid Work. In Picchio, A. (ed.), *Unpaid Work and the Economy: A Gender Analysis of the Standards of Living*. London: Routledge.

Gili, M., Roca, M., Basu, S., McKee, M. and Stuckler, D. (2013). The Mental Health Risks of Economic Crisis in Spain: Evidence from Primary Care Centres, 2006 and 2010. *European Journal of Public Health* 23(1): 103–108.

Giménez-Nadal, J. I. and Molina, J. A (2014). Regional Unemployment, Gender, and Time Allocation of the Unemployed. *Review of Economics of the Household* 12(1): 105–127.

Giubileo, F. (2011). Due o più modelli di politiche del lavoro in Europa? I servizi del lavoro in Italia, Germania, Francia, Svezia e Regno Unito. *Rivista del diritto della sicurezza sociale* 4(3): 759–777.

Giuliano, P. (2007). Living Arrangements in Western Europe: Does Cultural Origin Matter? *Journal of the European Economic Association* 5: 927–952.

Goergen, M., Brewster, C., Wood, G. and Wilkinson, A. J. (2012). Varieties of Capitalism and Investments in Human Capital. *Industrial Relations: A Journal of Economy and Society* 51(issue supplement 1): 501–527.

Goldthorpe, J. H. (1996). Class Analysis and the Reorientation of Class Theory: The Case of Persisting Differentials in Educational Attainment. *The British Journal of Sociology* 47(3): 481–505.

Goos, M. and Manning, A. (2007). Lousy and Lovely Jobs: The Rising Polarization of Work in Britain. *Review of Economics and Statistics* 89(1): 118–133.

Gora, M., Lewandoski, P. and Lis, M. (2016). Temporary Employment Boom in Poland: A Job Quality-Quantity Trade Off. *Proceedings of IZA/OECD/World Bank/UCW Workshop*. Rome.

Gordon, R. J. and Dew-Becker, I. (2008). The Role of Labor Market Changes in the Slowdown of European Productivity Growth. *CEPR Discussion* Paper n. 6722.

Gorry, A. (2013). Minimum Wages and Youth Unemployment. *European Economic Review* 64(C): 57–75.

Gottschalk, P. and Maloney, T. (1985). Involuntary Terminations, Unemployment and Job Matching: A Test of Job Search Theory. *Journal of Labor Economics* 3(2): 109–123.

Green, F. (2007). *Demanding Work: The Paradox of Job Quality in the Affluent Economy*. Princeton, NJ: Princeton University Press.

Green, C. and Heywood, J. S. (2011). Flexible Contracts and Subjective Well-being. *Economic Inquiry* 49(3): 716–729.

Green, C. and Leeves, G. D. (2013). Job Security, Financial Security and Worker Well-being. New Evidence on the Effects of Flexible Employment. *Scottish Journal of Political Economy* 60(2): 121–138.

Greene, W. H. (1993). *Econometric Analysis*. Upper Saddle River, NJ: Prentice Hall.

Greene, W. H. (2010). Testing Hypotheses About Interaction Terms in Nonlinear Models. *Economic Letters* 107(2): 291–296.

Gregg, P. and Tominey, E. (2005). The Wage Scar from Male Youth Unemployment. *Labour Economics* 12(4): 487–509.

Hall, J. and Nayyar, S. (2015). Working for Happiness. UNDP, *Human Development Reports*.

Hall, P. A. and Soskice, D. W. (2001). *Varieties of Capitalism: The Institutional Foundations of Comparative Advantage*. Oxford: Oxford University Press.

Hamermesh, D. (1997). Economic Aspects of Job Satisfaction. In Ashenfelter, O. and Oates, W. (eds), *Essays in Labor Market Analysis*. Oxford: Wiley.

Hammarstrom, A. (1994). Health Consequences of Youth Unemployment: Review from a Gender Perspective. *Social Science and Medicine* 38(5): 699–709.

Hammer, T. (2003). *Youth Unemployment and Social Exclusion in Europe*. Bristol: Policy Press.

Hanglberger, D. (2011). Does Job Satisfaction Adapt to Working Conditions? An Empirical Analysis for Rotating Shift Work, Flexitime, and Temporary Employment in UK. *FFB-Discussion Paper* n. 87.

Hanushek, E. A., Woessmann, L. and Zhang, L. (2011). General Education, Vocational Education, and Labor Market Outcomes over the Life Cycle. *NBER Working Paper* n. 17504.

Hanushek, E. A., Schwerdt, G., Woessmann, L. and Zhang, L. (2017). General Education, Vocational Education, and Labor Market Outcomes Over the Life Cycle. *Journal of Human Resources* 52(1): 48–87.

Heckman, J. J. (1979). Sample Selection Bias as a Specification Error. *Econometrica* 47(1): 153–161.

Heckman, J. J. and Borjas, G. J. (1980). Does Unemployment Cause Future Unemployment? Definitions, Questions and Answers from a Continuous Time Model of Heterogeneity and State Dependence. *Economica* 47(187): 247–283.

Heckman, J. J. and Singer, B. (1984). A Method of Minimizing the Impact of Distributional Assumptions for Duration Data. *Econometrica* 52(2): 271–320.

Heitmüller, A. (2005). A Note on Decompositions in Fixed Effects Models in the Presence of Time-Invariant Characteristics. *IZA Discussion Paper* n. 1886.

Hellevik, T. (2005). På egne ben. Unges etableringsfase i Norge. *Norsk institutt for forskning om oppvekst, velferd og aldring (NOVA) Rapport* n. 22/05, Oslo: Norwegian Social Research.

Hennan, D. F., Raffe, D. and Smyth, E. (1996). Cross-National Research on School-to-work Transitions: An Analytical Framework. *Paper commissioned by the OECD secretariat to provide Background for the Transition Thematic Review*, Paris: OECD.

Hertz, T., Jayasundera, T., Piraino, P., Selcuk, S., Smith, N. and Verashchagina, A. (2007). The Inheritance of Educational Inequality: International Comparisons and Fifty-Year Trends. *The B.E. Journal of Economic Analysis & Policy* 7(2): 1–48.

Holzer, H. J. (1988). Search Method Use by Unemployed Youth. *Journal of Labor Economics* 6(1): 1–20.

Hutengs, O. and Stadtmann, G. (2014). Youth and Gender Specific Unemployment and Okun's Law in Scandinavian Countries. *Comparative Economic Studies* 56(4): 567–580.

Iannelli, C. and Raffe, D. (2007). Vocational Upper-Secondary Education and the Transition from School Source. *European Sociological Review* 23(1): 49–63.

Ichino, A., Mealli, F. and Nannicini, T. (2008). From Temporary Help Jobs to Permanent Employment: What Can We Learn from Matching Estimators and Their Sensitivity?. *Journal of Applied Econometrics* 23(3): 305–327.

IMF (2010). Unemployment Dynamics During Recessions and Recoveries: Okun's Law and Beyond. *World Economic Outlook: Rebalancing Growth*: Chapter 3.

International Labour Office (2004). Starting Right: Decent Work for Young People. *Background paper prepared for the Tripartite Meeting on Youth Employment: The way forward*. Geneva: International Labour Office.

International Labour Office (2013). *Global Employment Trends for Youth 2013: A Generation at Risk*. Geneva: International Labour Office.

International Labour Office (2015). Employment Protection Legislation: Summary Indicators in the Area of Terminating Regular Contracts (Individual Dismissals). *Inclusive Labour Markets, Labour Relations and Working Conditions Branch (INWORK)*, Geneva: International Labour Office.

Ioannidou, A. and Stavrou, S. (2013). *Reformperspektiven der Berufsbildung in Griechenland*. Berlin: Friedrich Ebert Stiftung.

ISCED (2012). *International Standard Classification of Education 2011*. Montreal: Unesco Institute for Statistics.

ISFOL (2013). *La dinamica degli avviamenti dei contratti di lavoro. Anno 2012*. Rome: ISFOL.

Ivlevs, A. and King, R. (2012). Does More Schooling Make You Run for the Border? Evidence from Post-independence Kosovo. *Journal of Development Studies* 48(8): 1108–1120.

Jacob, M. and Kleinert, C. (2013). Demographic Changes, Labor Markets and Their Consequences on Post-school Transitions in West Germany 1975–2005. *Research in Social Stratification and Mobility* 32: 65–83.

Jahn, E. J., Riphahn, R. T. and Schnabel, C. (2012). Feature: Flexible Forms of Employment: Boon and Bane. *The Economic Journal* 122(562): F115–F124.

Jahoda, M. (1982). *Employment and Unemployment: A Social-psychological Analysis.* London: Cambridge University Press.

Jimeno, J. F. and Rodríguez-Palenzuela, D. (2002). Youth Unemployment in the OECD: Demographic Shifts, Labour Market Institutions, and Macroeconomic Shocks. *European Central Bank Working Paper* n. 155.

Kahn, L. M. (2012). Temporary Jobs and Job Search Effort in Europe. *Labour Economics* 19(1): 113–128.

Kahn, L. M. (2016). The Structure of the Permanent Job Wage Premium: Evidence from Europe. *Industrial Relations: A Journal of Economy and Society* 55(1): 149–178.

Kaiser, L. C. (2007). Gender-Job Satisfaction Differences Across Europe: An Indicator for Labor Market Modernization. *International Journal of Manpower* 28(1): 75–94.

Kalleberg, A. L. (2003). Flexible Firms and Labor Market Segmentation Effects of Workplace Restructuring on Jobs and Workers. *Work and Occupations* 30(2): 154–175.

Kalleberg, A. L. and Sorensen, A. B. (1979). The Sociology of Labor Markets. *Annual Review of Sociology* 5: 351–379.

Karamessini, M. (2008). The Southern European Social Model: Changes and Continuities in Recent Decades. *International Labour Review* 147(1): 43–70.

Kautto, M., Fritzell, J., Hvinden, B., Kvist, J. and Uusitalo, H. (2001). *Nordic Welfare States in the European Context.* London and New York: Routledge.

Kelly, E. and McGuinness, S. (2015). Impact of the Great Recession on Unemployed and NEET Individuals' Labour Market Transitions in Ireland. *Economic Systems* 39 (1): 59–71.

Kelly, E., Kingston, G., Russell, H. and McGinnity, F. (2015). The Equality Impact of the Employment Crisis. *Journal of the Statistical and Social Inquiry Society of Ireland* 44(5): 71–85.

Kelly, E., McGuinness, S., O'Connell, P. J., Haugh, D. and González Pandiella, A. (2014). Transitions In and Out of Unemployment Among Young People in the Irish Recession. *Comparative Economic Studies* 56(4): 616–634.

Kerckhoff, A. C. (1995). Institutional Arrangements and Stratification Processes in Industrial Societies. *Annual Review of Sociology* 21(1): 323–347.

Kingston, G., O'Connell, P. J. and Kelly, E. (2013). *Ethnicity and Nationality in the Irish Labour Market: Evidence from the QNHS Equality Module.* Dublin: Economic and Social Research Institute & Equality Authority.

Korenman, S. and Neumark, D. (1997). Cohort Crowding and Youth Labor Markets: A Cross-national Analysis. *NBER Working Paper* n. 6031.

Kornai, J. (2006). The Great Transformation of Central Eastern Europe. *Economics of Transition* 14(2): 207–244.

Krueger, A. B. and Mueller, A. I. (2014). A Contribution to the Empirics of Reservation Wages. *IZA Discussion Paper* n. 7957.

Krueger, A. B. and Mueller, A. I. (2016). A Contribution to the Empirics of Reservation Wages. *American Economic Journal: Economic Policy* 8(1): 142–179.

Krugman, P. (1994). Past and Prospective Causes of High Unemployment. *Economic Review*, Federal Reserve Bank of Kansas City IV(1): 23–43.

Kvist, J., Fritzell, J., Hvinden, B. and Kangas, O. (2012). *Changing Social Equality: The Nordic Welfare Model in the 21st Century.* Bristol: The Policy Press.

Lakey, J. (2001). *Youth Unemployment, Labour Market Programmes and Health.* London: Policy Studies Institute.

Lalive, R. (2002). Do Wages Compensate for Workplace Amenities? University of Zurich, *mimeo.*

Langsether, Å and Sandlie, H. C. (2006). Boforhold i leiemarkedet. In Gulbrandsen, L. (ed.), *Bolig og levekår i Norge 2004. En artikkelsamling.* NOVA Rapport 3, Oslo: Norwegian Social Research.

Launov, A. and Waelde, K. (2013). Thumbscrews for Agencies or for Individuals? How to Reduce Unemployment?. *IZA Discussion Paper* n. 7659.

Launov, A. and Waelde, K. (2016). The Employment Effect of Reforming a Public Employment Agency. *European Economic Review* 84: 140–164.

Layard, R., Nickell, S. N. and Jackman, R. (2005). *Unemployment, Macroeconomic Performance and the Labour Market.* Oxford: Oxford University Press.

Layte, R., O'Connell, P. J. and Russell, H. (2008). Temporary Jobs in Ireland: Does Class Influence Job Quality. *Economics and Social Review* 39(2): 81–104.

Leao, J. and Nogueira, G. (2013). Youth Unemployment in Southern Europe. *GEE Working Paper* n. 51.

Lee, J. (2000). The Robustness of Okun's Law: Evidence from OECD Countries. *Journal of Macroeconomics* 22(2): 331–356.

Leuven, E. and Oosterbeek, H. (2011). Overeducation and Mismatch in the Labor Market. In Hanushek, E., Machin, S. and Woessmann, L. (eds), *Handbook of the Economics of Education.* Amsterdam: Elsevier Science 4: 283–326.

Lindbeck, A. and Snower, D. J. (2001). Insiders Versus Outsiders. *Journal Economic Perspective* 15(1): 165–188.

Linz, S. J. (2003). Job Satisfaction Among Russian Workers. *International Journal of Manpower* 24(6): 626–652.

Linz, S. J. and Semykina, A. (2012). What Makes Workers Happy? Anticipated Rewards and Job Satisfaction. *Industrial Relations* 51(4): 811–844.

Lisi, D. (2013). The Impact of Temporary Employment and Employment Protection on Labour Productivity: Evidence from an Industry-level Panel of EU Countries. *Journal of Labour Market Research* 46(2): 119–144.

Liu, D. (2012). Education as Unemployment Insurance: A Model with Endogenous Educational Requirement for Job Application and Its Policy Implications. University of California, Department of Economics, *mimeo.*

Long, S. and Freese, J. (2006). *Regression Models for Categorical Dependent Variables Using STATA.* College Station, TX: STATA Press.

Lucas, R. E., Clark, A. E., Georgellis, Y. and Diener, E. (2004). Unemployment Alters the Set Point for Life Satisfaction. *Psychological Science* 15(1): 8–13.

Luce, R. (1959). *Individual Choice Behavior: A Theoretical Analysis.* New York: John Wiley.

Mac Guinness, S. (2006). Overeducation in the Labour Market. *Journal of Economic Survey* 20(3): 387–418.

Manacorda, M. and Moretti, E. (2006). Why Do Most Italian Youths Live with Their Parents? Intergenerational Transfers and Living Arrangements. *Journal of the European Economic Association* 4(4): 800–829.

Mandrone, E. (2008). La riclassificazione del lavoro tra occupazione standard e atipica: l'indagine Isfol-Plus 2006. *Collana studi Isfol* n. 2008/1.

Mandrone, E. (2011). La ricerca del lavoro in Italia: l'intermediazione pubblica, privata e informale. *Politica Economica* 27(1): 83–124.

Mandrone, E. (ed.) (2012). *Labour Economics PLUS Empirical Studies*. Rome: ISFOL Temi e Ricerche 3.

Mandrone, E. and Marocco, M. (2012a). Atipicità, flessibilità e precarietà: una lettura economica e giuridica attraverso l'indagine ISFOL-PLUS. *ISFOL Working Paper.*

Mandrone, E. and Marocco, M. (2012b). L'atipicità e i suoi derivati. www.la voce.info.

Manfredi, T. and Quintini, G. (2009). Going Separate Ways? School-to-work Transitions in the United States and Europe. *OECD Social, Employment and Migration Working Papers* n. 90.

Manfredi, T., Scarpetta, S. and Sonnet, A. (2010). Rising Youth Unemployment During The Crisis: How to Prevent Negative Long-term Consequences on a Generation?. *OECD Social, Employment and Migration Working Papers* n. 106.

Marelli, E. and Signorelli, M. (2011). Youth Unemployment Before and After the Crisis. In Manzella, P. and Rustico, L. (eds), *Productivity, Investment in Human Capital and the Challenge of Youth Employment.* Newcastle upon Tyne: Cambridge Scholars Publishing: 57–84.

Marelli, E. and Signorelli, M. (2013). The Unemployment Impact of Financial Crises. In Fadda, S. and Tridico, P. (eds), *Financial Crises, Labour Markets and Institutions*. Oxon and New York: Routledge: 192–211.

Marelli, E. and Signorelli, M. (2016). Youth Unemployment and the Disadvantages of the Young in the Labour Market. In Fadda, S. and Tridico, P. (eds), *Varieties of Economic Inequality*. Oxon and New York: Routledge: 197–216.

Marelli, E. and Vakulenko, E. (2016). Youth Unemployment in Italy and Russia: Aggregate Trends and Individual Determinants. *The Economics and Labour Relations Review* 27(3): 387–405.

Marelli, E., Patuelli, R. and Signorelli, M. (2012a). Regional Unemployment in the EU Before and After the Global Crisis. *Post-Communist Economies* 24(2): 155–175.

Marelli, E., Signorelli, M. and Tyrowicz, J. (2012b). Crises and Joint Employment-productivity Dynamics: A Comparative Perspective for European Countries. *Comparative Economic Studies* 54: 361–394.

Marelli, E., Choudhry Tanveer, M. and Signorelli, M. (2013). Youth and the Total Unemployment Rate: The Impact of Policies and Institutions. *Rivista internazionale di Scienze Sociali* 121(1): 63–86.

Marsden, D., Lucifora, C., Oliver-Alonso, J. and Guillotin, Y. (2002). *The Economic Costs of the Skills Gap in the EU*. Milano: Istituto per la Ricerca Sociale.

Martin, J. P., Martin, S. and Quintini, G. (2007). The Changing Nature of the School-to-work Transition Process in OECD Countries. *IZA Discussion Paper* n. 2582.

Mayer, K. U. (2009). New Directions in Life Course Research. *Annual Review of Sociology* 35: 413–433.

McGinnity, F., Mertens, A. and Gundert, S. (2005). A Bad Start? Fixed-Term Contracts and the Transition from Education to Work in West Germany. *European Sociological Review* 21(4): 359–374.

McGuinness, S. and Sloane, P. J. (2010). Esiste overeducation? Un'analisi comparata. In AlmaLaurea *XII Rapporto sulla condizione occupazionale dei laureati. Investimenti in capitale umano nel futuro di Italia ed Europa*, Bologna: Il Mulino.

McKee-Ryan, F., Song, Z., Wanberg, C. R. and Kinicki, A. J. (2005). Psychological and Physical Well-being During Unemployment: A Meta-analytic Study. *Journal of Applied Psychology* 90(1): 53–76.

Mencarini, L. and Tanturri, M. (2006). Una casa per diventare grandi. I giovani italiani, l'autonomia abitativa e il ruolo della famiglia d'origine. *Polis* 20(3): 405–430.

Mertens, A. and McGinnity, F. (2004). Wages and Wage Growth of Fixed-term Workers in East and West Germany. *Applied Economics Quarterly* 50(2): 139–163.

Millàn, M., Congregado, E. and Romàn, C. (2012). Determinants of Self-employment Survival in Europe. *Small Business Economics* 38(2): 231–258.

Mincer, J. (1958). Investment in Human Capital and Personal Income Distribution. *The Journal of Political Economy* 66(4): 281–302.

Mincer, J. (1974). *Schooling, Experience, and Earnings*. New York: NBER Press.

Mincer, J. (1991). Education and Unemployment. *National Bureau of Economic Research* n. 3838.

Modena, F. and Rondinelli, C. (2011). Leaving Home and Housing Prices. The Experience of Italian Youth Emancipation. Bank of Italy, Economic Research Department, *Temi di discussione/Economic Working Papers* n. 818.

Möller, J. (2010). The German Labor Market Response in the World Recession: Demystifying a Miracle. *Zeitschrift für Arbeitsmark Forschung (ZAF)* 42(4): 325–336.

Mooi-Reci, I. and Dekker, R. (2015). Fixed-Term Contracts: Short-Term Blessings or Long-Term Scars? Empirical Findings from the Netherlands 1980–2000. *British Journal of Industrial Relations* 53(1): 112–135.

Mroz, T. A. and Savage, T. H. (2006). The Long-Term Effects of Youth Unemployment. *Journal of Human Resources* 41(2): 259–293.

Mulder, C. H. and Hooimejer, P. (2002). Leaving Home in the Netherlands: Timing and First Housing. *Journal of Housing and the Built Environment* 17(3): 237–268.

Müller, W. and Gangl, M. (2003). The Transition from School to Work: A European Perspective. In Müller, W. and Gangl, M. (eds), *Transitions from Education to Work in Europe. The Integration of Youth into EU Labour Markets*. Oxford: Oxford University Press: 1–19.

Müller, W. and Shavit, Y. (1998). The Institutional Embeddedness of the Stratification Process: A Comparative Study of Qualifications and Occupations in Thirteen Countries. In Shavit, Y. and Müller, W. (eds), *From School to Work: A Comparative Study of Educational Qualifications and Occupational Destinations*. Oxford: Clarendon. Press: 1–48.

Nardi, B., Lucarelli, C., Talamonti, M., Arimatea, E., Fiori, V. and Moltedo-Perfetti, A. (2015). NEETs versus EETs: An Observational Study in Italy on the Framework of the HEALTH25 European Project. *Research in Post-Compulsory Education* 20(4): 377–399.

Naticchioni, P., Ricci, A. and Rustichelli, E. (2008). Studiare, l'investimento che non rende. www.lavoce.info.

Newell, A. and Pastore, F. (1999). Structural Change and Structural Unemployment in Poland. *Studi Economici* 54(69/3): 81–99.

Newell, A. T. and Pastore, F. (2006). Regional Unemployment and Industrial Restructuring in Poland. *Eastern European Economics* 44(3): 5–28.

Ng, T. W. H. and Feldman, D. C. (2007). The School-to-work Transition: A Role Identity Perspective. *Journal of Vocational Behavior* 71(1): 114–134.

Nickell, S. (1979). Education and Lifetime Patterns of Unemployment. *Journal of Political Economy* 87(5): S117–S131.

Nickell, S. (1997). Unemployment and Labor Market Rigidities: Europe versus North America. *Journal of Economic Perspectives* 11(3): 55–74.

Nickell, S., Nunziata, L. and Ochel, W. (2005). Unemployment on the OECD since the 1960s. What Do We Know?. *The Economic Journal* 115 (January): 1–27.

Nickell, W. (2006). The CEP-OECD Institutions Data Set (1960–2004). Centre for Economic Performance, London School of Economics and Political Science, *CEP Discussion Paper* 759.

Nicolitsas, D. (2007). Youth Participation in the Greek Labour Market: Developments and Obstacles. *Economic Bulletin* (2007)29: 37–88.

Nilsson, K. and Strandh, M. (1999). Nest Leaving in Sweden: The Importance of Early Educational and Labor Market Careers. *Journal of Marriage and Family* 61(4): 1068–1079.

Noelke, C. (2011). The Consequences of Employment Protection Legislation for the Youth Labour Market. *MZSE Working Papers* n. 144.

Noelke, C. (2015). Employment Protection Legislation and the Youth Labour Market. *European Sociological Review* 32(4): 471–485.

O'Higgins, N. S. (2001). *Youth Unemployment and Employment Policy: A Global Perspective*. Geneva: International Labour Office.

O'Higgins, N. S. (2010). The Impact of the Economic and Financial Crisis on Youth Employment: Measures for Labour Market Recovery in the European Union, Canada and the United States. *ILO Employment Working Paper* n. 70.

O'Higgins, N. S. (2012). This Time It's Different? Youth Labor Markets During the Great Recession. *Comparative Economic Studies* 54(2): 395–412.

OECD (1994). *The OECD Jobs Study. Facts, Analysis, Strategies*. Paris: OECD Publishing.

OECD (2008). *Education at a Glance*. Paris: OECD Publishing.

OECD (2009). *Education at a Glance*. Paris: OECD Publishing.

OECD (2010). *Off to a Good Start? Jobs for Youth*. Paris: OECD Publishing.

OECD (2012a). *The Challenge of Promoting Youth Employment in the G20 Countries*. Paris: OECD Publishing.

OECD (2012b). Financial and Human Resources Invested in Education. In OECD *Education at a Glance: OECD Indicators*. Chapter 7, Paris: OECD Publishing.

OECD (2013a). *OECD Employment Outlook*. Paris: OECD Publishing.

OECD (2013b). Protecting Jobs, Enhancing Flexibility: A New Look at Employment Protection Legislation. In *OECD. Employment Outlook 2013*. Chapter 2, Paris: OECD Publishing: 65–126.

OECD (2014a). Non-regular Employment, Job Security and the Labour Market Divide. In OECD. *Employment Outlook 2014*. Chapter 4, Paris: OECD Publishing: 141–209.

OECD (2014b). *OECD Employment Outlook*. Paris: OECD Publishing.

OECD (2015a). Adapting to the Changing Face of Work: Policies to Make the Most of Part-time and Temporary Work. *OECD Policy Brief*.

OECD (2015b). *OECD Employment Outlook*. Paris: OECD publishing.

OECD (2016). *OECD Employment Outlook*. Paris: OECD Publishing.

Oinonen, E. (2003). Extended Present, Faltering Future. Family Formation in the Process of Attaining Adult Status in Finland and Spain Young. *Nordic Journal of Youth Research* 11(2): 121–140.

Origo, F. and Pagani, L. (2009). Flexicurity and Job Satisfaction in Europe: The Importance of Perceived and Actual Job Stability for Well-being at Work. *Labour Economics* 16(5): 547–555.

Ortiz, L. (2010). Not the Right Job, but a Secure One: Over-education and Temporary Employment in France, Italy and Spain. *Work, Employment and Society* 24(1): 47–64.

Oswald, A. J. (1997). Happiness and Economic Performance. *Economic Journal* 107(445): 1815–1831.

Pagán, R. (2013). Job Satisfaction and Domains of Job Satisfaction for Older Workers with Disabilities in Europe. *Journal of Happiness Studies* 14(3): 861–891.

Pagán, R. and Malo, M. A. (2009). Job Satisfaction and Disability: Lower Expectations About Jobs or a Matter of Health?. *The Spanish Economic Review* 11(4): 51–74.

Parisi, M. L. (2016). Labor Productivity, Temporary Work and Youth Unemployment: The Experience of Southern Europe. Paper submitted to *European Youth Labor Markets: Problems and Policies.* Chapter 12, book proposal to Springer.

Parisi, M. L., Marelli, E. and Demidova, O. (2014). Labor Productivity of Young and Adult Temporary Workers and Youth Unemployment: A Cross-Country Analysis. In Caroleo, F. E. and De Siano, R. (eds), *New Challenges for the Labor Market: Spatial and Institutional Perspectives.* Naples: CRISEI: 9–44.

Parker, S. and Van Praag, C. (2006). Schooling, Capital Constraints and Entrepreneurial Performance: The Endogenous Triangle. *Journal of Business and Economic Statistics* 24(4): 416–431.

Pastore, F. (2010). Assessing the Impact of Incomes Policy: The Italian Experience. *International Journal of Manpower* 31(7): 793–817.

Pastore, F. (2011). *Fuori dal tunnel.* Torino: Giappichelli.

Pastore, F. (2012). To Study or to Work? Education and Labour Market Participation of Young People in Poland. *Eastern European Economics* 50(3): 49–78.

Pastore, F. (2013). *Employment Services in View of the School-to-Work Transition: A Comparative Analysis.* Rome: FORMEZ PA.

Pastore, F. (2015a). *The Youth Experience Gap: Explaining National Differences in the School-to-Work Transition.* Heidelberg: Physica Verlag.

Pastore, F. (2015b). The European Youth Guarantee: Labor Market Context, Conditions and Opportunities in Italy. *IZA Journal of European Labor Studies* 4(11), May.

Paul, K. I. and Moser, K. (2009). Unemployment Impairs Mental Health: Meta-analyses. *Journal of Vocational Behavior* 74(3): 264–282.

Pemberton, S. (2008). Social Inclusion and the 'Get Heard' Process: Implications for the Horizontal and Vertical Integration of Governance and Policy and the UK. *Public Policy and Administration* 23(2): 127–143.

Pena-Boquete, Y. (2016). Further Developments in the Dynamics of Female Labour Force Participation. *Empirical Economics* 50(2): 463–501.

Perugini, C. and Pompei, F. (eds) (2015). *Inequalities During and After Transition in Central and Eastern Europe.* Heidelberg: Springer Verlag.

Perugini, C. and Pompei, F. (2016). Employment Protection and Wage Inequality Within Education Groups in Europe. *Journal of Policy Modeling* 38(5): 810–836.

Perugini, C. and Pompei, F. (2017). Temporary Jobs, Institutions, and Wage Inequality Within Education Groups in Central-Eastern Europe. *World Development* 92: 40–59.

Pesaran, M. H. and Shin, Y. (1999). An Autoregressive Distributed Lag Modelling Approach to Cointegration Analysis. In Strom, S. (ed.), *Econometrics and Economic Theory in the 20th Century: The Ragnar Frisch Centennial Symposium.* Chapter 11, Cambridge: Cambridge University Press: 371–413.

Pfeiffer, F. and Seiberlich, R. (2009). A Socio-economic Analysis of Youth Disconnectedness. *ZEW Discussion Paper* n. 09-070.

Pica, G. (2016). Non è un mercato del lavoro per giovani. www.lavoce.info.

Piopiunik, M. and Ryan, P. (2012). Improving the Transition Between Education/Training and the Labour Market: What Can We Learn from Various National Approaches?. European Expert Network on Economics of Education (EENEE), *Analytical Report* n. 13.

Pissarides, C. (2000). *Equilibrium Unemployment Theory*. Cambridge, MA: MIT Press.

Pissarides, C. (2013). Unemployment in the Great Recession. *Economica* 80(319): 385–403.

Piurko, Y., Schwartz, S. and Davidov, E. (2011). Basic Personal Values and the Meaning of Left-right Political Orientations in 20 Countries. *Political Psychology* 20(20): 1–25.

Plantenga, J., Remery, C. and Samek, M. L. (2013). *Starting Fragile Gender Differences in the Youth Labour Market Final Report*. Luxembourg: Publications Office of the European Union.

Quintini, G. (2011). Over-qualified or Under-skilled: A Review of Existing Literature. *OECD Social, Employment and Migration Working Papers* n. 121.

Quintini, G. and Martin, S. (2014). Same but Different: School-to-work Transitions in Emerging and Advanced Economies. *OECD Social, Employment and Migration Working Papers* n. 154.

Quintini, G., Martin, J. P. and Martin, S. (2007). The Changing Nature of the School-to-Work Transition Process in OECD Countries. *IZA Discussion Paper* n. 2582.

Raffe, D. (2003). Pathways Linking Education and Work: A Review of Concepts, Research, and Policy Debates. *Journal of Youth Studies* 6(1): 3–19.

Raffe, D. (2008). The Concept of Transition System. *Journal of Education and Work* 21(4): 277–296.

Reagan, P. B. (1992). On-the-job Training, Layoff by Inverse Seniority, and the Incidence of Unemployed. *Journal of Economics and Business* 44(4): 317–324.

Refrigeri, L. and Aleandri, G. (2013). Educational Policies and Youth Unemployment. *Procedia – Social and Behavioral Sciences* 93: 1263–1268.

Riddell, C. and Song, X. (2011). The Impact of Education on Unemployment Incidence and Re-employment Success: Evidence from the U.S. Labour Market. *Labour Economics* 18(4): 453–463.

Rodríguez-Planas, N., Schmidl, R. and Zimmermann, K. F. (2015). A Roadmap to Vocational Education and Training Systems Around the World. *ILR Review* 68(2): 314–337.

Roodman, D. (2009a). How to Do Xtabond2: An Introduction to Difference and System GMM in Stata. *Stata Journal* 9(1): 86–136.

Roodman, D. (2009b). A Note on the Theme of Too Many Instruments. *Oxford Bulletin of Economics and Statistics* 71(1): 135–158.

Rosenbaum, J. E. and Takehiko, K. (1989). From High School to Work: Market and Institutional Mechanisms in Japan. *American Journal of Sociology* 94(6): 1334–1365.

Rosina, A. and Fraboni, R. (2004). Is Marriage Losing Its Centrality in Italy?. *Demographic Research* 11(6): 149–172.

Rosina, A. and Rivellini, G. (2004). Living Arrangements, Transgressive Behavior and Sexuality. In Crisafulli, C. and Dalla Zuanna, G. (eds), *Sex and the Italian Students*. Messina: University of Messina, Department of Statistics.

Russell, H. and O'Connell, P. J. (2001). Getting a Job in Europe: The Transition from Unemployment to Work Among Young People in Nine European Countries. *Work, Employment and Society* 15(1): 1–24.

Russell, H., McGinnity, F. and Kingston, G. (2014). *Gender and the Quality of Work: From Boom to Recession*. Dublin: Economic and Social Research Institute and the Equality Authority.

Ryan, P. (2001). The School-to-work Transition: A Cross-national Perspective. *Journal of Economic Literature* 39(1): 34–92.

Ryan, P. (2007). Has the Youth Labour Market Deteriorated in Recent Decades? Evidence from Developed Countries. *Arbetsrapport/Institutet för Framtidsstudier* n. 2007/5.

Sachs, A. and Smolny, W. (2014). Youth Unemployment in the OECD: The Role of Institutions. *ZEW Discussion Papers* n. 14-080.

Salvatori, A. (2010). Labour Contract Regulations and Workers' Wellbeing: International Longitudinal Evidence. *Labour Economics* 17: 667–678.

Sandlie, H. C. (2011). Hvordan går det med ungdommens etablering på boligmarkedet?. *Tidsskrift for ungdomsforskning* 11(2): 49–69.

Saraceno, C. (2000). Being Young in Italy: The Paradoxes of a Familistic Society. *European Journal of Social Quality* 2(2): 120–132.

Scarpetta, S., Sonnet, A. and Manfredi, T. (2010). Rising Youth Unemployment During the Crisis: How to Prevent Negative Long-term Consequences on a Generation?. *OECD Social, Employment and Migration Working Papers* n. 106.

Scharle, A. and Weber, T. (2011). Youth Guarantees: PES Approaches and Measures for Low Skilled Young People. Thematic Synthesis Paper. The European Commission Mutual Learning Programme.

Scherer, S. (2004). Stepping-Stones or Traps? The Consequences of Labour Market Entry Positions on Future Careers in West Germany, Great Britain and Italy. *Work, Employment & Society* 18(2): 369–394.

Schneider, S. and Tieben, N. (2011). A Healthy Sorting Machine? Social Inequality in the Transition to Upper Secondary Education in Germany. *Oxford Review of Education* 37(2): 139–166.

Schroeder, C. (2008). The Influence of Parents on Cohabitation in Italy: Insights from Two Regional Contexts. *Demographic Research* 19(48): 1693–1726.

Schwarz, G. (1978). Estimating the Dimension of a Model. *Annals of Statistics* 6(2): 461–464.

Scruggs, L., Detlef, J. and Kuitto, K. (2014). *Comparative Welfare Entitlements Dataset 2. Version 2014–03*. University of Connecticut and University of Greifswald.

Semykina, A. and Wooldridge, J. M. (2010). Estimating Panel Data Models in the Presence of Endogeneity and Selection. *Journal of Econometrics* 157(2): 375–380.

Sen, A. (1999). *Development as Freedom*. New York: Oxford University Press.

Senik, C. (2004). When Information Dominates Comparison: Learning from Russian Subjective Panel Data. *Journal of Public Economics* 88(9–10): 2099–2123.

Shavit, Y. and Blossfeld, H. P. (eds) (1993). *Persistent Inequality: Changing Educational Attainment in Thirteen Countries*. Boulder, CO: Westview Press.

Shimer, R. (2001). The Impact of Young Workers on the Aggregate Labor Market. *Quarterly Journal of Economics* 116(3): 969–1007.

Signorelli, M. and. Choudhry Tanveer, M. (2015). Youth Labour Market and the Great Recession. *Economic Systems* 39: 1–2.

Signorelli, M., Choudhry Tanveer, M. and Marelli, E. (2012). The Impact of Financial Crises on Female Labour. *European Journal of Development Research* 24(3): 413–433.

Sousa-Poza, A. and Sousa-Poza, A. A. (2003). Gender Differences in Job Satisfaction in Great Britain, 1991–2000: Permanent or Transitory?. *Applied Economics Letters* 10(11): 691–694.

Spence, M. (1973). Job Market Signalling. *Quarterly Journal of Economics* 87(3): 355–374.

Stancanelli, E. G. F. (2002). Do Temporary Jobs Pay? Wages and Career Perspectives of Temporary Workers. *Tilburg University Working Paper*.

Stocké, V. (2007). Explaining Educational Decision and Effects of Families' Social Class Position: An Empirical Test of the Breen–Goldthorpe Model of Educational Attainment. *European Sociological Review* 23(4): 505–519.

Stone, J., Berrington, A. and Falkingham, J. (2011). The Changing Determinants of UK Young Adults' Living Arrangements. *Demographic Research* 25(20): 629–666.

Styczynska, I. (2013). Enhancing Youth Opportunities in Employment: Determinants and Policy Implications. *Intereconomics* 48(4): 216–223.

Terza, J., Basu, A. and Rathouz, P. (2010). Two-stage Residual Inclusion Estimation: Addressing Endogeneity in Health Econometric Modeling. *Journal of Health Economics* 27(3): 531–543.

Texmon, I. (1995). Ut av redet. En demografisk analyse av flytting fra foreldrehjemmet. Statistics Norway, *Reports* n. 95/4.

Tronti, L. (2010). The Italian Productivity Slowdown: The Role of the Bargaining Model. *International Journal of Manpower* 31(7): 770–792.

Trostel, P. and Walker, I. (2006). Education and Work. *Education Economics* 14(4): 377–399.

Trostel, P., Walker, I. and Wooley, P. (2002). Estimates of the Economic Return to Schooling for 28 Countries. *Labour Economics* 9(1): 1–6.

UNESCO (2013). International Standard Classification of Education 2011. www.uis. unesco.org/Education/Documents/isced-fields-of-education-training-2013.pdf.

Urbanos-Garrido, R. M. and López-Valcárcel, B. G. (2015). The Influence of the Economic Crisis on the Association Between Unemployment and Health: An Empirical Analysis for Spain. *European Journal of Health Economics* 16(2): 175–184.

Van Ark, B. (2003). ICT and Productivity in Europe and the United States: Where Do the Differences Come from?. *CESifo Economic Studies* 49(3): 295–318.

Van de Ven, W. P. M. M. and Van Pragg, B. M. S. (1981). The Demand for Deductibles in Private Health Insurance: A Probit Model with Sample Selection. *Journal of Econometrics* 17(2): 229–252.

Van de Werfhorst, H. G. and Mijs, J. (2010). Achievement Inequality and the Institutional Structure of Educational Systems: A Comparative Perspective. *Annual Review of Sociology* 36: 407–428.

van Ours, J. C. (2015). The Great Recession Was Not So Great. Tilburg University, *Center for Economic Research Discussion Paper*. 2015-006.

Van Praag, B. M. S. and Ferrer-i-Carbonell, A. (2004). *Happiness Quantified: A Satisfaction Calculus Approach*. Oxford: Oxford University Press.

Van Praag, B. M. S. and Ferrer-i-Carbonell, A. (2006). An Almost Integration-free Approach to Ordered Response Models. *Tibergen Institute Discussion Paper* n. 2006-047/3.

Van Praag, B. M. S. and Ferrer-i-Carbonell, A. (2008). A Multi-dimensional Approach to Subjective Poverty. In Kakwani, N. and Silber, J. (eds), *Quantitative Approaches to Multidimensional Poverty Measurement*, New York: Palgrave Macmillan.

Verbrugge, L. M. (1985). Gender and Health: An Update on Hypotheses and Evidence. *Journal of Health and Social Behavior* 26(3): 156–182.

Verick, S. (2011). Who Is Hit Hardest during a Financial Crisis? The Vulnerability of Young Men and Women to Unemployment in an Economic Downturn. In Islam, I. and Verick, S. (eds), *From the Great Recession to Labour Market Recovery: Issues, Evidence and Policy Options*. London: ILO/Palgrave Macmillan: 119–145.

Vogel, J. (2002). European Welfare Regimes and the Transition to Adulthood: A Comparative and Longitudinal Perspective. *Social Indicators Research* 59(3): 275–299.

Vryonides, M. and Gouvias, D. (2012). Parents' Aspirations for Their Children's Educational and Occupational Prospects in Greece: The Role of Social Class. *International Journal of Educational Research* 53: 319–329.

Waddell, G. and Burton, K. (2006). *Is Work Good for Your Health and Well-being?*. London: The Stationery Office.

Wagner, M. and Huinink, J. (1991). Neuere Trends beim Auszug aus dem Elternhaus. In Buttler, G., Hoffman-Nowotny, H. J. and Schmitt-Rink, G. (eds), *Acta Demographica*. Heidelberg: Physica Verlag: 39–62.

Wanberg, C. R. (2012). The Individual Experience of Unemployment. *Annual Review of Psychology* 63: 369–396.

Wilkinson, A. and Wood, G. (2012). Institutions and Employment Relations: The State of the Art. *Industrial Relations: A Journal of Economy and Society* 51(s1): 373–388.

Winkelmann, L. and Winkelmann, R. (1998). Why Are the Unemployed So Unhappy? Evidence from Panel Data. *Economica* 65(257): 1–15.

Winkelmann, R. (2014). Unemployment and Happiness. Successful Policies for Helping the Unemployed Need to Confront the Adverse Effects of Unemployment on Felling of Life Satisfaction. *IZA World of Labor. Evidence-based Policy Making* n. 94.

Woelfl, A., Wanner, I., Kozluk, T. and Nicoletti, G. (2009). Ten Years of Product Market Reforms in OECD Countries: Insights from a Revised PMR Indicator. *OECD Economics Department Working Paper* n. 695.

Wooden, M. and Warren, D. (2004). Non-standard Employment and Job Satisfaction: Evidence from the HILDA Survey. *The Journal of Industrial Relations* 46(3): 275–297.

Wooldridge, J. M. (2010). *Econometric Analysis of Cross Section and Panel Data*. Cambridge, MA: MIT Press.

Zibrowius, M. (2013). Ethnic Background and Youth Unemployment in Germany. *BGPE Discussion Paper* n. 138.

Zimmermann, K. F., Biavaschi, C., Eichhorst, W., Giulietti, C., Kendzia, M. J., Muravyev, A., Pieters, J., Rodríguez-Planas, N. and Schmidl, R. (2013). Youth Unemployment and Vocational Training. *Foundations and Trends in Microeconomics* 9(1–2): 1–157.

Index